DUNCAN B. HEPPLEWHITE

THE COLLINS LONGMAN ATLAS

FOR SECONDARY SCHOOLS

Editorial Adviser

Richard Kemp
County Adviser for Humanities
Buckinghamshire

Copyright © Collins-Longman Atlases 1987, 1989

First published 1987

Reprinted 1987 (twice), 1988, 1989 (twice)

Wm Collins Sons and Co Ltd
PO Box
Glasgow
G4 0NB

Longman Group UK Ltd
Longman House
Burnt Mill
Harlow
Essex
CM20 2JE

Photographic Credits

Focal Point: p40 top, p45, p85
J Allan Cash: p117
NRSC: p40 bottom, p44
Picturepoint: p116, p118 left, p119 left and right
Frank Spooner Pictures: p118 right, p119 centre
University of Dundee: p11

Printed and bound in Scotland by William Collins Sons & Co. Ltd.

Contents

4 Symbols

REFERENCE MAPS

Relief and physical features

▲ 8848   Spot height (metres)

   Pass

   Permanent ice cap

Relief

Metres	
5000	
3000	
2000	
1000	
500	
200	
0	Sea Level
200	
4000	
7000	
Metres	

Relief and physical names   *ALPS*   *Zaïre Basin*   *Nicobar Islands*   *Mt. Cook*

Water features

   Submarine contour

. *11034*   Ocean depth (metres)

   Reef

   River

   Intermittent river

   Falls/Dam

   Gorge

   Canal

   Lake/Reservoir

   Intermittent lake

   Marsh/Swamp

Water names   *PACIFIC OCEAN*   *Red Sea*   *Lake Erie*   *Amazon*

Communications

Tunnel   Railway

Tunnel   Road

   Proposed road/desert track

⊕   Main airport

   Motorway

   Main road

Administration

   International boundary

   Undefined or disputed boundary

   Internal boundary

▨ ◉ ◎ ⊙   National capitals

   County or Region boundary

Country name   CHILE   Internal division   IOWA   Territorial admin.   *(Fr.)*

Settlement

▨ **Dhākā**   Over 1 000 000 inhabitants

◉ **Khulna**   500 000–1 000 000 inhabitants

◎ Imphal   100 000–500 000 inhabitants

⊙ Thimbu   Under 100 000 inhabitants

Built-up area

▨   Over 1 000 000 inhabitants

◉   500 000–1 000 000 inhabitants

◎   100 000–500 000 inhabitants

⊙   25 000–100 000 inhabitants

○   10 000–25 000 inhabitants

•   Under 10 000 inhabitants

BRITISH ISLES REFERENCE MAPS (pp. 12–15)

Additional or different symbols used on these maps

Relief

Metres	
1000	
500	
200	
100	
0	Sea Level
20	
50	
Metres	

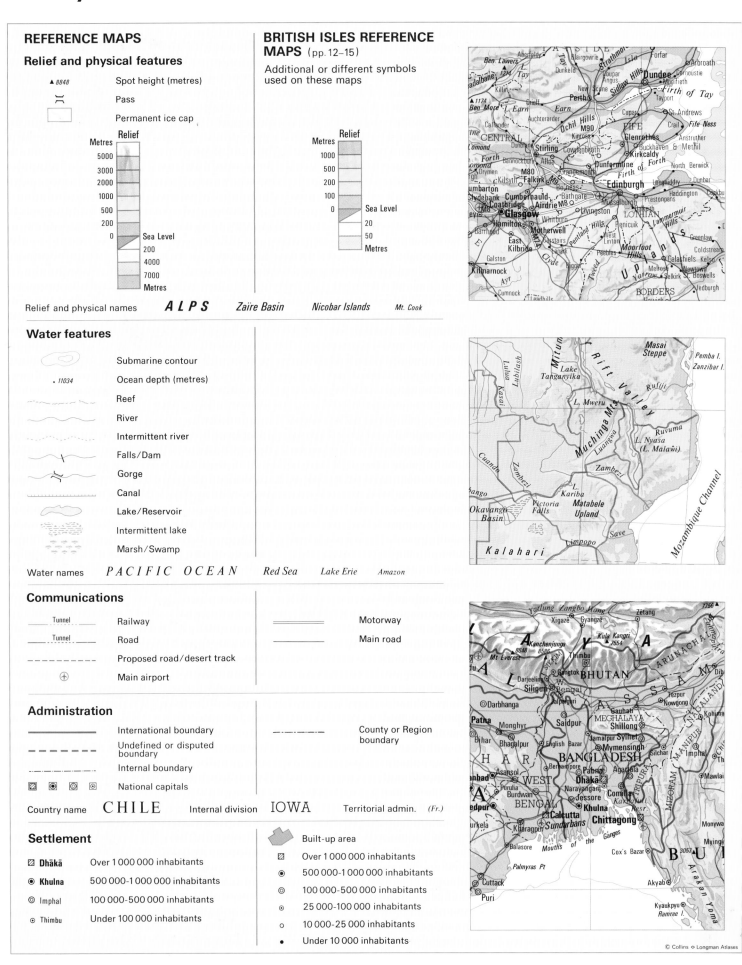

© Collins ◇ Longman Atlases

To draw a map of the world, or of a part of the world, the real area has to be reduced in size, or scaled down, to fit onto the map sheet or atlas page. The **scale** of any map therefore tells us precisely how much the real area has been reduced in size.

The scale of this map is 1:2 000 000 or 1cm represents 20 km

To use a map to work out the size of areas or distances on the real ground, we need to refer to the scale of that particular map. Map scales can be shown in several ways:

As a **linear scale** — a horizontal line is marked off in units which show how the real ground distances are represented on the map, as in the example below.

As a **statement of scale** — the linear scale above would be written as *1 cm to 1 km*. This means that 1 cm on the map represents 1 km on the real ground.

As a **representative fraction** — for example the scale shown above would be *1:100 000*. This means that every 1 unit of measurement on the map represents 100 000 units on the real ground.

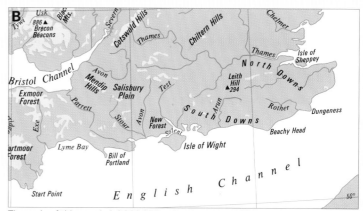

The scale of this map is 1:4 000 000 or 1cm represents 40 km

As the scale becomes smaller the amount of real ground that can be fitted onto the map becomes larger. But in making the scale smaller, the accuracy of the map, and the detail it can show, have to be reduced.

The four examples on this page show what happens when the map scale is made smaller. As the scale decreases from the top to the bottom of the page, the details shown on the maps become less precise and more generalised.

The scale of this map is 1:16 000 000 or 1cm represents 160 km

On Map A, at a scale of *1:2 000 000,* the Isle of Wight is shown as a county of England, and detail of roads, the location of towns and relief is clearly shown. It is possible to distinguish bays and inlets around the coast.

On Map B, at a scale of *1:4 000 000,* a larger area of the south of England is shown. Thus the coastline of the Isle of Wight has been generalised, and there are few details about the island other than its name.

On Map C, at a scale of *1:16 000 000,* it is possible to show the whole of England and part of the mainland of Europe. The coastline of the Isle of Wight is very generalised, and the island is no longer named.

On Map D, at a scale of *1:85 000 000,* all of Europe can be shown, but the Isle of Wight is represented only by a small dot. At this small scale it is impossible to show any detail of the actual shape of the island, but its location is marked.

The scale of this map is 1:85 000 000 or 1cm represents 850 km

Lines of latitude and longitude are imaginary lines drawn around a globe or on maps of the whole, or part of the world. Like the grid lines on Ordnance Survey maps they can be used to locate a place accurately.

LATITUDE

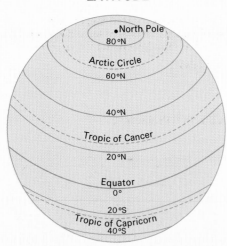

LONGITUDE

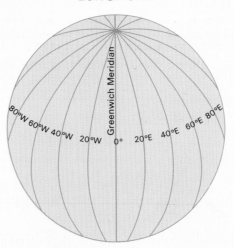

THE EARTH'S GRID SYSTEM

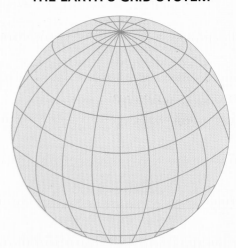

Lines of **latitude** (or *parallels*) are drawn parallel to the Equator. They are numbered in **degrees** either *north* or *south* of the Equator.
The Equator is numbered 0°, the North Pole 90°N and the South Pole 90°S.

Other important lines of latitude are the Tropic of Cancer (23½°N) and the Tropic of Capricorn (23½°S), the Arctic Circle (66½°N) and the Antarctic Circle (66½°S).

Lines of **longitude** (or *meridians*) are drawn from the North Pole to the South Pole. The prime meridian, numbered 0°, runs through the Greenwich Observatory in London and is called the Greenwich Meridian. Lines of longitude are numbered in **degrees** either *east* or *west* of the Greenwich Meridian. The 180° line of longitude, exactly opposite the Greenwich Meridian on the other side of the globe, is the International Date Line.

When lines of latitude and longitude are drawn on a globe or map they form a grid, with the parallels and meridians meeting at right angles. By using a combination of a place's latitude and longitude that place can be accurately located on the globe or map.

To be really accurate each degree of latitude and longitude can be divided into smaller units called **minutes**. There are 60 minutes in one degree. For example the location of Moscow is 55° 45′ north of the Equator, and 37° 42′ east of the Greenwich Meridian — this latitude and longitude reference is usually shortened to 55 45N 37 42E.

THE HEMISPHERES

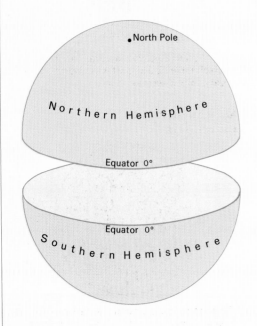

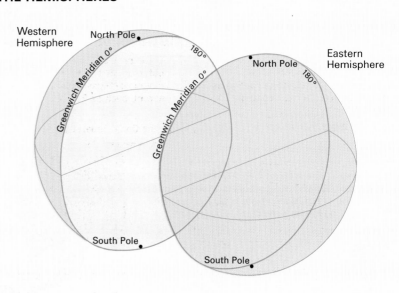

By splitting the globe along the line of the Equator the earth can be divided into two halves, called the Northern and Southern **hemispheres**. If the globe is divided into two from the North Pole to the South Pole, along the 0° and 180° lines of longitude, the halves are called the Eastern Hemisphere and the Western Hemisphere.

An atlas map of the world shows the whole world on the flat surface of the page. Yet in reality the earth is actually a sphere. This means that a system has to be used to turn the round surface of the earth into a flat map of the world, or part of the world. This cannot be done without some distortion — on a map some parts of the world have been stretched, other parts have been compressed. A system for turning the globe into a flat map is called a **projection**.

There are many different projections, each of which distort different things to achieve a flat map. Correct area, correct shape, correct distances or correct directions can be achieved by a projection; but, by achieving any one of these things the others have to be distorted. When choosing the projection to use for a particular map it is important to think which of these things it is most important to have correct.

The projections below illustrate the main types of projections, and include some of those used in this atlas.

PROJECTION GROUPS

Cylindrical Projection

Cylindrical projections are constructed by projecting the surface of the globe on to a cylinder just touching the globe.

Conic Projection

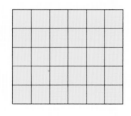

Conic projections are constructed by projecting part of the globe on to a cone which just touches a circle on the globe.

Azimuthal Projection

Azimuthal projections are constructed by projecting part of the globe on to a plane which touches the globe only at one point.

EXAMPLES OF PROJECTIONS

Mercator Conformal Cylindrical
World

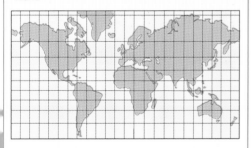

The Mercator projection avoids distorting the shape but makes the areas near the poles larger than they should be.
This projection is used for navigation as directions can be plotted as straight lines.

Winkel Equal Area
World pp. 120-121

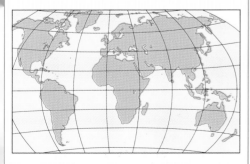

Equal area projections such as Winkel are useful for world maps where it is important to show the correct relative sizes of areas.

Conic Equal Area
Europe pp. 32-33

Conic projections are best suited for areas between 30° and 60° north and south with longer east-west extent than north-south extent, such as Europe.

Bonne Conic Equal Area
North America p. 79

The Bonne projection is a special kind of conic projection best suited for areas with a greater north-south than east-west extent such as North America.

Lambert Azimuthal Equal Area
Africa p. 94

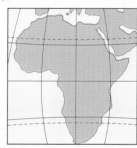

Lambert's projection is useful for areas which have similar east-west, north-south dimensions such as Africa.

Azimuthal Equidistant
Antarctica p. 128

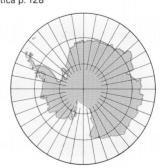

This projection is a good choice for showing travel routes from a central point as points on the map are in constant relative position and distance from the centre.

ORKNEY ISLANDS

SHETLAND ISLANDS

ATLANTIC

OCEAN

NORTH

SEA

IRISH SEA

ENGLISH Channel

St. George's Channel

Bristol Channel

North Channel

The Minch

© Collins ◇ Longman Atlases

Scale 1:4 000 000

0   50   100   150 km

Conic Projection

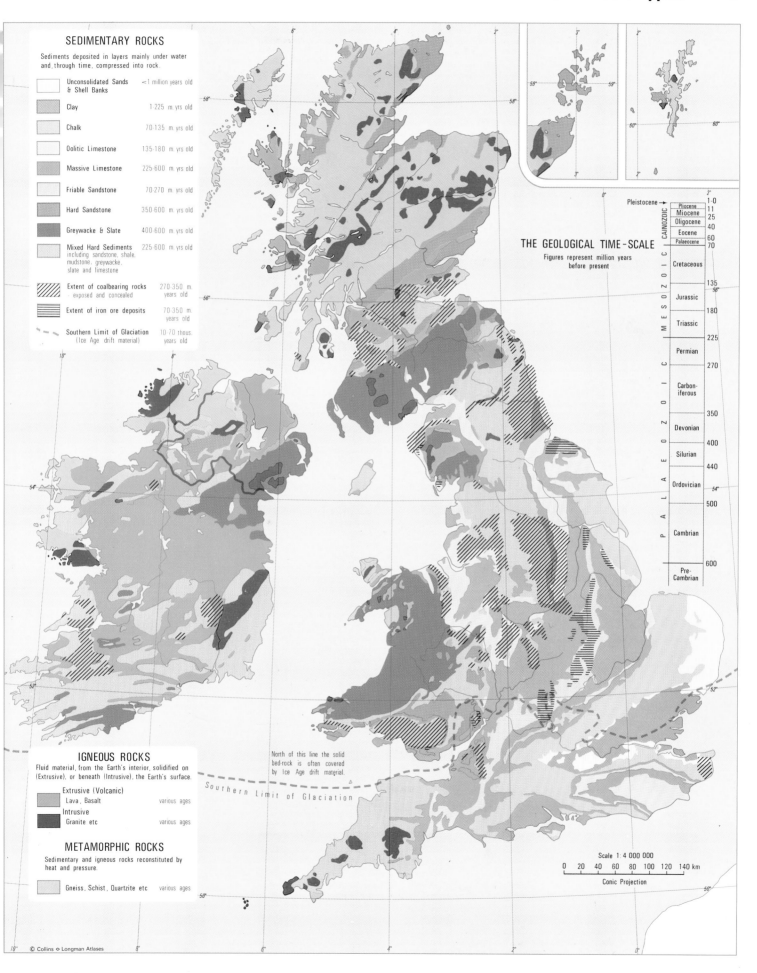

SEDIMENTARY ROCKS

Sediments deposited in layers mainly under water and, through time, compressed into rock.

	Unconsolidated Sands & Shell Banks	<1 million years old
	Clay	1-225 m. yrs old
	Chalk	70-135 m. yrs old
	Oolitic Limestone	135-180 m. yrs old
	Massive Limestone	225-600 m. yrs old
	Friable Sandstone	70-270 m. yrs old
	Hard Sandstone	350-600 m. yrs old
	Greywacke & Slate	400-600 m. yrs old
	Mixed Hard Sediments including sandstone, shale, mudstone, greywacke, slate and limestone	225-600 m. yrs old

	Extent of coalbearing rocks - exposed and concealed	270-350 m. years old
	Extent of iron ore deposits	70-350 m. years old
	Southern Limit of Glaciation (Ice Age drift material)	10-70 thous. years old

THE GEOLOGICAL TIME-SCALE

Figures represent million years before present

Pleistocene →

CAINOZOIC	Pliocene	1·0
	Miocene	11
	Oligocene	25
	Eocene	40
	Palaeocene	60
		70
MESOZOIC	Cretaceous	
		135
	Jurassic	
		180
	Triassic	
		225
PALAEOZOIC	Permian	
		270
	Carboniferous	
		350
	Devonian	
		400
	Silurian	
		440
	Ordovician	
		500
	Cambrian	
		600
	Pre-Cambrian	

IGNEOUS ROCKS

Fluid material, from the Earth's interior, solidified on (Extrusive), or beneath (Intrusive), the Earth's surface.

| | Extrusive (Volcanic) Lava, Basalt | various ages |
| | Intrusive Granite etc | various ages |

METAMORPHIC ROCKS

Sedimentary and igneous rocks reconstituted by heat and pressure.

| | Gneiss, Schist, Quartzite etc | various ages |

North of this line the solid bed-rock is often covered by Ice Age drift material.

Southern Limit of Glaciation

Scale 1:4 000 000

0 20 40 60 80 100 120 140 km

Conic Projection

© Collins ◇ Longman Atlases

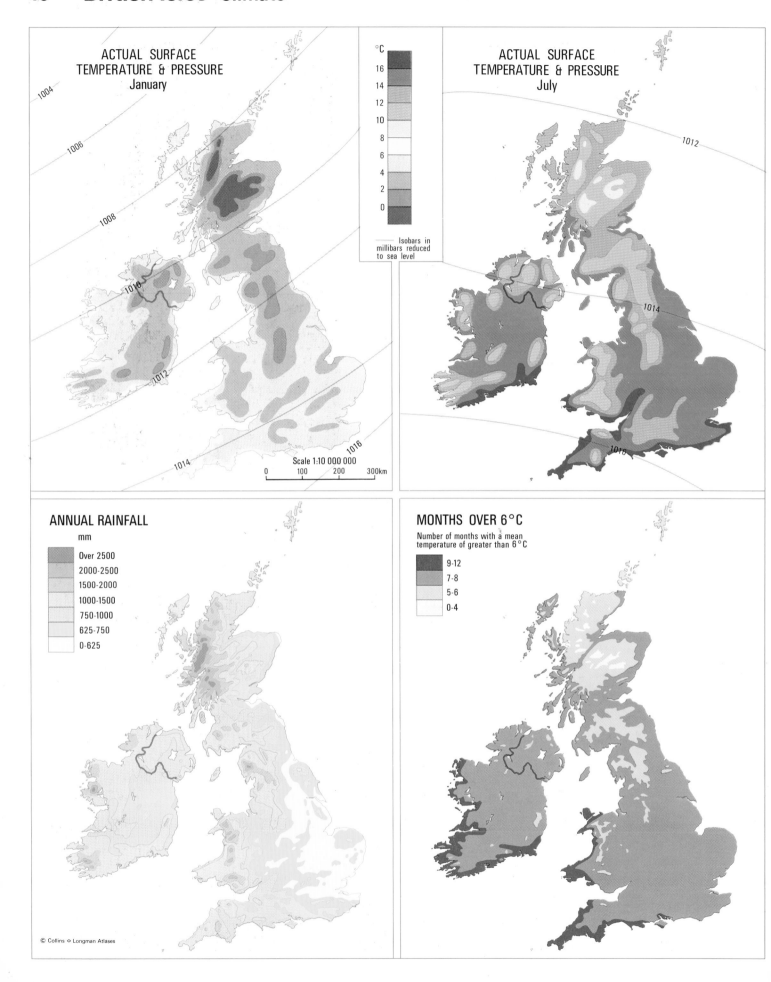

ACTUAL SURFACE
TEMPERATURE & PRESSURE
January

ACTUAL SURFACE
TEMPERATURE & PRESSURE
July

°C

16
14
12
10
8
6
4
2
0

Isobars in
millibars reduced
to sea level

Scale 1:10 000 000

0   100   200   300km

ANNUAL RAINFALL

mm

Over 2500
2000-2500
1500-2000
1000-1500
750-1000
625-750
0-625

MONTHS OVER 6°C

Number of months with a mean
temperature of greater than 6°C

9-12
7-8
5-6
0-4

© Collins ◊ Longman Atlases

WEATHER MAP

H Anticyclone
L Depression

—1012— Pressure in millibars

Cold front

Warm front

Occluded front

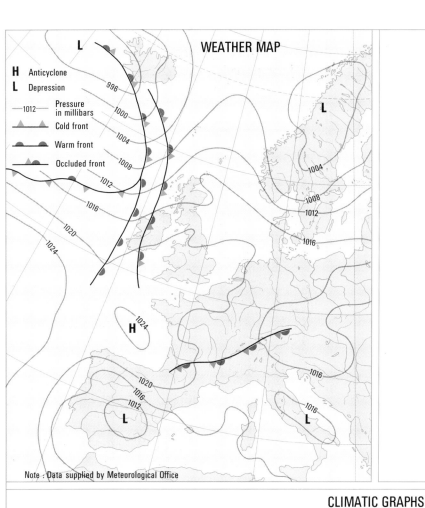

Note : Data supplied by Meteorological Office

WEATHER SATELLITE PHOTOGRAPH

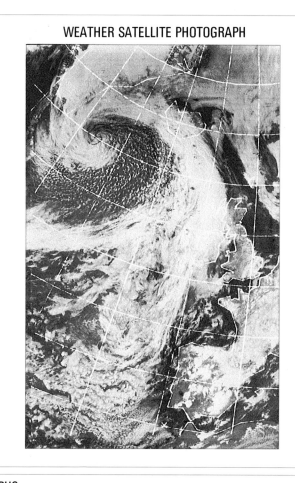

CLIMATIC GRAPHS

Height in metres above sea level.

Mean monthly temperature.

Average monthly rainfall.

ABERDEEN 14m
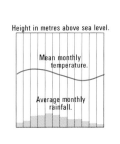

BELFAST 19m
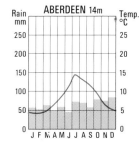

BIRMINGHAM 157m
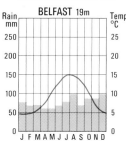

CARDIFF 16m
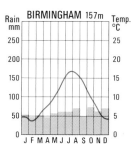

FORT WILLIAM 52m
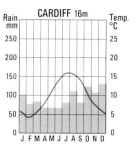

GLASGOW 55m
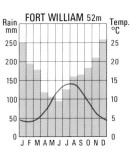

HOLYHEAD 5m
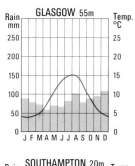

MARGATE 16m
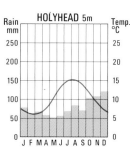

NORWICH 28m
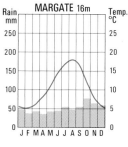

PENZANCE 17m
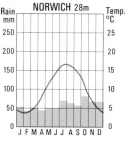

SOUTHAMPTON 20m
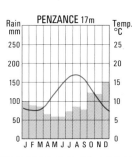

STORNOWAY 16m
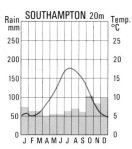

TYNEMOUTH 15m
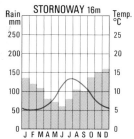

YORK 17m
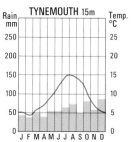

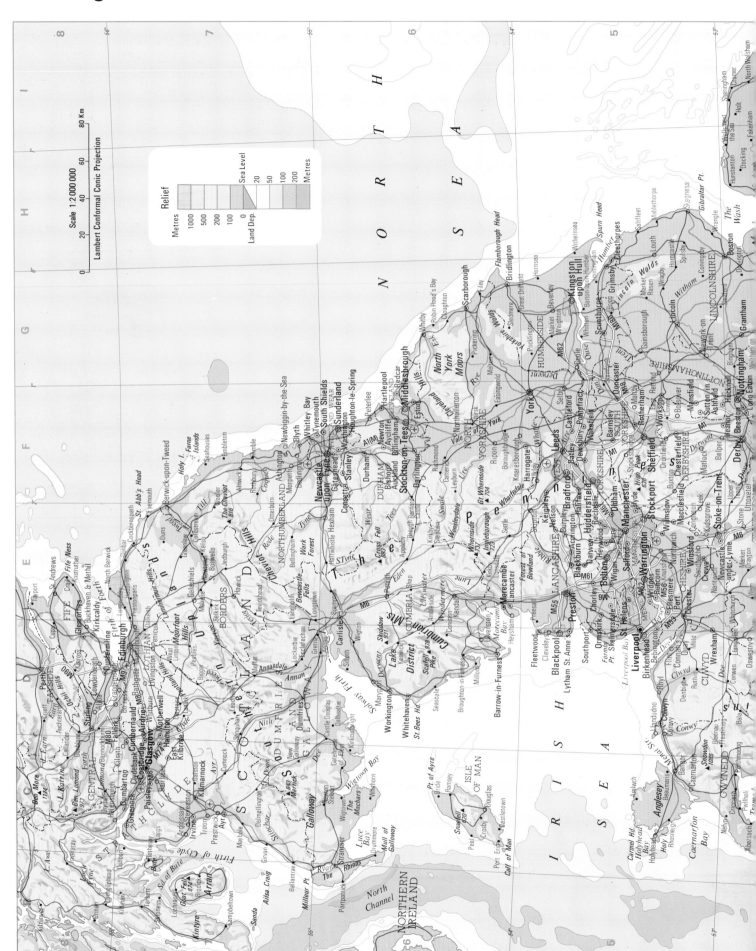

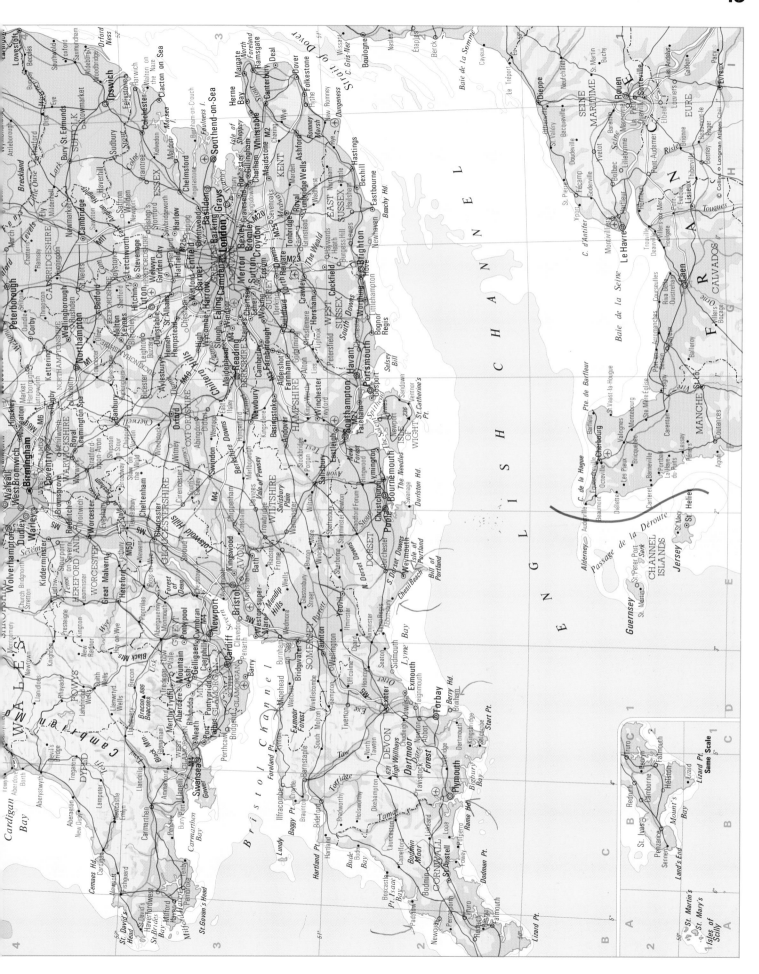

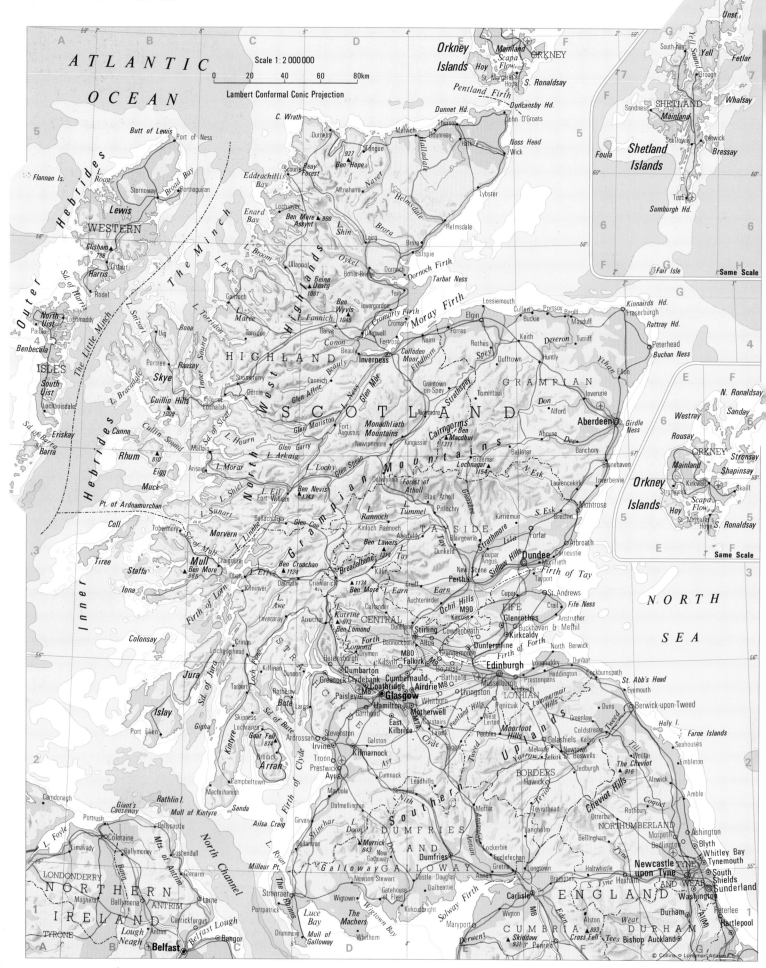

ATLANTIC

OCEAN

Scale 1:2 000 000

0   20   40   60   80km

Lambert Conformal Conic Projection

NORTH

SEA

© Collins ◦ Longman Atlases

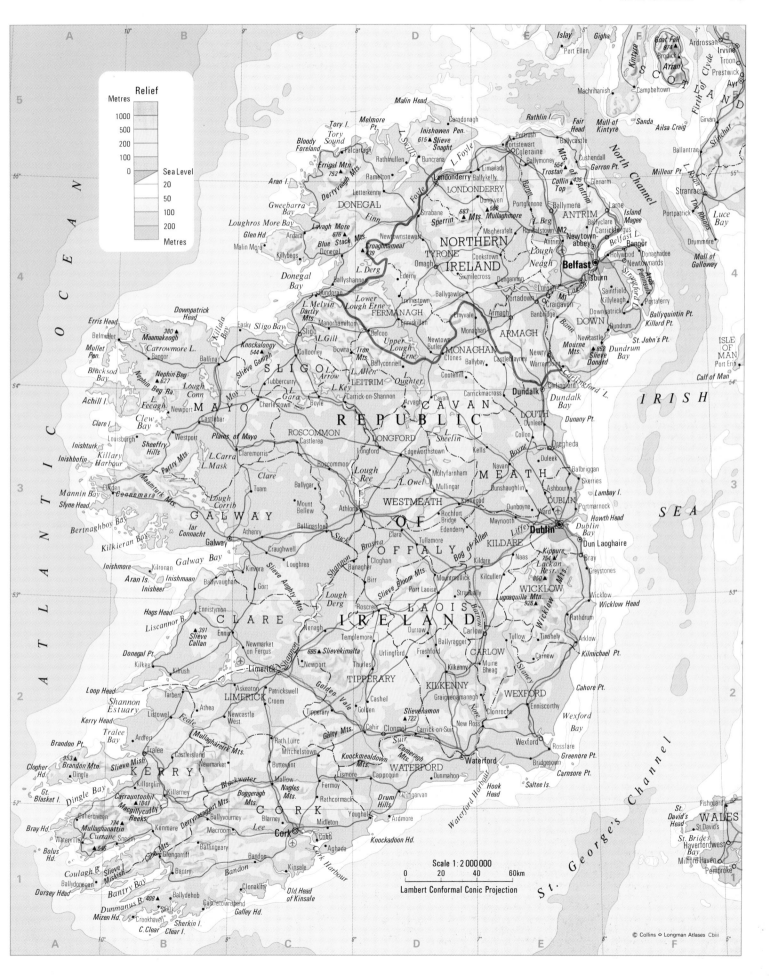

Relief

Metres
1000
500
200
100
0 Sea Level
20
50
100
200
Metres

Scale 1:2 000 000

0   20   40   60km

Lambert Conformal Conic Projection

© Collins ◇ Longman Atlases Cbiii

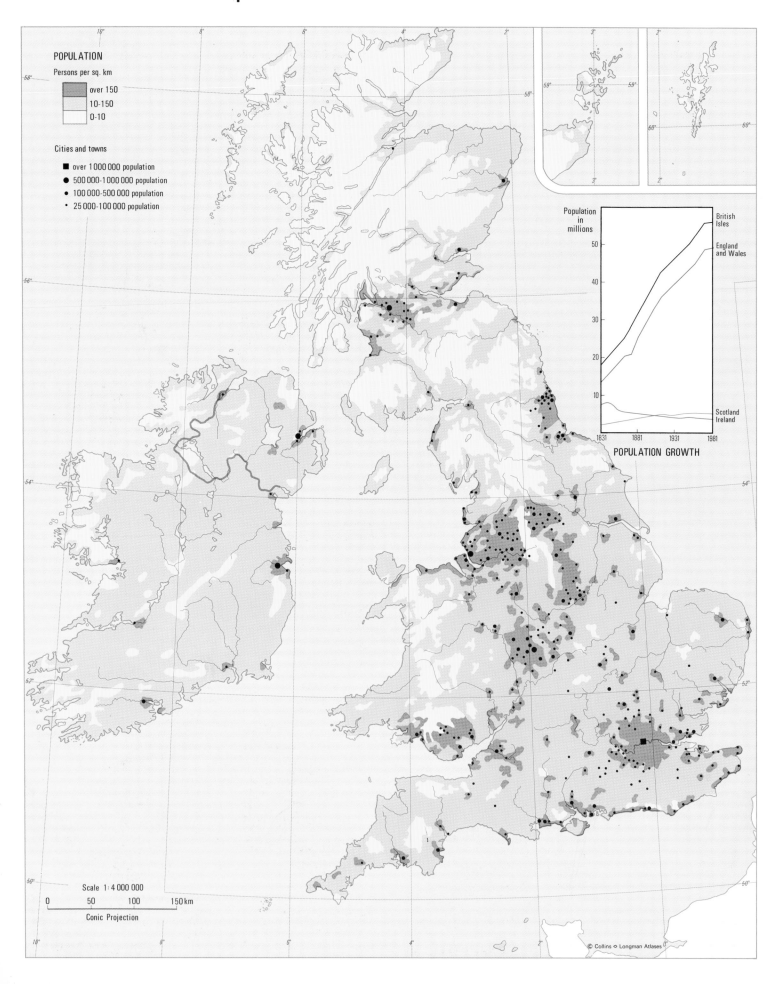

POPULATION

Persons per sq. km

over 150

10-150

0-10

Cities and towns

■ over 1 000 000 population

● 500 000-1 000 000 population

• 100 000-500 000 population

· 25 000-100 000 population

Population in millions

British Isles

England and Wales

Scotland
Ireland

50

40

30

20

10

1831   1881   1931   1981

POPULATION GROWTH

Scale 1: 4 000 000

0   50   100   150 km

Conic Projection

© Collins ◇ Longman Atlases

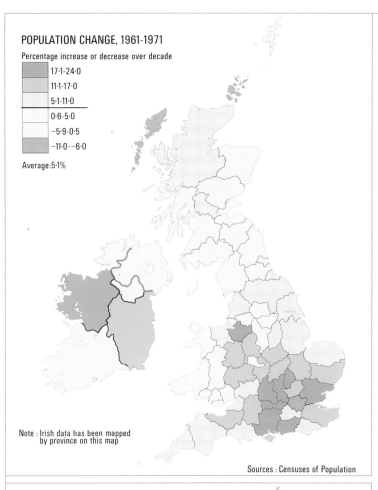

POPULATION CHANGE, 1961-1971

Percentage increase or decrease over decade

- 17·1-24·0
- 11·1-17·0
- 5·1-11·0
- 0·6-5·0
- −5·9-0·5
- −11·0--6·0

Average: 5·1%

Note : Irish data has been mapped
by province on this map

Sources : Censuses of Population

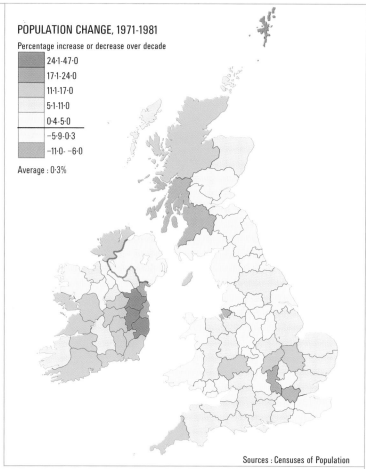

POPULATION CHANGE, 1971-1981

Percentage increase or decrease over decade

- 24·1-47·0
- 17·1-24·0
- 11·1-17·0
- 5·1-11·0
- 0·4-5·0
- −5·9-0·3
- −11·0--6·0

Average : 0·3%

Sources : Censuses of Population

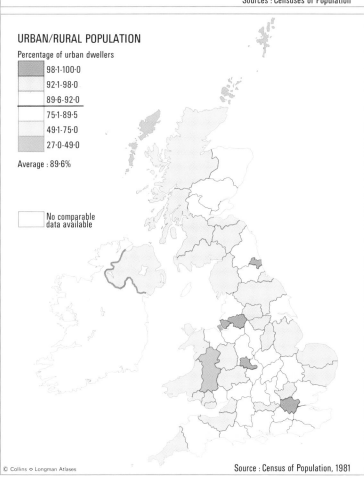

URBAN/RURAL POPULATION

Percentage of urban dwellers

- 98·1-100·0
- 92·1-98·0
- 89·6-92·0
- 75·1-89·5
- 49·1-75·0
- 27·0-49·0

Average : 89·6%

No comparable
data available

Source : Census of Population, 1981

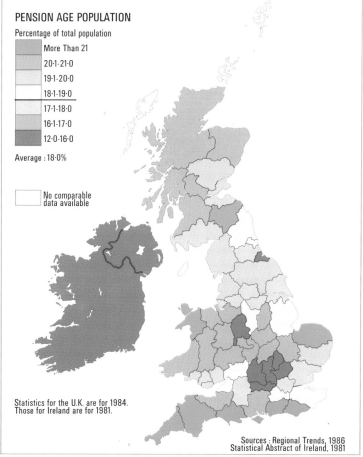

PENSION AGE POPULATION

Percentage of total population

- More Than 21
- 20·1-21·0
- 19·1-20·0
- 18·1-19·0
- 17·1-18·0
- 16·1-17·0
- 12·0-16·0

Average : 18·0%

No comparable
data available

Statistics for the U.K. are for 1984.
Those for Ireland are for 1981.

Sources : Regional Trends, 1986
Statistical Abstract of Ireland, 1981

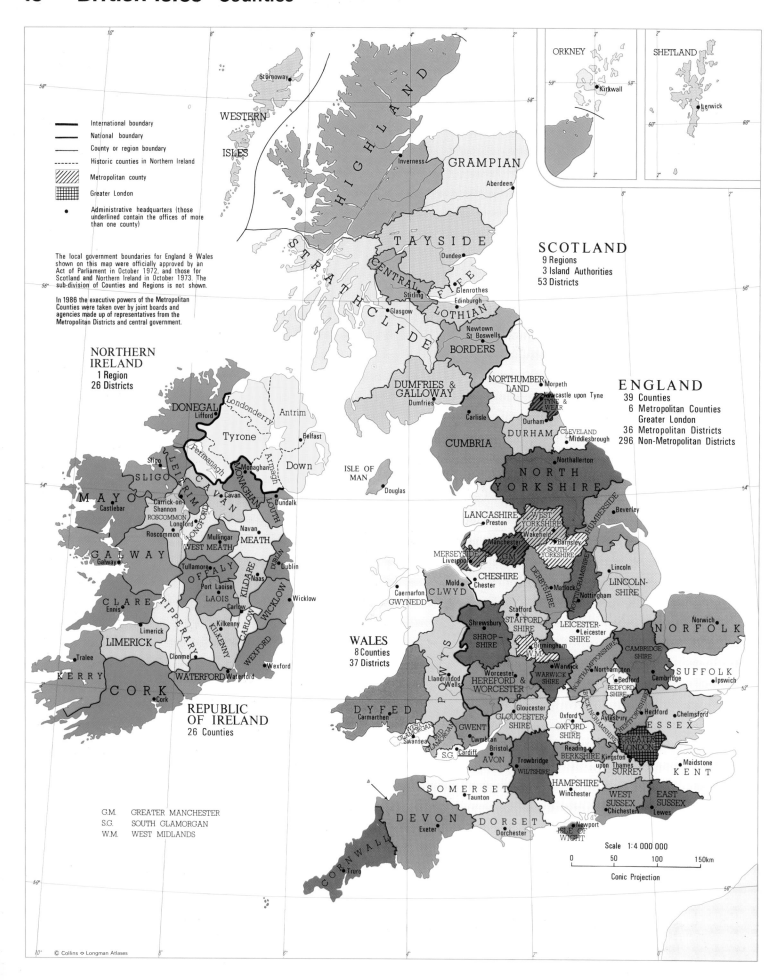

Legend

— International boundary
— National boundary
— County or region boundary
--- Historic counties in Northern Ireland
▨ Metropolitan county
▦ Greater London
• Administrative headquarters (those underlined contain the offices of more than one county)

The local government boundaries for England & Wales shown on this map were officially approved by an Act of Parliament in October 1972, and those for Scotland and Northern Ireland in October 1973. The sub-division of Counties and Regions is not shown.

In 1986 the executive powers of the Metropolitan Counties were taken over by joint boards and agencies made up of representatives from the Metropolitan Districts and central government.

NORTHERN IRELAND
1 Region
26 Districts

SCOTLAND
9 Regions
3 Island Authorities
53 Districts

ENGLAND
39 Counties
6 Metropolitan Counties
Greater London
36 Metropolitan Districts
296 Non-Metropolitan Districts

WALES
8 Counties
37 Districts

REPUBLIC OF IRELAND
26 Counties

G.M. GREATER MANCHESTER
S.G. SOUTH GLAMORGAN
W.M. WEST MIDLANDS

Scale 1:4 000 000
0   50   100   150km
Conic Projection

© Collins ◇ Longman Atlases

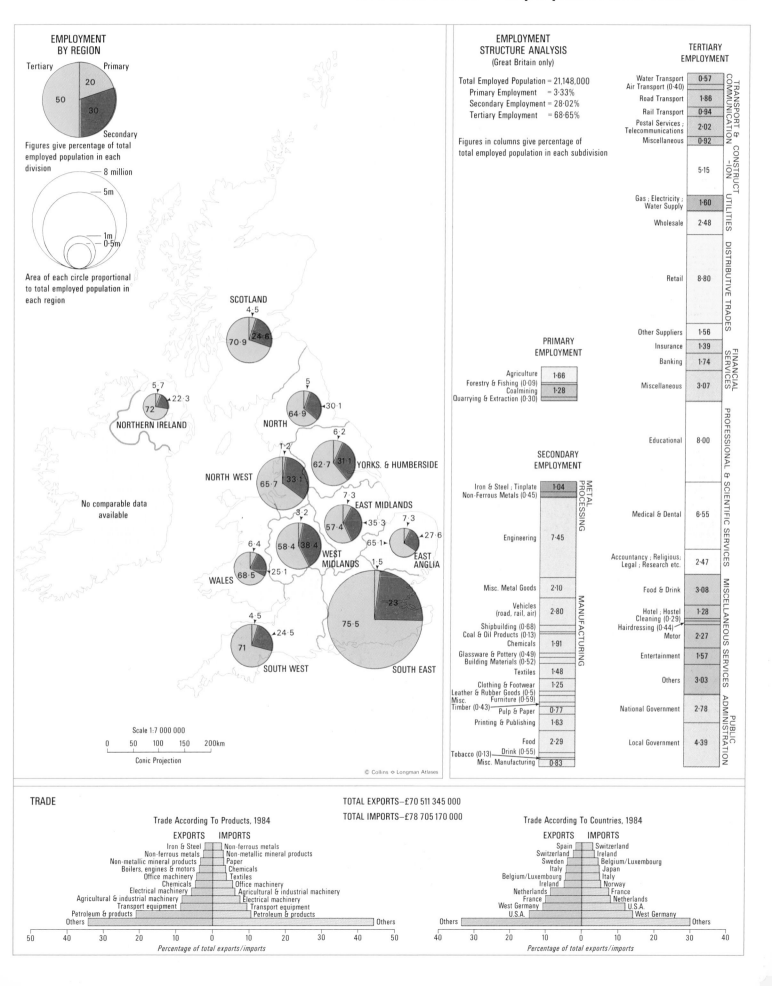

EMPLOYMENT BY REGION

Tertiary   Primary
50   20
30
Secondary

Figures give percentage of total employed population in each division

8 million
5m
1m
0.5m

Area of each circle proportional to total employed population in each region

No comparable data available

SCOTLAND
4.5
70.9   24.6

NORTHERN IRELAND
5.7
72   22.3

NORTH
5
64.9   30.1

YORKS. & HUMBERSIDE
6.2
62.7   31.1

NORTH WEST
1.2
65.7   33.1

EAST MIDLANDS
7.3
57.4   35.3

EAST ANGLIA
7.3
65.1   27.6

WEST MIDLANDS
3.2
58.4   38.4

WALES
6.4
68.5   25.1

SOUTH EAST
1.5
75.5   23

SOUTH WEST
4.5
71   24.5

Scale 1:7 000 000
0   50   100   150   200km
Conic Projection

© Collins ◇ Longman Atlases

EMPLOYMENT STRUCTURE ANALYSIS
(Great Britain only)

Total Employed Population = 21,148,000
Primary Employment = 3·33%
Secondary Employment = 28·02%
Tertiary Employment = 68·65%

Figures in columns give percentage of total employed population in each subdivision

PRIMARY EMPLOYMENT

Agriculture — 1·66
Forestry & Fishing (0·09)
Coalmining — 1·28
Quarrying & Extraction (0·30)

SECONDARY EMPLOYMENT

METAL PROCESSING
Iron & Steel ; Tinplate — 1·04
Non-Ferrous Metals (0·45)

MANUFACTURING
Engineering — 7·45
Misc. Metal Goods — 2·10
Vehicles (road, rail, air) — 2·80
Shipbuilding (0·68)
Coal & Oil Products (0·13)
Chemicals — 1·91
Glassware & Pottery (0·49)
Building Materials (0·52)
Textiles — 1·48
Clothing & Footwear — 1·25
Leather & Rubber Goods (0·5)
Misc. Furniture (0·59)
Timber (0·43) — Pulp & Paper — 0·77
Printing & Publishing — 1·63
Food — 2·29
Tobacco (0·13) — Drink (0·55)
Misc. Manufacturing — 0·83

TERTIARY EMPLOYMENT

TRANSPORT & COMMUNICATION
Water Transport — 0·57
Air Transport (0·40)
Road Transport — 1·86
Rail Transport — 0·94
Postal Services ; Telecommunications — 2·02
Miscellaneous — 0·92

CONSTRUCTION — 5·15

UTILITIES
Gas ; Electricity ; Water Supply — 1·60

DISTRIBUTIVE TRADES
Wholesale — 2·48
Retail — 8·80
Other Suppliers — 1·56

FINANCIAL SERVICES
Insurance — 1·39
Banking — 1·74
Miscellaneous — 3·07

PROFESSIONAL & SCIENTIFIC SERVICES
Educational — 8·00
Medical & Dental — 6·55
Accountancy ; Religious; Legal ; Research etc. — 2·47

MISCELLANEOUS SERVICES
Food & Drink — 3·08
Hotel ; Hostel — 1·28
Cleaning (0·29)
Hairdressing (0·44)
Motor — 2·27
Entertainment — 1·57
Others — 3·03

PUBLIC ADMINISTRATION
National Government — 2·78
Local Government — 4·39

TRADE

TOTAL EXPORTS—£70 511 345 000
TOTAL IMPORTS—£78 705 170 000

Trade According To Products, 1984

EXPORTS   IMPORTS

Iron & Steel | Non-ferrous metals
Non-ferrous metals | Non-metallic mineral products
Non-metallic mineral products | Paper
Boilers, engines & motors | Chemicals
Office machinery | Textiles
Chemicals | Office machinery
Electrical machinery | Agricultural & industrial machinery
Agricultural & industrial machinery | Electrical machinery
Transport equipment | Transport equipment
Petroleum & products | Petroleum & products
Others | Others

50   40   30   20   10   0   10   20   30   40   50
Percentage of total exports/imports

Trade According To Countries, 1984

EXPORTS   IMPORTS

Spain | Switzerland
Switzerland | Ireland
Sweden | Belgium/Luxembourg
Italy | Japan
Belgium/Luxembourg | Italy
Ireland | Norway
Netherlands | France
France | Netherlands
West Germany | U.S.A.
U.S.A. | West Germany
Others | Others

40   30   20   10   0   10   20   30   40
Percentage of total exports/imports

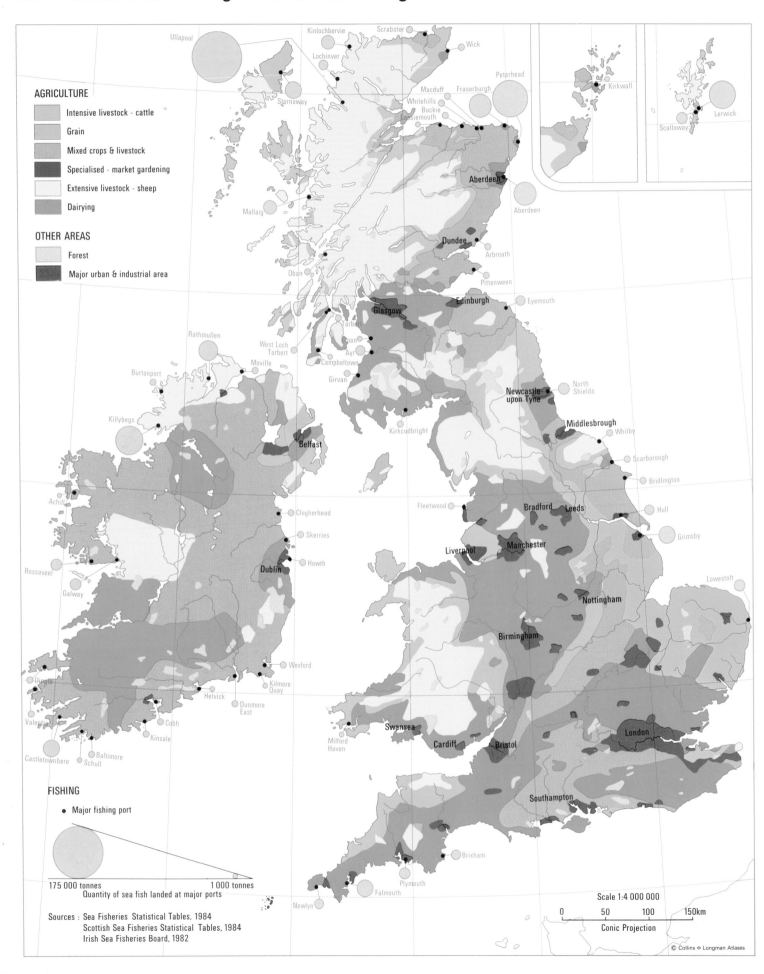

AGRICULTURE

- Intensive livestock - cattle
- Grain
- Mixed crops & livestock
- Specialised - market gardening
- Extensive livestock - sheep
- Dairying

OTHER AREAS

- Forest
- Major urban & industrial area

FISHING

- Major fishing port

175 000 tonnes   1 000 tonnes
Quantity of sea fish landed at major ports

Sources : Sea Fisheries Statistical Tables, 1984
Scottish Sea Fisheries Statistical Tables, 1984
Irish Sea Fisheries Board, 1982

Scale 1:4 000 000

0   50   100   150km

Conic Projection

© Collins ○ Longman Atlases

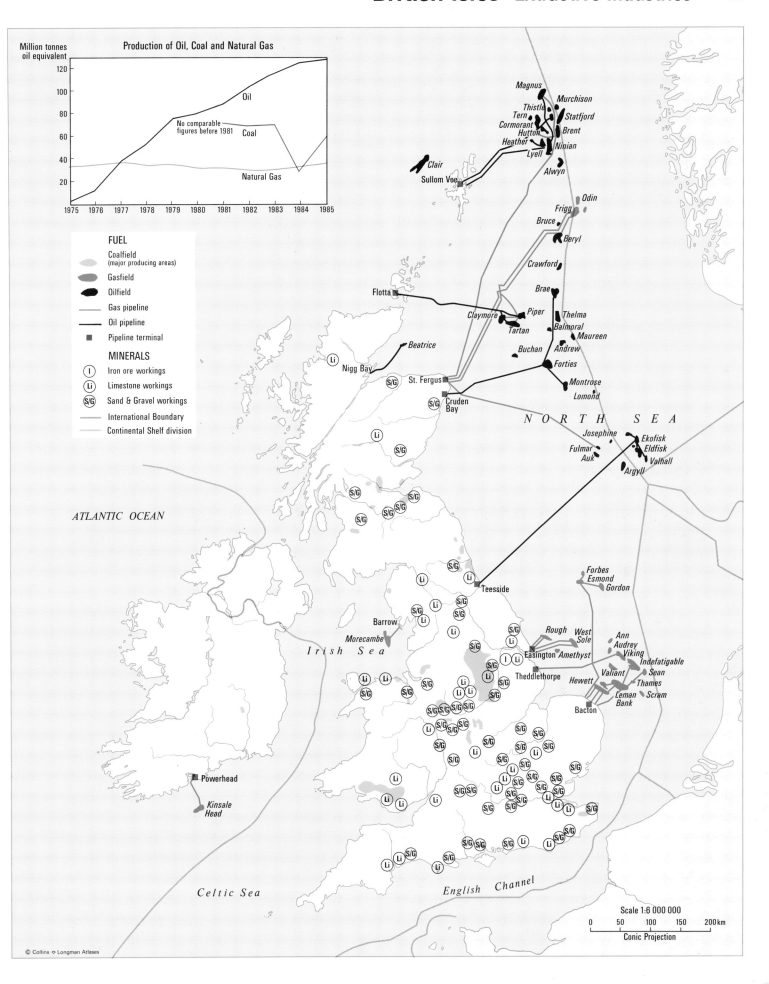

Production of Oil, Coal and Natural Gas

Million tonnes oil equivalent

120 100 80 60 40 20

1975 1976 1977 1978 1979 1980 1981 1982 1983 1984 1985

Oil

No comparable figures before 1981

Coal

Natural Gas

FUEL

Coalfield (major producing areas)

Gasfield

Oilfield

Gas pipeline

Oil pipeline

Pipeline terminal

MINERALS

I Iron ore workings

Li Limestone workings

S/G Sand & Gravel workings

International Boundary

Continental Shelf division

ATLANTIC OCEAN

Irish Sea

Celtic Sea

English Channel

NORTH SEA

Magnus
Murchison
Thistle
Tern
Statfjord
Cormorant
Brent
Hutton
Heather
Ninian
Lyell
Alwyn

Clair
Sullom Voe

Odin
Frigg
Bruce
Beryl
Crawford
Brae
Thelma
Claymore
Piper
Balmoral
Tartan
Maureen
Buchan
Andrew
Forties
Montrose
Lomond

Flotta

Beatrice
Nigg Bay
St. Fergus
Cruden Bay

Josephine
Fulmar
Ekofisk
Auk
Eldfisk
Valhall
Argyll

Teesside

Forbes
Esmond
Gordon

Barrow
Morecambe
Rough
West Sole
Ann
Audrey
Viking
Easington
Amethyst
Indefatigable
Theddlethorpe
Valiant
Sean
Hewett
Thames
Leman Bank
Scram
Bacton

Powerhead
Kinsale Head

Scale 1:6 000 000

0 50 100 150 200 km

Conic Projection

© Collins ◇ Longman Atlases

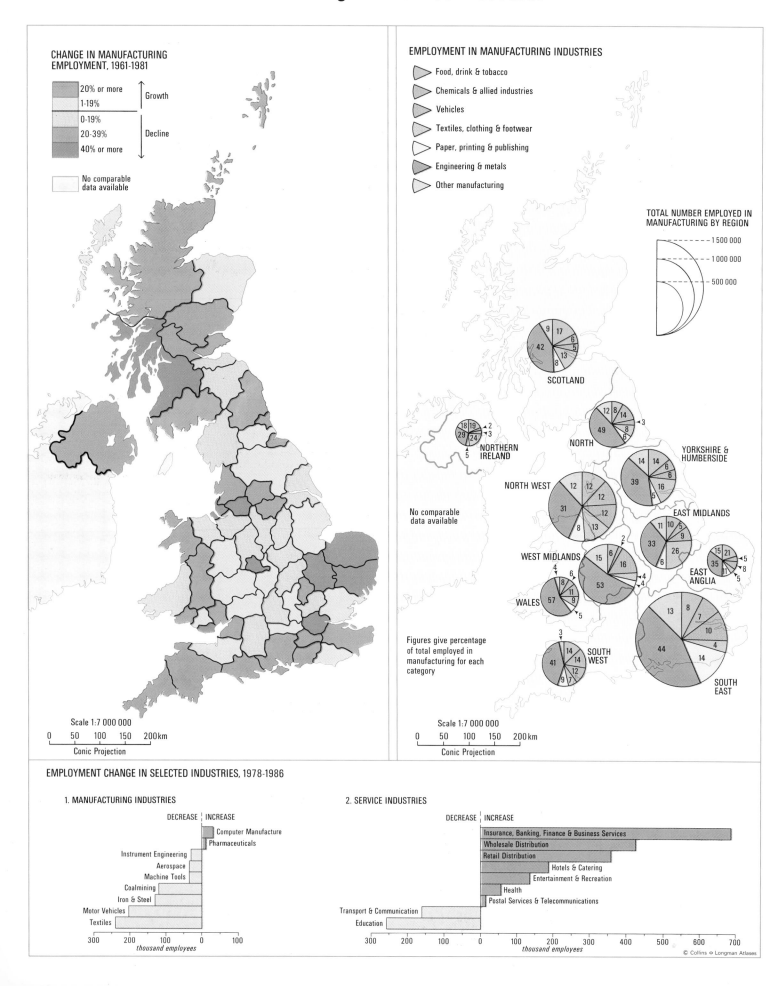

CHANGE IN MANUFACTURING EMPLOYMENT, 1961-1981

- 20% or more — Growth
- 1-19%
- 0-19% — Decline
- 20-39%
- 40% or more

No comparable data available

Scale 1:7 000 000

0   50   100   150   200km

Conic Projection

EMPLOYMENT IN MANUFACTURING INDUSTRIES

- Food, drink & tobacco
- Chemicals & allied industries
- Vehicles
- Textiles, clothing & footwear
- Paper, printing & publishing
- Engineering & metals
- Other manufacturing

TOTAL NUMBER EMPLOYED IN MANUFACTURING BY REGION

- 1 500 000
- 1 000 000
- 500 000

SCOTLAND — 9, 17, 6, 5, 13, 8, 42

NORTHERN IRELAND — 18, 19, 2, 3, 24, 5, 29

No comparable data available

NORTH — 12, 8, 14, 3, 8, 6, 49

YORKSHIRE & HUMBERSIDE — 14, 14, 6, 6, 16, 5, 39

NORTH WEST — 12, 12, 12, 13, 8, 31

EAST MIDLANDS — 11, 10, 5, 9, 26, 6, 33

WEST MIDLANDS — 15, 6, 16, 4, 4, 53, 2

EAST ANGLIA — 15, 21, 5, 8, 11, 5, 35

WALES — 4, 6, 8, 11, 9, 5, 57

SOUTH WEST — 3, 14, 14, 12, 7, 9, 41

SOUTH EAST — 13, 8, 7, 10, 4, 14, 44

Figures give percentage of total employed in manufacturing for each category

Scale 1:7 000 000

0   50   100   150   200km

Conic Projection

EMPLOYMENT CHANGE IN SELECTED INDUSTRIES, 1978-1986

1. MANUFACTURING INDUSTRIES

DECREASE | INCREASE

- Computer Manufacture
- Pharmaceuticals
- Instrument Engineering
- Aerospace
- Machine Tools
- Coalmining
- Iron & Steel
- Motor Vehicles
- Textiles

300   200   100   0   100
thousand employees

2. SERVICE INDUSTRIES

DECREASE | INCREASE

- Insurance, Banking, Finance & Business Services
- Wholesale Distribution
- Retail Distribution
- Hotels & Catering
- Entertainment & Recreation
- Health
- Postal Services & Telecommunications
- Transport & Communication
- Education

300   200   100   0   100   200   300   400   500   600   700
thousand employees

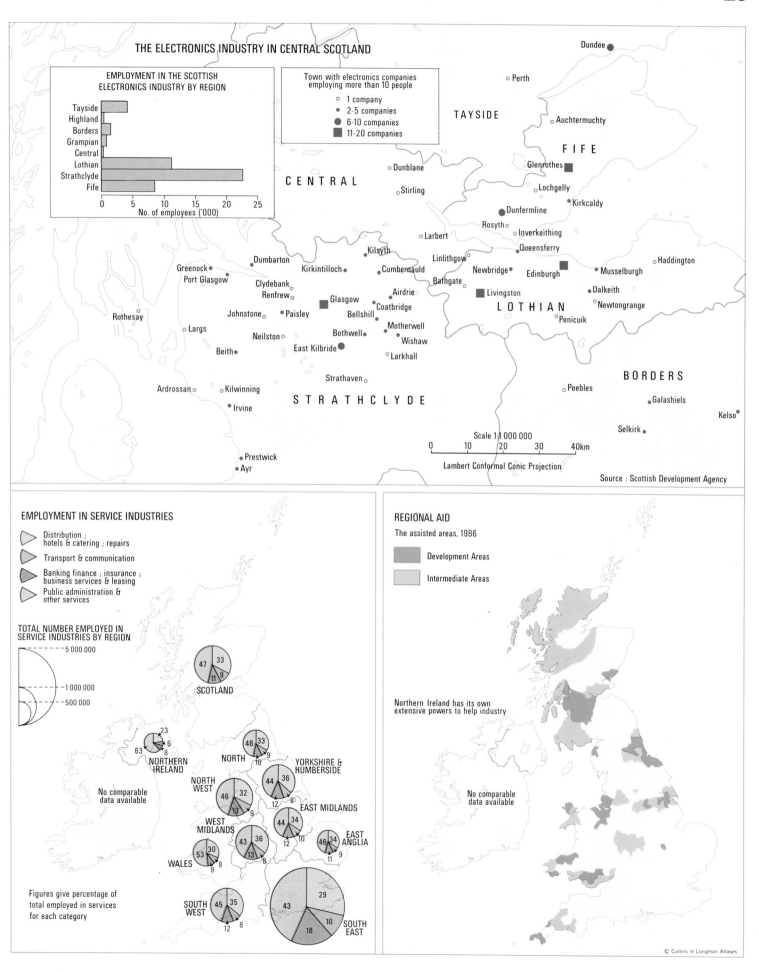

THE ELECTRONICS INDUSTRY IN CENTRAL SCOTLAND

EMPLOYMENT IN THE SCOTTISH ELECTRONICS INDUSTRY BY REGION

Tayside
Highland
Borders
Grampian
Central
Lothian
Strathclyde
Fife

No. of employees ('000)
0   5   10   15   20   25

Town with electronics companies employing more than 10 people
○ 1 company
• 2-5 companies
● 6-10 companies
■ 11-20 companies

Dundee
Perth
Auchtermuchty

TAYSIDE

FIFE
Glenrothes
Lochgelly
Kirkcaldy
Dunfermline
Rosyth
Inverkeithing
Queensferry
Haddington

CENTRAL
Dunblane
Stirling
Larbert
Linlithgow
Newbridge
Edinburgh
Musselburgh
Bathgate

Dumbarton
Kilsyth
Cumbernauld
Kirkintilloch
Greenock
Port Glasgow
Clydebank
Renfrew
Glasgow
Airdrie
Coatbridge
Bellshill
Livingston
Dalkeith
Newtongrange

LOTHIAN
Penicuik

Rothesay
Johnstone
Paisley
Motherwell
Wishaw
Largs
Neilston
Bothwell
Beith
East Kilbride
Larkhall

Ardrossan
Kilwinning
Strathaven

BORDERS
Peebles
Galashiels
Kelso
Selkirk

Irvine

STRATHCLYDE

Scale 1:1 000 000
0   10   20   30   40km

Lambert Conformal Conic Projection

Prestwick
Ayr

Source : Scottish Development Agency

EMPLOYMENT IN SERVICE INDUSTRIES

▷ Distribution ; hotels & catering ; repairs
▷ Transport & communication
▷ Banking finance ; insurance ; business services & leasing
▷ Public administration & other services

TOTAL NUMBER EMPLOYED IN SERVICE INDUSTRIES BY REGION

— 5 000 000
— 1 000 000
— 500 000

SCOTLAND
47 33
11 9

NORTHERN IRELAND
23 6
63 8

No comparable data available

NORTH
48 33
10 9

YORKSHIRE & HUMBERSIDE
44 36
12 8

NORTH WEST
46 32
13 9

EAST MIDLANDS
44 34
12 10

WEST MIDLANDS
43 36
13 8

EAST ANGLIA
46 34
11

WALES
53 30
9 8

SOUTH WEST
45 35
12 8

SOUTH EAST
43 29
18 10

Figures give percentage of total employed in services for each category

---

REGIONAL AID

The assisted areas, 1986

▨ Development Areas
▨ Intermediate Areas

Northern Ireland has its own extensive powers to help industry

No comparable data available

© Collins ○ Longman Atlases

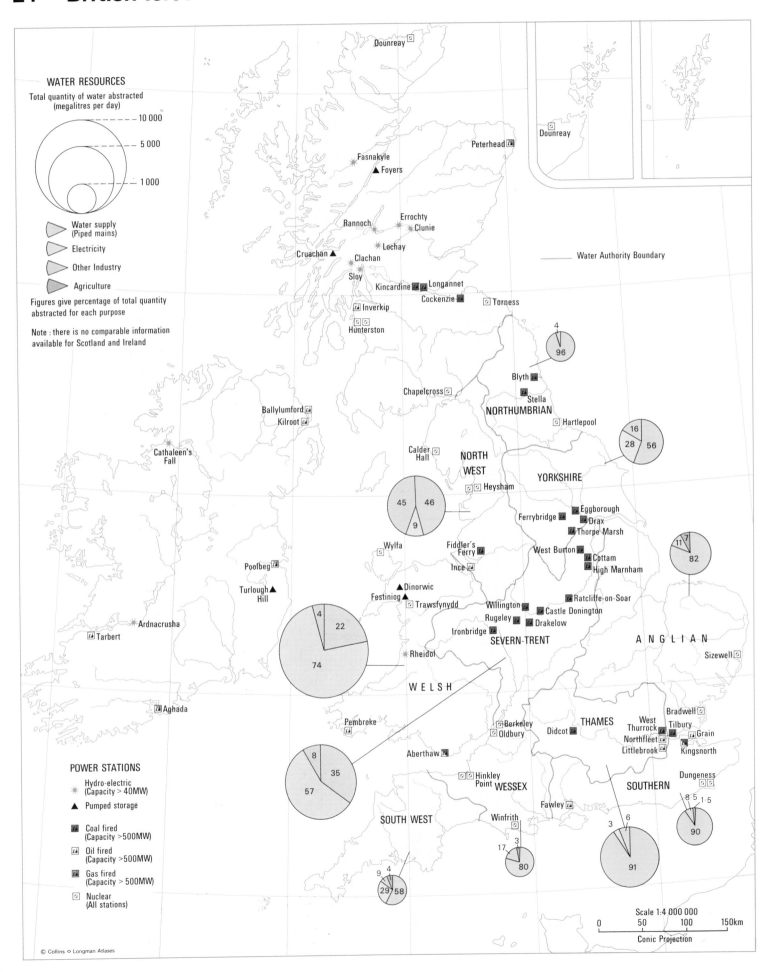

WATER RESOURCES

Total quantity of water abstracted
(megalitres per day)

— 10 000
— 5 000
— 1 000

Water supply
(Piped mains)

Electricity

Other Industry

Agriculture

Figures give percentage of total quantity
abstracted for each purpose

Note : there is no comparable information
available for Scotland and Ireland

Water Authority Boundary

POWER STATIONS

✳ Hydro-electric
(Capacity > 40MW)

▲ Pumped storage

▣ Coal fired
(Capacity >500MW)

▣ Oil fired
(Capacity >500MW)

▣ Gas fired
(Capacity > 500MW)

▢ Nuclear
(All stations)

Dounreay

Dounreay

Peterhead

Fasnakyle
▲ Foyers

Errochty
Rannoch ✳ Clunie
✳ Lochay
Cruachan ▲ Clachan
Sloy
Kincardine ▣▣ Longannet
Cockenzie ▣ Torness
Inverkip
Hunterston

4
96

Blyth
Stella
NORTHUMBRIAN
Chapelcross Hartlepool

Ballylumford
Kilroot

16
28 56

Cathaleen's
Fall

Calder
Hall NORTH
WEST YORKSHIRE
Heysham

45 46
9

Eggborough
Ferrybridge Drax
Thorpe Marsh

Wylfa
Fiddler's
Ferry West Burton
Ince Cottam
High Marnham

11 7
82

Poolbeg

Turlough ▲
Hill ▲ Dinorwic
Festiniog ▲
Trawsfynydd Willington Ratcliffe-on-Soar
Rugeley Castle Donington
Ironbridge Drakelow
SEVERN-TRENT A N G L I A N

4
22
Ardnacrusha
Tarbert
74 Rheidol Sizewell

W E L S H

Aghada

Pembroke West Bradwell
Berkeley Thurrock Tilbury
Oldbury Didcot Northfleet Grain
Aberthaw Littlebrook Kingsnorth

8
35 Hinkley THAMES Dungeness
Point WESSEX SOUTHERN
57 Fawley 8 5 1·5

Winfrith 90
SOUTH WEST 3 6
3
17 3 91
9 4 80
29 58

Scale 1:4 000 000
0   50   100   150km
Conic Projection

© Collins ◊ Longman Atlases

ROADS

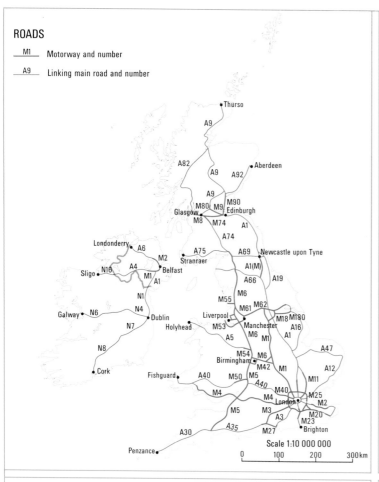

—M1— Motorway and number

—A9— Linking main road and number

Scale 1:10 000 000

0   100   200   300km

RAILWAYS

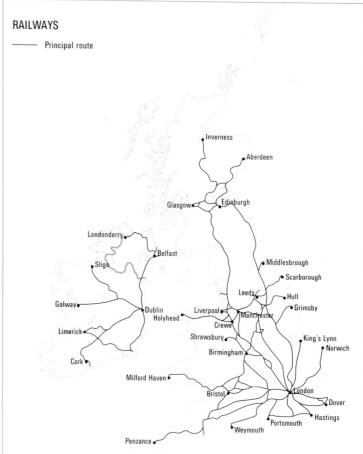

—— Principal route

AIRPORTS

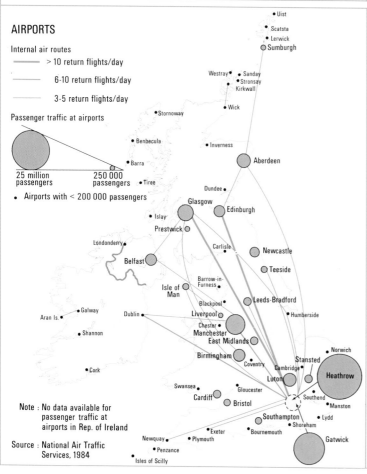

Internal air routes

——— > 10 return flights/day

——— 6-10 return flights/day

——— 3-5 return flights/day

Passenger traffic at airports

25 million passengers   250 000 passengers

• Airports with < 200 000 passengers

Note : No data available for passenger traffic at airports in Rep. of Ireland

Source : National Air Traffic Services, 1984

PORTS

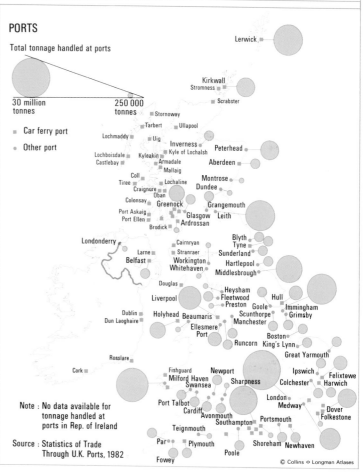

Total tonnage handled at ports

30 million tonnes   250 000 tonnes

■ Car ferry port

● Other port

Note : No data available for tonnage handled at ports in Rep. of Ireland

Source : Statistics of Trade Through U.K. Ports, 1982

© Collins ○ Longman Atlases

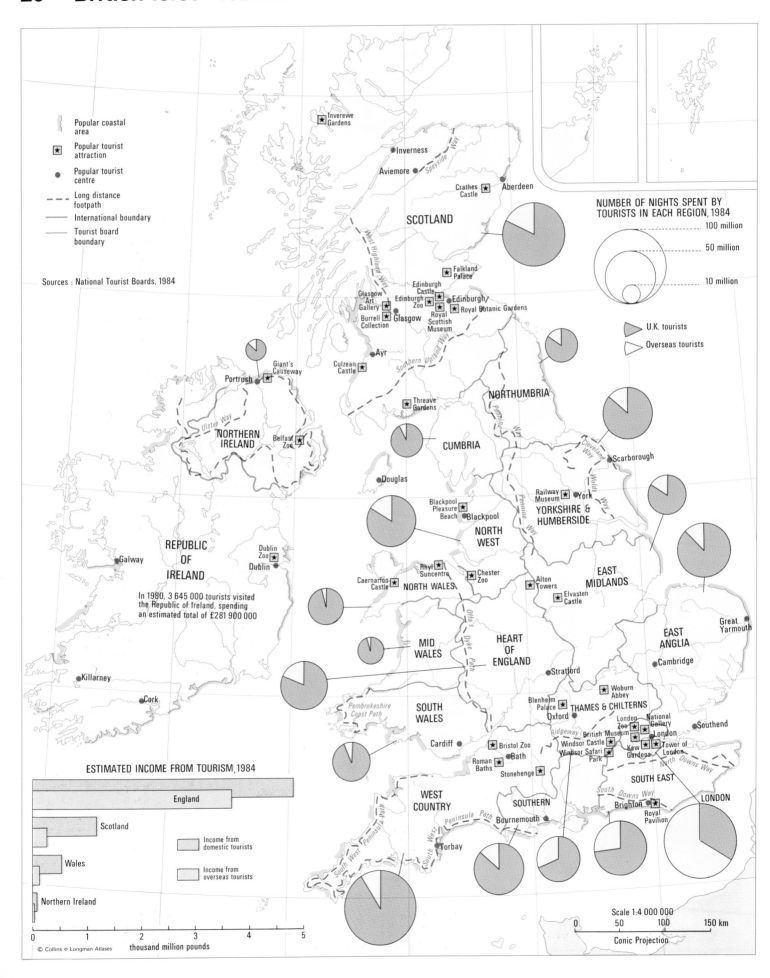

Popular coastal area

Popular tourist attraction

Popular tourist centre

Long distance footpath

International boundary

Tourist board boundary

Sources : National Tourist Boards, 1984

NUMBER OF NIGHTS SPENT BY TOURISTS IN EACH REGION, 1984
100 million
50 million
10 million

U.K. tourists

Overseas tourists

Inverewe Gardens

Inverness
Aviemore
Speyside Way

Crathes Castle
Aberdeen

SCOTLAND

West Highland Way

Falkland Palace

Glasgow Art Gallery
Edinburgh Castle
Edinburgh Zoo
Edinburgh
Royal Botanic Gardens

Burrell Collection
Glasgow
Royal Scottish Museum

Ayr

Southern Upland Way

Culzean Castle

Giant's Causeway

Portrush

NORTHUMBRIA

Threave Gardens

Ulster Way

NORTHERN IRELAND

Belfast Zoo

CUMBRIA

Pennine Way

Cleveland Way

Scarborough

REPUBLIC OF IRELAND

In 1980, 3 645 000 tourists visited the Republic of Ireland, spending an estimated total of £281 900 000

Galway

Dublin Zoo
Dublin

Douglas

Railway Museum
York

Wolds Way

YORKSHIRE & HUMBERSIDE

Blackpool Pleasure Beach
Blackpool

NORTH WEST

Pennine Way

Rhyl Suncentre

Chester Zoo

EAST MIDLANDS

Alton Towers

Elvaston Castle

Killarney

Caernarfon Castle
NORTH WALES

Offa's Dyke Path

MID WALES

HEART OF ENGLAND

EAST ANGLIA

Great Yarmouth

Cork

Stratford

Cambridge

Pembrokeshire Coast Path

SOUTH WALES

Woburn Abbey

Blenheim Palace
Oxford
THAMES & CHILTERNS

London Zoo
National Gallery
British Museum
London
Tower of London
Kew Gardens

Southend

Cardiff

Ridgeway

Bristol Zoo
Bath
Roman Baths
Stonehenge

Windsor Castle
Windsor Safari Park

North Downs Way

SOUTH EAST

WEST COUNTRY

South West Peninsula Path

SOUTHERN

South Downs Way

Brighton
Royal Pavilion

LONDON

Bournemouth

Torbay

ESTIMATED INCOME FROM TOURISM, 1984

England

Scotland

Wales

Northern Ireland

Income from domestic tourists

Income from overseas tourists

0   1   2   3   4   5
thousand million pounds

© Collins ◇ Longman Atlases

Scale 1:4 000 000

0   50   100   150 km

Conic Projection

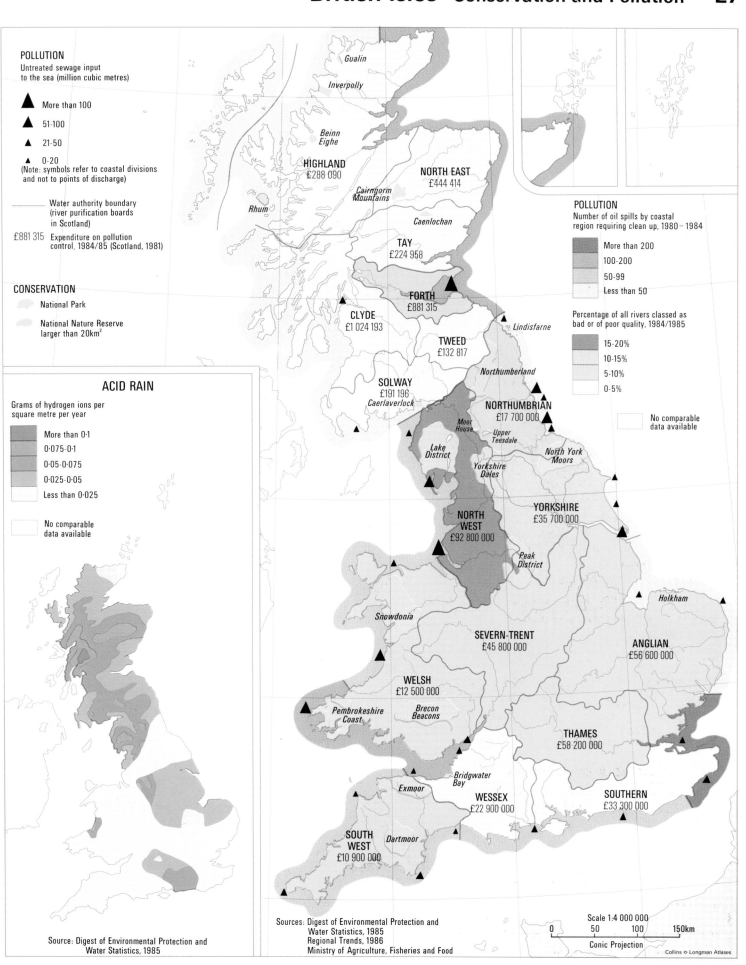

POLLUTION

Untreated sewage input
to the sea (million cubic metres)

▲ More than 100

▲ 51-100

▲ 21-50

▲ 0-20

(Note: symbols refer to coastal divisions
and not to points of discharge)

— Water authority boundary
(river purification boards
in Scotland)

£881 315 Expenditure on pollution
control, 1984/85 (Scotland, 1981)

CONSERVATION

National Park

National Nature Reserve
larger than 20km²

POLLUTION

Number of oil spills by coastal
region requiring clean up, 1980–1984

More than 200

100-200

50-99

Less than 50

Percentage of all rivers classed as
bad or of poor quality, 1984/1985

15-20%

10-15%

5-10%

0-5%

No comparable
data available

ACID RAIN

Grams of hydrogen ions per
square metre per year

More than 0·1

0·075-0·1

0·05-0·075

0·025-0·05

Less than 0·025

No comparable
data available

Gualin

Inverpolly

*Beinn
Eighe*

HIGHLAND
£288 090

Rhum

*Cairngorm
Mountains*

NORTH EAST
£444 414

Caenlochan

TAY
£224 958

CLYDE
£1 024 193

FORTH
£881 315

Lindisfarne

TWEED
£132 817

Northumberland

SOLWAY
£191 196

Caerlaverock

NORTHUMBRIAN
£17 700 000

*Moor
House*

*Upper
Teesdale*

*Lake
District*

*North York
Moors*

*Yorkshire
Dales*

YORKSHIRE
£35 700 000

NORTH
WEST
£92 800 000

*Peak
District*

Snowdonia

SEVERN-TRENT
£45 800 000

Holkham

ANGLIAN
£56 600 000

WELSH
£12 500 000

*Pembrokeshire
Coast*

*Brecon
Beacons*

THAMES
£58 200 000

*Bridgwater
Bay*

Exmoor

WESSEX
£22 900 000

SOUTHERN
£33 300 000

SOUTH
WEST
£10 900 000

Dartmoor

Sources: Digest of Environmental Protection and
Water Statistics, 1985
Regional Trends, 1986
Ministry of Agriculture, Fisheries and Food

Scale 1:4 000 000

0   50   100   150km

Conic Projection

Collins ◊ Longman Atlases

Source: Digest of Environmental Protection and
Water Statistics, 1985

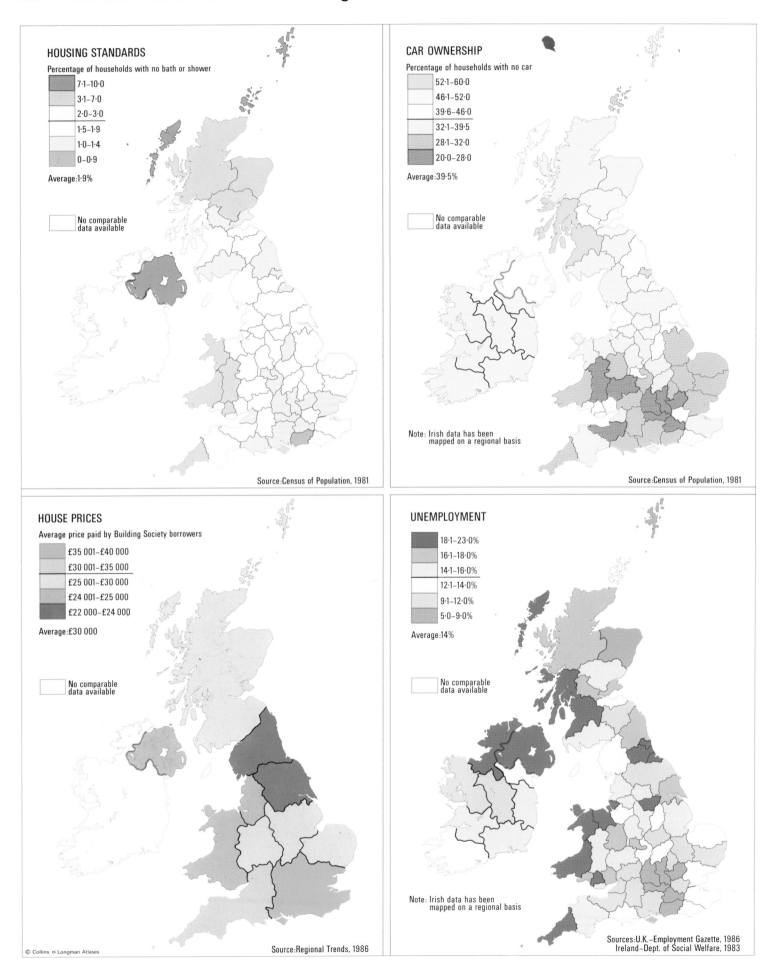

HOUSING STANDARDS

Percentage of households with no bath or shower

- 7·1–10·0
- 3·1–7·0
- 2·0–3·0
- 1·5–1·9
- 1·0–1·4
- 0–0·9

Average:1·9%

No comparable data available

Source:Census of Population, 1981

CAR OWNERSHIP

Percentage of households with no car

- 52·1–60·0
- 46·1–52·0
- 39·6–46·0
- 32·1–39·5
- 28·1–32·0
- 20·0–28·0

Average:39·5%

No comparable data available

Note: Irish data has been mapped on a regional basis

Source:Census of Population, 1981

HOUSE PRICES

Average price paid by Building Society borrowers

- £35 001–£40 000
- £30 001–£35 000
- £25 001–£30 000
- £24 001–£25 000
- £22 000–£24 000

Average:£30 000

No comparable data available

© Collins ◇ Longman Atlases

Source:Regional Trends, 1986

UNEMPLOYMENT

- 18·1–23·0%
- 16·1–18·0%
- 14·1–16·0%
- 12·1–14·0%
- 9·1–12·0%
- 5·0–9·0%

Average:14%

No comparable data available

Note: Irish data has been mapped on a regional basis

Sources:U.K.–Employment Gazette, 1986
Ireland–Dept. of Social Welfare, 1983

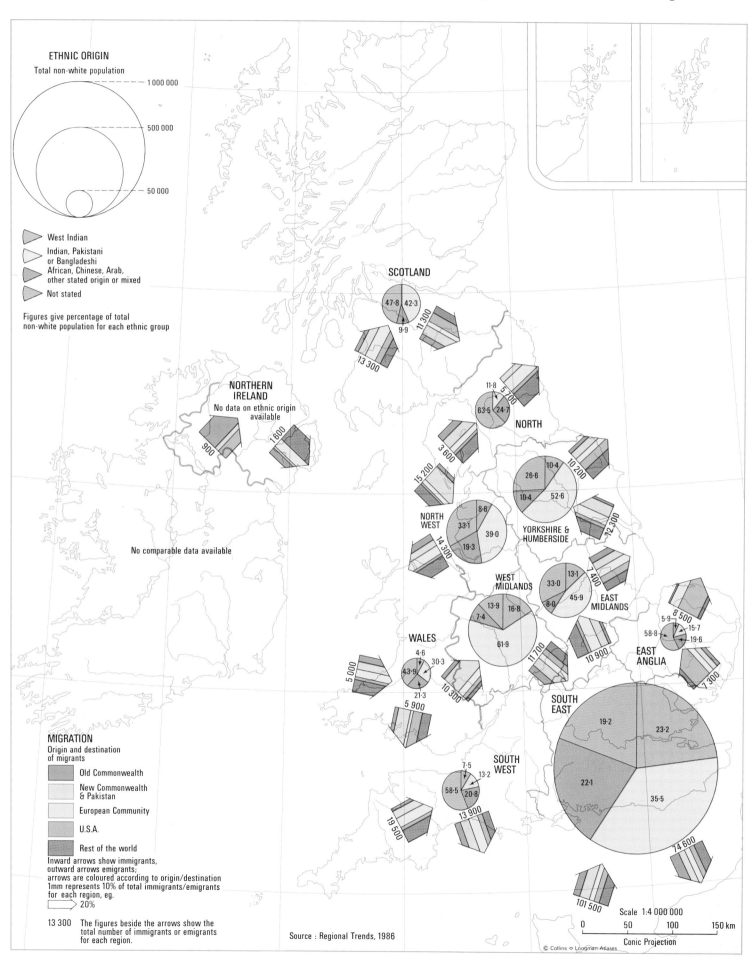

ETHNIC ORIGIN
Total non-white population

1 000 000
500 000
50 000

West Indian

Indian, Pakistani
or Bangladeshi

African, Chinese, Arab,
other stated origin or mixed

Not stated

Figures give percentage of total
non-white population for each ethnic group

SCOTLAND
47·8 42·3
9·9
11 300
13 300

NORTHERN
IRELAND
No data on ethnic origin
available
900
1 600

No comparable data available

NORTH
11·8 5 700
63·5 24·7
3 600

15 200

YORKSHIRE &
HUMBERSIDE
26·6 10·4 10 200
10·4 52·6
12 300

NORTH
WEST
8·6
33·1
19·3 39·0
14 300

EAST
MIDLANDS
13·1 7 400
33·0
8·0 45·9
10 900

WEST
MIDLANDS
13·9 16·8
7·4
61·9
11 700

EAST
ANGLIA
5·9 8 500
58·8 15·7
19·6
7 300

WALES
4·6
30·3
43·9
21·3
10 300
5 000
5 900

SOUTH
EAST
19·2 23·2
22·1 35·5
74 600

SOUTH
WEST
7·5
13·2
58·5 20·8
13 900
19 500

101 500

MIGRATION
Origin and destination
of migrants

Old Commonwealth

New Commonwealth
& Pakistan

European Community

U.S.A.

Rest of the world

Inward arrows show immigrants,
outward arrows emigrants;
arrows are coloured according to origin/destination
1mm represents 10% of total immigrants/emigrants
for each region, eg.

20%

13 300   The figures beside the arrows show the
total number of immigrants or emigrants
for each region.

Source : Regional Trends, 1986

Scale 1:4 000 000
0   50   100   150 km
Conic Projection

© Collins ◇ Longman Atlases

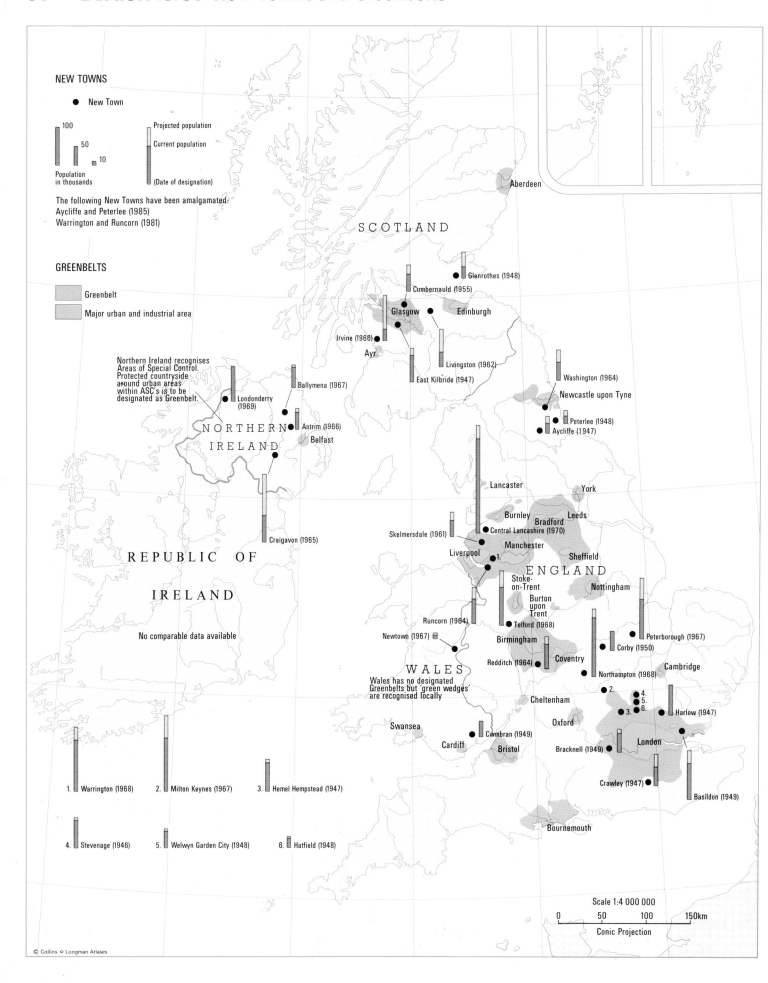

NEW TOWNS

● New Town

100
50
10
Population
in thousands

Projected population
Current population
(Date of designation)

The following New Towns have been amalgamated:
Aycliffe and Peterlee (1985)
Warrington and Runcorn (1981)

GREENBELTS

Greenbelt

Major urban and industrial area

Northern Ireland recognises
Areas of Special Control.
Protected countryside
around urban areas
within ASC's is to be
designated as Greenbelt.

SCOTLAND

Aberdeen

Glenrothes (1948)
Cumbernauld (1955)
Glasgow
Edinburgh
Irvine (1966)
Ayr
Livingston (1962)
East Kilbride (1947)
Washington (1964)
Newcastle upon Tyne
Peterlee (1948)
Aycliffe (1947)

Ballymena (1967)
Londonderry
(1969)
NORTHERN
IRELAND
Antrim (1966)
Belfast

Lancaster
York
Burnley
Bradford
Leeds
Central Lancashire (1970)
Skelmersdale (1961)
Liverpool
Manchester
1.
ENGLAND
Sheffield
Stoke-
on-Trent
Nottingham
Burton
upon
Trent
Runcorn (1964)
Telford (1968)
Newtown (1967)
Birmingham
Peterborough (1967)
Corby (1950)
Redditch (1964)
Coventry
Northampton (1968)
Cambridge
2.
4.
5.
3.   6.
Harlow (1947)
Cheltenham
Oxford
London
Bracknell (1949)
Crawley (1947)
Basildon (1949)

Craigavon (1965)

REPUBLIC   OF

IRELAND

No comparable data available

WALES
Wales has no designated
Greenbelts but 'green wedges'
are recognised locally

Swansea
Cardiff
Cwmbran (1949)
Bristol

Bournemouth

1. Warrington (1968)   2. Milton Keynes (1967)   3. Hemel Hempstead (1947)

4. Stevenage (1946)   5. Welwyn Garden City (1948)   6. Hatfield (1948)

Scale 1:4 000 000
0   50   100   150km
Conic Projection

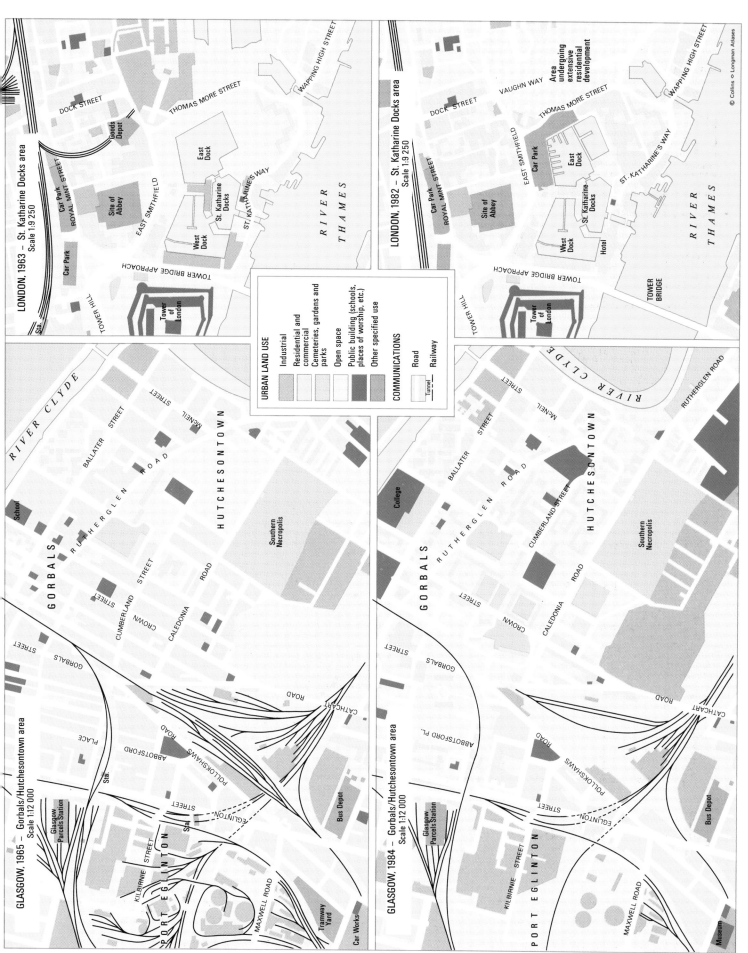

LONDON, 1963 – St. Katharine Docks area
Scale 1:9 250

DOCK STREET
THOMAS MORE STREET
WAPPING HIGH STREET
Goods Depot
Car Park
ROYAL MINT STREET
EAST SMITHFIELD
Site of Abbey
Car Park
East Dock
St. Katharine Docks
ST. KATHARINE'S WAY
West Dock
TOWER BRIDGE APPROACH
Sta.
TOWER HILL
Tower of London
RIVER THAMES

LONDON, 1982 – St. Katharine Docks area
Scale 1:9 250

DOCK STREET
VAUGHN WAY
Area undergoing extensive residential development
THOMAS MORE STREET
WAPPING HIGH STREET
Car Park
ROYAL MINT STREET
EAST SMITHFIELD
Car Park
East Dock
Site of Abbey
St. Katharine Docks
ST. KATHARINE'S WAY
West Dock
Hotel
Hotel
TOWER BRIDGE APPROACH
TOWER HILL
Tower of London
TOWER BRIDGE
RIVER THAMES

URBAN LAND USE

- Industrial
- Residential and commercial
- Cemeteries, gardens and parks
- Open space
- Public building (schools, places of worship, etc.)
- Other specified use

COMMUNICATIONS

- Road
- Railway
- Tunnel

GLASGOW, 1965 – Gorbals/Hutchesontown area
Scale 1:12 000

RIVER CLYDE
School
BALLATER STREET
STREET
McNEIL
RUTHERGLEN ROAD
GORBALS
CUMBERLAND STREET
CROWN STREET
CALEDONIA ROAD
HUTCHESONTOWN
Southern Necropolis
STREET
GORBALS STREET
ABBOTSFORD PLACE
POLLOKSHAWS ROAD
Sta.
EGLINTON STREET
CATHCART ROAD
Glasgow Parcels Station
KILBIRNIE STREET
PORT EGLINTON
MAXWELL ROAD
Bus Depot
Tramway Yard
Car Works

GLASGOW, 1984 – Gorbals/Hutchesontown area
Scale 1:12 000

RIVER CLYDE
STREET
McNEIL
RUTHERGLEN ROAD
College
BALLATER STREET
GORBALS
CUMBERLAND STREET
CROWN STREET
CALEDONIA ROAD
RUTHERGLEN ROAD
HUTCHESONTOWN
Southern Necropolis
STREET
GORBALS STREET
ABBOTSFORD PL.
POLLOKSHAWS ROAD
EGLINTON STREET
CATHCART ROAD
Glasgow Parcels Station
KILBIRNIE STREET
PORT EGLINTON
MAXWELL ROAD
Bus Depot
Museum

© Collins ○ Longman Atlases

Relief

Metres
5000
3000
2000
1000
500
200
0
Sea Level
Land Dep.
200
4000
7000
Metres

Scale 1:16 000 000

0 200 400 600 800 km

Conic Projection

ARCTIC

North Cape

NORWEGIAN SEA

Arctic Circle

Inari

Vesterålen
Lofoten
Vestfjorden

Kebnekaise 2123

Lapla

Muonio
Torne

Storavan
Ume
Skellefte
Lule

Kemi

Frohavet

Oulujärvi

Gulf of Bothnia

Storsjön
Indals
Ljusnan

Näsijärvi
Kalla

Dovrefjell
Jotunheimen
Glittertind 2470

Sognefjorden

Mjösa
Gløma
Klar
Dal

Åland Is.

Gulf of Finlar

L. Peipu

Hardangerfjorden

Otra
Ostfjorden
Läger

Vänern
Göta

Vättern

Mälaren

Gotland

Saaremaa

Gulf of Riga

Lindesnes

Skagerrak

Kattegat

Lagan
Öland

BALTIC SEA

Limfjorden
Jutland

Zealand
Bornholm

Funen

Neman

FAROE Is.

Shetland Is.

Orkney Is.

Moray Firth

Hebrides

Ben Nevis 1343

Grampian Mountains

Firth of Forth

Clyde

Southern Uplands

Malin Head

Galway Bay

Shannon

Wicklow Mts.

Irish Sea

Cape Clear

Celtic Sea

St. George's Channel

The Pennines

Snowdon 1085

Cambrian Mts.

Trent

Severn

The Wash

The Fens

Thames

Land's End

Isles of Scilly

English Channel

Channel Is.

Str. of Dover

Frisian Is.

IJsselmeer

Kiel Canal

Elbe

Oder

NORTH SEA

Harz Mts.

Spree

Warta

Vistula

NORTH EU

Neman

Bug

ATLANTIC OCEAN

Bay of Biscay

Brittany

Seine
Marne

Loire

Loire

Vienne

Gironde

Garonne

Dordogne

Meuse
Rhine
Ardennes
Mosel
Taunus
Weser

Ore Mts.

Bohemian Forest

Sudeten Mts.

Oder

Silesian Plateau

Vistula

Gerlachovka 2663

Carpathian

Morava

Morava

Tisza

Hungarian Plain

Drava

Danube

Mures

Transylvanian
Iron Gate

Balka

Danube

C. Finisterre

Cantabrian Mts.

Gulf of Gascony

Massif Central

Mont Dore 1886

Pyrénées

Pico de Aneto 3404

Iberian Mts.

Ebro

Douro

Douro

Tagus

Iberian Peninsula

Guadiana

C. Roca

C. St. Vincent

Sierra Morena

Gulf of Cadiz

Guadalquivir

Mulhacén 3482
Sierra Nevada

Str. of Gibraltar

C. Palos

Ebro Delta

Balearic Is.

Minorca

C. de la Nao
Ibiza
Majorca

Gulf of Lions

C. Creus

Saône

Jura Mts.

L. Geneva

Rhône

Mt. Blanc 4807

ALPS

Vosges
Black Forest

L. Constance

Inn

Brenner Pass

Gross Glockner 3798

Mt. Rosa 4634

Dolomites

Adige

Danube

Drava

Sava

Durance

Cevennes

Rhône

Po

Brenner

G. of Genoa

Ligurian Sea

Arno

Tiber

Apennines

2914 Mt. Corno

1277 Vesuvius

ADRIATIC SEA

Dinaric Alps

Drina

Durmitor 2522

L. Shkoder

Rhodope

Mesala 2925

Struma
Axiós

Corsica

Str. of Bonifacio

Sardinia

Tyrrhenian Sea

G. of Taranto

Stromboli 926

Sicily

Mt. Etna 3340

Str. of Otranto

Corfu

Ionian Islands

Mt. Olympus 2911

Pindus Mts.

Mt. At

Killini 2376

Euboea

Ionian Sea

C. Spartivento

C. Passero

C. Bon

Mejerda

MEDITERRAN

Oum er Rbia

Rif Mts.

Sebou

Cheliff

Tell Atlas

Chott ech Chergui

High Atlas

Saharan Atlas

Toubkal 4165

C. Matapan

Snaefell 1803

Vatnajökull

Mt. Hekla 1491

Surtsey

Straumnes

© Collins ◊ Longman Atlases

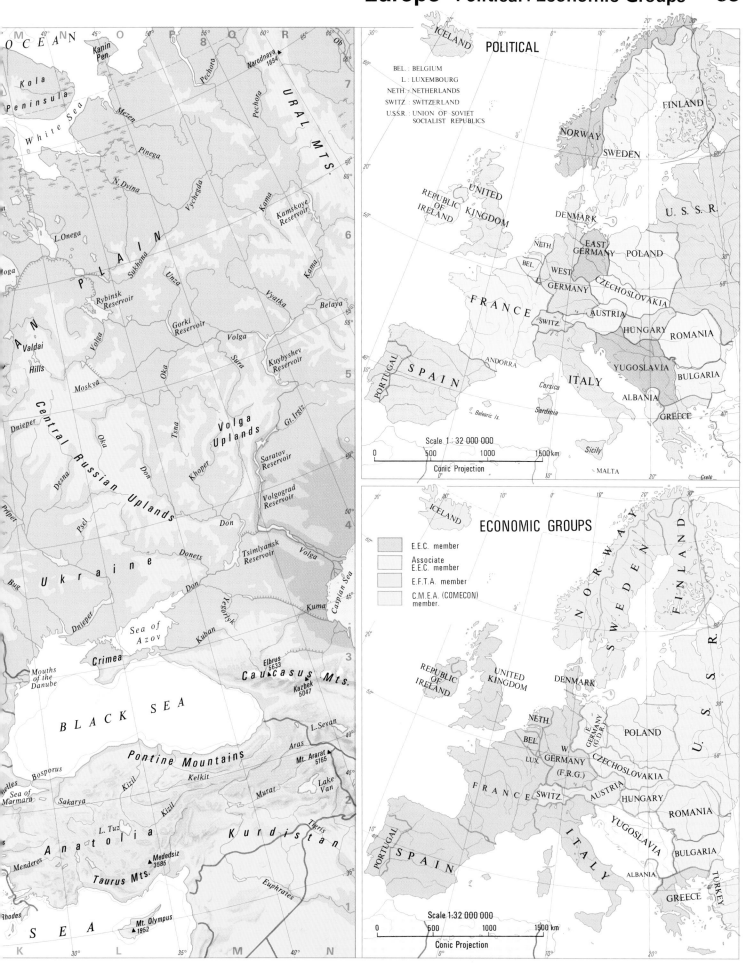

POLITICAL

BEL. : BELGIUM
L : LUXEMBOURG
NETH : NETHERLANDS
SWITZ : SWITZERLAND
U.S.S.R : UNION OF SOVIET
SOCIALIST REPUBLICS

ICELAND

NORWAY
SWEDEN
FINLAND

REPUBLIC
OF
IRELAND
UNITED
KINGDOM
DENMARK
U.S.S.R.

NETH.
BEL.
L
WEST
GERMANY
EAST
GERMANY
POLAND
CZECHOSLOVAKIA

FRANCE
SWITZ.
AUSTRIA
HUNGARY
ROMANIA

PORTUGAL
SPAIN
ANDORRA
ITALY
YUGOSLAVIA
BULGARIA
ALBANIA
GREECE

Corsica
Sardinia
Balearic Is.
Sicily
MALTA
Crete

Scale 1 : 32 000 000

0   500   1000   1500 km

Conic Projection

ECONOMIC GROUPS

E.E.C. member

Associate
E.E.C. member

E.F.T.A. member

C.M.E.A. (COMECON)
member.

ICELAND

NORWAY
SWEDEN
FINLAND

REPUBLIC
OF
IRELAND
UNITED
KINGDOM
DENMARK
U.S.S.R.

NETH.
BEL.
LUX.
W.
GERMANY
(F.R.G.)
E.
GERMANY
(G.D.R.)
POLAND
CZECHOSLOVAKIA

FRANCE
SWITZ.
AUSTRIA
HUNGARY
ROMANIA

PORTUGAL
SPAIN
ITALY
YUGOSLAVIA
BULGARIA
ALBANIA
GREECE
TURKEY

Scale 1:32 000 000

0   500   1000   1500 km

Conic Projection

(Left physical map labels)

OCEAN
Kanin Pen.
Kola Peninsula
White Sea
Mezen
Pinega
N. Dvina
Vychegda
Pechora
Narodnaya 1894
URAL MTS.
PLAIN
L.Onega
Sukhona
Kama
Kamskoye Reservoir
Kama
Rybinsk Reservoir
Gorki Reservoir
Unza
Vyatka
Belaya
Valdai Hills
Volga
Volga
Oka
Sura
Kuybyshev Reservoir
Moskva
Moskva
Dnieper
Desna
Oka
Tsna
Khoper
Volga Uplands
Gt. Irgiz
Saratov Reservoir
Central Russian Uplands
Psel
Don
Don
Donets
Tsimlyansk Reservoir
Volgograd Reservoir
Volga
Ukraine
Bug
Dnieper
Yegorlyk
Kuma
Caspian Sea
Sea of Azov
Kuban
Crimea
Mouths of the Danube
Elbrus 5633
Caucasus Mts.
Kazbek 5047
BLACK SEA
L.Sevan
Aras
Mt. Ararat 5165
Bosporus
Pontine Mountains
Kizil
Kelkit
Murat
Lake Van
Sea of Marmara
Sakarya
Kizil
L. Tuz
Anatolia
Kurdistan
Tigris
Menderes
Mededsiz 3585
Taurus Mts.
Euphrates
Rhodes
Mt. Olympus 1952
SEA

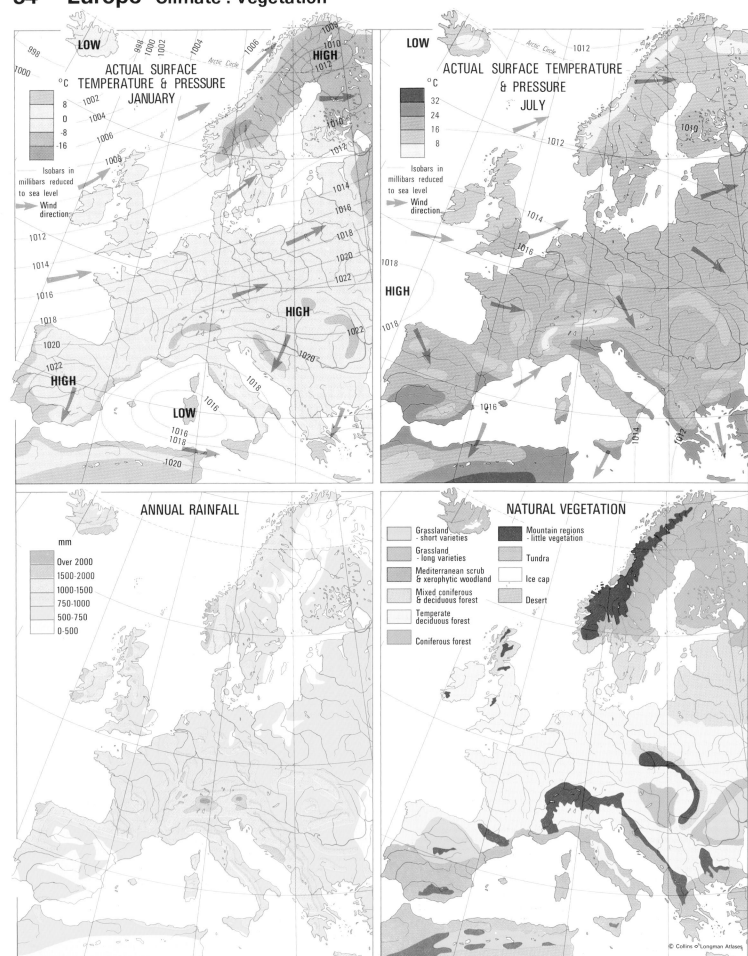

ACTUAL SURFACE
TEMPERATURE & PRESSURE
JANUARY

°C
8
0
-8
-16

Isobars in
millibars reduced
to sea level
Wind
direction

LOW
HIGH
HIGH
LOW
HIGH

998
1000
1002
1004
1006
1008
1010
1012
1014
1016
1018
1020
1022

ACTUAL SURFACE TEMPERATURE
& PRESSURE
JULY

°C
32
24
16
8

Isobars in
millibars reduced
to sea level
Wind
direction

LOW
HIGH
Arctic Circle

ANNUAL RAINFALL

mm
Over 2000
1500-2000
1000-1500
750-1000
500-750
0-500

NATURAL VEGETATION

Grassland
- short varieties

Grassland
- long varieties

Mediterranean scrub
& xerophytic woodland

Mixed coniferous
& deciduous forest

Temperate
deciduous forest

Coniferous forest

Mountain regions
- little vegetation

Tundra

Ice cap

Desert

© Collins ↔ Longman Atlases

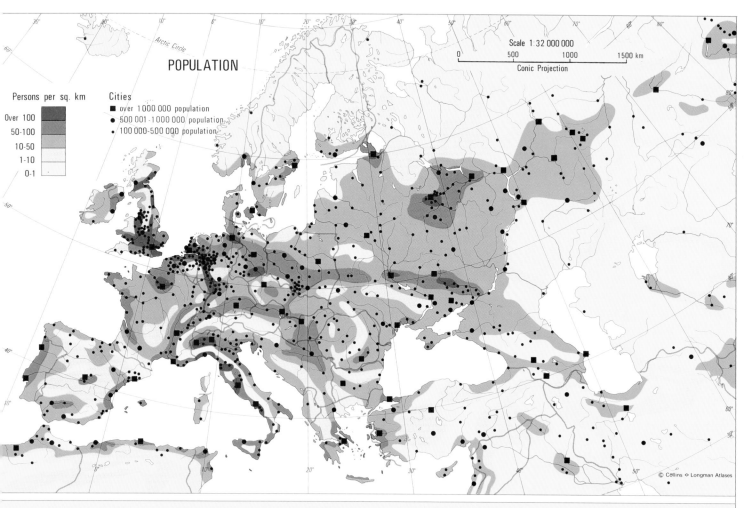

POPULATION

Persons per sq. km

Over 100
50-100
10-50
1-10
0-1

Cities
■ over 1 000 000 population
● 500 001 - 1 000 000 population
• 100 000 - 500 000 population

Scale 1 : 32 000 000
0   500   1000   1500 km
Conic Projection

© Collins ◇ Longman Atlases

POPULATION STATISTICS

COUNTRY	TOTAL POPULATION	% URBAN POPULA-TION	LIFE EXPECTATION AT BIRTH		% OF TOTAL POPULATION BY AGE GROUP				
			MALE	FEMALE	0-14	15-34	35-54	55-74	75+
ALBANIA	2 841 000	33.8	68.00	71.50	na	na	na	na	na
AUSTRIA	7 549 000	54.9	69.18	76.59	20.0	30.4	24.2	19.2	6.2
BELGIUM	9 856 000	94.6	68.60	75.08	20.0	31.1	24.2	18.9	5.8
BULGARIA	8 939 000	64.6	68.68	73.91	22.1	28.8	26.4	18.7	4.0
CZECHOSLOVAKIA	15 415 000	66.7	67.00	74.34	24.3	30.8	23.2	17.4	4.3
DENMARK	5 114 000	82.6	71.40	77.40	19.7	30.2	24.9	19.3	5.9
EAST GERMANY	16 699 000	76.6	69.09	75.10	19.3	31.1	25.8	17.4	6.4
FINLAND	4 863 000	59.9	69.53	77.77	20.0	33.4	24.6	17.8	4.2
FRANCE	54 652 000	73.4	70.41	78.47	21.8	31.3	23.5	17.3	6.1
GREECE	9 840 000	na	70.13	73.64	22.4	28.4	26.5	17.7	5.0
HUNGARY	10 690 000	54.3	66.14	73.68	22.0	28.8	25.4	19.1	4.7
ICELAND	237 000	88.7	73.91	79.45	26.9	34.9	20.3	13.7	4.2
IRELAND, REPUBLIC OF	3 508 000	55.6	68.77	73.52	30.6	31.0	19.1	15.5	3.8
ITALY	56 559 000	na	69.69	75.91	21.4	29.6	25.4	18.6	5.0
LUXEMBOURG	365 000	77.8	66.80	72.80	19.0	31.2	26.8	18.2	4.8
NETHERLANDS	14 362 000	88.4	72.70	79.30	21.8	34.0	23.3	16.3	4.6
NORWAY	4 129 000	70.7	72.64	79.41	21.3	30.4	22.0	20.2	6.1
POLAND	36 571 000	59.3	67.24	75.20	24.7	33.7	23.0	15.0	3.6
PORTUGAL	10 099 000	29.7	65.09	72.86	25.9	32.1	22.3	16.2	3.5
ROMANIA	22 553 000	48.5	67.42	72.18	27.0	28.8	25.0	15.9	3.3
SPAIN	38 228 000	91.4	70.41	76.21	25.6	29.8	23.7	16.7	4.2
SWEDEN	8 329 000	82.7	73.05	79.08	19.2	28.4	24.2	21.6	6.6
SWITZERLAND	6 505 000	57.1	72.00	78.70	19.0	30.8	26.3	18.2	5.7
U.S.S.R.	272 500 000	64.1	64.00	74.00	na	na	na	na	na
UNITED KINGDOM	55 610 000	89.6	69.86	75.80	20.2	30.1	23.6	20.1	6.0
WEST GERMANY	61 421 000	na	70.18	76.85	16.9	30.7	27.0	19.2	6.2
YUGOSLAVIA	22 855 000	na	67.72	73.15	24.4	32.8	25.9	13.8	3.1

Source : U.N. Demographic Yearbook 1983   Figures are the latest available census figures or estimates.

AGRICULTURE Arable & livestock rearing

- Subsistence - mixed crops & livestock
- Commercial - grain dominant
- Commercial - mixed crops & livestock
- Specialised - plantation & market gardening
- Nomadic herding
- Extensive livestock rearing
- Intensive livestock rearing
- Dairying

FORESTRY

- Softwoods for sawlogs, pulp, paper & newsprint
- Mixed softwoods & hardwoods for sawlogs

FISHING

- Large scale commercial
- Small scale

MINERAL EXTRACTION

(A)	Asbestos	(Ng)	Natural gas
(B)	Bauxite	(N)	Nickel
(Ch)	Chromium	(P)	Petroleum
(C)	Coal	(Ph)	Phosphates
(Cb)	Cobalt	(Pl)	Platinum
(Cp)	Copper	(Pt)	Potash
(D)	Diamonds	(S)	Salt
(G)	Gold	(Sl)	Silver
(I)	Iron	(Ti)	Tin
(L)	Lead	(Tu)	Tungsten
(Mn)	Manganese	(U)	Uranium
(Mr)	Mercury	(Z)	Zinc

OTHER AREAS

- Tundra & alpine
- Desert & semi-desert
- Major urban and industrial area

Scale 1:16 000 000

0   200   400   600   800 km

Conic Projection

Map labels: Oslo, Stockholm, Copenhagen, Malmö, Gdansk, Berlin, Warsaw, Hamburg, Prague, Katowice, Vienna, Budapest, Bucha(rest), Sofia, Athe(ns), Clydeside, Tyneside, West Yorkshire, Merseyside, West Midlands, London, Rotterdam Europoort, Lille, Liège, Ruhr, Frankfurt, Mannheim-Karlsruhe, Stuttgart, Munich, Paris, Lyon, Milan, Turin, Genoa, Marseille, Rome, Naples, Oporto, Lisbon, Madrid, Barcelona, Casablanca, Algiers

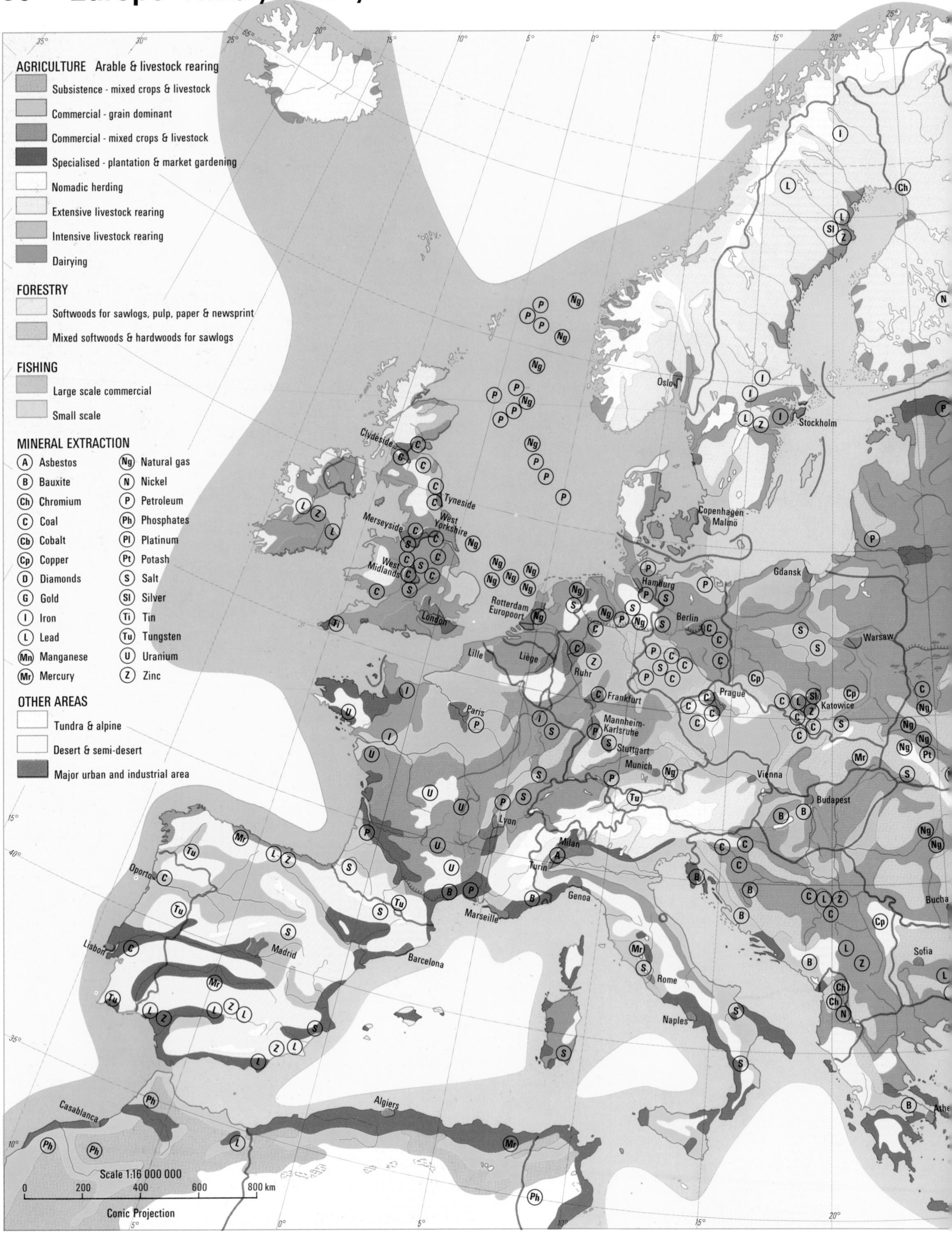

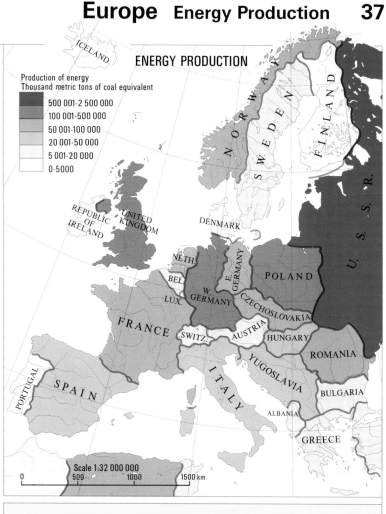

ENERGY PRODUCTION

Production of energy
Thousand metric tons of coal equivalent

- 500 001-2 500 000
- 100 001-500 000
- 50 001-100 000
- 20 001-50 000
- 5 001-20 000
- 0-5000

Scale 1:32 000 000

0   500   1000   1500 km

ENERGY PRODUCTION STATISTICS

Figures in thousand metric tons of coal equivalent for 1982

COUNTRY	TOTAL	SOLIDS mainly coal	LIQUIDS mainly petroleum	GAS	ELEC-TRICITY
ALBANIA	6 689	800	5 089	529	271
AUSTRIA	8 884	1 385	1 876	1 825	3 798
BELGIUM	8 637	6 539	na	42	2 056
BULGARIA	18 441	16 211	436	97	1 697
CZECHOSLOVAKIA	66 265	64 176	134	776	1 179
DENMARK	2 454	0	2 451	na	3
EAST GERMANY	89 855	84 231	80	3 992	1 552
FINLAND	3 990	450	na	na	3 540
FRANCE	55 885	20 595	3 460	19 440	21 390
GREECE	7 153	5 225	1 490	na	438
HUNGARY	22 934	10 036	4 102	8 776	20
ICELAND	398	na	na	na	398
IRELAND, REPUBLIC OF	4 162	1 382	na	2 632	148
ITALY	28 878	454	2 810	19 019	6 595
LUXEMBOURG	61	na	na	na	61
NETHERLANDS	92 046	0	14 605	76 961	480
NORWAY	83 102	472	35 728	35 488	11 432
POLAND	171 080	164 639	418	5 703	320
PORTUGAL	1 034	190	na	na	844
ROMANIA	92 606	17 331	17 859	55 958	1 458
SPAIN	25 558	18 804	2 226	1	4 527
SWEDEN	11 697	27	20	na	11 650
SWITZERLAND	6 311	na	na	na	6 311
U.S.S.R.	2 013 473	495 618	892 263	594 193	31 399
UNITED KINGDOM	311 328	103 261	154 404	47 561	6 102
WEST GERMANY	163 702	127 475	6 190	19 801	10 236
YUGOSLAVIA	35 005	22 901	6 326	2 381	3 397

Source : UN Statistical Yearbook 1982

C Collins ◇ Longman Atlases

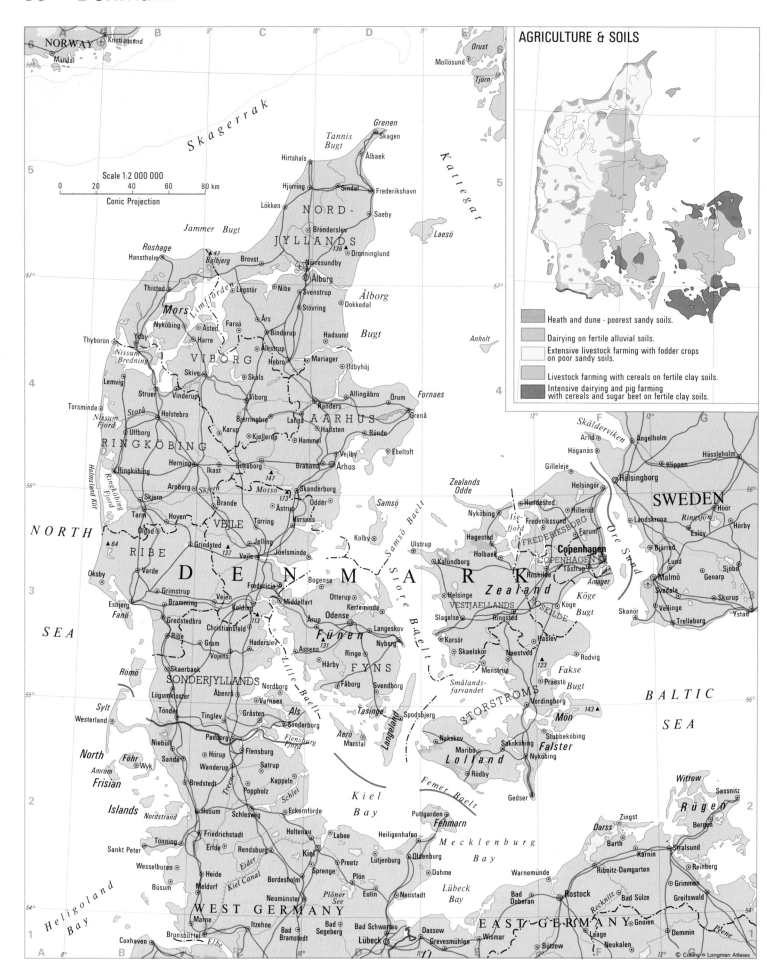

ZUIDER ZEE SCHEME

West Frisian Islands

Vlieland

Leeuwarden

Harlingen

Wadden Sea

Texel

Sneek

Barrier Dam 30km (1927-32)

Heerenveen

Den Helder

NORTH SEA

WIERINGERMEER
(1921-30)
20,000 ha.

Ijsselmeer
(120,000 ha.)

Proefpolder Andijk
(1927-40ha.)

NORTH EAST POLDER
(1937-42)
48,000 ha

Emmeloord

Enkhuizen

-4·5
Urk

Schokland

Heerhugowaard

Hoorn

Kampen

Alkmaar

-5·0

Heiloo

MARKERWAARD
?
40,000 ha.

Lelystad

EASTERN
FLEVOLAND
(1950-57)
54,000 ha.

Beverwijk

Marken

Nunspeet

SOUTHERN
FLEVOLAND
(1959-68)
43,000 ha.

Amsterdam

Almere

Harderwijk

Bussum

Huizen

Ermelo

Laren

Amersfoort

Legend:
- Land reclamation (1200-1600)
- Land reclamation (1600-1900)
- Land reclamation (1900-1970)
- Land reclamation until the year 2000
- Fresh water
- Residential area
- Important road
- Coastline in 1920
- Dyke
- Pumping station
- Lock
- -4·5 Lowest height in metres

Scale 1:1 200 000

0   10   20   30km

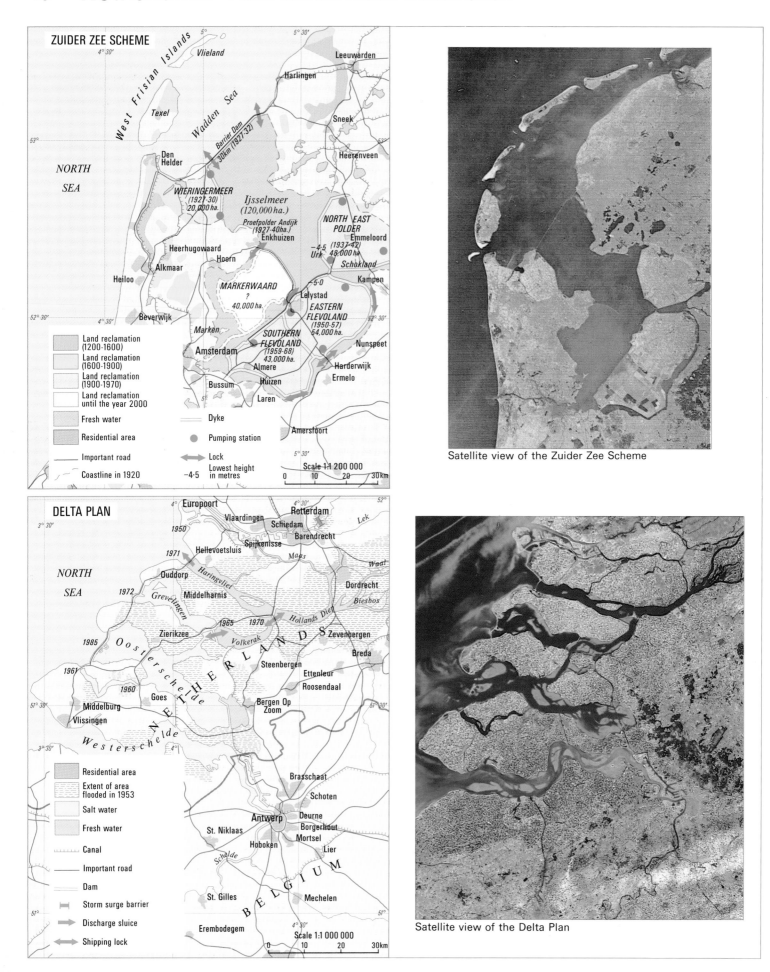

Satellite view of the Zuider Zee Scheme

DELTA PLAN

Europoort

Vlaardingen

Rotterdam

1950

Schiedam

Lek

Spijkenisse

Barendrecht

1971

Hellevoetsluis

Maas

Ouddorp

Haringvliet

Dordrecht

Waal

NORTH SEA

1972

Greveⅼingen

Middelharnis

Biesbos

Zierikzee

1965   1970

Hollands Diep

Volkerak

Zevenbergen

1985

Oosterschelde

Breda

1961

Steenbergen

Ettenleur

1960

Goes

Roosendaal

Middelburg

Bergen Op Zoom

Vlissingen

Westerschelde

NETHERLANDS

Brasschaat

Schoten

Antwerp

Deurne

St. Niklaas

Borgerhout

Mortsel

Hoboken

Lier

Schelde

BELGIUM

St. Gilles

Mechelen

Erembodegem

Legend:
- Residential area
- Extent of area flooded in 1953
- Salt water
- Fresh water
- Canal
- Important road
- Dam
- Storm surge barrier
- Discharge sluice
- Shipping lock

Scale 1:1 000 000

0   10   20   30km

Satellite view of the Delta Plan

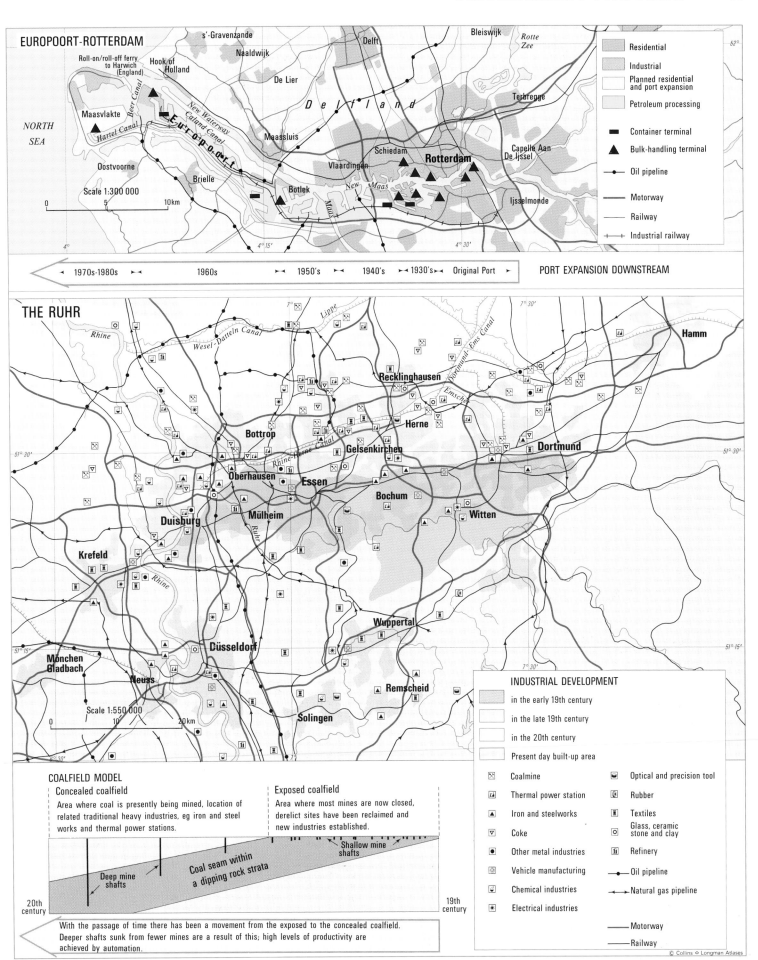

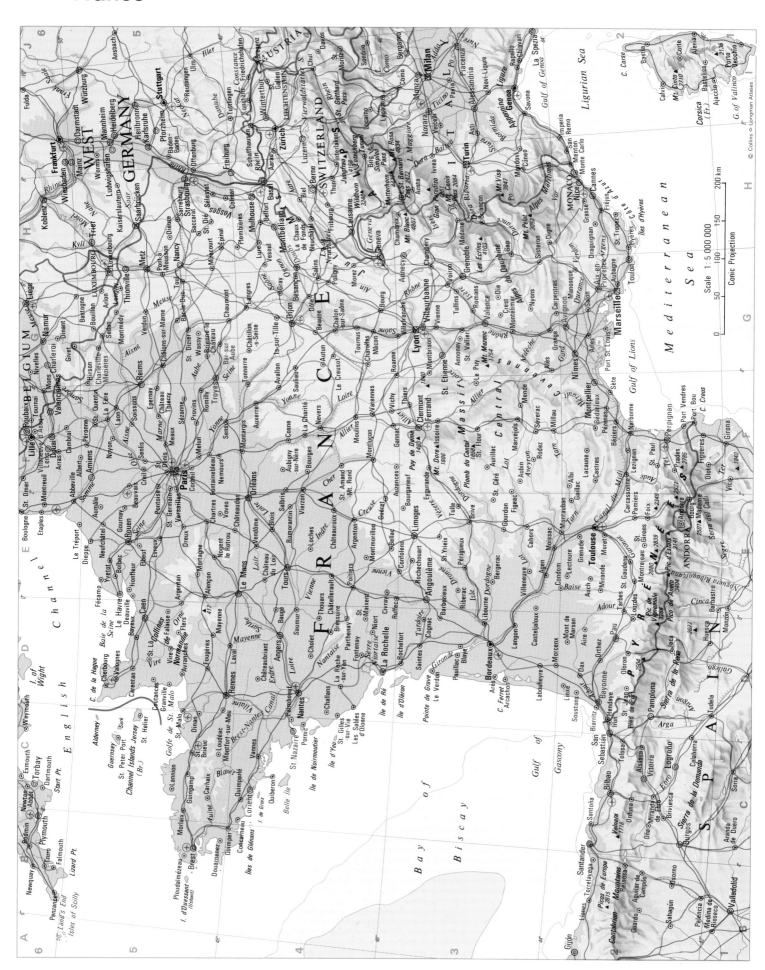

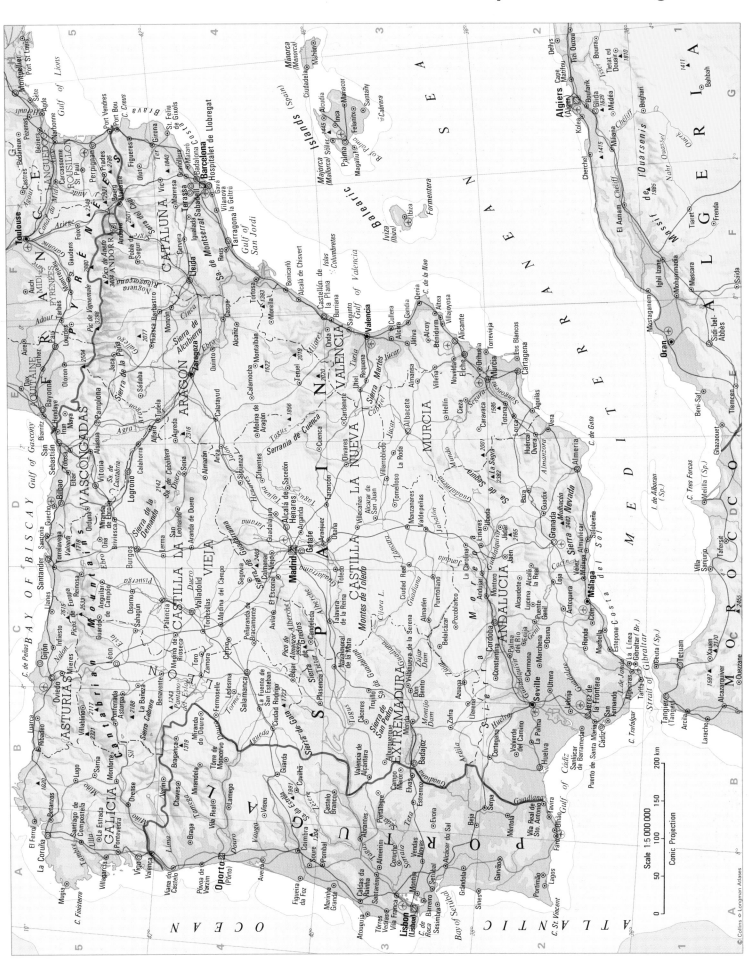

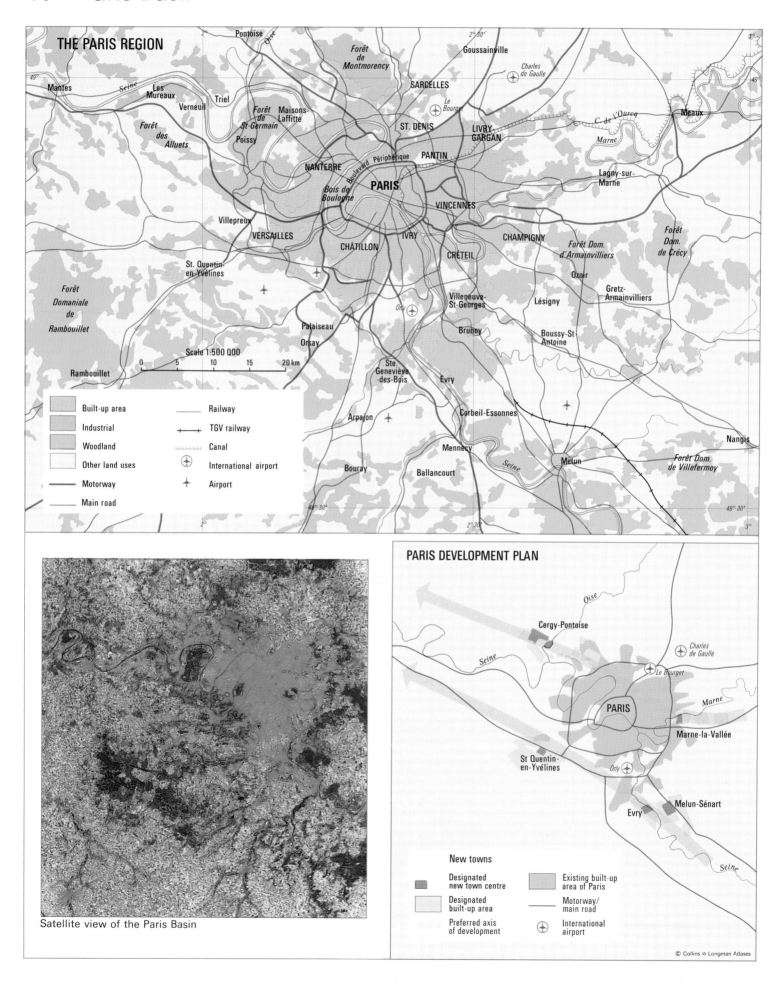

THE PARIS REGION

Pontoise
Oise
2°
Forêt de Montmorency
Goussainville
Charles de Gaulle
2°30'
3°
49°
Mantes
Seine
Les Mureaux
Triel
Verneuil
Forêt de St-Germain
Maisons-Laffitte
SARCELLES
Le Bourget
ST. DENIS
LIVRY-GARGAN
C. de l'Ourcq
Meaux
49°
Forêt des Alluets
Poissy
NANTERRE
PANTIN
Marne
Lagny-sur-Marne
Boulevard Périphérique
PARIS
Bois de Boulogne
VINCENNES
Villepreux
VERSAILLES
CHÂTILLON
IVRY
CHAMPIGNY
CRÉTEIL
Forêt Dom. d'Armainvilliers
Forêt Dom. de Crécy
St. Quentin-en-Yvélines
Ozoir
Gretz-Armainvilliers
Orly
Villeneuve-St-Georges
Lésigny
Boussy-St-Antoine
Palaiseau
Orsay
Brunoy
Ste. Geneviève-des-Bois
Évry
Arpajon
Corbeil-Essonnes
Nangis
Mennecy
Melun
Bouray
Ballancourt
Seine
Forêt Dom. de Villefermoy
48°30'
2°
2°30'
3°

Scale 1:500 000
0   5   10   15   20 km

Rambouillet
Forêt Domaniale de Rambouillet

Legend
- Built-up area
- Industrial
- Woodland
- Other land uses
- Motorway
- Main road
- Railway
- TGV railway
- Canal
- ⊕ International airport
- ✈ Airport

Satellite view of the Paris Basin

PARIS DEVELOPMENT PLAN

Oise
Cergy-Pontoise
Seine
Charles de Gaulle
Le Bourget
PARIS
Marne
Marne-la-Vallée
St Quentin-en-Yvélines
Orly
Evry
Melun-Sénart
Seine

New towns
- Designated new town centre
- Designated built-up area
- Preferred axis of development
- Existing built-up area of Paris
- Motorway/main road
- ⊕ International airport

© Collins ◇ Longman Atlases

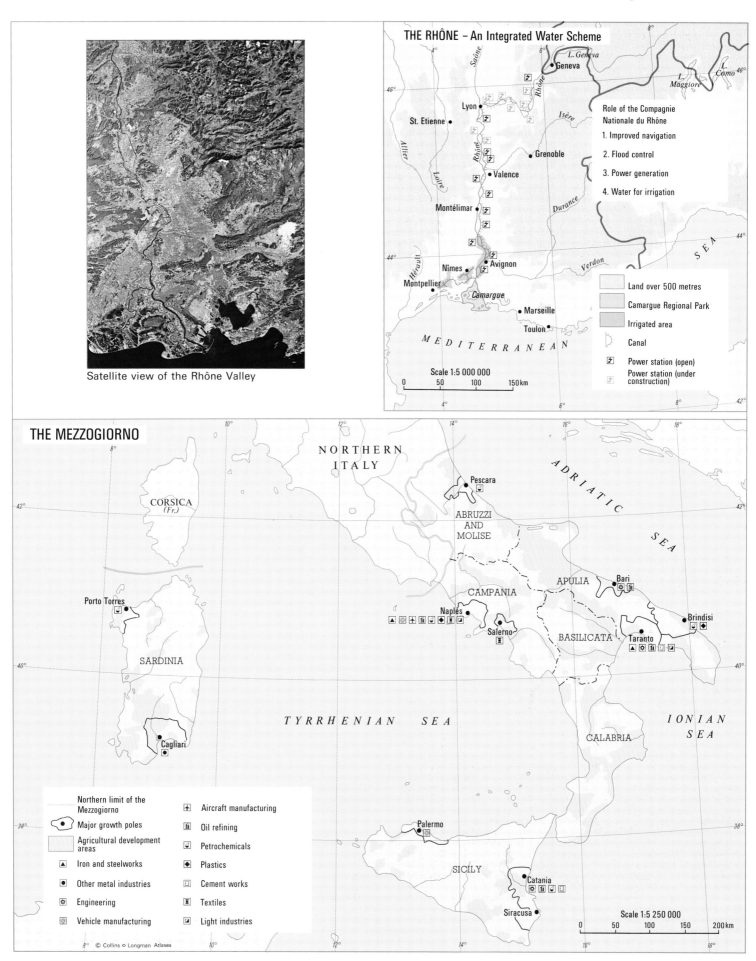

Satellite view of the Rhône Valley

THE RHÔNE – An Integrated Water Scheme

L. Geneva
Geneva
L. Como
L. Maggiore
Saône
Rhône
Isère
Lyon
St. Etienne
Grenoble
Rhône
Valence
Montélimar
Durance
Allier
Loire
Hérault
Nîmes
Avignon
Verdon
Montpellier
Camargue
Marseille
Toulon
SEA
MEDITERRANEAN

Role of the Compagnie Nationale du Rhône

1. Improved navigation
2. Flood control
3. Power generation
4. Water for irrigation

Land over 500 metres
Camargue Regional Park
Irrigated area
Canal
Power station (open)
Power station (under construction)

Scale 1:5 000 000
0   50   100   150 km

THE MEZZOGIORNO

CORSICA (Fr.)

NORTHERN ITALY

Pescara

ABRUZZI AND MOLISE

ADRIATIC SEA

APULIA
Bari

CAMPANIA
Naples
Salerno
BASILICATA
Taranto
Brindisi

Porto Torres

SARDINIA

Cagliari

TYRRHENIAN SEA

CALABRIA

IONIAN SEA

Palermo

SICILY

Catania

Siracusa

Northern limit of the Mezzogiorno
Major growth poles
Agricultural development areas
Iron and steelworks
Other metal industries
Engineering
Vehicle manufacturing
Aircraft manufacturing
Oil refining
Petrochemicals
Plastics
Cement works
Textiles
Light industries

Scale 1:5 250 000
0   50   100   150   200 km

46 Italy and The Balkans

Relief

Metres	
5000	
3000	
2000	
1000	
500	
200	
0	Sea Level
Land Dep.	200
	4000
	7000
	Metres

AUSTRIA

FRANCE

SWITZ

ITALY

Corsica (Fr.)

Sardinia (Italy)

ALGERIA

TUNISIA

LIGURIAN SEA

TYRRHENIAN SEA

MEDITERRANEAN

ADRIATIC

Gulf of Venice

Gulf of Lions

Gulf of Genoa

Sicily

MALTA

HUNGARY

Nagykanizsa Hódmezővásárhely White Crișul Odorhei U.S.S.R.
Kaposvár Szekszárd Szeged Makó Arad Alba Sighișoara Sfântu Bolgrad L.
  Baja Subotica Timișoara Mureș Iulia Gheorghe Focșani Izmail Sasyk
Pécs Kikinda Deva Sibiu Red Tower Brașov Alps Râmnicu Galați Reni
Virovitica Sombor Timiș Lugoj Pass Negoiu Sarat Brăila Tulcea Mouths of
  Drava Novi Zrenjanin 2460 Mt Mindra 2548 Buzău Faurei the Danube Sulina
Osijek Sad Transylvanian 2518 ROMANIA Ploești Portiței St Gheorghe's
Brod Danube Ruma Vršac Tirgu-Jiu Pitești Dîmbovița Mouth Mouth
Dubica Banja Doboj Tuzla Orșova Turnu Olt Arges Bucharest Cernavodă Constanța
  Luka Belgrade Severin Iron Slatina Oltenița Călărași
Travnik Valjevo Gate Craiova Jiu Silistra Danube Mangalia
  Sarajevo Višegrad Kragujevac Negotin Caracal Giurgiu Ruse Tolbukhin C. Kaliakra
Sinj Alps Čvrsnica Kraljevo Morava Zaječar Vidin Calafat Corabia Turnu Zimnicea Razgrad Balchik
  2228 Nereiva Pljevlja Kruševac Timok Lom Oryakhovo Măgurele Svishtov Kolarovgrad
Mostar Durmitor Tara Novi Kuršumlija Ogosta Pleven Tûrnovo Varna BLACK
Metković 2522 Pazar Niš Balkan Vratsa Iskûr Lovech Osûm Karnobat SEA
Nikšić Ibar Kosovska- Pirot Dragoman Botevgrad Mountains Sliven
Mljet Durmitor Mitrovica Leskovac Pass Sofia 2376 Kazanlûk Shipka Pass Tundzha Yambol Burgas
  Kotor Titograd 2658 Pristina Vranje Dimitrovo Radomir Stara Zagora
Dubrovnik Cetinje Peć (Pernik) Trajan's Gate Dimitrovgrad Elkhovo
Bar Prizren Kumanovo Kyustendil Musala BULGARIA C. Iğneada
  Shkodër Drin 2640 Blagoevgrad 2925 Plovdiv Maritsa Edirne Kirklareli
SEA Shëngjin Skopje 2252 Rhodope Khaskovo Arda Midye Bosporus
  C. Rodonit Titov Kočani Smolyan Mts. Luleburgaz Catalca Istanbul
  C. Palit Veles Strumica Petrich Mesta Xanthi Komotini Tekirdağ Üsküdar
Bari Prilep Vardar Crna Kilkis Sérrai Dráma Kaválla Alexandroúpolis Keșan SEA OF MARMARA
Monopoli Durrës ALBANIA Ohrid Bitola Edhessa Gallipoli Dardanelles Marmara Bandirma
  Tiranë Ohridsko Prespa L. Florina Thásos G. of Saros Çanakkale Bursa
Brindisi Elbasan L. Kastoria Kozáni Thessaloniki C. Plati Samothráki Imroz 1767 Balikesir
Lecce Berat 2417 Korçë Mt Olympus G. of Singitikos G. Mt Athos Límnos Edremit
Táranto Otranto Seman Pindus Smólikas 2917 Thessaloniki G. of 2033 TURKEY
  Vlorë 2633 Aliákmon Toronaíos Áyios Soma
Gulf of Vijose Ossa Evstrátios Lésvos Ayvalik
Taranto Gallipoli 1978 G. of Izmir Bergama Akhisar
  C. Sta Maria Corfu Ioánnina Trikkala Pinios Lárisa AEGEAN Mitilíni Dikili Manisa
di Leuca Corfu Igoumenitsa Kardhítsa Fársala Vólos Psará Alașehir
Neto Árta Akhelóös Mts N. Sporades Khíos Izmir Turgutlu Ödemiș
Crotone Préveza Lamía Skíros SEA Manisa Menderes
  C. Rizzuto Levkás Pass of Parnassós Euboea Psará Aydin Söke
Ganzaro Thermopylae 2457 2510 Khalkis 1743 Khíos Sámos Milâs
  Návpaktos GREECE Marathon C. Kafirévs Ándros Ikaría Muğla
IONIAN Mesolóngion Gulf of Athens Tínos G. of Kerme
  Kefallinía G. of Patras Corinth Mégara Piraeus Kéa Mármaris
SEA Pátras Corinth Aíyina Kíthnos Kos Rhodes
  Killíni Argos Návplion Cyclades Náxos Kos Rhodes
Zákinthos 2376 Páros Lindos
  Pírgos Spárti Milos Ios Amorgós Dodecanese
Kiparissía Alfiós Thira
Scale 1:5 250 000 Kalámai SEA OF CRETE
  Pílos Skhiza G. of Messina Andikíthira Canea Karpáthos
0 50 100 150 200 km C. Matapan G. of Lakonia C. Spátha Réthimnon
Conic Projection C. Maléa Kíthira Iráklion Idhi
  2456
SEA Crete

48

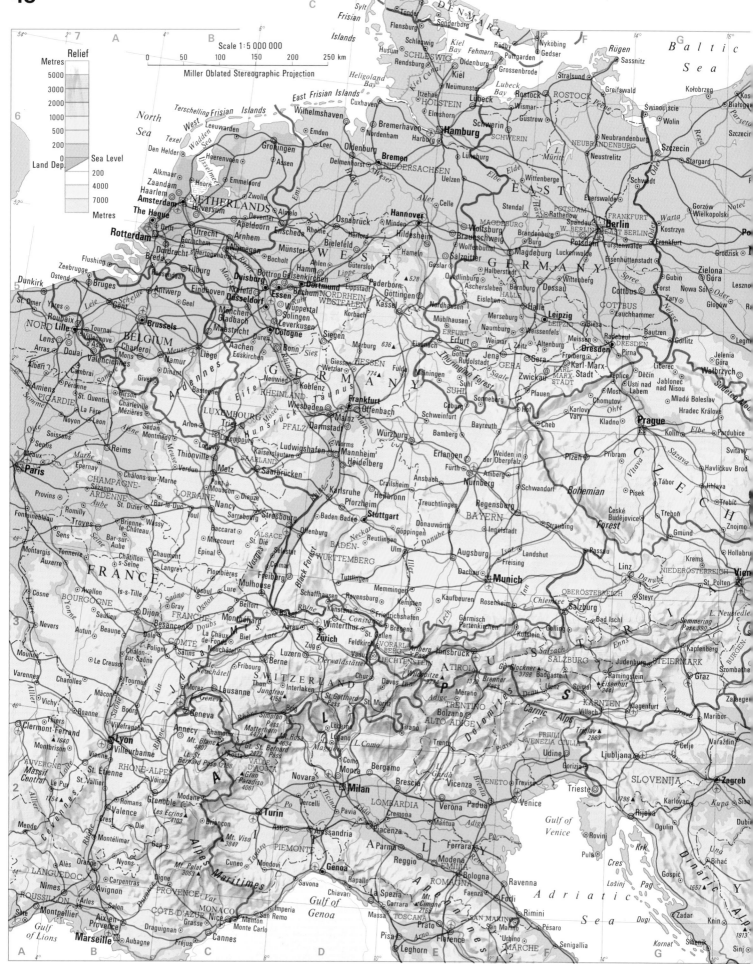

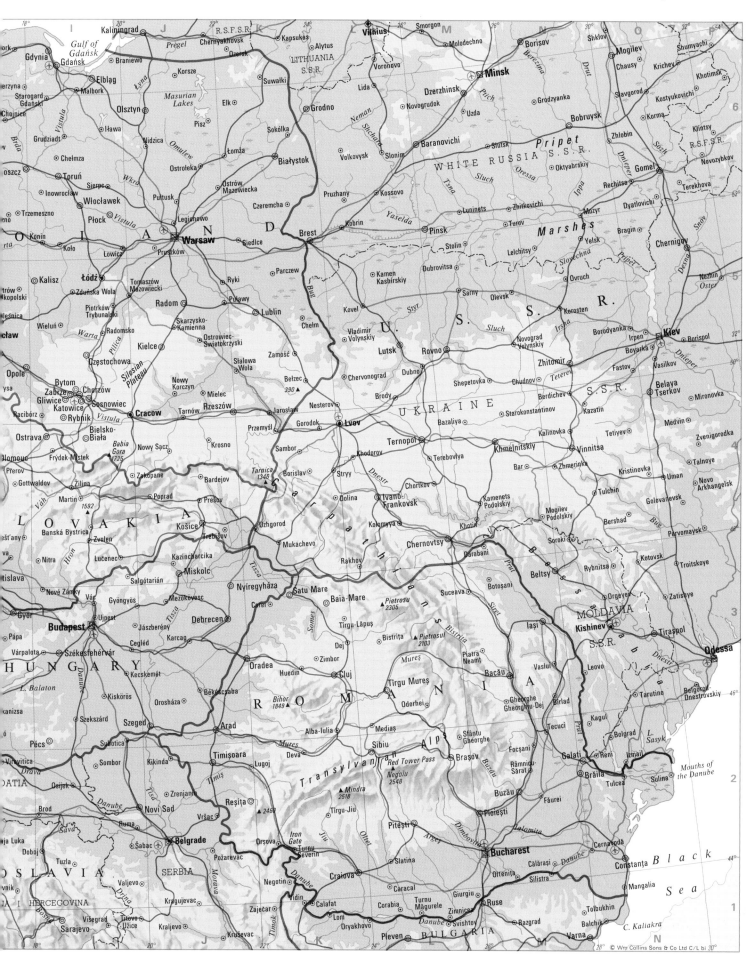

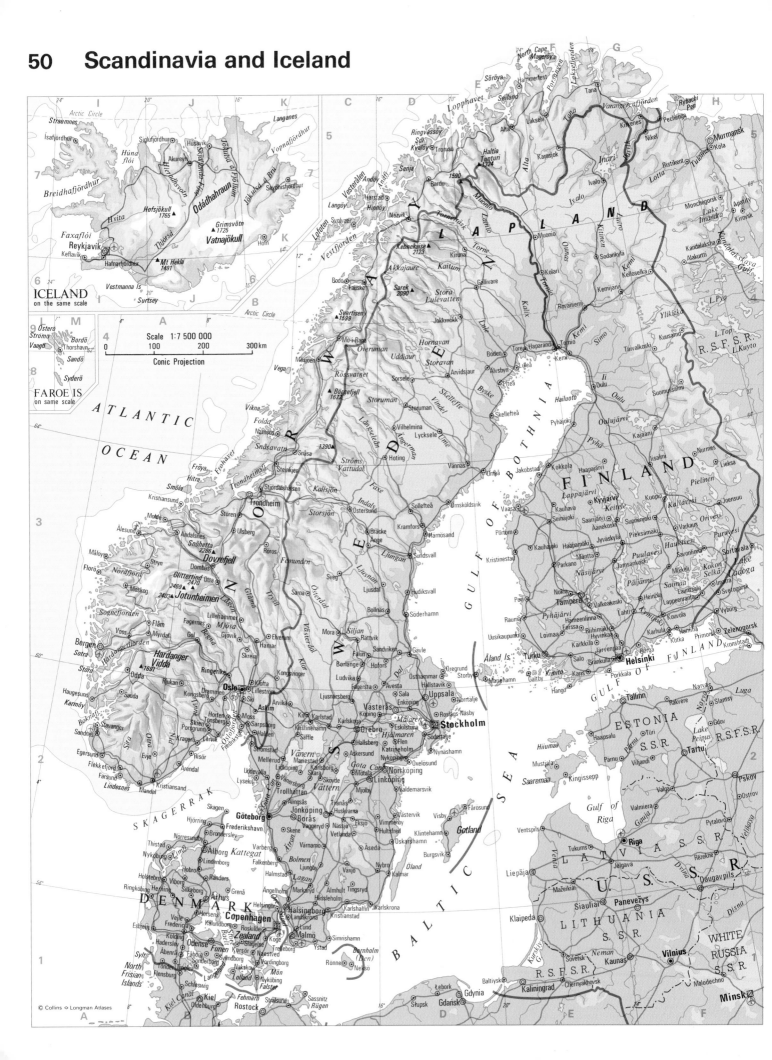

ICELAND
on the same scale

FAROE IS
on same scale

Scale 1:7 500 000
0   100   200   300km
Conic Projection

© Collins ◇ Longman Atlases

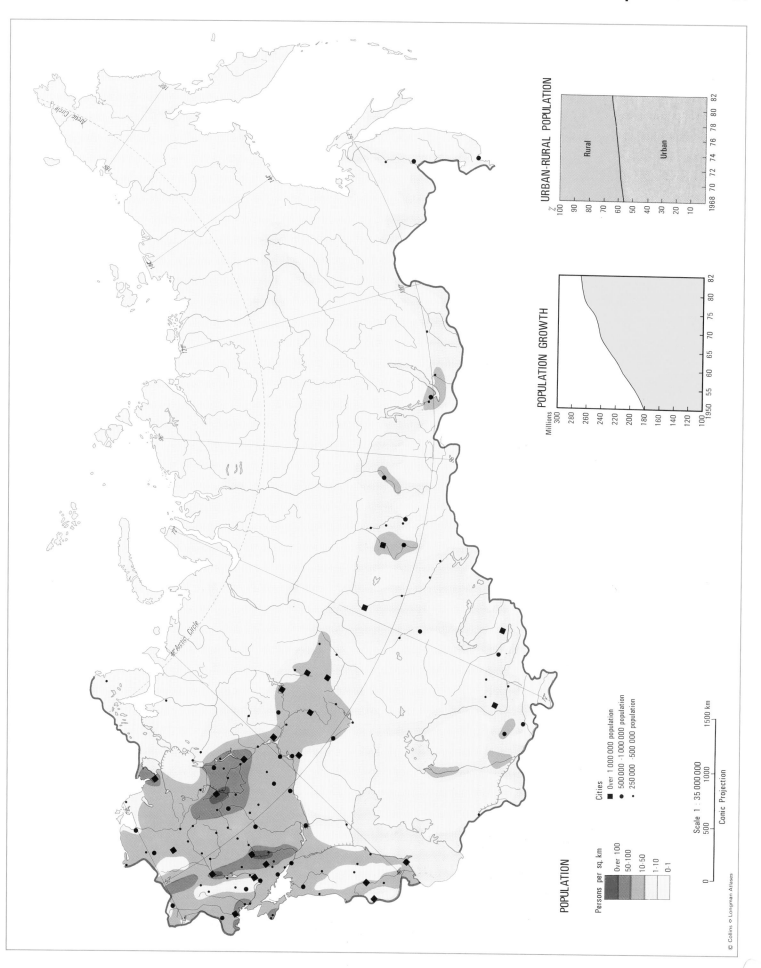

URBAN-RURAL POPULATION

Rural

Urban

%
100
90
80
70
60
50
40
30
20
10

1968 70 72 74 76 78 80 82

POPULATION GROWTH

Millions
300
280
260
240
220
200
180
160
140
120
100

1950 55 60 65 70 75 80 82

POPULATION

Persons per sq. km

Over 100
50-100
10-50
1-10
0-1

Cities
■ Over 1 000 000 population
● 500 000 - 1 000 000 population
• 250 000 - 500 000 population

Scale 1 : 35 000 000

0   500   1000   1500 km

Conic Projection

© Collins ◇ Longman Atlases

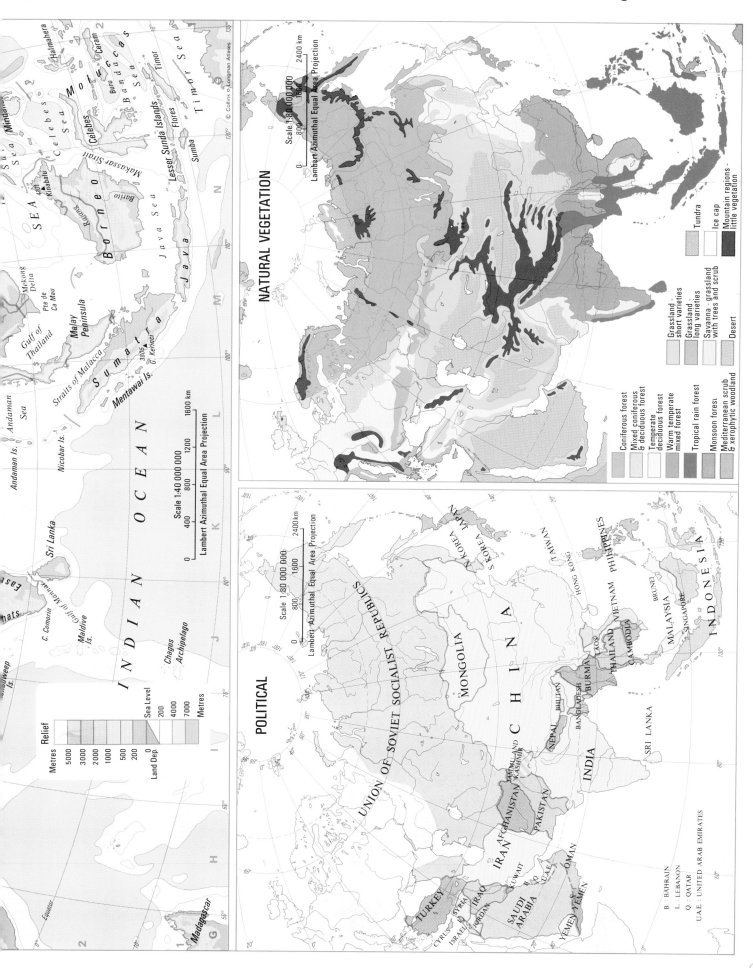

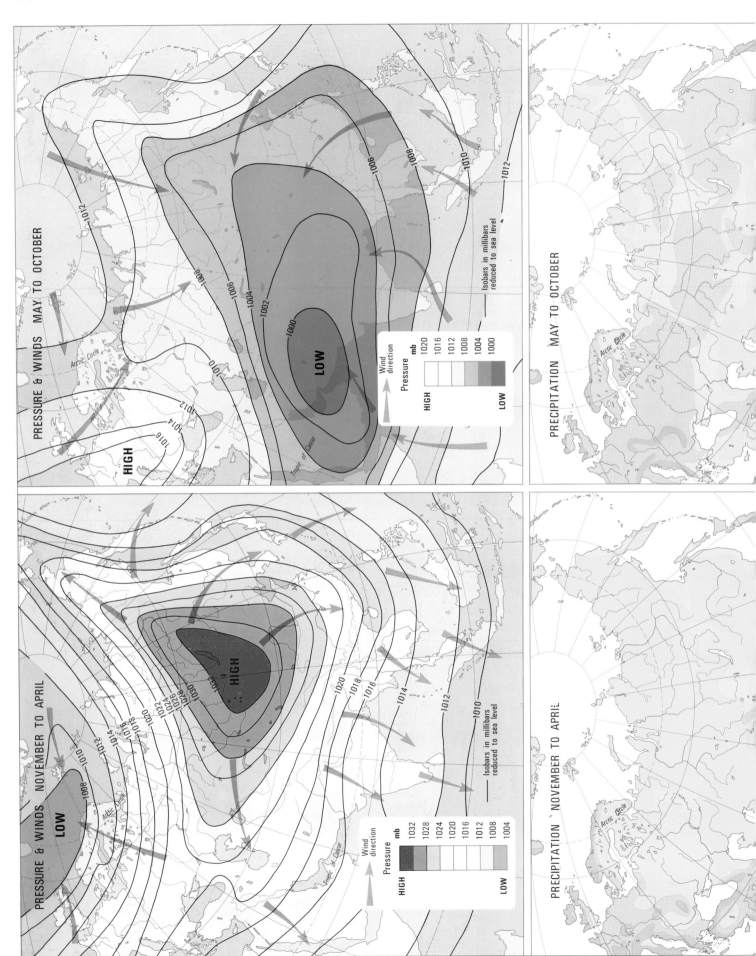

PRESSURE & WINDS MAY TO OCTOBER

Isobars in millibars reduced to sea level

Wind direction

Pressure

	mb
HIGH	1020
	1016
	1012
	1008
	1004
LOW	1000

LOW

HIGH

PRECIPITATION MAY TO OCTOBER

PRESSURE & WINDS NOVEMBER TO APRIL

LOW

HIGH

Isobars in millibars reduced to sea level

Wind direction

Pressure

	mb
HIGH	1032
	1028
	1024
	1020
	1016
	1012
	1008
LOW	1004

PRECIPITATION NOVEMBER TO APRIL

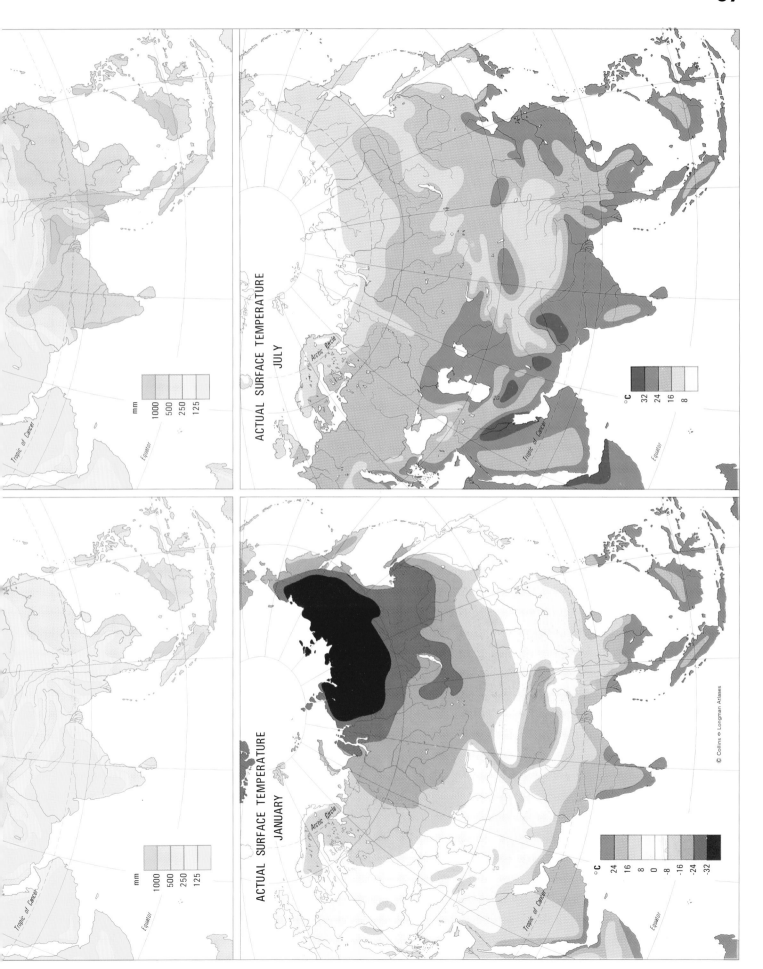

ACTUAL SURFACE TEMPERATURE
JULY

mm
1000
500
250
125

°C
32
24
16
8

Tropic of Cancer

Equator

Arctic Circle

ACTUAL SURFACE TEMPERATURE
JANUARY

mm
1000
500
250
125

°C
24
16
8
0
-8
-16
-24
-32

Tropic of Cancer

Equator

Arctic Circle

© Collins ◊ Longman Atlases

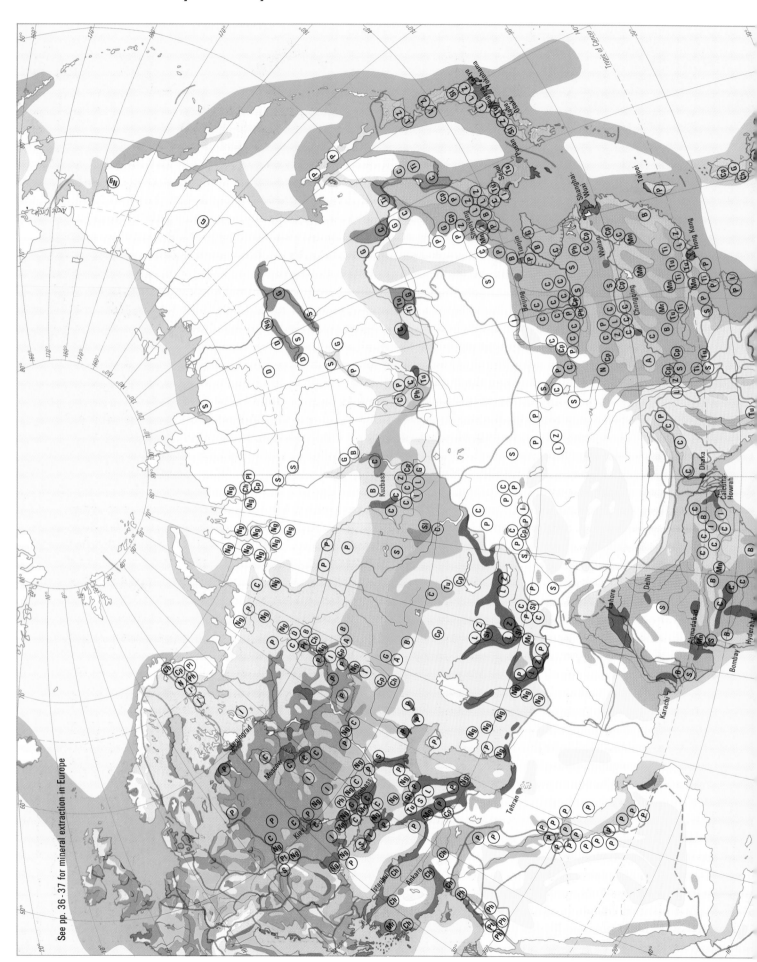

See pp. 36 - 37 for mineral extraction in Europe

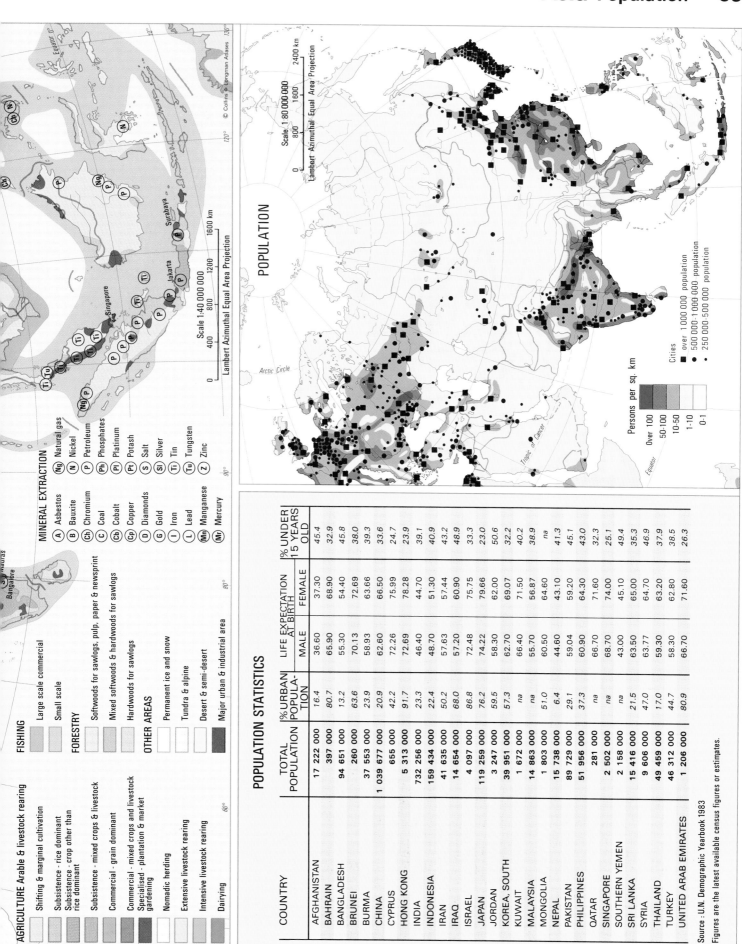

POPULATION

Scale 1:80 000 000

Lambert Azimuthal Equal Area Projection

Persons per sq. km
- Over 100
- 50-100
- 10-50
- 1-10
- 0-1

Cities
- ■ over 1 000 000 population
- ● 500 000-1 000 000 population
- • 250 000-500 000 population

AGRICULTURE Arable & livestock rearing
- Shifting & marginal cultivation
- Subsistence - rice dominant
- Subsistence - crop other than rice dominant
- Subsistence - mixed crops & livestock
- Commercial - grain dominant
- Commercial - mixed crops and livestock
- Specialised - plantation & market gardening
- Nomadic herding
- Extensive livestock rearing
- Intensive livestock rearing
- Dairying

FISHING
- Large scale commercial
- Small scale

FORESTRY
- Softwoods for sawlogs, pulp, paper & newsprint
- Mixed softwoods & hardwoods for sawlogs
- Hardwoods for sawlogs

OTHER AREAS
- Permanent ice and snow
- Tundra & alpine
- Desert & semi-desert
- Major urban & industrial area

MINERAL EXTRACTION
- (A) Asbestos
- (B) Bauxite
- (Ch) Chromium
- (C) Coal
- (Cb) Cobalt
- (Cp) Copper
- (D) Diamonds
- (G) Gold
- (I) Iron
- (L) Lead
- (Mn) Manganese
- (Mr) Mercury
- (Ng) Natural gas
- (N) Nickel
- (P) Petroleum
- (Ph) Phosphates
- (Pl) Platinum
- (Pt) Potash
- (S) Salt
- (Si) Silver
- (Ti) Tin
- (Tu) Tungsten
- (Z) Zinc

Scale 1:40 000 000

Lambert Azimuthal Equal Area Projection

© Collins · Longman Atlases

POPULATION STATISTICS

COUNTRY	TOTAL POPULATION	% URBAN POPULATION	LIFE EXPECTATION AT BIRTH MALE	LIFE EXPECTATION AT BIRTH FEMALE	% UNDER 15 YEARS OLD
AFGHANISTAN	17 222 000	16.4	36.60	37.30	45.4
BAHRAIN	397 000	80.7	65.90	68.90	32.9
BANGLADESH	94 651 000	13.2	55.30	54.40	45.8
BRUNEI	260 000	63.6	70.13	72.69	38.0
BURMA	37 553 000	23.9	58.93	63.66	39.3
CHINA	1 039 677 000	20.9	62.60	66.50	33.6
CYPRUS	655 000	42.2	72.26	75.99	24.7
HONG KONG	5 313 000	91.7	72.69	78.28	23.9
INDIA	732 256 000	23.3	46.40	44.70	39.1
INDONESIA	159 434 000	22.4	48.70	51.30	40.9
IRAN	41 635 000	50.2	57.63	57.44	43.2
IRAQ	14 654 000	68.0	57.20	60.90	48.9
ISRAEL	4 097 000	86.8	72.48	75.75	33.3
JAPAN	119 259 000	76.2	74.22	79.66	23.0
JORDAN	3 247 000	59.5	58.30	62.00	50.6
KOREA, SOUTH	39 951 000	57.3	62.70	69.07	32.2
KUWAIT	1 672 000	na	66.40	71.50	40.2
MALAYSIA	14 863 000	na	55.70	56.87	38.9
MONGOLIA	1 803 000	51.0	60.50	64.60	41.3
NEPAL	15 738 000	6.4	44.60	43.10	45.1
PAKISTAN	89 729 000	29.1	59.04	59.20	43.0
PHILIPPINES	51 956 000	37.3	60.90	64.30	32.3
QATAR	281 000	na	66.70	71.60	na
SINGAPORE	2 502 000	na	68.70	74.00	25.1
SOUTHERN YEMEN	2 158 000	na	43.00	45.10	49.4
SRI LANKA	15 416 000	21.5	63.50	65.00	35.3
SYRIA	9 606 000	47.0	63.77	64.70	46.9
THAILAND	49 459 000	17.0	59.30	63.20	37.9
TURKEY	46 312 000	44.7	58.30	62.80	38.5
UNITED ARAB EMIRATES	1 206 000	80.9	66.70	71.60	26.3

Source : U.N. Demographic Yearbook 1983

Figures are the latest available census figures or estimates.

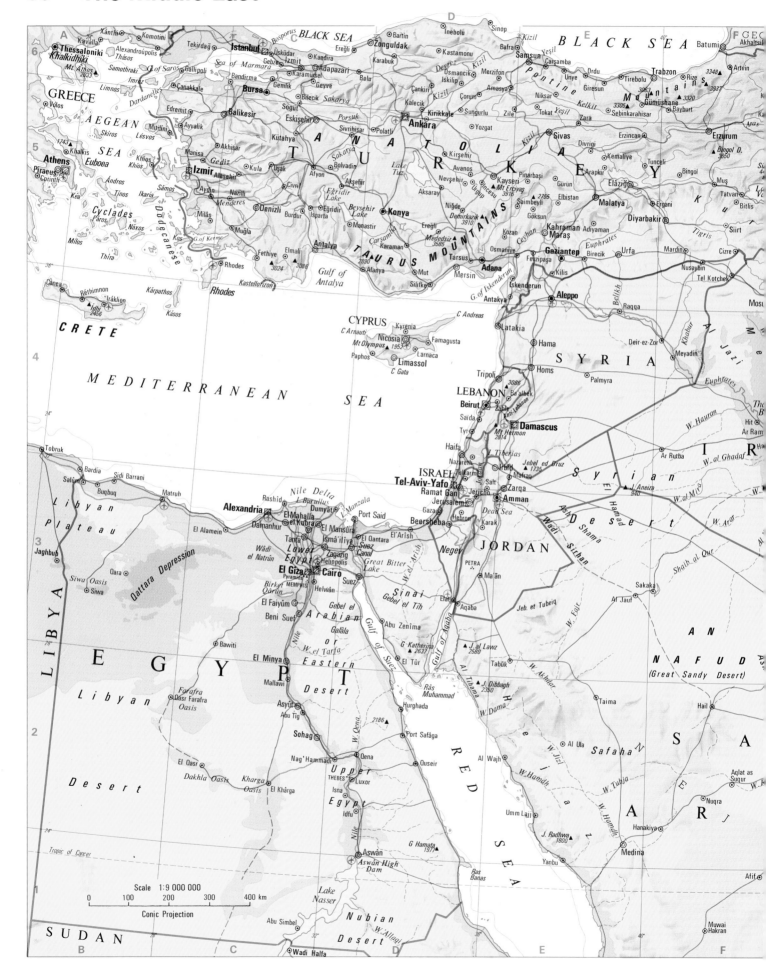

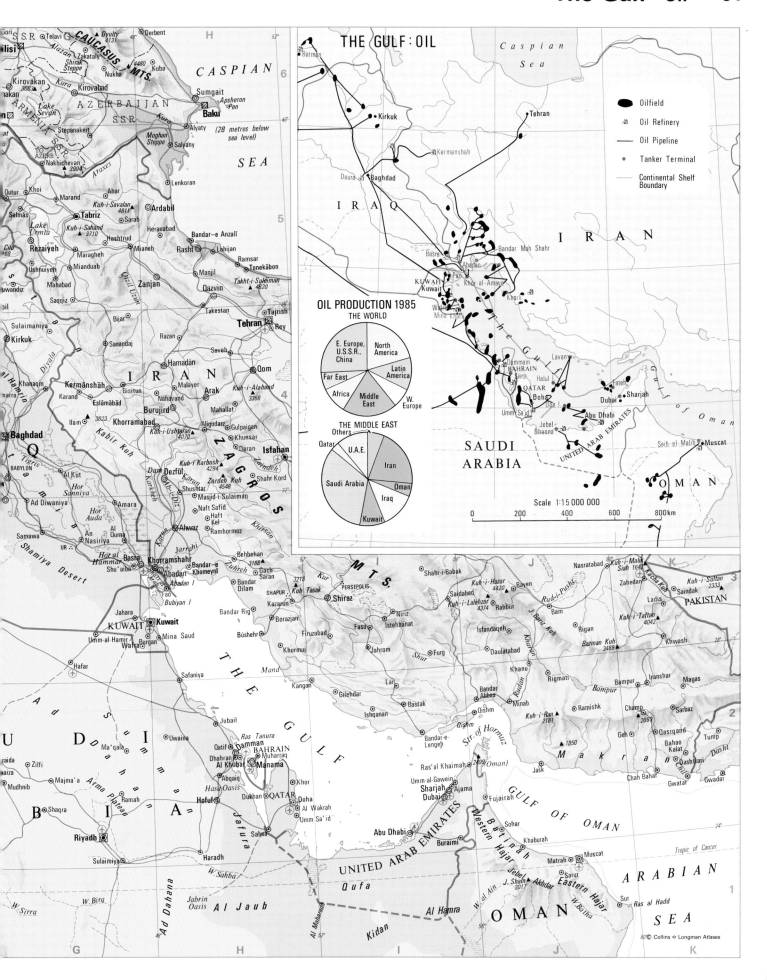

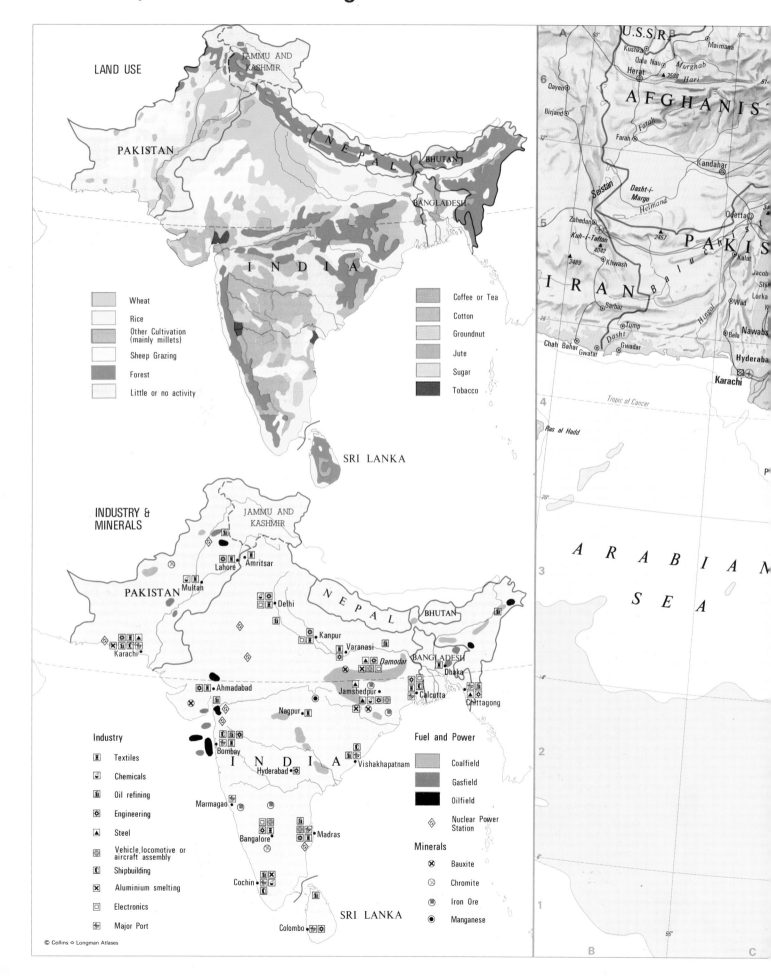

LAND USE

JAMMU AND KASHMIR

PAKISTAN

NEPAL

BHUTAN

BANGLADESH

INDIA

Wheat

Rice

Other Cultivation (mainly millets)

Sheep Grazing

Forest

Little or no activity

Coffee or Tea

Cotton

Groundnut

Jute

Sugar

Tobacco

SRI LANKA

INDUSTRY & MINERALS

JAMMU AND KASHMIR

PAKISTAN

Lahore Amritsar

Multan

Delhi

NEPAL

Kanpur

Varanasi

BHUTAN

Karachi

Ahmadabad

Damodar

BANGLADESH

Dhaka

Jamshedpur

Calcutta

Chittagong

Nagpur

Bombay

Hyderabad

INDIA

Vishakhapatnam

Industry

▣ Textiles

☑ Chemicals

▥ Oil refining

▧ Engineering

▲ Steel

◉ Vehicle, locomotive or aircraft assembly

⛴ Shipbuilding

✖ Aluminium smelting

▢ Electronics

▦ Major Port

Marmagao

Bangalore

Madras

Cochin

SRI LANKA

Colombo

Fuel and Power

Coalfield

Gasfield

Oilfield

◇ Nuclear Power Station

Minerals

⊗ Bauxite

⊘ Chromite

▣ Iron Ore

◉ Manganese

U.S.S.R.

Kushka Maimana

Qala Nau Murghab

Herat ▲3588 Hari

Qayen

Birjand

AFGHANIS

Farah Farah

Kandahar

Seistan

Dasht-i-Margo

Helmand

Quetta

Zahedan

Kuh-i-Taftan
4042

2457

PAKIS

▲3489 Khwash

Kalat

IRAN

Jacob

Larka

Sarbaz

Wad

Shi

Tump

Nawabs

Chah Bahar Gwatar Dasht Gwadar

Bela

Hyderaba

Karachi

B a l u

Tropic of Cancer

Ras al Hadd

ARABIAN

SEA

66°

© Collins ◊ Longman Atlases

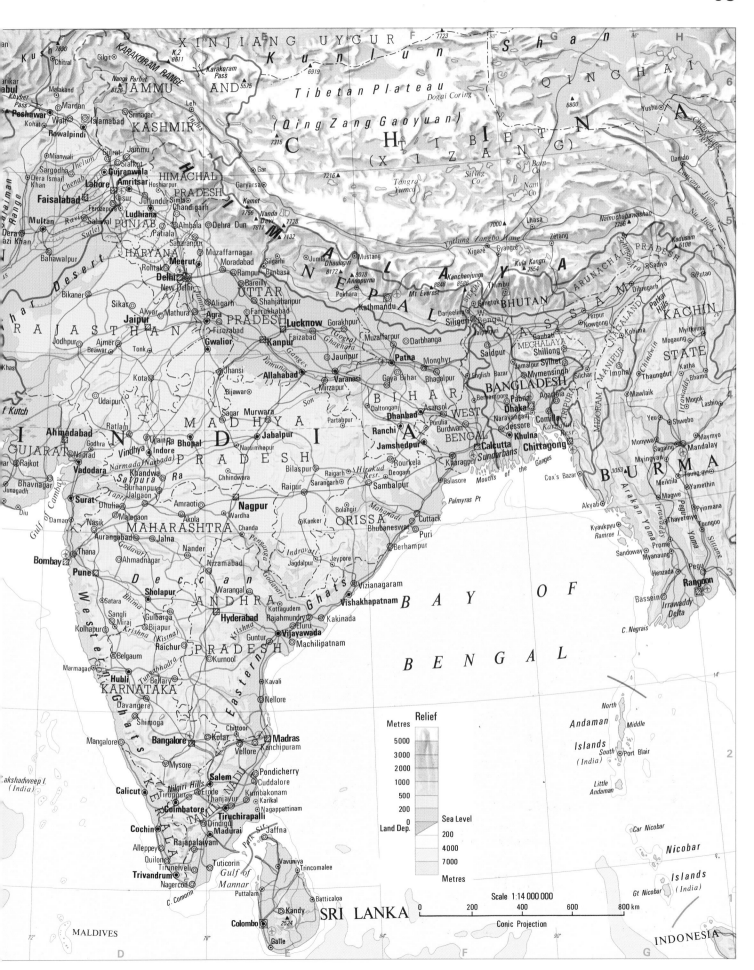

XINJIANG UYGUR

Kun lun Shan

K2 8611
Karakoram Pass
Karakoram Range
Nanga Parbat 8126
JAMMU AND KASHMIR

Tibetan Plateau
Dogai Coring
QINGHAI
Yushu
Qamdo

(Qing Zang Gaoyuan)

C H T I B E T N A
(X I Z A N G)

7315
7216

Siling Co
Nam Co
Bam Co

Tangra Yumco

7000
Lhasa
Zêtang
Namchabawashan 7756

HIMACHAL PRADESH
Kamet 7756
Nanda Devi 7817
7728
7132

Yarlung Zangbo Jiang
Xigaze
Gyangze

ARUNACHAL PRADESH
Kadusam 5108
Putao
Dibrugarh
Sadiya

Khyber Pass
Peshawar
Kohat
Rawalpindi
Islamabad
Wah

Mianwali
Sargodha
Gujrat
Sialkot
Jammu
Srinagar
Leh
Gar
Garyarsa

Jumla
Mustang
Dhaulagiri 8172
Annapurna 8078
Pokhara

Kanchenjunga 8586
Mt Everest 8848
Thimbu
Gangtok
BHUTAN

ASSAM
Tezpur
Nowgong
Gauhati
Shillong
MEGHALAYA

NAGALAND
Kohima
Mokokchung

KACHIN STATE
Myitkyina
Mogaung
Chindwin

Faisalabad
Lahore
Amritsar
Gujranwala
Kasur
Ludhiana
Ferozepore
Hoshiarpur
Jullundur
Simla
Chandigarh
Ambala
Dehra Dun
Sahawal
PUNJAB
Patiala
Saharanpur

HARYANA
Muzaffarnagar
Meerut
Rohtak
Delhi
New Delhi

Multan
Bahawalpur
Bikaner
Sikar
Jaipur
Alwar
Mathura
Agra

RAJASTHAN
Jodhpur
Ajmer
Beawar
Tonk
Kota

Jaisalmer
Moradabad
Rampur
Bareilly
Shahjahanpur
Aligarh
UTTAR PRADESH
Farrukhabad
Lucknow
Gorakhpur
Faizabad
Jaunpur
Allahabad
Kanpur
Gwalior
Jhansi

Silgarhi
Banbasa

Kathmandu
NEPAL
Muzaffarpur
Darbhanga
Patna
Monghyr
Saidpur
Darjeeling
Siliguri
Jalpaiguri
W Bengal
Rangpur

Mymensingh
Sylhet
Silchar
MANIPUR
Imphal
Thaungdut
Katha
Bhamo
Mawlaik
Yeu
Shwebo
Maymyo
Mandalay
Sagaing
Monywa
Myingyan

Ahmadabad
GUJARAT
Godhra
Ujjain
Indore
Bhopal
Vindhya Ra
MADHYA PRADESH
Jabalpur
Narsimhapur
Allahabad
Varanasi
Mirzapur
Gaya
Bihar
Bhagalpur
BIHAR
Daltonganj
Dhanbad
Ranchi
Asansol
Purulia
Burdwan
WEST BENGAL
Narayanganj
Jessore
Khulna
BANGLADESH
Pabna
Dhaka
Comilla
TRIPURA
Agartala
MIZORAM
Aijal
3053
BURMA
Akyab
Arakan Yoma
Irrawaddy
Pegu Yoma
Shwebo
Lashio
Mogok

Nadiad
Vadodara
Bhavnagar
Junagadh
Rajkot
Diu
Daman
Surat
Dhulia
Malegaon
Nasik
Narmada (Nabada)
Satpura Ra
Khandwa
Burhanpur
Jalgaon
Amraoti
Akola
Nagpur
Wardha
Chhindwara
Bilaspur
Raigarh
Sarangarh
Raipur
Chanda
Kanker
Bolangir
Hirakud Resr
Deogarh
Sambalpur
Rourkela
Kharagpur
Balasore
Mouths of the Ganges
Sunderbans
Calcutta
Chittagong
Cox's Bazar
Kyaukpyu
Ramree I.

Bombay
Pune
Thana
Ahmadnagar
Aurangabad
Jalna
Nander
Nizamabad
MAHARASHTRA
Deccan
Godavari
Satara
Sangli
Miraj
Sholapur
Gulbarga
Bijapur
Warangal
ANDHRA PRADESH
Hyderabad
Jagdalpur
Jeypore
Berhampur
Bhubaneswar
Cuttack
Puri
ORISSA
Mahanadi
Indravati
Palmyras Pt
Sandoway
Prome
Myanaung
Henzada
Bassein
C. Negrais
Rangoon
Irrawaddy Delta
Pegu

BAY OF BENGAL

Bhima
Kolhapur
Belgaum
Raichur
Bellary
Krishna (Kistna)
Kurnool
Kavali
Nellore
Guntur
Vijayawada
Machilipatnam
Eluru
Rajahmundry
Kakinada
Vishakhapatnam
Vizianagaram
Eastern Ghats

Marmagao
Hubli
Davangere
Shimoga
KARNATAKA
Western Ghats
Tungabhadra
Chittoor
Kolar
Bangalore
Mangalore
Mysore
Vellore
Kanchipuram
Madras
Pondicherry
Cuddalore

Andaman Islands (India)
North Andaman
Middle Andaman
Port Blair
South Andaman
Little Andaman

Lakshadweep I. (India)
Calicut
Nilgiri Hills
Tiruppur
Coimbatore
Erode
Salem
Thanjavur
Kumbakonam
Karikal
TAMIL NADU
Tiruchirapalli
Dindigul
Madurai
Cochin
Alleppey
Quilon
Rajapalayam
Nagappattinam
Tuticorin
Tirunelveli
Trivandrum
Nagercoil
C. Comorin

Car Nicobar
Nicobar Islands (India)
Gt Nicobar

Gulf of Mannar
Jaffna
Vavuniya
Trincomalee
Batticaloa
Puttalam
Kandy 2524
SRI LANKA
Colombo
Galle

Park St.

MALDIVES

INDONESIA

Relief

Metres	
5000	
3000	
2000	
1000	
500	
200	
Sea Level	
Land Dep.	200
	4000
	7000

Metres

Scale 1:14 000 000
0   200   400   600   800 km
Conic Projection

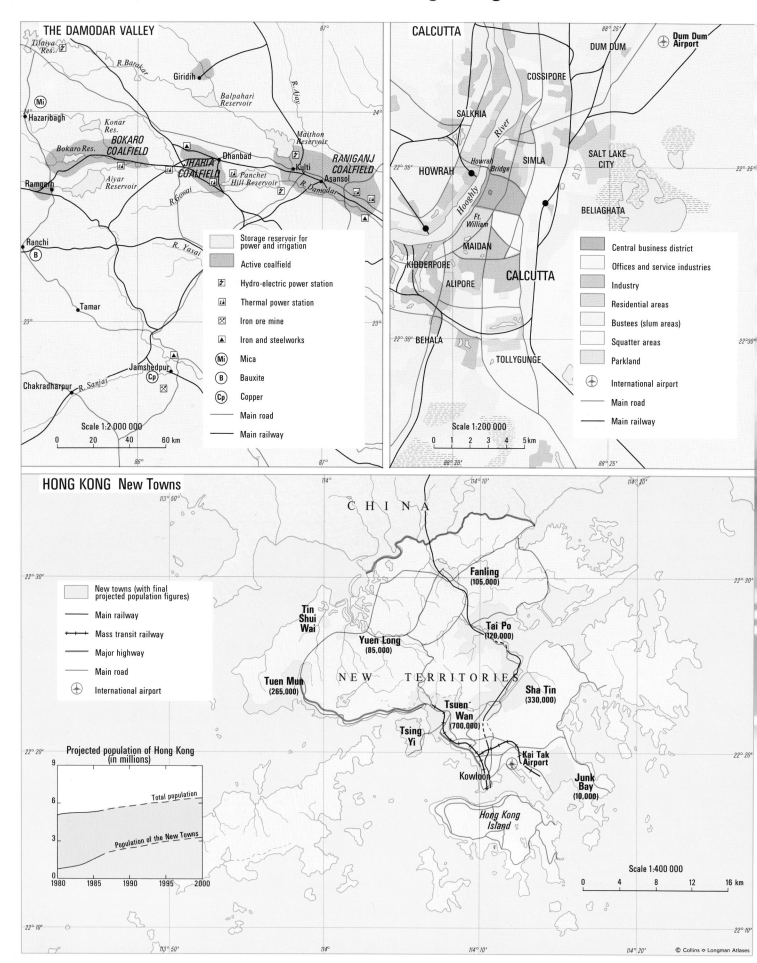

THE DAMODAR VALLEY

Tilaiya Res.
R. Barakar
Giridih
Balpahari Reservoir
R. Ajay
Mi
Hazaribagh
Konar Res.
BOKARO COALFIELD
Maithon Reservoir
Bokaro Res.
Dhanbad
RANIGANJ COALFIELD
JHARIA COALFIELD
Kulti
Ramgarh
Aiyar Reservoir
Panchet Hill Reservoir
Asansol
R. Gowai
R. Damodar
Ranchi
B
R. Yasai
Tamar
Jamshedpur
Cp
Chakradharpur
R. Sanjai

Storage reservoir for power and irrigation
Active coalfield
Hydro-electric power station
Thermal power station
Iron ore mine
Iron and steelworks
Mi   Mica
B   Bauxite
Cp   Copper
Main road
Main railway

Scale 1:2 000 000
0   20   40   60 km

CALCUTTA

DUM DUM
Dum Dum Airport
COSSIPORE
SALKHIA
River
SIMLA
SALT LAKE CITY
HOWRAH
Howrah Bridge
Hooghly
Ft. William
BELIAGHATA
MAIDAN
KIDDERPORE
CALCUTTA
ALIPORE
BEHALA
TOLLYGUNGE

Central business district
Offices and service industries
Industry
Residential areas
Bustees (slum areas)
Squatter areas
Parkland
International airport
Main road
Main railway

Scale 1:200 000
0   1   2   3   4   5 km

HONG KONG New Towns

CHINA

New towns (with final projected population figures)
Main railway
Mass transit railway
Major highway
Main road
International airport

Fanling (105,000)
Tin Shui Wai
Tai Po (120,000)
Yuen Long (85,000)
NEW TERRITORIES
Tuen Mun (265,000)
Sha Tin (330,000)
Tsuen Wan (700,000)
Tsing Yi
Kai Tak Airport
Kowloon
Junk Bay (10,000)
Hong Kong Island

Projected population of Hong Kong (in millions)

Total population
Population of the New Towns
9
6
3
0
1980   1985   1990   1995   2000

Scale 1:400 000
0   4   8   12   16 km

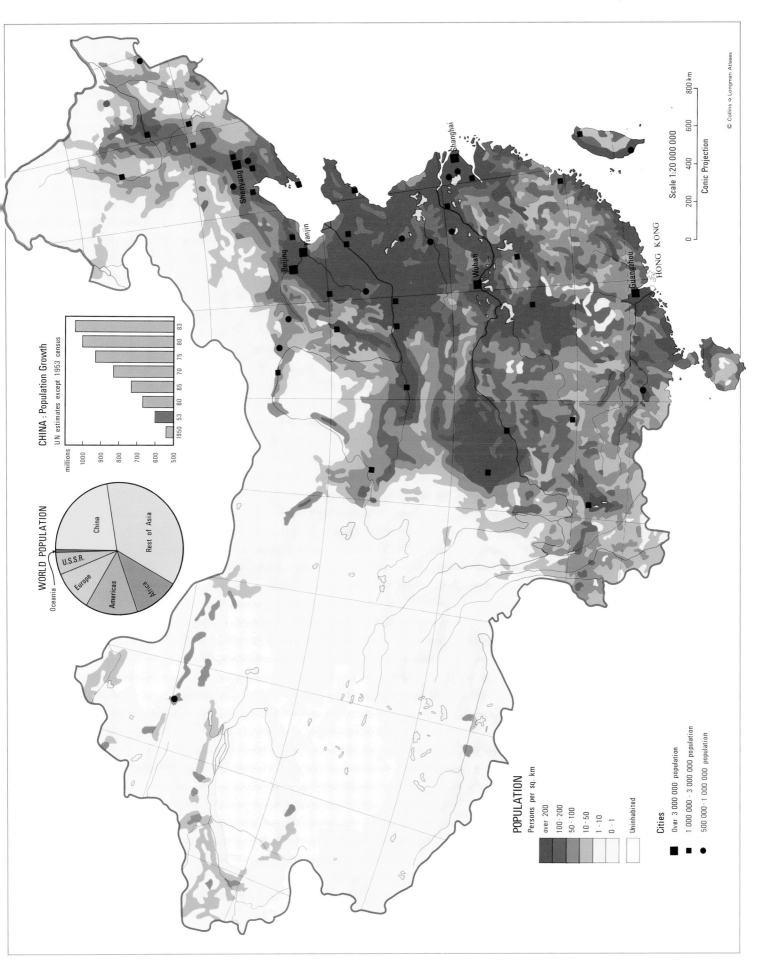

China Population

Scale 1:20 000 000

0   200   400   600   800 km

Conic Projection

© Collins ◇ Longman Atlases

Shanghai

Shenyang

Tianjin

Beijing

Wuhan

Guangzhou

HONG KONG

CHINA : Population Growth

UN estimates except 1953 census

millions
1000
900
800
700
600
500

1950   53   60   65   70   75   80   83

WORLD POPULATION

Oceania
China
U.S.S.R.
Europe
Americas
Africa
Rest of Asia

POPULATION

Persons per sq. km

over 200
100 - 200
50 - 100
10 - 50
1 - 10
0 - 1
Uninhabited

Cities

■ Over 3 000 000 population
■ 1 000 000 - 3 000 000 population
● 500 000 - 1 000 000 population

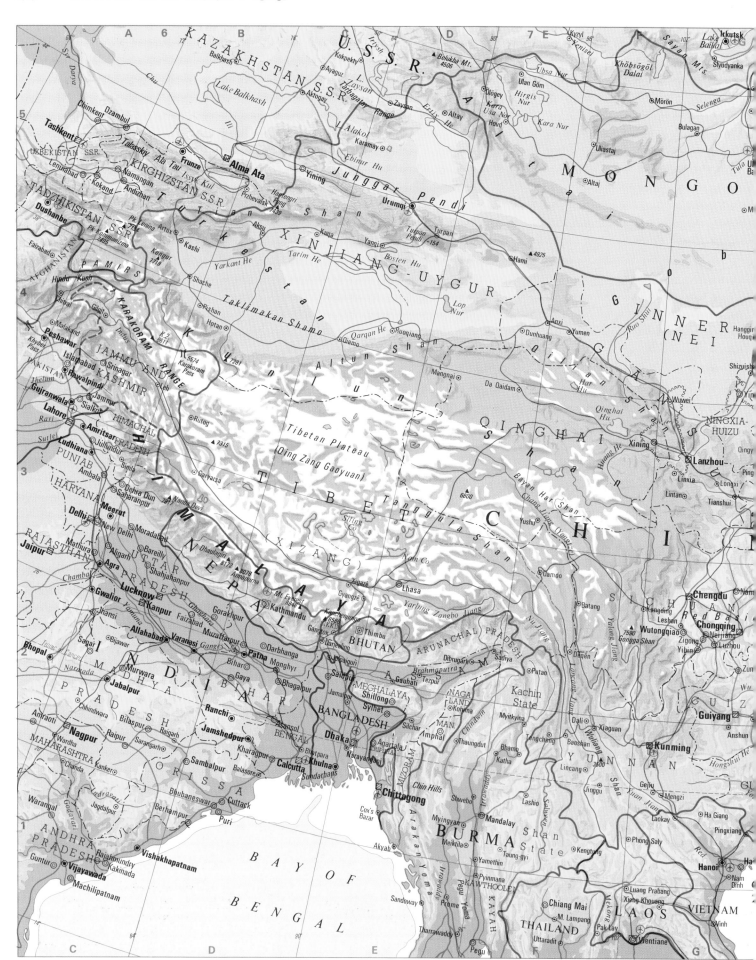

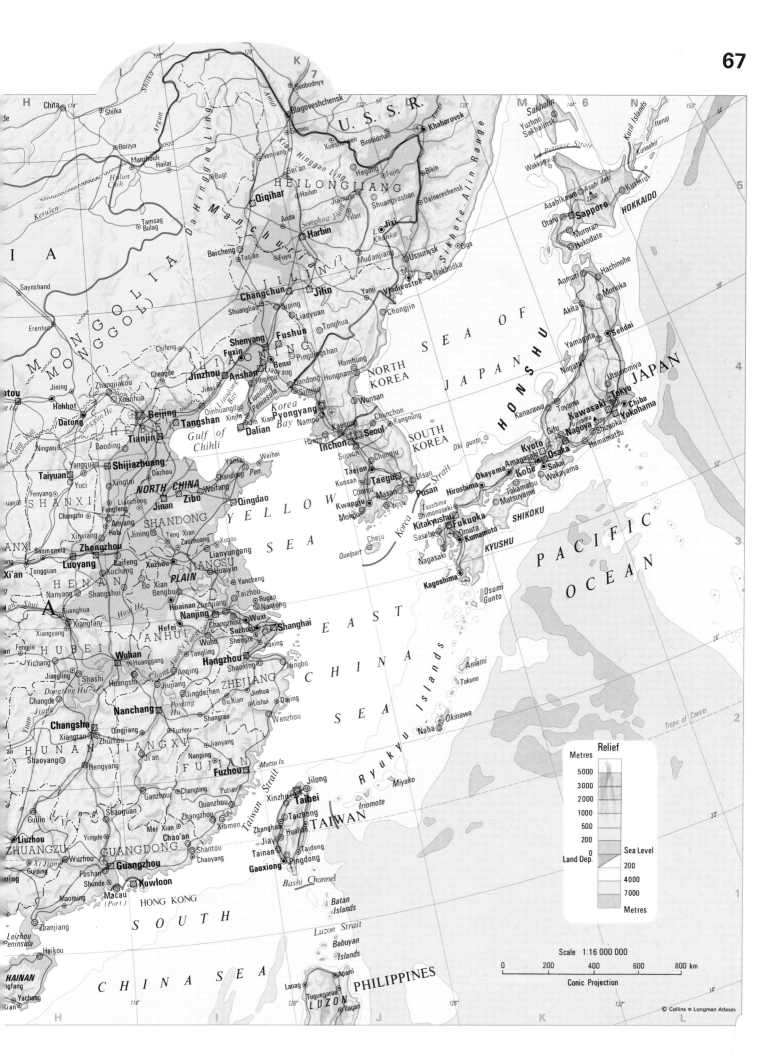

Scale 1:15 000 000

0   200   400   600   800 km

Bonne Projection

© Collins ◇ Longman Atlases

G
Taizhong
nanghua
ayi
nan
ngdong

TAIWAN

Batan Is.

uzon *Strait*

Babuyan Is.

C. Engaño

aoag Aparri
Tuguegarao
Pulog Ilagan
2929
Fernando Bayombong
jupan
San Carlos
Cabanatuan
Quezon City
Manila
San Pablo Daet
Lucena Naga *Catanduanes*
as Legaspi
indoro *Burias* Jrosin
Bulan
Panay Masbate Catarman
Iloilo Cadiz Calbayog *Samar*
Bacolod Cebu Catbalogan Guiuan
Negros *Leyte* Tacloban *C. Johnson*
Tanay Bohol Dinagat Depth
Dumaguete Tagbilaran Siargao 10497
Dipolog Butuan
Ozamiz Cagayan de Oro
Pagadian Iligan
Zamboanga *Moro* Cotabato Datu
Basilan *Gulf* Piang
Jolo *Sulu* General
Arch. Santos

LUZON

PHILIPPINES

MINDANAO

CHINA

TAIWAN

Hanoi
MACAU HONG
KONG

BURMA
Rangoon Vientiane
LAOS
THAILAND VIETNAM
Andaman Is. Bangkok
(India) CAMBODIA
Phnom
Penh

Manila

PHILIPPINES

BRUNEI
Kuala Lumpur Bandar Seri
Begawan
MALAYSIA
SINGAPORE

INDONESIA

Jakarta

PAPUA
NEW
GUINEA

Port
Moresby

AUSTRALIA

ASEAN
(Association of South East Asian Nations)

National Capital

Scale 1 : 40 000 000
0 500 1000 km

Philippine Trench

BELAU Koror

Sorol
Ifalik
Lamotrek

Eauripik

Caroline Islands
(U.S. Trust Territory)

PACIFIC

OCEAN

Sonsorol

Merir

Tobi

Helen Reef

Karakelong Talaud
Is
Sangi
Sangihe
Is

CELEBES
SEA

Manado
Buol Tondano
omini 2207 Kuandang Belang
Gorontalo 1970

MOLUCCAS

Morotai

Jailolo Tobelo
Ternate Halmahera
Soasiu Weda

Togian Is
Poh
Tuli Peleng
Poso Taliabu Obi
ESI Banggai Is Sula Is
G. of
Tolo CERAM SEA
ni Binaija
mbola Namlea 3055
Mekongga Ceram Bula
2790 Ambon
Kolaka Buru
Kendari
Kolaka Wowoni

Muna Butung
abaena Tukangbesi
Baubau Is
abia

SI
A

Maumere
Ende Alor
Sawu Nikiniki
Roti 2365 Timor
Sawu Sea Kupang

Waigeo

Dampier Str Kwoka
3000
Klamono Arfak
Sorong 2939
Vogelkop Wasian

Misoöl
Teluk Berau
Kokas Babo
Fakfak Wasior

Kaimana

Adi

Kokenau

Kolepom
C. Vals Okaba
Merauke

Manokwari

Biak Bosnik
Mokmer
Japen

Schouten Is

Serui
Teluk
Irian

Mamberamo

Jayapura

Sarmi

Vanimo

Aitape

Wewak

IRIAN
Maoke Range
Sudirman Mts. Jayawijaya
Puntjak Jaya Mts.
5030 Mandala Pk
4702
JAYA

Mapik

Sepik
Angoram

PAPUA NEW
Wabag Mt
Laiagam Hagen
5030 Mt. Wilhelm
Mendi 4694
Tanahmerah

NEW GUINEA GUINEA
Wabag Kainantu
Mt.
Goroka
Bulolo Lae

Mappi Kikori Baimuru

Digoel Kerema

Fly Gulf of
Papua
Daru Port Moresby

Kila Kila

Mulgrave Is Banks I
Torres Str. Thursday I
Prince of Wales C. York

ARAFURA SEA

Coral
Sea

Relief
Metres
5000
3000
2000
1000
500
200
Land Dep. Sea Level
200
4000
7000
Metres

Manus
Lorengau
Admiralty Is

Bismarck
Sea

1340

Madang

Bismarck R
Huon Pen
Finschhafen
Wau
3993
Popondetta

Equator

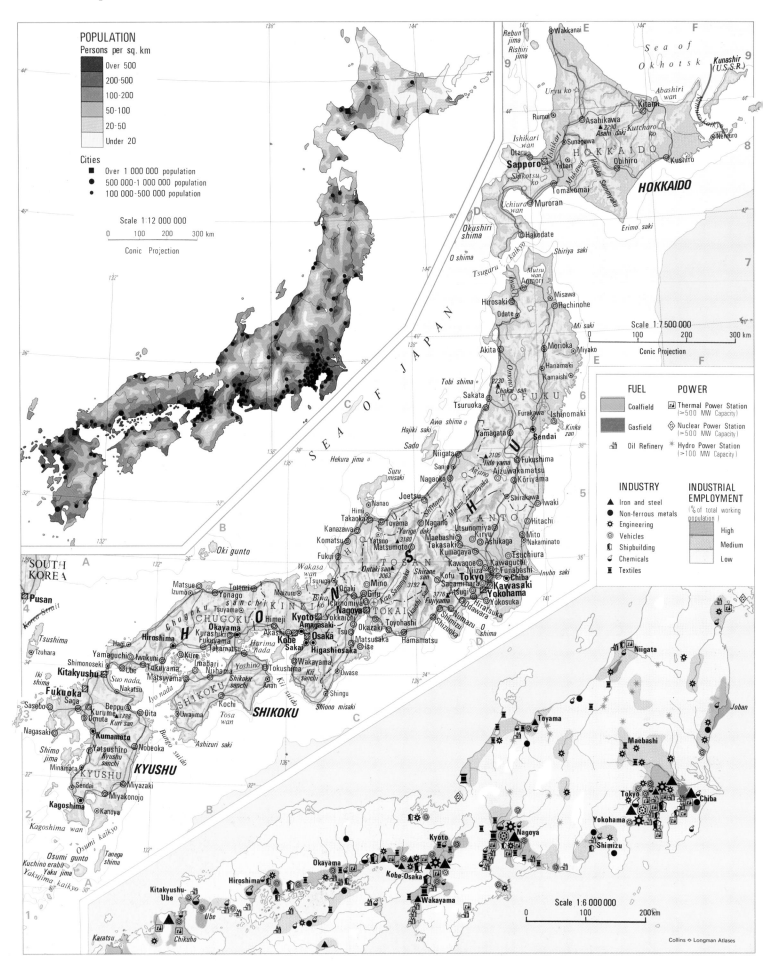

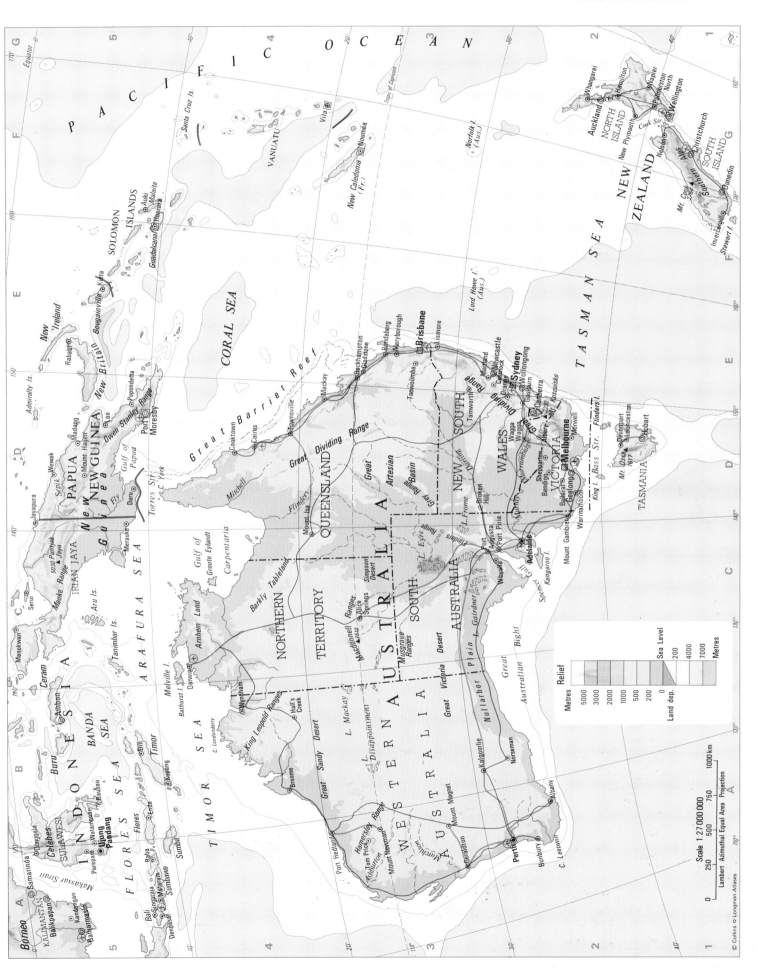

PACIFIC OCEAN

Equator

INDONESIA

Borneo
KALIMANTAN
Balikpapan
Kandangan
Banjarmasin
Samarinda
Dongqala
Parepare
Watampone
Ujung
Pandang
SULAWESI
Celebes
Manokwari
Serui
Ceram
Ambon
Buru
BANDA
SEA
Bau Bau
Bili
Timor
Kupang
Flores
Ende
Sumba
Sumbawa
Raba
Mataram
Singaraja
Denpasar
Bali
FLORES SEA
MAKASSAR STRAIT

New Ireland
New Britain
Rabaul
Admiralty Is.
Jayapura
Manokwan
IRIAN JAYA
Maoke Range
5030 Puncak Jaya
Aru Is.
Tanimbar Is.
Merauke

SOLOMON
ISLANDS
Kieta
Bougainville
Buka
Guadalcanal
Honiara
Auki
Malaita

PAPUA NEW GUINEA
Sepik
Wewak
Madag
Mount Hagen
Owen Stanley Range
Popondetta
Port Moresby
Gulf of Papua
Fly
Daru
C. York
Torres Str.

Santa Cruz Is.

VANUATU
Vila
Nouméa
New Caledonia (Fr.)

Norfolk I. (Aus.)

Tropic of Capricorn

CORAL SEA

Great Barrier Reef

Cooktown
Cairns
Townsville
Mackay
Rockhampton
Gladstone
Bundaberg
Maryborough
Brisbane
Lismore

ARAFURA SEA

Gulf of Carpentaria
Groote Eylandt
Arnhem Land
Melville I.
Bathurst I.
Darwin
C. Londonderry
Wyndham
Hall's Creek
King Leopold Ranges

TIMOR SEA

NORTHERN TERRITORY
Barkly Tableland
Mitchell
Flinders
Mount Isa

QUEENSLAND
Great Dividing Range
Great Artesian Basin
Grey Range
Toowoomba

NEW SOUTH WALES
Tamworth
Newcastle
Maitland
Sydney
Wollongong
Canberra
Orange
Bathurst
Dividing Range
Murrumbidgee
Wagga Wagga
Mt. Kosciusko
2230
Albury
Bendigo

VICTORIA
Ballarat
Geelong
Melbourne
Morwell
Shepparton
Warrnambool
Mount Gambier

King Str.
Bass Str.
Flinders I.

TASMANIA
Devonport
Launceston
Mt. Ossa 1617
Hobart

NEW ZEALAND
Whangarei
Auckland
Hamilton
NORTH ISLAND
New Plymouth
Napier
Palmerston North
Wellington
Cook Str.
Nelson
Mt. Cook 3765
SOUTH ISLAND
Christchurch
Southern Alps
Invercargill
Stewart I.
Dunedin

TASMAN SEA

Lord Howe I. (Aus.)

Alice Springs
Macdonnell Ranges 1510
Musgrave Ranges
Simpson Desert
L. Eyre
Flinders Range
L. Frome

SOUTH AUSTRALIA
L. Mackay
L. Disappointment
Great Sandy Desert
Great Victoria Desert
L. Gairdner
Port Augusta
Port Pirie
Whyalla
Adelaide
Spencer Gulf
Kangaroo I.

WESTERN AUSTRALIA
Broome
Port Hedland
Hamersley Range
Tom Price
Mount Newman
Mount Magnet
Murchison
Geraldton
Perth
Kalgoorlie
Norseman
Nullarbor Plain
Great Australian Bight
Great Bight
Albany
Bunbury
C. Leeuwin

Ashburton

Scale 1:27 000 000

Lambert Azimuthal Equal Area Projection

1000 km
750
500
250
0

Relief

Metres
5000
3000
2000
1000
500
200
Sea Level
Land dep.
200
4000
7000
Metres

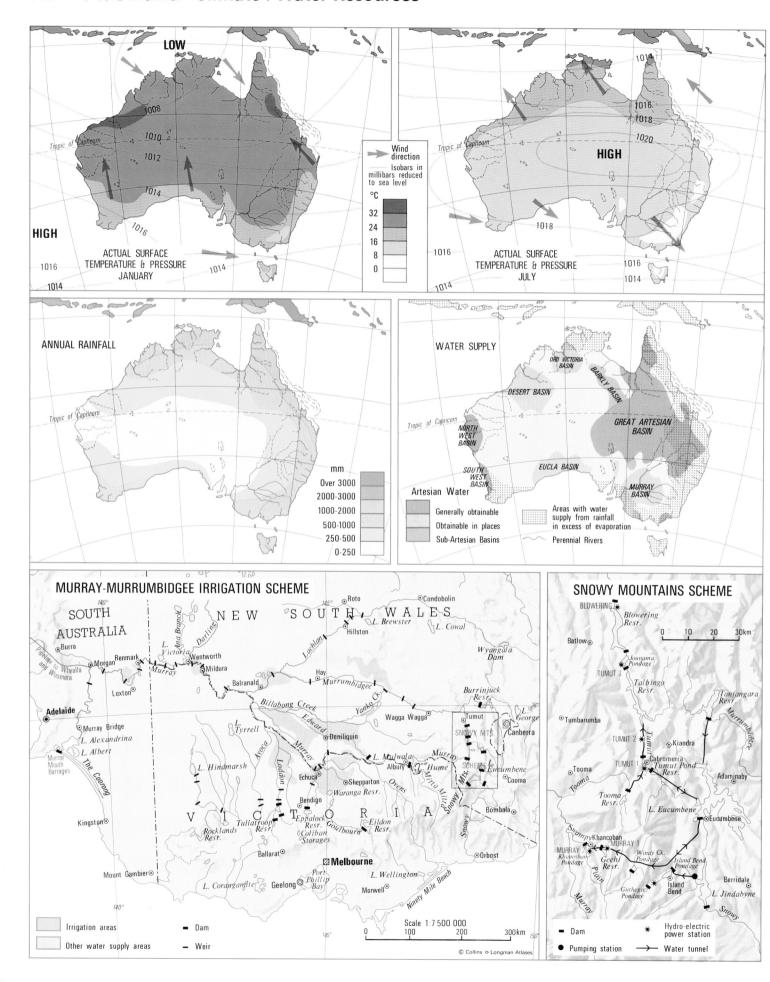

ACTUAL SURFACE TEMPERATURE & PRESSURE JANUARY

LOW

HIGH

1016
1014

Tropic of Capricorn

1008
1010
1012
1014
1016

ACTUAL SURFACE TEMPERATURE & PRESSURE JULY

HIGH

1014
1016
1018
1020

1018

1016
1014

Wind direction	
Isobars in millibars reduced to sea level	

°C
32
24
16
8
0

ANNUAL RAINFALL

Tropic of Capricorn

mm
Over 3000
2000-3000
1000-2000
500-1000
250-500
0-250

WATER SUPPLY

ORD VICTORIA BASIN
BARKLY BASIN
DESERT BASIN
GREAT ARTESIAN BASIN
NORTH WEST BASIN
SOUTH WEST BASIN
EUCLA BASIN
MURRAY BASIN

Tropic of Capricorn

Artesian Water

Generally obtainable
Obtainable in places
Sub-Artesian Basins

Areas with water supply from rainfall in excess of evaporation

Perennial Rivers

MURRAY-MURRUMBIDGEE IRRIGATION SCHEME

SOUTH AUSTRALIA

NEW SOUTH WALES

°Roto
°Condobolin
L. Brewster
°Hillston
L. Cowal

Burra
L. Victoria
Ana Branch
Darling
Wentworth
Renmark
Morgan
Murray
Mildura
Loxton
Balranald
Hay
Lachlan
Murrumbidgee
Wyangala Dam
Burrinjuck Resr.

Pipeline to Whyalla and Woomera

Adelaide
Murray Bridge
L. Alexandrina
L. Albert
Murray Mouth Barrages
The Coorong
Kingston
Mount Gambier

L. Tyrrell
Billabong Creek
Edward
Yanko Ck.
Wagga Wagga
Tumut
SNOWY MTS
Canberra
L. George

Avoca
Loddon
Murray
Deniliquin
L. Mulwala
Albury
Hume
Murray
Mitta Mitta
Snowy Mts.
Eucumbene
Cooma
SCHEME
L. Hindmarsh
Echuca
Shepparton
Ovens
Bombala

VICTORIA
Bendigo
Waranga Resr.
Eppalock Resr.
Coliban Storages
Tullaroop Resr.
Goulburn
Eildon Resr.
Rocklands Resr.
Ballarat
Snowy
Orbost

Melbourne
Port Phillip Bay
Geelong
L. Corangamite
L. Wellington
Morwell
Ninety Mile Beach

Irrigation areas
Other water supply areas
Dam
Weir

Scale 1:7 500 000
0 100 200 300km

© Collins ◇ Longman Atlases

SNOWY MOUNTAINS SCHEME

BLOWERING
Blowering Resr.
Batlow
0 10 20 30km
Jounama Pondage
TUMUT 3
Talbingo Resr.
Tantangara Resr.
Tumbarumba
Murrumbidgee
TUMUT 2
Tumut
Kiandra
TUMUT 1
Cabramurra
Tumut Pond Resr.
Tooma
Adaminaby
Tooma Resr.
L. Eucumbene
Swampy Plain
Khancoban
MURRAY 1
Eucumbene
MURRAY
Khancoban Pondage
Windy Ck. Pondage
Island Bend Pondage
Geehi Resr.
Guthega Pondage
Island Bend
Berridale
Murray
Snowy
L. Jindabyne

Dam
Pumping station
Hydro-electric power station
Water tunnel

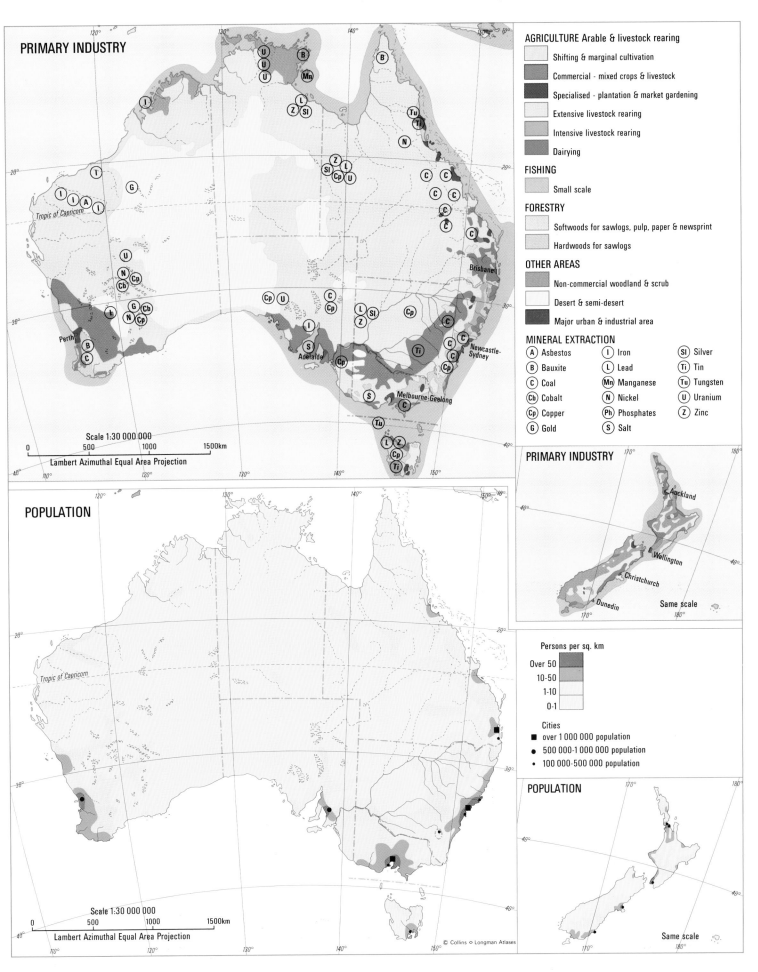

PRIMARY INDUSTRY

POPULATION

AGRICULTURE Arable & livestock rearing
- Shifting & marginal cultivation
- Commercial - mixed crops & livestock
- Specialised - plantation & market gardening
- Extensive livestock rearing
- Intensive livestock rearing
- Dairying

FISHING
- Small scale

FORESTRY
- Softwoods for sawlogs, pulp, paper & newsprint
- Hardwoods for sawlogs

OTHER AREAS
- Non-commercial woodland & scrub
- Desert & semi-desert
- Major urban & industrial area

MINERAL EXTRACTION
(A) Asbestos	(I) Iron	(Sl) Silver
(B) Bauxite	(L) Lead	(Ti) Tin
(C) Coal	(Mn) Manganese	(Tu) Tungsten
(Cb) Cobalt	(N) Nickel	(U) Uranium
(Cp) Copper	(Ph) Phosphates	(Z) Zinc
(G) Gold	(S) Salt	

Tropic of Capricorn

Perth

Brisbane

Newcastle-Sydney

Adelaide

Melbourne-Geelong

PRIMARY INDUSTRY

Auckland
Wellington
Christchurch
Dunedin   Same scale

Persons per sq. km
- Over 50
- 10-50
- 1-10
- 0-1

Cities
- ■ over 1 000 000 population
- ● 500 000-1 000 000 population
- • 100 000-500 000 population

POPULATION

Same scale

Scale 1:30 000 000
0   500   1000   1500km
Lambert Azimuthal Equal Area Projection

© Collins ◇ Longman Atlases

The 34 countries surrounding the Pacific Ocean and the 23 island states scattered across it have become a region of great economic and political importance. Approximately 2.4 billion people live in the region – more than half of the world's population. The region produces half of the world's total wealth (GNP) and has an abundance of natural resources, including 21% of the world's oil resources, 63% of its wool, 67% of its cotton, 87% of its natural rubber and 94% of its natural silk.

The graphs on these two pages show the importance of the trade between the major countries in the region. (The graphs show the trade between countries as a percentage of total trade for each selected country).

CANADA
Total Imports £33 362 million
Total Exports £40 701 million

% of total trade

IMPORTS — U.S.A., Japan
EXPORTS — U.S.A., Japan

U.S.A.
Total Imports £145 600 million
Total Exports £121 270 million

% of total trade

IMPORTS — Canada, Japan, Taiwan, South Korea, Hong Kong, Indonesia
EXPORTS — Canada, Japan, South Korea, Australia, Taiwan, Singapore

JAPAN
Total Imports £74 899 million
Total Exports £78 975 million

% of total trade

IMPORTS — U.S.A., Indonesia, Australia, China, Canada, South Korea, Malaysia, Taiwan
EXPORTS — U.S.A., South Korea, Hong Kong, Australia, Singapore, Indonesia, Taiwan, China, Canada

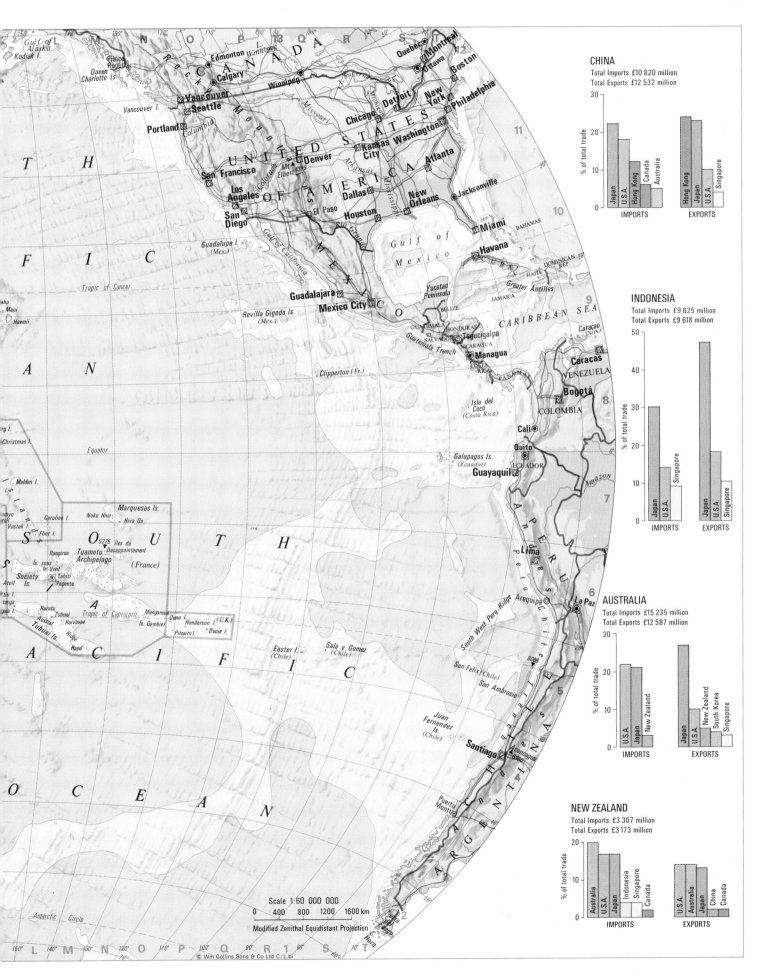

CHINA
Total Imports £10 820 million
Total Exports £12 532 million

% of total trade

IMPORTS: Japan, U.S.A., Hong Kong, Canada, Australia
EXPORTS: Hong Kong, Japan, U.S.A., Singapore

INDONESIA
Total Imports £9 625 million
Total Exports £9 618 million

% of total trade

IMPORTS: Japan, U.S.A., Singapore
EXPORTS: Japan, U.S.A., Singapore

AUSTRALIA
Total Imports £15 235 million
Total Exports £12 587 million

% of total trade

IMPORTS: U.S.A., Japan, New Zealand
EXPORTS: Japan, U.S.A., New Zealand, South Korea, Singapore

NEW ZEALAND
Total Imports £3 307 million
Total Exports £3 173 million

% of total trade

IMPORTS: Australia, U.S.A., Japan, Indonesia, Singapore, Canada
EXPORTS: U.S.A., Australia, Japan, China, Canada

Scale 1:60 000 000

0   400   800   1200   1600 km

Modified Zenithal Equidistant Projection

© Wm Collins Sons & Co Ltd C/L bi

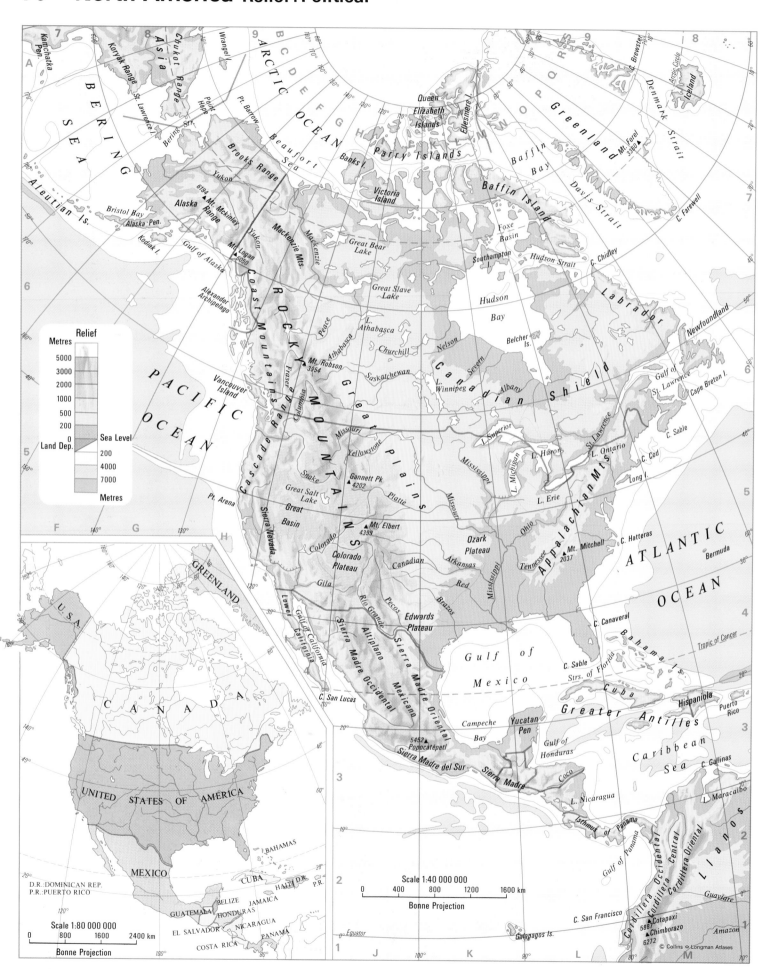

Scale 1:40 000 000

0   400   800   1200   1600 km

Bonne Projection

Scale 1:80 000 000

0   800   1600   2400 km

Bonne Projection

Relief
Metres

5000
3000
2000
1000
500
200
0   Sea Level
Land Dep.
200
4000
7000

Metres

D.R.:DOMINICAN REP.
P.R.:PUERTO RICO

© Collins ◇ Longman Atlases

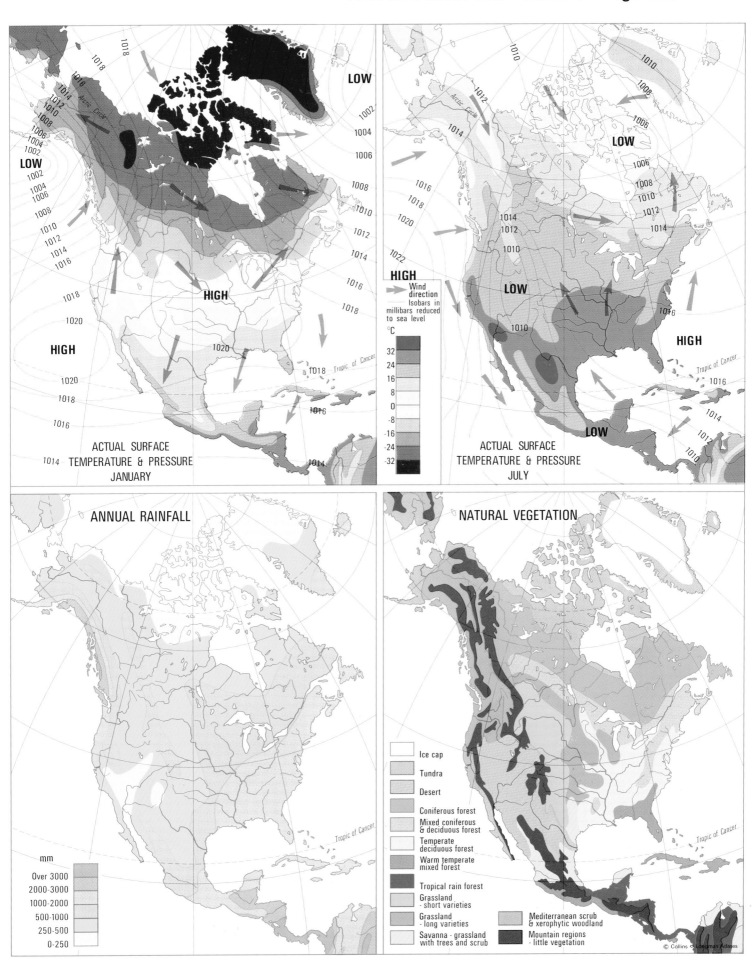

LOW
LOW
HIGH
HIGH
HIGH

ACTUAL SURFACE
TEMPERATURE & PRESSURE
JANUARY

LOW
LOW
HIGH
LOW

ACTUAL SURFACE
TEMPERATURE & PRESSURE
JULY

HIGH

Wind direction
Isobars in millibars reduced to sea level

°C

| 32 |
| 24 |
| 16 |
| 8 |
| 0 |
| -8 |
| -16 |
| -24 |
| -32 |

ANNUAL RAINFALL

mm

| Over 3000 |
| 2000-3000 |
| 1000-2000 |
| 500-1000 |
| 250-500 |
| 0-250 |

NATURAL VEGETATION

Ice cap
Tundra
Desert
Coniferous forest
Mixed coniferous & deciduous forest
Temperate deciduous forest
Warm temperate mixed forest
Tropical rain forest
Grassland - short varieties
Grassland - long varieties
Savanna - grassland with trees and scrub
Mediterranean scrub & xerophytic woodland
Mountain regions - little vegetation

Tropic of Cancer

© Collins Longman Atlases

POPULATION DISTRIBUTION

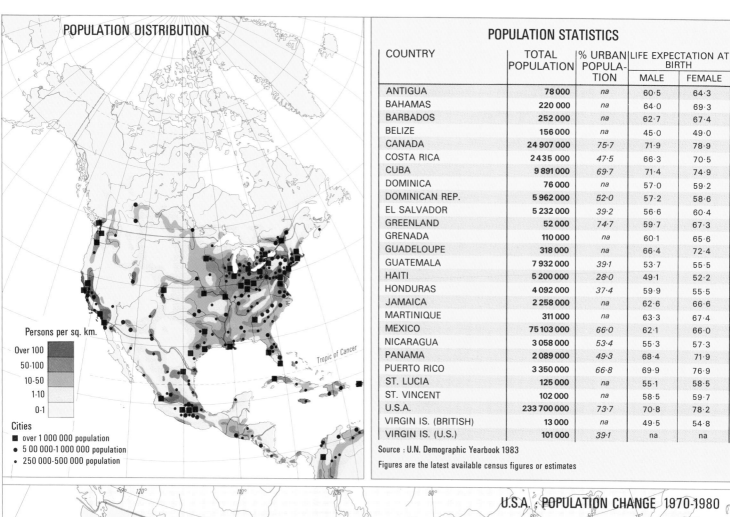

Persons per sq. km.

- Over 100
- 50-100
- 10-50
- 1-10
- 0-1

Cities

- ■ over 1 000 000 population
- ● 5 00 000-1 000 000 population
- • 250 000-500 000 population

POPULATION STATISTICS

COUNTRY	TOTAL POPULATION	% URBAN POPULA-TION	LIFE EXPECTATION AT BIRTH	
			MALE	FEMALE
ANTIGUA	78 000	na	60·5	64·3
BAHAMAS	220 000	na	64·0	69·3
BARBADOS	252 000	na	62·7	67·4
BELIZE	156 000	na	45·0	49·0
CANADA	24 907 000	75·7	71·9	78·9
COSTA RICA	2 435 000	47·5	66·3	70·5
CUBA	9 891 000	69·7	71·4	74·9
DOMINICA	76 000	na	57·0	59·2
DOMINICAN REP.	5 962 000	52·0	57·2	58·6
EL SALVADOR	5 232 000	39·2	56·6	60·4
GREENLAND	52 000	74·7	59·7	67·3
GRENADA	110 000	na	60·1	65·6
GUADELOUPE	318 000	na	66·4	72·4
GUATEMALA	7 932 000	39·1	53·7	55·5
HAITI	5 200 000	28·0	49·1	52·2
HONDURAS	4 092 000	37·4	59·9	55·5
JAMAICA	2 258 000	na	62·6	66·6
MARTINIQUE	311 000	na	63·3	67·4
MEXICO	75 103 000	66·0	62·1	66·0
NICARAGUA	3 058 000	53·4	55·3	57·3
PANAMA	2 089 000	49·3	68·4	71·9
PUERTO RICO	3 350 000	66·8	69·9	76·9
ST. LUCIA	125 000	na	55·1	58·5
ST. VINCENT	102 000	na	58·5	59·7
U.S.A.	233 700 000	73·7	70·8	78·2
VIRGIN IS. (BRITISH)	13 000	na	49·5	54·8
VIRGIN IS. (U.S.)	101 000	39·1	na	na

Source : U.N. Demographic Yearbook 1983

Figures are the latest available census figures or estimates

U.S.A. : POPULATION CHANGE 1970-1980

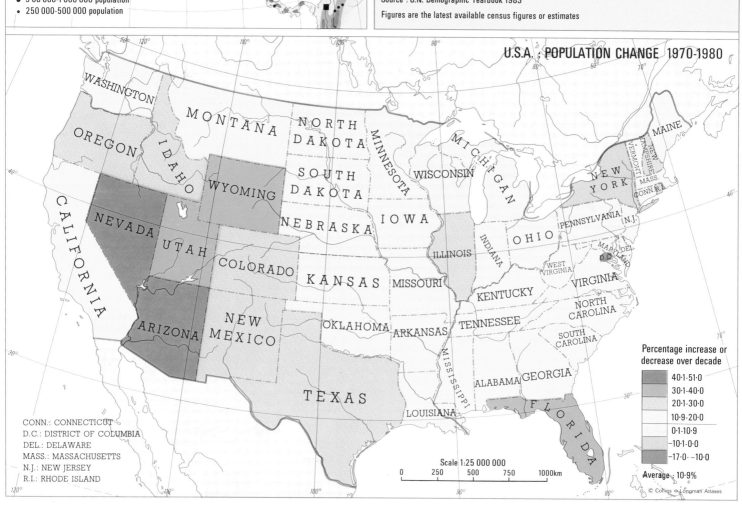

CONN.: CONNECTICUT
D.C.: DISTRICT OF COLUMBIA
DEL.: DELAWARE
MASS.: MASSACHUSETTS
N.J.: NEW JERSEY
R.I.: RHODE ISLAND

Scale 1:25 000 000

0   250   500   750   1000km

Percentage increase or decrease over decade

- 40·1-51·0
- 30·1-40·0
- 20·1-30·0
- 10·9-20·0
- 0·1-10·9
- -10·1-0·0
- -17·0--10·0

Average : 10·9%

© Collins ○ Longman Atlases

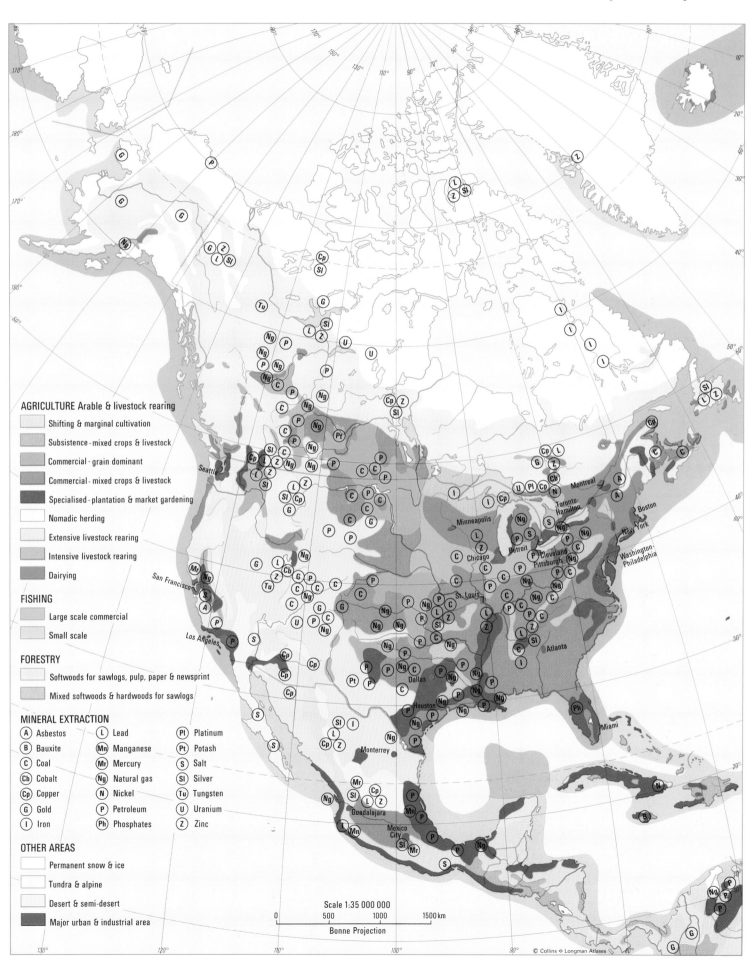

AGRICULTURE Arable & livestock rearing

- Shifting & marginal cultivation
- Subsistence - mixed crops & livestock
- Commercial - grain dominant
- Commercial - mixed crops & livestock
- Specialised - plantation & market gardening
- Nomadic herding
- Extensive livestock rearing
- Intensive livestock rearing
- Dairying

FISHING

- Large scale commercial
- Small scale

FORESTRY

- Softwoods for sawlogs, pulp, paper & newsprint
- Mixed softwoods & hardwoods for sawlogs

MINERAL EXTRACTION

(A) Asbestos	(L) Lead	(Pl) Platinum
(B) Bauxite	(Mn) Manganese	(Pt) Potash
(C) Coal	(Mr) Mercury	(S) Salt
(Cb) Cobalt	(Ng) Natural gas	(Sl) Silver
(Cp) Copper	(N) Nickel	(Tu) Tungsten
(G) Gold	(P) Petroleum	(U) Uranium
(I) Iron	(Ph) Phosphates	(Z) Zinc

OTHER AREAS

- Permanent snow & ice
- Tundra & alpine
- Desert & semi-desert
- Major urban & industrial area

Scale 1:35 000 000

0   500   1000   1500 km

Bonne Projection

© Collins ◇ Longman Atlases

© Collins ◇ Longman Atlases

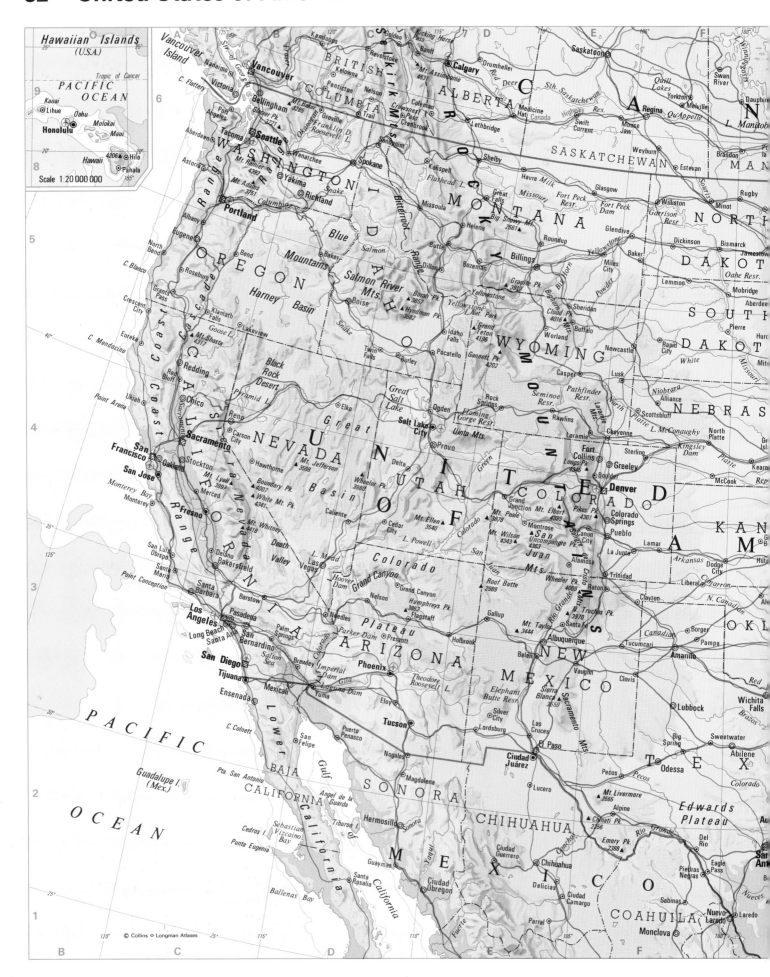

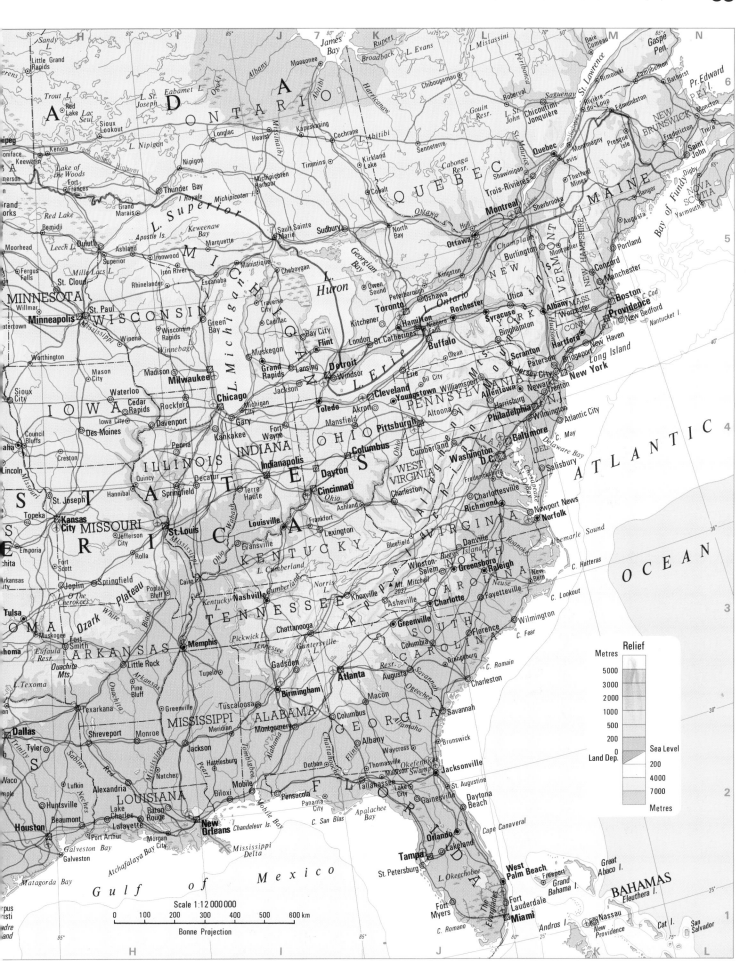

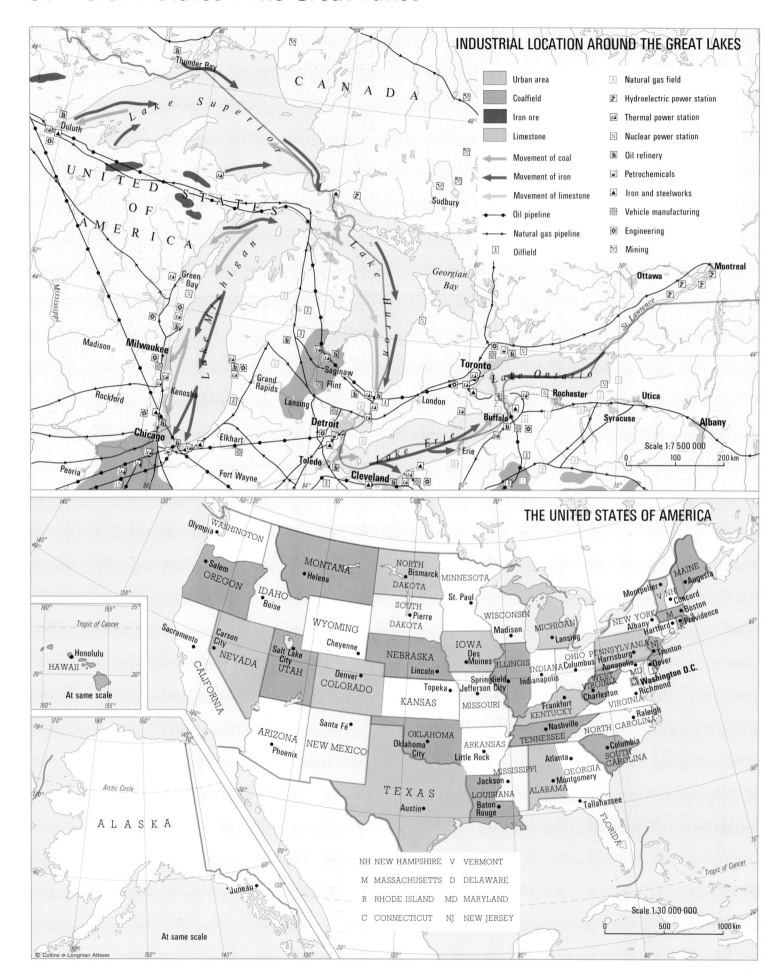

INDUSTRIAL LOCATION AROUND THE GREAT LAKES

Urban area
Coalfield
Iron ore
Limestone

Movement of coal
Movement of iron
Movement of limestone
Oil pipeline
Natural gas pipeline
Oilfield

Natural gas field
Hydroelectric power station
Thermal power station
Nuclear power station
Oil refinery
Petrochemicals
Iron and steelworks
Vehicle manufacturing
Engineering
Mining

C A N A D A

Thunder Bay

Lake Superior

Duluth

U N I T E D   S T A T E S

O F

A M E R I C A

Sudbury

Georgian Bay

Lake Michigan

Lake Huron

Green Bay

Madison

Milwaukee

Rockford

Kenosha

Grand Rapids

Saginaw

Flint

Lansing

Ottawa

Montreal

St. Lawrence

Toronto

Lake Ontario

Rochester

Utica

Chicago

Elkhart

Detroit

London

Buffalo

Syracuse

Albany

Peoria

Fort Wayne

Toledo

Lake Erie

Erie

Cleveland

Mississippi

Scale 1:7 500 000
0   100   200 km

THE UNITED STATES OF AMERICA

Olympia • WASHINGTON

Salem • OREGON

IDAHO
Boise •

MONTANA
Helena •

NORTH DAKOTA
Bismarck •

MINNESOTA
St. Paul •

SOUTH DAKOTA
Pierre •

WISCONSIN
Madison •

MICHIGAN
Lansing •

MAINE
Augusta •

Montpelier • V   NH   Concord
Boston
NEW YORK   M   Providence
Albany •   Hartford   C   R

Sacramento •

Carson City •

NEVADA

WYOMING
Cheyenne •

IOWA
Des Moines •

ILLINOIS

OHIO
Columbus

PENNSYLVANIA
Harrisburg   Trenton   NJ

Salt Lake City •
UTAH

Denver •
COLORADO

NEBRASKA
Lincoln •

Springfield •
Jefferson City

INDIANA
Indianapolis •

Annapolis
MD   Dover   D
Washington D.C.
WEST VIRGINIA   Richmond
Charleston •

CALIFORNIA

Topeka •

KANSAS

MISSOURI

Frankfort •
KENTUCKY

VIRGINIA

Raleigh •
NORTH CAROLINA

ARIZONA
Phoenix •

Santa Fé •

NEW MEXICO

OKLAHOMA
Oklahoma City •

ARKANSAS
Little Rock •

TENNESSEE
Nashville •

Atlanta •

Columbia •
SOUTH CAROLINA

Tropic of Cancer

Honolulu •
HAWAII

At same scale

ALASKA

Juneau •

At same scale

TEXAS

Austin •

MISSISSIPPI
Jackson •

LOUISIANA
Baton Rouge •

ALABAMA
Montgomery •

GEORGIA

Tallahassee •

FLORIDA

Tropic of Cancer

Arctic Circle

NH   NEW HAMPSHIRE   V   VERMONT
M   MASSACHUSETTS   D   DELAWARE
R   RHODE ISLAND   MD   MARYLAND
C   CONNECTICUT   NJ   NEW JERSEY

Scale 1:30 000 000
0   500   1000km

© Collins ◇ Longman Atlases

AGRICULTURE

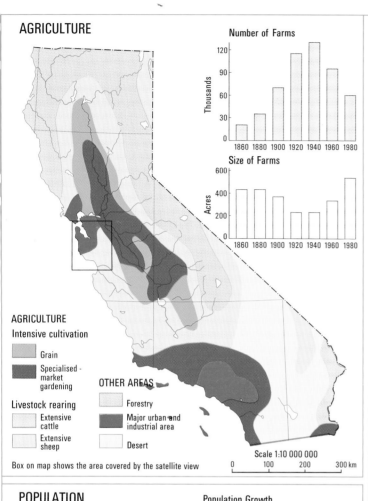

Number of Farms

Thousands

120
90
60
30
0

1860 1880 1900 1920 1940 1960 1980

Size of Farms

Acres

600
400
200
0

1860 1880 1900 1920 1940 1960 1980

AGRICULTURE

Intensive cultivation

- Grain
- Specialised - market gardening

Livestock rearing

- Extensive cattle
- Extensive sheep

OTHER AREAS

- Forestry
- Major urban and industrial area
- Desert

Box on map shows the area covered by the satellite view

Scale 1:10 000 000

0   100   200   300 km

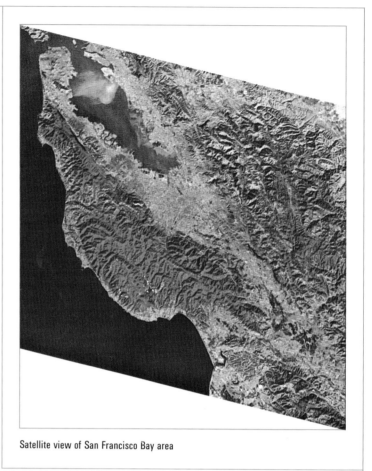

Satellite view of San Francisco Bay area

POPULATION

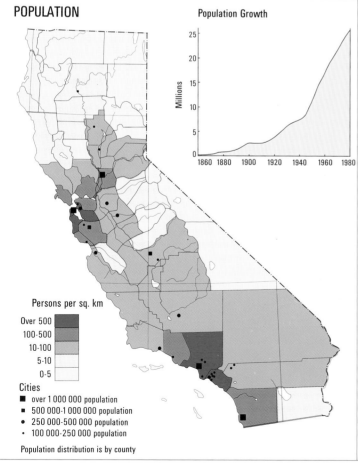

Population Growth

Millions

25
20
15
10
5
0

1860 1880 1900 1920 1940 1960 1980

Persons per sq. km

- Over 500
- 100-500
- 10-100
- 5-10
- 0-5

Cities

- ■ over 1 000 000 population
- ■ 500 000-1 000 000 population
- ● 250 000-500 000 population
- • 100 000-250 000 population

Population distribution is by county

WATER SUPPLY

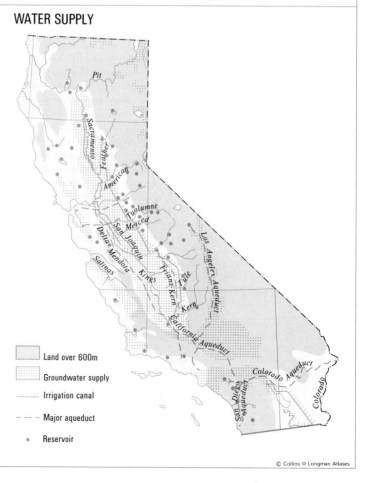

- Land over 600m
- Groundwater supply
- Irrigation canal
- Major aqueduct
- ● Reservoir

© Collins ◇ Longman Atlases

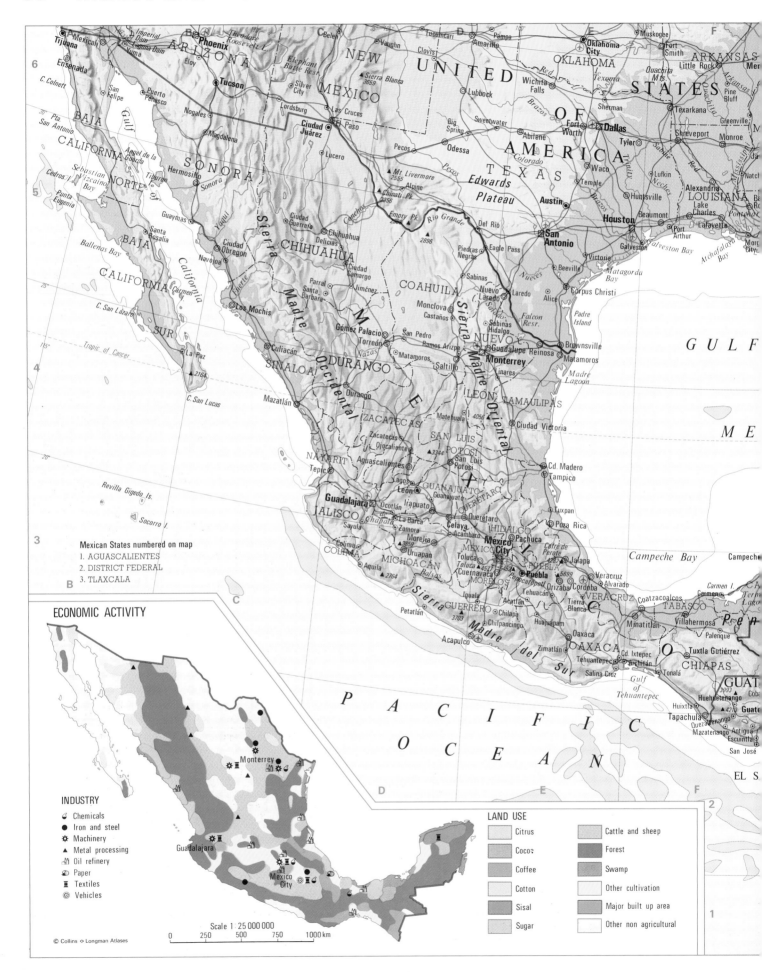

Mexican States numbered on map
1. AGUASCALIENTES
2. DISTRICT FEDERAL
3. TLAXCALA

ECONOMIC ACTIVITY

INDUSTRY
- ⌒ Chemicals
- ● Iron and steel
- ✿ Machinery
- ▲ Metal processing
- ⚚ Oil refinery
- ⬭ Paper
- ☰ Textiles
- ✪ Vehicles

LAND USE

Citrus		Cattle and sheep
Cocoa		Forest
Coffee		Swamp
Cotton		Other cultivation
Sisal		Major built up area
Sugar		Other non agricultural

Scale 1 : 25 000 000

0   250   500   750   1000 km

© Collins ◇ Longman Atlases

TENNESSEE
Pickwick L.
Asheville
Chattanooga
Guntersville L.
Greenville
Charlotte
Fayetteville
New Bern
C. Lookout

NORTH CAROLINA
SOUTH CAROLINA
Columbia
Florence
Wilmington
C. Fear

Tupelo
Tuscaloosa
Birmingham
Gadsden
ALABAMA
Atlanta
GEORGIA
Augusta
Savannah
Ogeechee
C. Romain
Charleston

Montgomery
Columbus
Albany
Macon
Savannah
Altamaha

Mobile
Pensacola
Thomasville
Madison
Waycross
Brunswick

Biloxi
Panama City
Tallahassee
Lake City
St. Augustine
Jacksonville

Mississippi Delta
Mobile Bay
C. San Blas
Apalachee Bay
Gainesville
Daytona Beach
Cape Canaveral

ATLANTIC

OCEAN

F L O R I D A
Orlando
Tampa
Lakeland
St. Petersburg
West Palm Beach

Tampa B.
Lake Okeechobee
Fort Myers
Fort Lauderdale

The Everglades
Miami
C. Romano

O F

C. Sable
Key West
Florida Keys
New Providence
Nassau
BAHAMAS
Cat I.

Great Abaco I.
Freeport
Grand Bahama I.
Eleuthera I.
San Salvador

Straits of Florida
Andros I.
Exuma Is.
Rum Cay

C O

Gt. Exuma
Samana Cay
Long I.

Matanzas
Cardenas
Archo. de Sabana
Crooked I.
Plana Cays
Mayaguana I.

Havana (La Habana)
Marianao
Sagua la Grande
Caibarién
Acklin's I.
Turks and Caicos Is. (U.K.)

Pinar del Rio
Guane
Santa Clara
Morón
Little Inagua
Caicos Is.
Turks Is.

Nueva Gerona
Guines
Cienfuegos
Sancti Spiritus
Ciego de Avila
Nuevitas
Great Inagua

Yucatan Channel
G. San Antonio
Puerto Juárez
Archo. de los Canarreos
Isle of Pines
CUBA
Trinidad
Camaguey
Victoria de las Tunas
Holguín
Banes
Baracoa
Tortue
Puerto Plata

Tizimín
Cozumel I.
Jardines de la Reina
Manzanillo
Bayamo
S. Luis
Guantánamo
Cap Haitien
Valverde
Santiago
San Francisco de Macorís
Sámana

CATÁN
QUINTANA ROO
Sa. Maestra
Turquino 1971
Santiago de Cuba
C. Cruz
G. of Gonâve
Gonaïves
St. Marc
La Vega
La Romana

Chetumal Bay
Little Cayman
Cayman Brac
Greater
Jérémie
Port-au-Prince
2414
S. Cristóbal
S. Pedro
Saona
Mona

Corozal
Ambergris Cay
Grand Cayman
Georgetown
Cayman Is. (U.K.)
Les Cayes
2680
Barahona
Azua

BELIZE
Turneffe Is.
Montego Bay
St. Ann's Bay
Port Antonio
Hispaniola
Antilles

Punta Gorda
Pto. Cortés
Gulf of Honduras
Black River
JAMAICA Kingston

S. Pedro Sula
Tela
La Ceiba
Bay Is.

C. Camarón
Caratasca Lagoon
C. Gracias á Dios
C A R I B B E A N
S E A

Juticalpa
Mosquitia Plain
HONDURAS
2469
Tegucigalpa
Mosquito Coast

Comayagua
Danli
2400
Prinzapolca
Bluefields

Sta. Rosa
Chinandega
León
Escondido
Rama

NICARAGUA
1780
Managua
Río Grande

S. Salvador
Jinotepe
Lake Nicaragua

Granada
Rivas
San Juan del Norte

COSTA RICA
Liberia
San José
Límon

Nicoya Peninsula
Irazu 3432
Chirripó 3820

San Juan
Colon
P A N A M A
Panama City

Metres | Relief
5000
3000
2000
1000
500
200
0 | Sea Level
Land Dep. | 200
4000
7000

Scale 1:12 500 000
0 100 200 300 400 500 600km
Chamberlin Trimetric Projection

Puerto Rico Trench
Bayamo
San Juan
PUERTO RICO (U.S.A.)
Mayagüez
Ponce
Caguas
1338

Virgin Is.(U.K.)
St. Thomas
Virgin Is. (U.S.A.)
St. Croix
Anegada
Tortola
Virgin Gorda

Anguilla (U.K.)
St. Martin (Fr.)
St. Barthélemy (Fr.)
Sint Maarten (Neth.)
Saba (Neth.)
Sint Eustatius (Neth.)
ST. KITTS-NEVIS

Barbuda (U.K.)
ANTIGUA
St. John's
Montserrat (U.K.)

Leeward Islands

Pointe-à-Pitre
Marie Galante
Guadeloupe (Fr.) Basse-Terre
1484
Roseau **DOMINICA**

Fort-de-France
Martinique (Fr.)
Castries
ST. LUCIA

St. Kingstown
ST. VINCENT AND THE GRENADINES
St. George's

Bridgetown
BARBADOS

Windward Islands
GRENADA

TOBAGO
Port of Spain
San Fernando
TRINIDAD

La Blanquilla
Dragon's Mouth
Serpent's Mouth

Bonaire
Orchila
Margarita I.
Porlamar
Paria Pen.
Cumaná
G. of Paria

Los Roques
Tortuga
Araya Pen.
Pto. La Cruz
Maturin
Orinoco Delta

La Guaira
Barcelona

L e s s e r   A n t i l l e s

Tropic of Cancer

Windward Passage

8528
San Juan
Bayamon
Arecibo
1338
DOMINICAN REP.
Santo Domingo
Caguas
Mayagüez
Ponce
PUERTO RICO (U.S.A.)

Netherlands Antilles
Aruba
Curaçao
Bonaire
Willemstad

Guajira Peninsula
Castilletes
Paraguaná Pen.
Gulf of Venezuela
Punto Fijo
Coro
Puerto Cabello
Maracay
Valencia

Ríohacha
Sta. Marta
Cristóbal Colon 5775
Valledupar
San Felipe
Barquisimeto

Barranquilla
Baranoa
Maracaibo
Cabimas
Lagunillas
VENEZUELA

Cartagena
Turbaco
Sabanalarga
La Concepción
Machiques
Lake Maracaibo
Acarigua
Guanare

Carmen
Arjona
Augustín
Codazzi
Valera
Trujillo
Mérida
Barinas

Magangué
Cerete
Sincelejo
Ocaña
Bolívar 5007
Guanare
Apure

Montería
San Jorge
Mompós
Cúcuta
5002
Puerto de Nutrias

Puerto Rey
Barrancabermeja 4200
San Cristóbal
Pamplona
Arauca

Turbo
Bucaramanga
Piedecuesta
Meta

C O L O M B I A
1959
Socorro
5493

Golfito
David
Santiago
Azuero Peninsula
Coiba I.
Pta. Burica

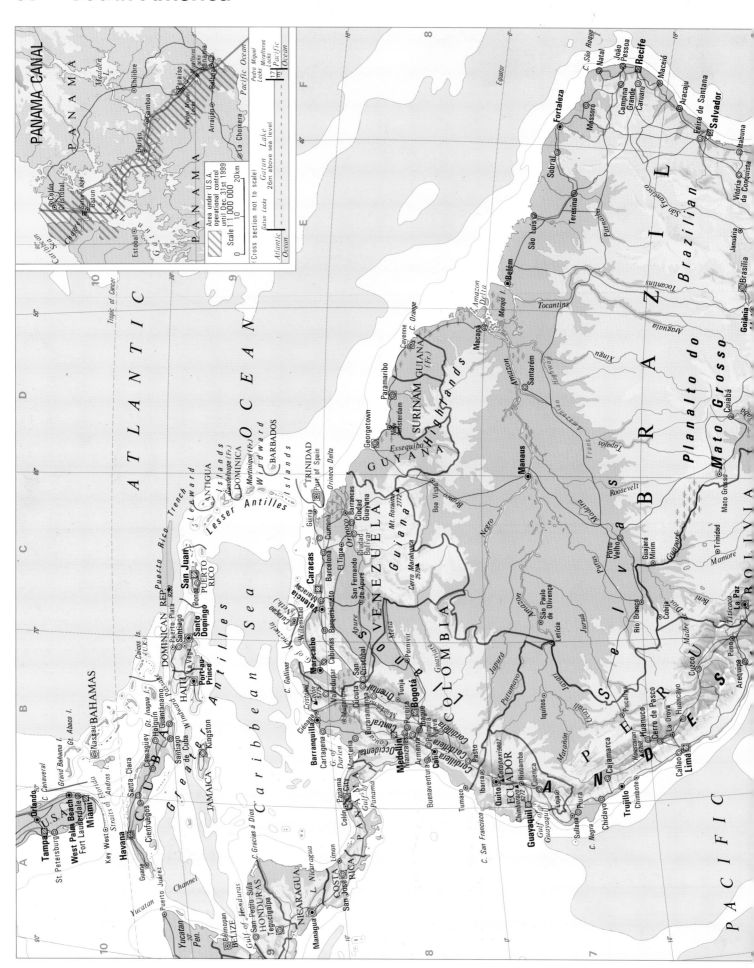

PANAMA CANAL

PANAMA

Madden L.
Chilibre
Gatún Locks
Gamboa
Pedro Miguel Locks
Paraiso
Miraflores Locks
Balboa
PANAMA
Panamá
Arraiján
Colón
Cristóbal
Gatún
Chagres
Gatún Lake
La Chorrera
Darién

Pacific Ocean

Caribbean Sea

Area under U.S.A.
operational control
until Dec. 31st 1999
Scale 1:1 000 000
0   10   20km

Gatun Lake
26m above sea level
(Cross section not to scale)

Pedro Miguel
Locks
Miraflores
Locks
Gatun
Locks

Pacific
Ocean
Atlantic
Ocean

ATLANTIC   OCEAN

PACIFIC

Tropic of Cancer

Equator

U.S.A.
Tampa
Orlando
C. Canaveral
St. Petersburg
West Palm Beach
Fort Lauderdale
Miami
Key West
Straits of Florida

Havana
Guane
CUBA
Santa Clara
Cienfuegos
Camagüey
Holguín
Santiago de Cuba
Guantánamo
Gt. Inagua I.
Caicos Is.

BAHAMAS
Nassau
Grand Bahama I.
Gt. Abaco I.
Andros I.

Yucatan
Puerto Juárez
Yucatan Pen.
Gulf of Honduras
BELIZE
Belmopan
San Pedro Sula
HONDURAS
Tegucigalpa
NICARAGUA
Managua
L. Nicaragua
COSTA RICA
San José
Limón
C. Gracias á Dios
Puerto Cabezas

JAMAICA
Kingston
HAITI
Port-au-Prince
DOMINICAN REP.
Santo Domingo
Santiago
La Vega
Windward Passage
9292

PUERTO RICO
San Juan
Ponce
ANTIGUA
Leeward Islands
DOMINICA
Guadeloupe (Fr.)
Martinique (Fr.)
BARBADOS
Windward Islands
Lesser Antilles
Antilles

Puerto Rico Trench

Greater Antilles

Caribbean Sea

TRINIDAD
Port of Spain
Güiria
Carúpano
Cumaná
Barcelona
Caracas
Valencia
Maracay
Maracaibo
Coro
Cabimas
Barquisimeto
Orinoco Delta
Curaçao (Neth.)
Willemstad
C. Gallinas
Cristóbal Colón

VENEZUELA
Ciudad
Guayana
Ciudad
Bolívar
El Tigre
San Fernando
de Apure
Cerro Marahuaca
2578
Mt. Roraima
2772

GUYANA HIGHLANDS
Georgetown
New
Amsterdam
Essequibo
Paramaribo
SURINAM
Cayenne
GUIANA (Fr.)
C. Orange
Macapá
Marajó I.
Amazon
Delta
Belém
São Luís
Teresina
Sobral
Fortaleza
Mossoró
C. São Roque
Natal
João Pessoa
Recife
Maceió
Campina Grande
Caruaru
Aracaju
Feira de Santana
Salvador
Itabuna
Vitória
da Conquista
Januária

COLOMBIA
Bogotá
Cúcuta
Bucaramanga
Barranquilla
Cartagena
Montería
Valledupar
Cabimas
San Cristóbal
Ocaña
Magangué
Tunja
Cordillera Central
Cordillera Occidental
Cordillera Oriental
Medellín
Manizales
Pereira
Armenia
Ibagué
Cali
Neiva
Palmira
Buenaventura
Popayán
Pasto
Tumaco
Ciénaga
Cauca

Amazon
Negro
Branco
Boa Vista
Santarém
Manaus
São Paulo
de Olivença
Leticia
Iquitos
Japurá
Putumayo
Içá
Juruá
Jutaí
Rio Branco
Cobija
Guajará Mirim
Porto Velho
Madeira
Roosevelt
Trinidad
Mamoré
Guaporé
Beni
Tapajós
Xingu
Tocantins
Araguaia
Goiânia
Brasília
Planalto do Mato Grosso
Cuiabá

B R A Z I L
Brazilian
Highlands
São Francisco
Parnaíba

B O L I V I A
La Paz
Titicaca
Cochabamba
Madre de Dios

P E R U
Pucallpa
Cerro de Pasco
La Oroya
Huánuco
Huancayo
Lima
Callao
Chimbote
Trujillo
Chiclayo
Chimbote
Huascarán
6768
A N D E S
Cajamarca
Cuzco
Puno
Arequipa

ECUADOR
Quito
Guayaquil
Cotopaxi 5897
Chimborazo
6272
Ambato
Riobamba
Cuenca
Loja
Ibarra
Portoviejo
C. San Francisco
C. San Lorenzo
Golfo de Guayaquil
Sullana
Piura
C. Negra
Tumbes

Orinoco
Apure
Meta
Arauca
Guaviare
Vichada
Caquetá
Vaupés
Barinas
Portuguesa
Guárico
Pamplona
Bucaramanga

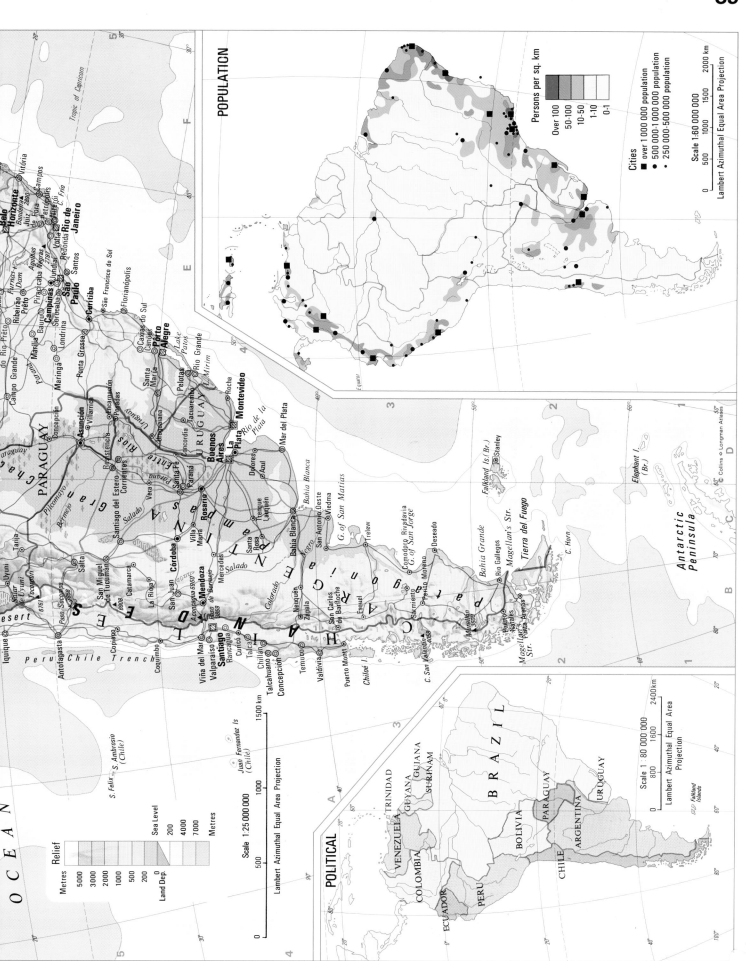

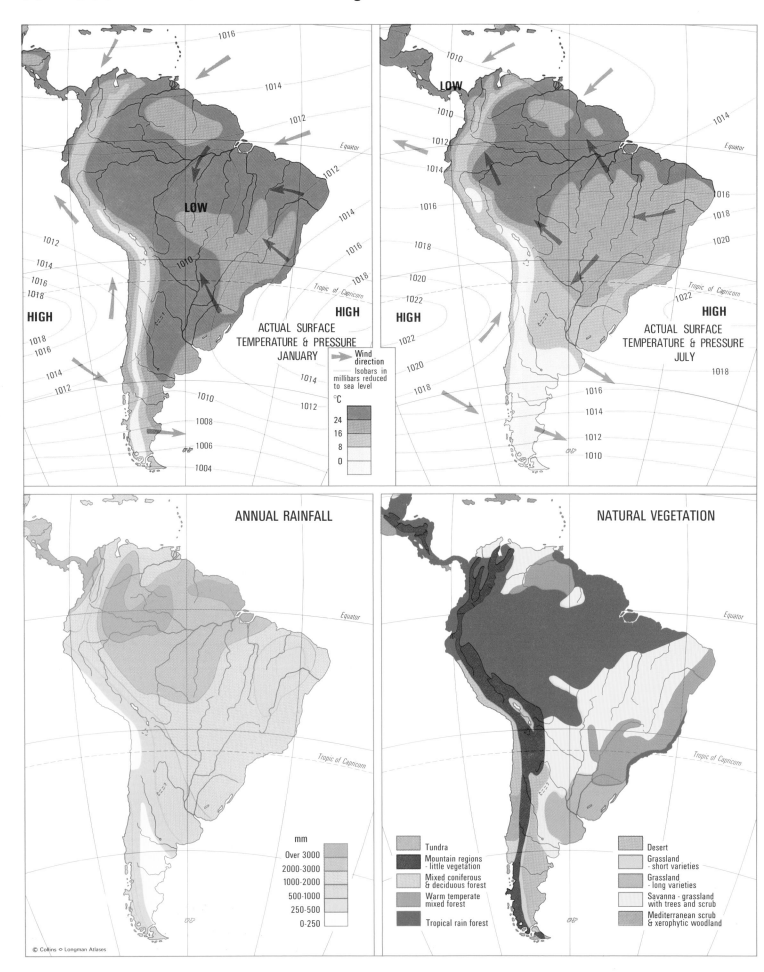

ACTUAL SURFACE TEMPERATURE & PRESSURE JANUARY

Wind direction
Isobars in millibars reduced to sea level

°C
24
16
8
0

ACTUAL SURFACE TEMPERATURE & PRESSURE JULY

HIGH   LOW   HIGH

ANNUAL RAINFALL

mm
Over 3000
2000-3000
1000-2000
500-1000
250-500
0-250

NATURAL VEGETATION

Tundra

Mountain regions - little vegetation

Mixed coniferous & deciduous forest

Warm temperate mixed forest

Tropical rain forest

Desert

Grassland - short varieties

Grassland - long varieties

Savanna - grassland with trees and scrub

Mediterranean scrub & xerophytic woodland

© Collins ○ Longman Atlases

AGRICULTURE Arable & livestock rearing

Shifting & marginal cultivation

Subsistence - rice dominant

Subsistence - crop other than rice dominant

Subsistence - mixed crops & livestock

Commercial - grain dominant

Commercial - mixed crops & livestock

Specialised - plantation & market gardening

Nomadic herding

Extensive livestock rearing

Intensive livestock rearing

Dairying

FISHING

Large scale commercial

Small scale

FORESTRY

Hardwoods for sawlogs

MINERAL EXTRACTION

(A) Asbestos   (L) Lead   (Sl) Silver

(B) Bauxite   (Mn) Manganese   (Ti) Tin

(Ch) Chromium   (Ng) Natural gas   (Tu) Tungsten

(Cp) Copper   (N) Nickel   (U) Uranium

(D) Diamonds   (P) Petroleum   (Z) Zinc

(G) Gold   (Ph) Phosphates

(I) Iron   (S) Salt

OTHER AREAS

Tundra & alpine

Desert & semi-desert

Major urban & industrial area

Scale 1:35 000 000

0   500   1000   1500km

Lambert Azimuthal Equal Area Projection

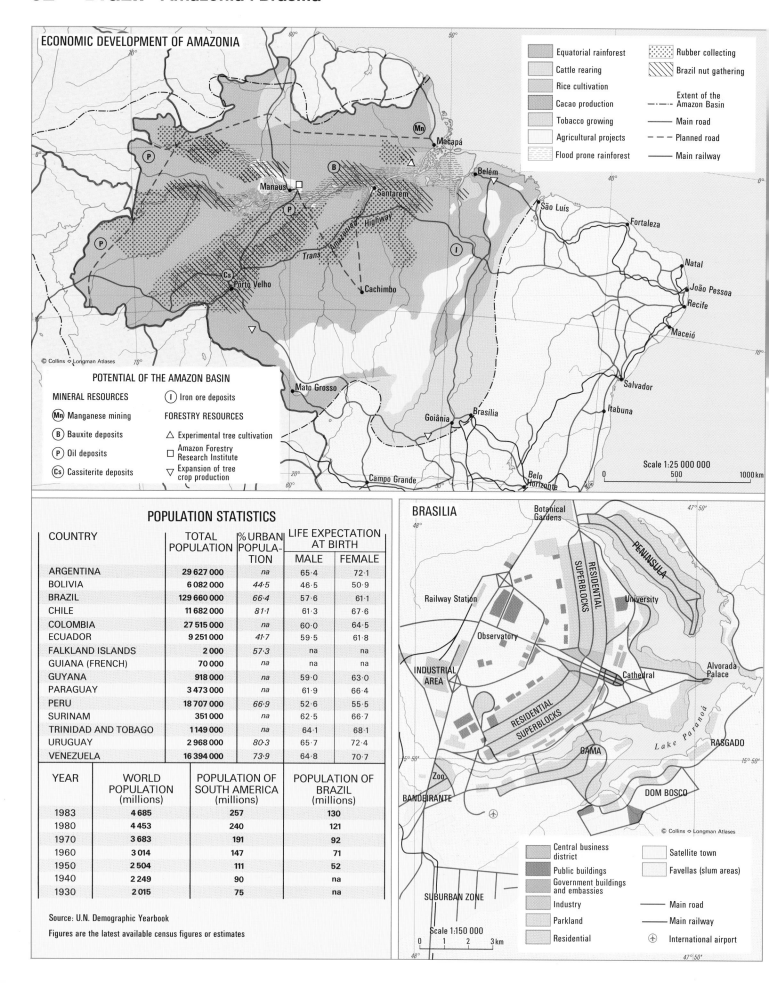

ECONOMIC DEVELOPMENT OF AMAZONIA

Legend:
- Equatorial rainforest
- Cattle rearing
- Rice cultivation
- Cacao production
- Tobacco growing
- Agricultural projects
- Flood prone rainforest
- Rubber collecting
- Brazil nut gathering
- —·—·— Extent of the Amazon Basin
- ——— Main road
- ‑ ‑ ‑ Planned road
- ——— Main railway

Map labels: Macapá, Manaus, Santarém, Belém, São Luís, Fortaleza, Natal, João Pessoa, Recife, Maceió, Salvador, Itabuna, Brasília, Goiânia, Mato Grosso, Cachimbo, Pôrto Velho, Campo Grande, Belo Horizonte, Trans Amazonian Highway

© Collins ◊ Longman Atlases

POTENTIAL OF THE AMAZON BASIN

MINERAL RESOURCES
- (Mn) Manganese mining
- (B) Bauxite deposits
- (P) Oil deposits
- (Cs) Cassiterite deposits
- (I) Iron ore deposits

FORESTRY RESOURCES
- △ Experimental tree cultivation
- ☐ Amazon Forestry Research Institute
- ▽ Expansion of tree crop production

Scale 1:25 000 000
0   500   1000km

POPULATION STATISTICS

COUNTRY	TOTAL POPULATION	%URBAN POPULATION	LIFE EXPECTATION AT BIRTH MALE	LIFE EXPECTATION AT BIRTH FEMALE
ARGENTINA	29 627 000	na	65·4	72·1
BOLIVIA	6 082 000	44·5	46·5	50·9
BRAZIL	129 660 000	66·4	57·6	61·1
CHILE	11 682 000	81·1	61·3	67·6
COLOMBIA	27 515 000	na	60·0	64·5
ECUADOR	9 251 000	41·7	59·5	61·8
FALKLAND ISLANDS	2 000	57·3	na	na
GUIANA (FRENCH)	70 000	na	na	na
GUYANA	918 000	na	59·0	63·0
PARAGUAY	3 473 000	na	61·9	66·4
PERU	18 707 000	66·9	52·6	55·5
SURINAM	351 000	na	62·5	66·7
TRINIDAD AND TOBAGO	1 149 000	na	64·1	68·1
URUGUAY	2 968 000	80·3	65·7	72·4
VENEZUELA	16 394 000	73·9	64·8	70·7

YEAR	WORLD POPULATION (millions)	POPULATION OF SOUTH AMERICA (millions)	POPULATION OF BRAZIL (millions)
1983	4 685	257	130
1980	4 453	240	121
1970	3 683	191	92
1960	3 014	147	71
1950	2 504	111	52
1940	2 249	90	na
1930	2 015	75	na

Source: U.N. Demographic Yearbook

Figures are the latest available census figures or estimates

BRASILIA

Map labels: Botanical Gardens, PENINSULA, RESIDENTIAL SUPERBLOCKS, University, Railway Station, Observatory, INDUSTRIAL AREA, Cathedral, Alvorada Palace, RESIDENTIAL SUPERBLOCKS, Lake Paranoá, GAMA, RASGADO, Zoo, BANDEIRANTE, DOM BOSCO, SUBURBAN ZONE

© Collins ◊ Longman Atlases

Legend:
- Central business district
- Public buildings
- Government buildings and embassies
- Industry
- Parkland
- Residential
- Satellite town
- Favellas (slum areas)
- ——— Main road
- ——— Main railway
- ⊕ International airport

Scale 1:150 000
0   1   2   3km

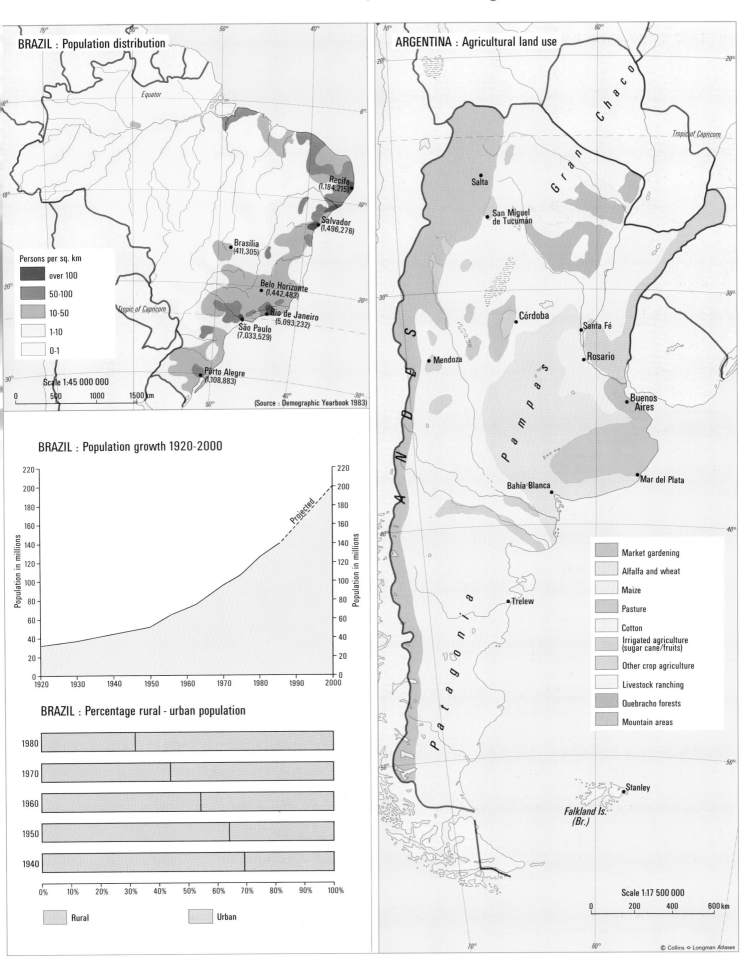

BRAZIL : Population distribution

Equator

Recife
(1,184,215)

Salvador
(1,496,276)

Brasília
(411,305)

Belo Horizonte
(1,442,483)

Rio de Janeiro
(5,093,232)

São Paulo
(7,033,529)

Tropic of Capricorn

Pôrto Alegre
(1,108,883)

Persons per sq. km

over 100
50-100
10-50
1-10
0-1

Scale 1:45 000 000

0   500   1000   1500 km

(Source : Demographic Yearbook 1983)

BRAZIL : Population growth 1920-2000

Projected

Population in millions

BRAZIL : Percentage rural - urban population

1980
1970
1960
1950
1940

0% 10% 20% 30% 40% 50% 60% 70% 80% 90% 100%

Rural   Urban

ARGENTINA : Agricultural land use

Gran Chaco

Tropic of Capricorn

Salta

San Miguel
de Tucumán

Córdoba

Santa Fé

Mendoza

Rosario

A N D E S

Buenos
Aires

P a m p a s

Bahía Blanca

Mar del Plata

P a t a g o n i a

Trelew

Market gardening
Alfalfa and wheat
Maize
Pasture
Cotton
Irrigated agriculture
(sugar cane/fruits)
Other crop agriculture
Livestock ranching
Quebracho forests
Mountain areas

Stanley

Falkland Is.
(Br.)

Scale 1:17 500 000

0   200   400   600 km

© Collins ◇ Longman Atlases

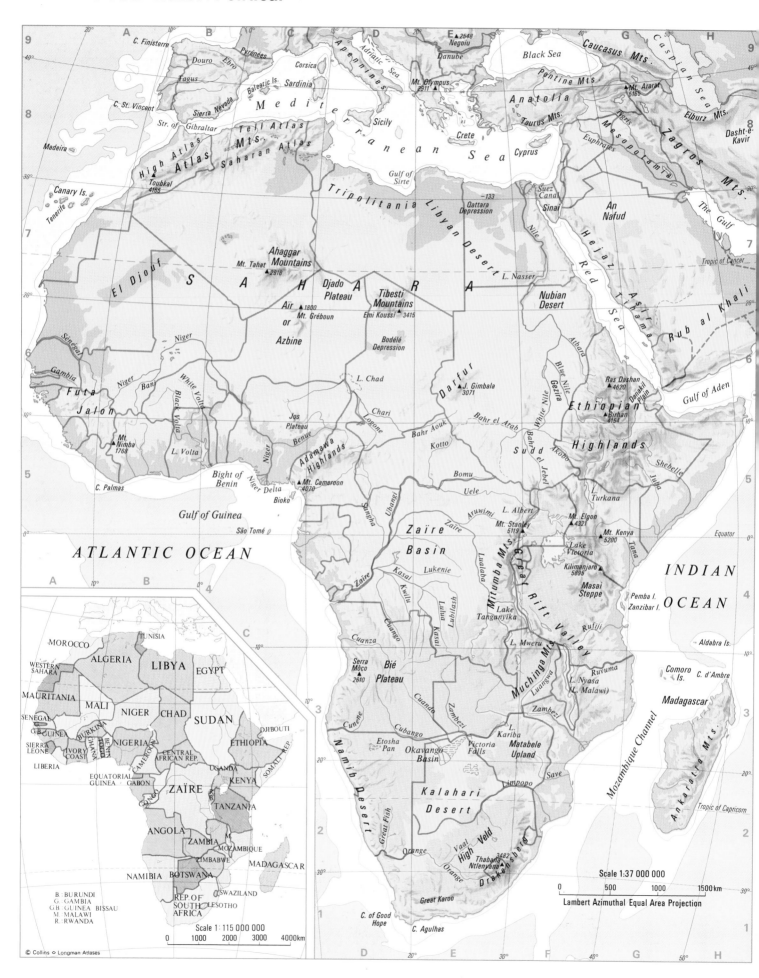

Scale 1:37 000 000

0   500   1000   1500km

Lambert Azimuthal Equal Area Projection

Scale 1:115 000 000

0   1000   2000   3000   4000km

B : BURUNDI
G : GAMBIA
GB : GUINEA BISSAU
M : MALAWI
R : RWANDA

© Collins ◇ Longman Atlases

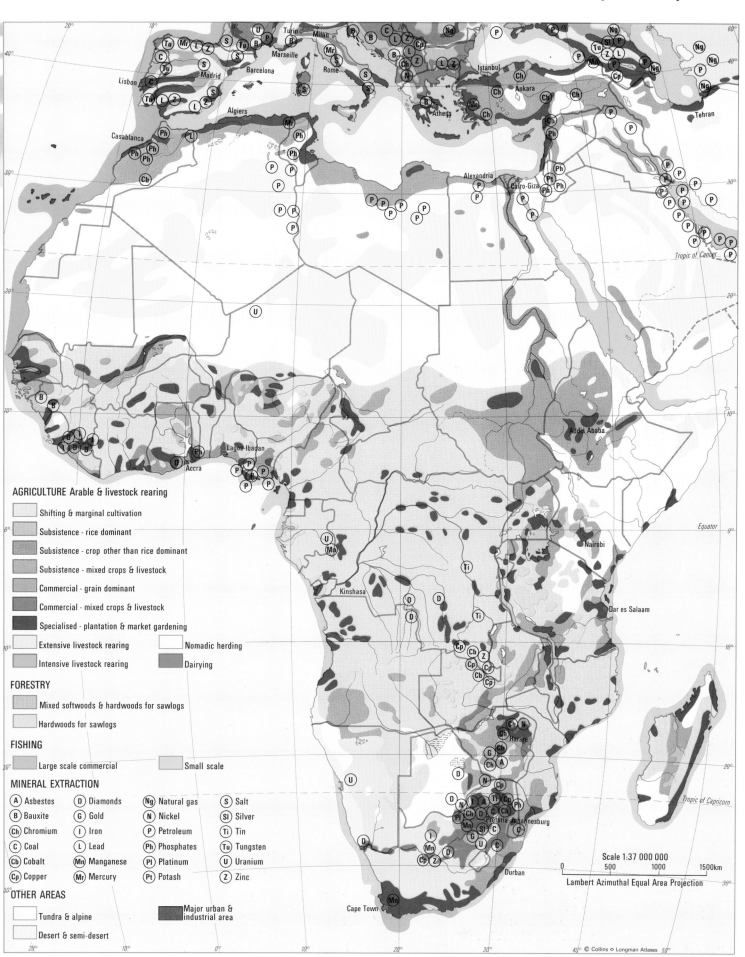

AGRICULTURE Arable & livestock rearing

Shifting & marginal cultivation

Subsistence - rice dominant

Subsistence - crop other than rice dominant

Subsistence - mixed crops & livestock

Commercial - grain dominant

Commercial - mixed crops & livestock

Specialised - plantation & market gardening

Extensive livestock rearing   Nomadic herding

Intensive livestock rearing   Dairying

FORESTRY

Mixed softwoods & hardwoods for sawlogs

Hardwoods for sawlogs

FISHING

Large scale commercial   Small scale

MINERAL EXTRACTION

(A) Asbestos   (D) Diamonds   (Ng) Natural gas   (S) Salt
(B) Bauxite   (G) Gold   (N) Nickel   (Sl) Silver
(Ch) Chromium   (I) Iron   (P) Petroleum   (Ti) Tin
(C) Coal   (L) Lead   (Ph) Phosphates   (Tu) Tungsten
(Cb) Cobalt   (Mn) Manganese   (Pl) Platinum   (U) Uranium
(Cp) Copper   (Mr) Mercury   (Pt) Potash   (Z) Zinc

OTHER AREAS

Tundra & alpine

Desert & semi-desert

Major urban & industrial area

Scale 1:37 000 000

0   500   1000   1500km

Lambert Azimuthal Equal Area Projection

© Collins ◇ Longman Atlases

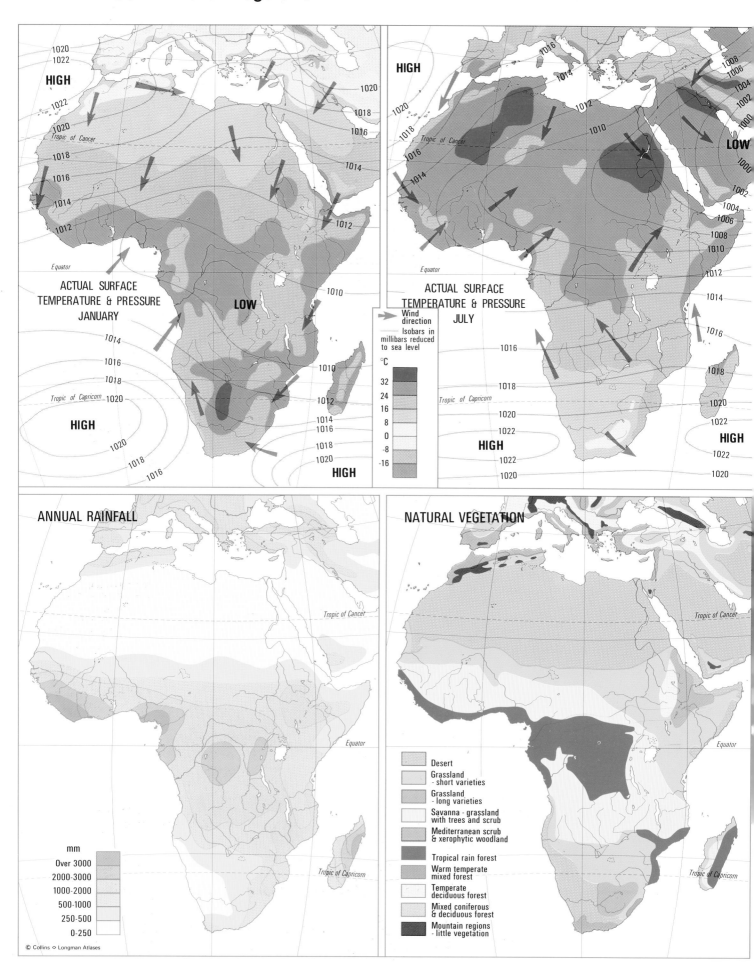

ACTUAL SURFACE
TEMPERATURE & PRESSURE
JANUARY

ACTUAL SURFACE
TEMPERATURE & PRESSURE
JULY

Wind
direction
Isobars in
millibars reduced
to sea level

°C

	32
	24
	16
	8
	0
	-8
	-16

HIGH
LOW
Tropic of Cancer
Equator
Tropic of Capricorn

ANNUAL RAINFALL

mm

	Over 3000
	2000-3000
	1000-2000
	500-1000
	250-500
	0-250

NATURAL VEGETATION

	Desert
	Grassland - short varieties
	Grassland - long varieties
	Savanna - grassland with trees and scrub
	Mediterranean scrub & xerophytic woodland
	Tropical rain forest
	Warm temperate mixed forest
	Temperate deciduous forest
	Mixed coniferous & deciduous forest
	Mountain regions - little vegetation

© Collins ○ Longman Atlases

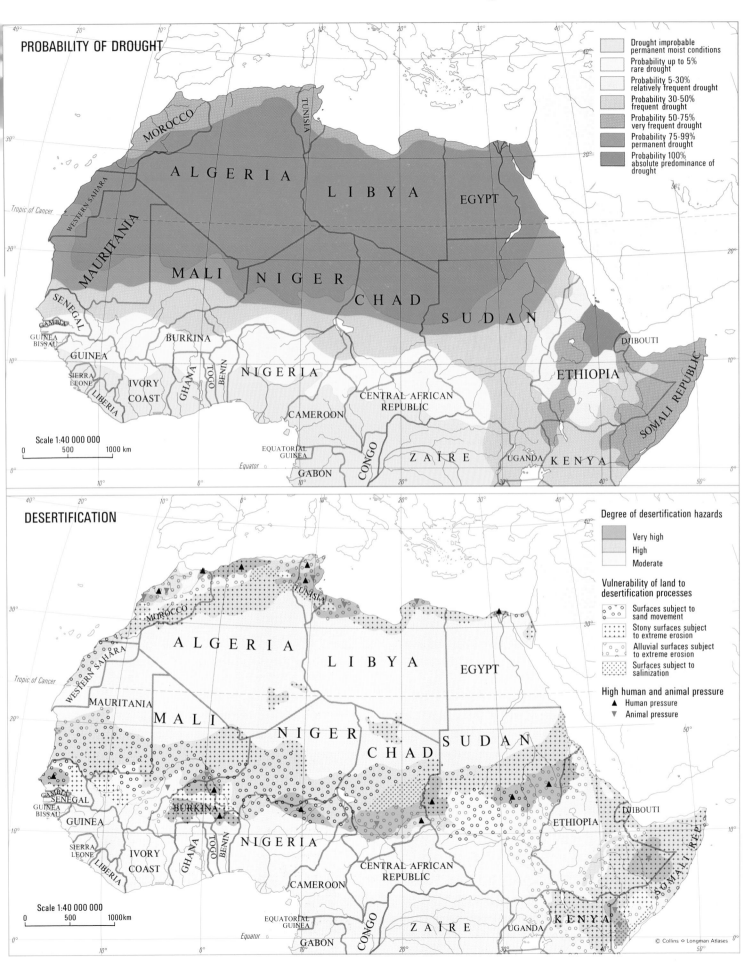

PROBABILITY OF DROUGHT

Drought improbable permanent moist conditions

Probability up to 5% rare drought

Probability 5-30% relatively frequent drought

Probability 30-50% frequent drought

Probability 50-75% very frequent drought

Probability 75-99% permanent drought

Probability 100% absolute predominance of drought

Scale 1:40 000 000

0   500   1000 km

DESERTIFICATION

Degree of desertification hazards

Very high

High

Moderate

Vulnerability of land to desertification processes

Surfaces subject to sand movement

Stony surfaces subject to extreme erosion

Alluvial surfaces subject to extreme erosion

Surfaces subject to salinization

High human and animal pressure

▲ Human pressure

▼ Animal pressure

Scale 1:40 000 000

0   500   1000km

© Collins ○ Longman Atlases

POPULATION DISTRIBUTION

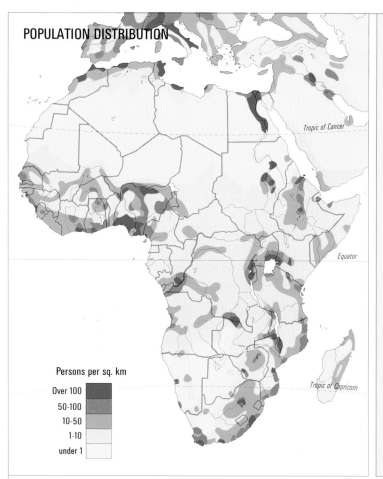

Persons per sq. km

- Over 100
- 50-100
- 10-50
- 1-10
- under 1

POPULATION STATISTICS

COUNTRY	TOTAL POPULATION	% URBAN POPULA-TION	LIFE EXPECTATION AT BIRTH	
			MALE	FEMALE
ALGERIA	20 500 000	52.0	58.5	61.4
ANGOLA	8 339 000	na	38.5	41.6
BOTSWANA	1 007 000	16.1	50.8	54.2
CENTRAL AFRICAN REP.	2 450 000	35.3	33.1	36.1
CONGO	1 651 000	na	43.0	46.1
EGYPT	44 533 000	44.3	51.6	53.8
EQUATORIAL GUINEA	375 000	na	40.4	43.6
ETHIOPIA	33 680 000	14.4	39.3	42.5
GABON	1 127 000	na	25.1	45.1
KENYA	18 784 000	15.5	46.9	51.2
LIBYA	3 342 000	29.8	53.8	57.0
MADAGASCAR	9 400 000	16.3	37.5	38.3
MALAŴI	6 429 000	8.5	40.9	44.2
MAURITANIA	1 719 000	22.8	40.4	43.6
MOROCCO	22 109 000	42.1	53.8	57.0
MOZAMBIQUE	13 311 000	13.2	45.8	49.1
NAMIBIA	1 465 000	na	45.0	47.5
REP. OF SOUTH AFRICA	30 802 000	53.1	49.8	53.2
SOMALI	5 269 000	na	39.3	42.5
SUDAN	20 362 000	20.2	43.9	46.4
TANZANIA	20 378 000	13.8	47.3	50.7
TUNISIA	6 886 000	49.8	57.6	58.6
UGANDA	14 625 000	na	48.3	51.7
WESTERN SAHARA	147 000	45.1	na	na
ZAÏRE	31 151 000	34.2	46.4	49.7
ZAMBIA	6 242 000	40.4	47.7	51.0
ZIMBABWE	7 740 000	23.6	51.3	55.6

Source : U.N. Demographic Yearbook 1983
Figures are the latest available census figures or estimates

CITIES OVER 100 000 - 1963

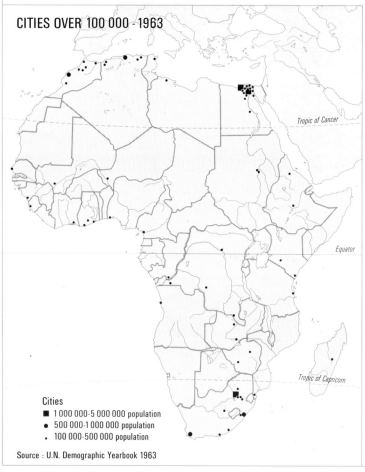

Cities
- ■ 1 000 000-5 000 000 population
- ● 500 000-1 000 000 population
- · 100 000-500 000 population

Source : U.N. Demographic Yearbook 1963

CITIES OVER 100 000 - 1983

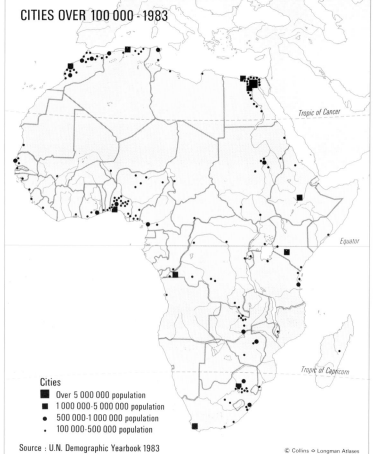

Cities
- ■ Over 5 000 000 population
- ■ 1 000 000-5 000 000 population
- ● 500 000-1 000 000 population
- · 100 000-500 000 population

Source : U.N. Demographic Yearbook 1983

© Collins ◇ Longman Atlases

Relief

Metres	
5000	
3000	
2000	
1000	
500	
200	
0	Sea Level
	200
	4000
	Metres

Scale 1:20 000 000

0   200   400   600   800km

Lambert Azimuthal Equal Area Projection

© Collins • Longman Atlases

Same scale

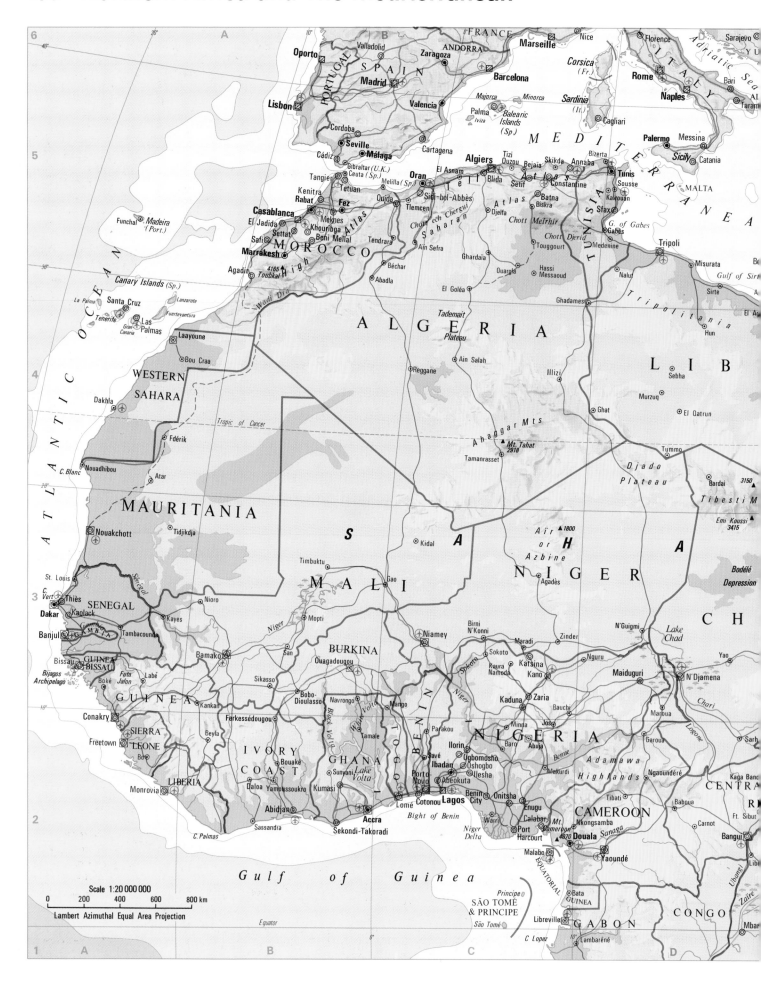

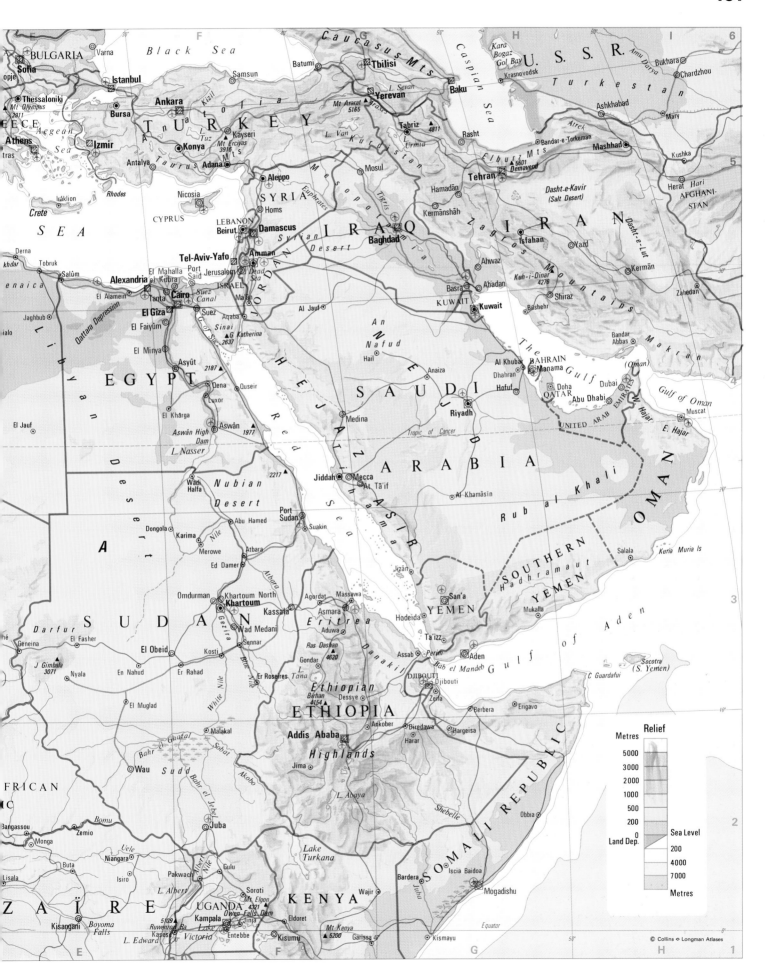

101

E F G H I 6

BULGARIA Varna
Sofia Istanbul Black Sea
opje Samsun Batumi Tbilisi
Thessaloniki Ankara Kızıl Caucasus Mts Caspian Sea Kara Bogaz Gol Bay U.S.S.R.
ECE Mt Olympus 2911 Bursa Tuz Anatolia Mt Ararat 5165 Yerevan Araxes Baku Krasnovodsk Turkestan Amu Darya Bukhara Chardzhou
Aegean Izmir Konya Mt Erciyas 3916 Kayseri Tabriz 4811 Rasht Ashkhabad Atrek Mary Kushka Mashhad
Athens Sea Antalya Taurus Mts Adana L. Van Urmia Demavend 5601 Tehran Elburz Mts Bandar-e-Torkeman Herat Hari AFGHANI-STAN
tras Aleppo Mosul Hamadān Dasht-e-Kavir (Salt Desert)
Iráklion Rhodes Nicosia SYRIA Homs Kermānshāh Isfahan Yazd Kermān Zahedan
Crete CYPRUS LEBANON Beirut Damascus Euphrates Mesopotamia IRAQ Baghdad Tigris Zagros IRAN Kuh-i-Dinar 4276 Shiraz Makran Bandar Abbas
SEA Derna Tobruk Tel-Aviv-Yafo Amman Syrian Desert Ahwaz The Gulf Bandar Abbas
khdar Salûm Alexandria El Mahalla el Kubra Port Said Jerusalem ISRAEL Dead Sea JORDAN Al Jauf Basra Abadan BAHRAIN Manama Dubai Gulf of Oman
enaica Jaghbub El Alamein Tanta Cairo Suez Canal Ma'an Kuwait KUWAIT Al Khubar Dhahran Hofuf QATAR Doha Abu Dhabi W. Hajar Muscat
El Gîza Suez Gulf of Suez Aqaba Sinai G. Katherina 2637 An Nafud Riyadh UNITED ARAB EMIRATES (Oman) E. Hajar
El Faiyûm Qattara Depression El Minya HEJAZ Hail SAUDI Tropic of Cancer
EGYPT Asyût 2187 Qena Medina Anaiza ARABIA OMAN
Libyan Luxor El Khârga Aswân Aswân High Dam 1977 Red ATIR Jiddah Mecca At Tā'if Al Khamāsin Rub al Khali Salala Kuria Muria Is
L. Nasser Sea Wadi Halfa 2217 Port Sudan SOUTHERN Hadhramaut
El Jauf Desert Nubian Desert Abu Hamed Suakin Jizán YEMEN San'a YEMEN Mukalla
Dongola Karima Nile Atbara Hodeida Ta'izz Aden Gulf of Aden C Guardafui Socotra (S. Yemen)
A Merowe Ed Damer Assab Perim Bab el Mandeb
Omdurman Khartoum North Agordat Massawa Asmara DJIBOUTI Djibouti Berbera Erigavo
SUDAN Khartoum Kassala Eritrea Aduwa Zeila
Darfur El Fasher Wad Medani Ras Dashan 4620 Ankober Diredawa SOMALI REPUBLIC
Geneina Sennar Gondar L. Tana Harar
J Gimbala 3071 El Obeid Kosti Er Roseires Danakil Berbera Hargeisa
Nyala En Nahud Er Rahad Blue Nile ETHIOPIA Birhan 4154 Dessye Highlands Obbia
El Muglad White Nile Jima Ankober
FRICAN Malakal Addis Ababa Relief
C Bahr el Ghazal Sobat Iscia Baidoa Metres 5000 3000 2000 1000 500 200 0 Sea Level 200 4000 7000 Metres
Wau Sudd Akobo Lake Turkana Shebelle Land Dep.
angassou Bomu Zemio Uele Bahr el Jebel Albert Nile Juba Bardera Jitha Mogadishu
Monga Niangara Buta Lisala L. Albert ZAÏRE Kisangani Boyoma Falls Ruwenzori 5109 Ba L. Edward Kasese UGANDA Kampala Lake Victoria Entebbe Jinja Owen Falls Dam Mt Elgon 4321 Soroti Gulu Pakwach Eldoret KENYA Kisumu Wajir Mt Kenya 5200 Garissa Kismayu Equator
© Collins ◇ Longman Atlases
ZAÏRE E F G H 1

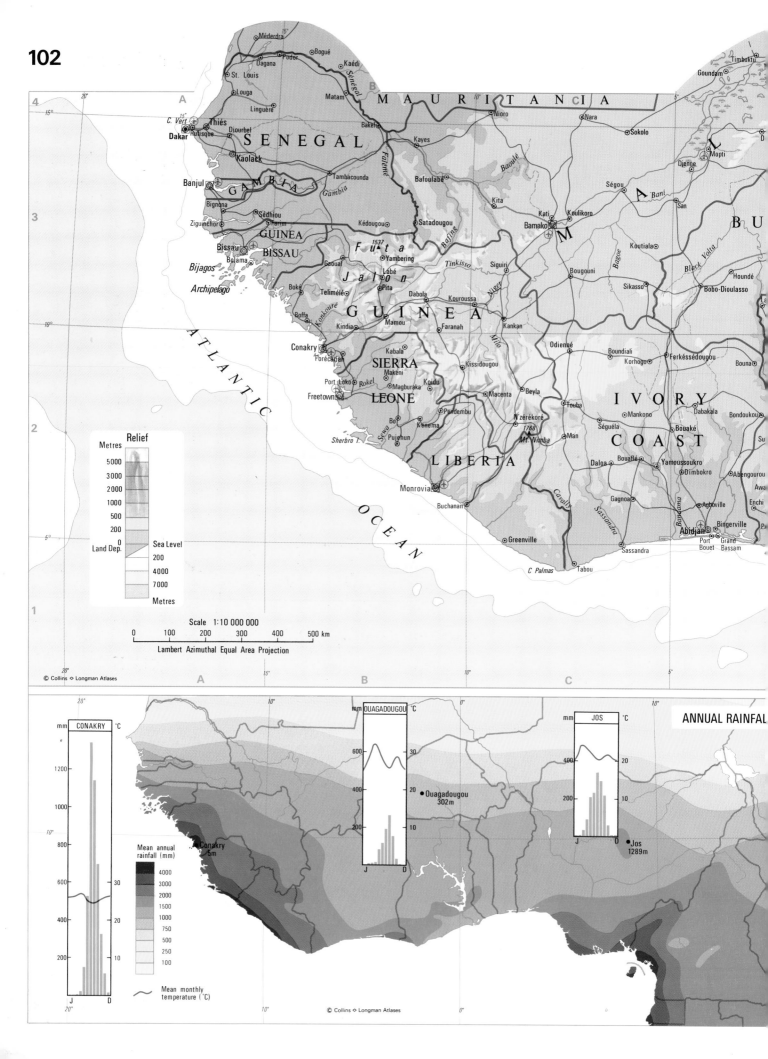

Relief

Metres
5000
3000
2000
1000
500
200
Land Dep. | 0 | Sea Level
200
4000
7000
Metres

Scale 1:10 000 000

0 100 200 300 400 500 km

Lambert Azimuthal Equal Area Projection

© Collins ◇ Longman Atlases

MAURITANIA

SENEGAL

Mèderdra
Podor
Bogué
Dagana
Kaédi
St. Louis
Louga
Matam
Linguère
C. Vert
Thiès
Nioro
Nara
Sokolo
Dakar
Rufisque
Diourbel
Kayes
Kaolack
Bakel
Goundam
Timbuktu

L I

Mopti
Djenne
Ségou
Bani
San
M A
Kita
Koulikoro
Bamako
Kati
BU

GAMBIA
Banjul
Tambacounda
Bafoulabé
Bignona
Gambia
Sédhiou
Ziguinchor
Farim
Kédougou
Satadougou
GUINEA
BISSAU
Bissau
Bolama
1537
Futa
Yambering
Tinkisso
Siguiri
Bougouni
Sikasso
Bobo-Dioulasso
Houndé
Bijagos
Jaloon
Gaoual
Labé
Pita
Dabola
Kouroussa
Archipelago
Boké
Telimélé
Kindia
Mamou
Faranah
Kankan
Odienné
Boundiali
Bouna
Boffa
GUINEA
Korhogo
Ferkéssédougou
Conakry
Forécariah
Kabala
Kissidougou
IVORY
Port Loko
Rokel
Makeni
Koidu
Macenta
Beyla
Touba
Mankono
Dabakala
Bondoukou
Magburaka
COAST
Freetown
SIERRA
LEONE
Bo
Pendembu
N'zérékoré
Séguéla
Bouaké
Kenema
1768
Man
Daloa
Bouaflé
Yamoussoukro
Pujehun
Mt. Nimba
Dimbokro
Abengourou
Sherbro I.
LIBERIA
Gagnoa
Agboville
Monrovia
Buchanan
Abidjan
Bingerville
Greenville
Port
Bouet
Grand
Bassam
Sassandra
C Palmas
Tabou

ATLANTIC

OCEAN

Bijagos

ANNUAL RAINFAL

mm CONAKRY °C
1200
1000
800
600
400
200
J   D

mm OUAGADOUGOU °C
600
400
200
Ouagadougou
302m
J   D

mm JOS °C
400
200
Jos
1289m
J   D

Conakry
5m

Mean annual
rainfall (mm)
4000
3000
2000
1500
1000
750
500
250
100

Mean monthly
temperature (°C)

© Collins ◇ Longman Atlases

N I G E R

CHAD

Bourem
a-Rharous
Gao
Yatakala
Tillabéri
Dori
Niamey
Dosso
Birni N'Konni
Maradi
Tessaoua
Zinder
Tanout
Gouré
Nguigmi
Bosso
Lake Chad
Moussoro
N'Djamena
Plain of Bornu
Bahr el Ghazal
Chari
Ergig
Chari
Maroua
Lai
Boumo
Garoua
Benue
Yola
Kontcha
Déo
Faro
Vina
Ngaoundéré
Péné
Tibati Dvérem
Banyo
Baboua
Bouar
C.A.R.
Carnot
Bertoua
Batouri
Berbérati
Nola
Yokadouma
Doumé
Mamfé
Sanaga
Yaoundé
Edéa
Nyong
Kribi
Campo
Bata
GABON
CONGO
Lomié
Kadeï
Boumba
Mbéré

Fada-N'Gourma
ouagadougou
Red Volta
White Volta
Tamale
Mango
Natitingou
Sokodé
Blitta
Atakpamé
Abomey
Aného
Lomé
Tema
Accra
Winneba
Cape Coast
kondi-Takoradi
Jbuasi
Kade
Kofoidua
Oda
Akuse
Ho
Kéte Krachi
Lake Volta
Volta

BENIN
TOGO
GHANA
BURKINA

Kandi
Nikki
Djougou
Parakou
Kaiama
Save
Sakété
Pobé
Porto-Novo
Cotonou
Ilaro
Abeokuta
Ijebu Ode
Okitipupa
Lagos

SOKOTO
Zamfara
Birnin Kebbi
Gaya
Yelwa
Kontagora
Zungeru
Jebba
Lafiagi
Bida
Baro
Ilorin
KWARA
Ogbomosho
Oyo
OYO
Iwo
Oshogbo
Ilesha
Ife
Ibadan
OGUN
ONDO
Akure
Owo
Benin City
BENDEL
Warri
Ughelli
IMO
Owerri
RIVERS
Yenagoa
Aba
Port Harcourt
Bonny
Brass
Niger Delta

Sokoto
Sokoto
Gusau
Kaura Namoda
Katsina
Kano
KANO
Hadejia
Nguru
Geidam
Dikwa
Maiduguri
BORNO
Damaturu
Potiskum
Azare
Buni
Biu
Mubi
Mandara Mts
Gombe
Bauchi
BAUCHI
Jos
Jos Plateau
1585
Kafanchan
Zaria
KADUNA
Kaduna
Minna
NIGER
Abuja
FED. CAP. TER.
Wamba
PLATEAU
Nasarawa
Lokoja
Kabba
Idah
Nsukka
Enugu
ANAMBRA
Onitsha
Afikpo
Abakaliki
BENUE
Makurdi
Ibi
Ogoja
Mamfé
Calabar
Uyo
Umuahia
CROSS RIVER
Ogoja
GONGOLA
Shebshi Mts
Adamawa Highlands
Bamenda Highlands
Bamenda
Foumban
Yoko
Bafia
Nkongsamba
Kumba
Bétaré Oya
Buea
Douala
Limbe
Malabo
3008
Mt Cameroon
4070
Dschang
2500

N I G E R I A

CAMEROON

EQUATORIAL GUINEA

Bight of Benin

Gulf of Guinea

Bight of Bonny

SÃO TOMÉ & PRINCIPE
Principe

Hadejia
Komadugu Gana
Gongola
Marigu
Kaduna
Benue
Donga
Katsina Ala
Mayo Daga
Kabba
Oshun
Niger
Ka
Mékrou
Niger

Gao
Tambacounda
Kano
Freetown
Ibadan
Abidjan
Douala

CLIMATIC REGIONS

Equatorial
(High annual rainfall. Constant high temperature. High humidity.)

Humid tropical
(High rainfall with two short dry seasons. Constant high temperature.)

Tropical
(One rainy season. One dry season. Hotter during dry season, cooler during wet season.)

Sahelian
(Short wet season for about three months. Very high temperatures.)

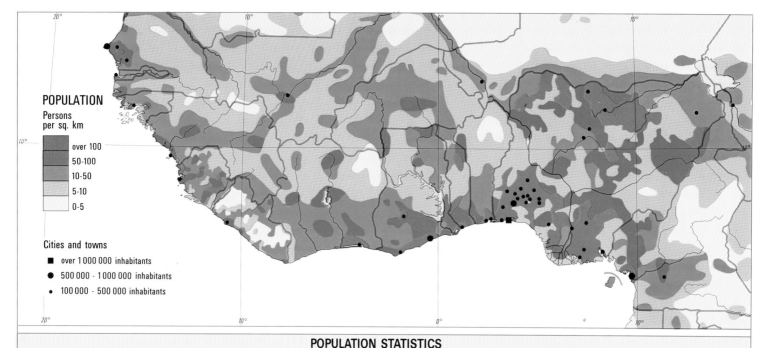

POPULATION

Persons per sq. km

- over 100
- 50-100
- 10-50
- 5-10
- 0-5

Cities and towns

- ■ over 1 000 000 inhabitants
- ● 500 000 - 1 000 000 inhabitants
- • 100 000 - 500 000 inhabitants

POPULATION STATISTICS

COUNTRY	TOTAL POPULATION	% URBAN POPULA-TION	LIFE EXPECTATION AT BIRTH		% OF TOTAL POPULATION BY AGE GROUP				
			MALE	FEMALE	0-14	15-34	35-54	55-74	75+
BENIN	3 720 000	39.4	39.0	42.1	48.8	28.0	14.1	6.5	2.6
BURKINA	6 607 000	6.4	32.1	31.1	45.4	30.3	16.3	6.5	1.5
CAMEROON	9 165 000	28.0	44.4	47.6	39.3	32.3	16.8	← 11.6 →	
CHAD	4 789 000	18.4	29.0	35.0	37.4	35.9	21.7	← 5 →	
GAMBIA	618 000	18.2	32.0	35.0	41.9	34.7	17.4	5.5	0.5
GHANA	12 700 000	31.4	48.3	51.7	na	na	na	na	na
GUINEA	5 177 000	na	36.7	39.8	na	na	na	na	na
GUINEA BISSAU	863 000	na	39.4	42.6	44.3	31.1	15.8	6.6	2.2
IVORY COAST	9 161 000	32.0	43.4	46.6	44.6	33.7	16.2	4.7	0.8
LIBERIA	2 057 000	29.1	45.8	44.0	40.9	33.7	17.5	6.6	1.3
MALI	7 528 000	17.7	46.9	49.7	44.1	17.6	← 38.3 →		
NIGER	5 772 000	na	39.0	42.1	43.0	na	na	na	na
NIGERIA	89 022 000	na	37.2	36.7	na	na	na	na	na
SENEGAL	6 316 000	34.3	39.7	42.9	43.2	31.9	16.4	6.9	1.6
SIERRA LEONE	3 472 000	na	30.6	33.5	40.6	31.5	17.9	7.4	2.6
TOGO	2 756 000	15.2	31.6	38.5	na	na	na	na	na

(Source: UN Demographic Yearbook 1983)

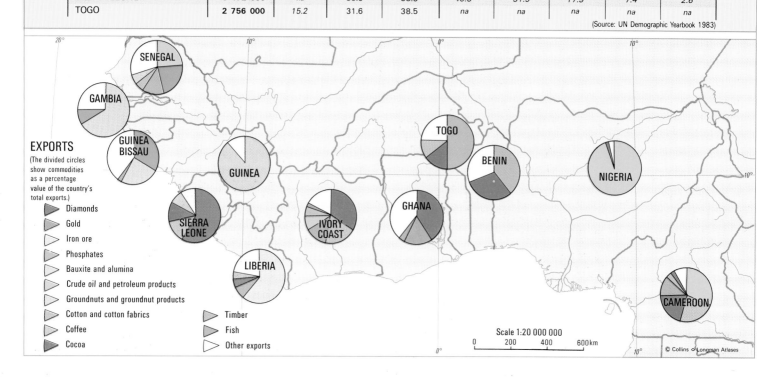

EXPORTS

(The divided circles show commodities as a percentage value of the country's total exports.)

- Diamonds
- Gold
- Iron ore
- Phosphates
- Bauxite and alumina
- Crude oil and petroleum products
- Groundnuts and groundnut products
- Cotton and cotton fabrics
- Coffee
- Cocoa
- Timber
- Fish
- Other exports

Scale 1:20 000 000

0   200   400   600km

© Collins ◇ Longman Atlases

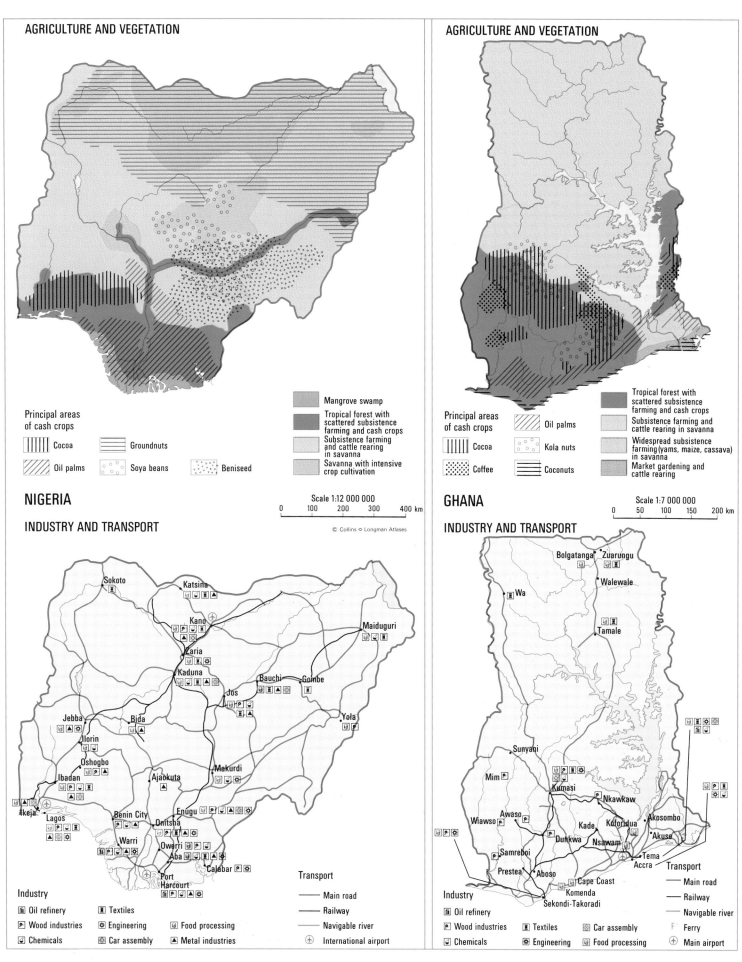

AGRICULTURE AND VEGETATION

Principal areas of cash crops
Cocoa		Groundnuts
Oil palms		Soya beans
		Beniseed

Mangrove swamp

Tropical forest with scattered subsistence farming and cash crops

Subsistence farming and cattle rearing in savanna

Savanna with intensive crop cultivation

NIGERIA

INDUSTRY AND TRANSPORT

Scale 1:12 000 000
0   100   200   300   400 km

© Collins ◇ Longman Atlases

Sokoto
Katsina
Kano
Maiduguri
Zaria
Kaduna
Bauchi   Gombe
Jos
Yola
Jebba   Bida
Ilorin
Oshogbo
Ibadan   Ajaokuta   Makurdi
Akeja
Lagos   Benin City   Enugu
Warri   Onitsha
Owerri
Aba
Port Harcourt   Calabar

Industry
- 🏭 Oil refinery
- 🪵 Wood industries
- ⬒ Chemicals
- ▣ Textiles
- ✦ Engineering
- ⊙ Car assembly
- ▤ Food processing
- ▲ Metal industries

Transport
— Main road
— Railway
— Navigable river
✈ International airport

AGRICULTURE AND VEGETATION

Principal areas of cash crops
Cocoa		Oil palms
Coffee		Kola nuts
		Coconuts

Tropical forest with scattered subsistence farming and cash crops

Subsistence farming and cattle rearing in savanna

Widespread subsistence farming (yams, maize, cassava) in savanna

Market gardening and cattle rearing

GHANA

INDUSTRY AND TRANSPORT

Scale 1:7 000 000
0   50   100   150   200 km

Bolgatanga   Zuarungu
Walewale
Wa
Tamale
Sunyani
Mim   Kumasi
Nkawkaw
Wiawso   Awaso   Akosombo
Kade   Koforidua   Akuse
Samreboi   Dunkwa   Nsawam
Prestea   Aboso   Tema
Cape Coast   Accra
Komenda
Sekondi-Takoradi

Industry
- 🏭 Oil refinery
- 🪵 Wood industries
- ⬒ Chemicals
- ▣ Textiles
- ✦ Engineering
- ⊙ Car assembly
- ▤ Food processing

Transport
— Main road
— Railway
— Navigable river
F Ferry
✈ Main airport

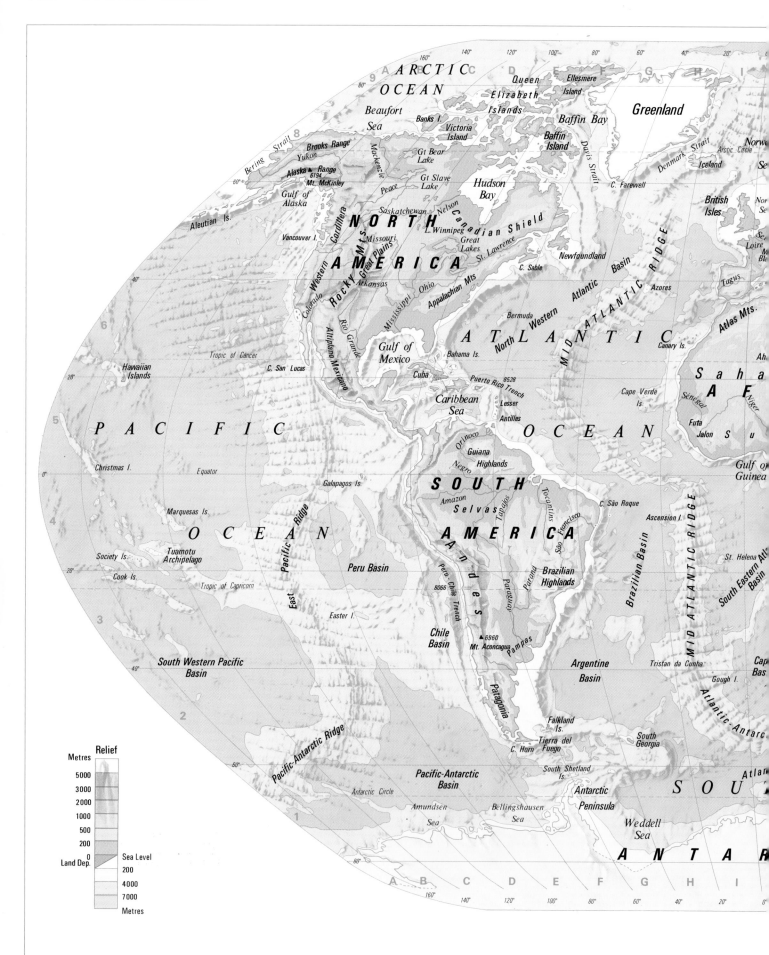

ARCTIC OCEAN
Queen Elizabeth Islands
Ellesmere Island
Greenland
Beaufort Sea
Banks I.
Victoria Island
Baffin Bay
Baffin Island
Davis Strait
Denmark Strait
Iceland
Arctic Circle
Norwe
Nor Se
Bering Strait
Brooks Range
Yukon
Alaska Range 6194
Mt. McKinley
Gulf of Alaska
Mackenzie
Gt Bear Lake
Gt Slave Lake
Peace
Hudson Bay
C. Farewell
British Isles
Aleutian Is.
Vancouver I.
NORTH AMERICA
Cordillera
Western Mts
Missouri
Saskatchewan
Nelson
L. Winnipeg
Canadian Shield
Great Lakes
St. Lawrence
Newfoundland
Atlantic Basin
MID ATLANTIC RIDGE
Loire
Rocky Mts
Great Plains
Arkansas
Mississippi
Ohio
Appalachian Mts
C. Sable
Azores
Tagus
Colorado
Rio Grande
Altiplano Mexicano
Tropic of Cancer
C. San Lucas
Gulf of Mexico
Bahama Is.
Bermuda
North Western Atlantic
A T L A N T I C
Atlas Mts.
Hawaiian Islands
Cuba
Puerto Rico Trench 8528
Lesser Antilles
Canary Is.
Saha
AF
Caribbean Sea
O C E A N
Cape Verde Is.
Sénégal
Niger
P A C I F I C
Orinoco
Guiana Highlands
Futa Jalon S u
Gulf of Guinea
Christmas I.
Equator
Galapagos Is.
Negro
SOUTH
C. São Roque
Ascension I.
Marquesas Is.
East Pacific Ridge
Amazon
Selvas
Tapajos
Tocantins
São Francisco
Brazilian Basin
St. Helena
South Eastern Atl
Society Is.
Tuamotu Archipelago
AMERICA
Andes
Brazilian Highlands
MID ATLANTIC RIDGE
Cook Is.
Tropic of Capricorn
Peru Basin
Peru Chile Trench
Paraguay
Paraná
Tristan da Cunha
Cap Bas
Easter I.
8066
Gough I.
Atlantic-Antarc
South Western Pacific Basin
Chile Basin
6960
Mt. Aconcagua
Pampas
Argentine Basin
Patagonia
Falkland Is.
South Georgia
Pacific-Antarctic Ridge
C. Horn
Tierra del Fuego
South Shetland Is.
SOU
Atlan
Pacific-Antarctic Basin
Antarctic Circle
Amundsen Sea
Bellingshausen Sea
Antarctic Peninsula
Weddell Sea
ANTAR

Relief

Metres	
5000	
3000	
2000	
1000	
500	
200	
0	Sea Level
Land Dep.	200
	4000
	7000
	Metres

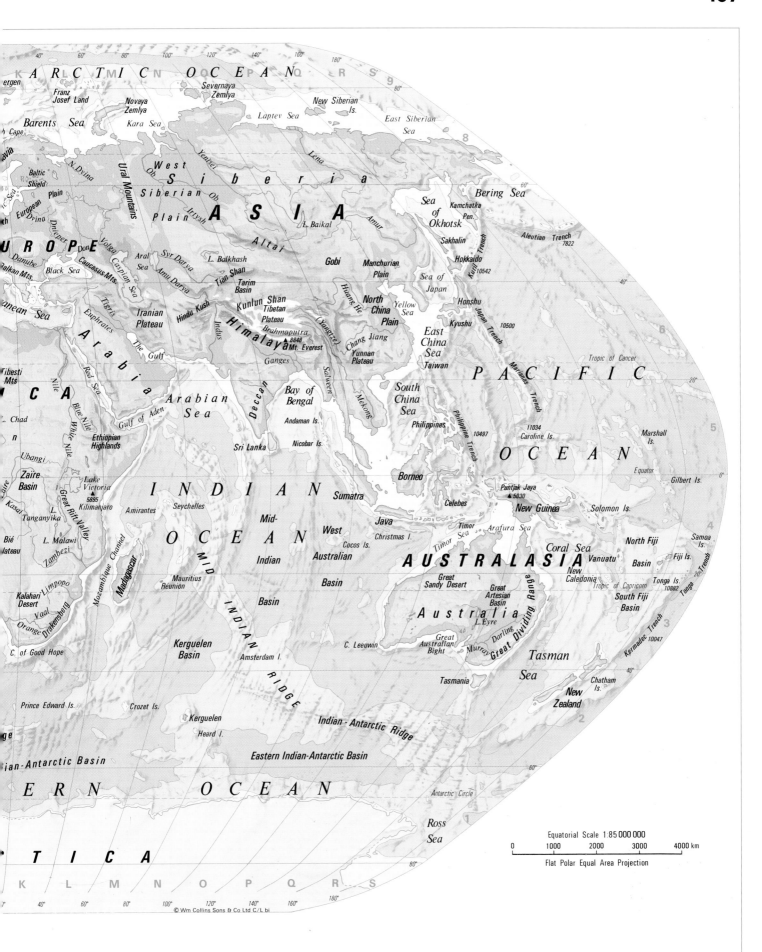

ARCTIC OCEAN

Spitsbergen Franz Josef Land · Novaya Zemlya · Severnaya Zemlya · New Siberian Is.

Barents Sea · Kara Sea · *Laptev Sea* · *East Siberian Sea* · *Bering Sea*

N. Cape · N. Dvina · West · *Ob* · Yenisei · Lena · *Amur* · Kamchatka Pen. · Sea of Okhotsk

Baltic Shield · *Ural Mountains* · *Siberia* · Sakhalin · Aleutian Trench 7822

European Plain · West Siberian Plain · **ASIA** · L. Baikal · Hokkaido · Kuril Trench 10542

EUROPE · *Volga* · Don · *Caspian Sea* · Aral Sea · *Syr Darya* · L. Balkhash · Altai · Gobi · Manchurian Plain · Sea of Japan

Danube · Caucasus Mts. · Black Sea · Amu Darya · Tian Shan · Tarim Basin · Huang He · North China Plain · Yellow Sea · Honshu · Japan Trench 10500

Balkan Mts. · Don · Tigris · Iranian Plateau · Hindu Kush · Kunlun Shan · Tibetan Plateau · (Yangtze) · Kyushu

Mediterranean Sea · *Euphrates* · The Gulf · *Indus* · *Himalaya* · Brahmaputra · 8848 ▲ Mt. Everest · Chang Jiang · East China Sea

AFRICA · Red Sea · Arabia · Ganges · Salween · Yunnan Plateau · Taiwan

Tibesti Mts · Nile · *Arabian Sea* · Deccan · Bay of Bengal · Mekong · South China Sea · **PACIFIC**

Chad · Blue Nile · Gulf of Aden · Andaman Is. · Philippines · Philippine Trench 10497 · Caroline Is. 11034 · Tropic of Cancer

White Nile · Ethiopian Highlands · Sri Lanka · Nicobar Is. · Marshall Is.

Ubangi · Zaire Basin · Lake Victoria · Seychelles · **OCEAN**

Zaire · L. Tanganyika · 5895 Kilimanjaro · Amirantes · **INDIAN** · Sumatra · Borneo · Puntjak Jaya ▲ 5030 · Solomon Is. · Gilbert Is. · Equator

Kasai · Great Rift Valley · Celebes · New Guinea

Bié Plateau · L. Malawi · Zambezi · Mid- · West · Java · Timor Sea · Arafura Sea · North Fiji Basin · Samoa Is.

OCEAN · Indian · Australian · Christmas I. · Cocos Is. · **AUSTRALASIA** · Coral Sea · Vanuatu · Fiji Is.

Kalahari Desert · Limpopo · Madagascar · MID INDIAN RIDGE · Basin · Great Sandy Desert · Great Artesian Basin · New Caledonia · Tropic of Capricorn · Tonga Is. 10882 · South Fiji Basin · Tonga Trench

Mozambique Channel · Mauritius Reunion · Basin · Australia · L. Eyre

Orange · Vaal · Drakensberg · Kerguelen Basin · Amsterdam I. · C. Leeuwin · Great Australian Bight · Murray · Darling · Great Dividing Range · Tasman Sea · Kermadec Trench 10047

C. of Good Hope · Kerguelen · Tasmania · Chatham Is.

Prince Edward Is. · Crozet Is. · Heard I. · New Zealand

Indian - Antarctic Ridge

Eastern Indian-Antarctic Basin

Atlantic-Antarctic Basin · **ERN OCEAN** · Antarctic Circle

ANTARCTICA · Ross Sea

Equatorial Scale 1:85 000 000

0 · 1000 · 2000 · 3000 · 4000 km

Flat Polar Equal Area Projection

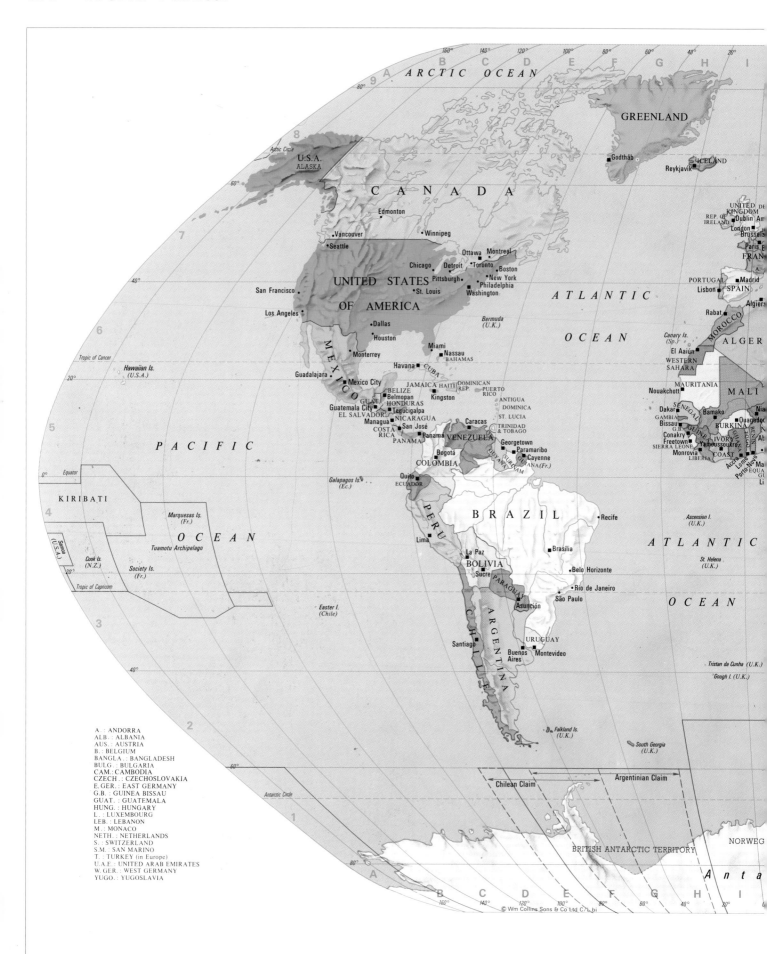

ARCTIC OCEAN

GREENLAND

Godthåb
Reykjavík
ICELAND

CANADA

Arctic Circle

U.S.A.
ALASKA

Edmonton

Vancouver • • Winnipeg
Seattle

UNITED
KINGDOM
REP. OF
IRELAND Dublin
London
Brussels
Paris
FRAN

Ottawa • Montreal
Chicago • Detroit • Toronto
Pittsburgh • • Boston
UNITED STATES • New York
OF AMERICA • St. Louis • Philadelphia
Washington

San Francisco •

Los Angeles •

ATLANTIC

OCEAN

PORTUGAL
Lisbon Madrid
SPAIN

Rabat Algiers
MOROCCO ALGER

Bermuda
(U.K.)

Dallas •

Houston •

Tropic of Cancer

Hawaiian Is.
(U.S.A.)

Monterrey •

Guadalajara •

Miami •
• Nassau
BAHAMAS
Havana • CUBA

Mexico City •
BELIZE
JAMAICA HAITI
Belmopan Kingston
Canary Is.
(Sp.)
El Aaiún
WESTERN
SAHARA

MAURITANIA
Nouakchott

MALI
Bamako

DOMINICAN
REP.
PUERTO
RICO
ANTIGUA
DOMINICA
ST. LUCIA

GUAT.
Guatemala City
EL SALVADOR
HONDURAS
Tegucigalpa
NICARAGUA
Managua
San José
COSTA
RICA
PANAMA
Panamá

Caracas •
TRINIDAD
& TOBAGO

Georgetown
Paramaribo
Cayenne
VENEZUELA

GUIANA (Fr.)

SENEGAL
Dakar
GAMBIA
G.B.
Bissau
Conakry
GUINEA BURKINA Ouagadou
Freetown
SIERRA LEONE
Monrovia
LIBERIA
IVORY
COAST Yamoussoukro TOGO BENIN
Accra
Lomé
Porto Novo
EQUA
GU

PACIFIC

Bogotá

COLOMBIA

Quito
ECUADOR

Galapagos Is.
(Ec.)

KIRIBATI

Marquesas Is.
(Fr.)

Samoa
(U.S.A.)

OCEAN

Tuamotu Archipelago

Cook Is.
(N.Z.)
Society Is.
(Fr.)

Tropic of Capricorn

Easter I.
(Chile)

Equator

PERU

Lima •

La Paz
BOLIVIA
Sucre
PARAGUAY
Asunción

BRAZIL

• Recife

• Brasília

• Belo Horizonte

• Rio de Janeiro
São Paulo

Ascension I.
(U.K.)

ATLANTIC

St. Helena
(U.K.)

OCEAN

Santiago •
CHILE
ARGENTINA
Buenos
Aires
URUGUAY
Montevideo

Tristan da Cunha (U.K.)

Gough I. (U.K.)

Falkland Is.
(U.K.)

South Georgia
(U.K.)

Argentinian Claim

Chilean Claim

Antarctic Circle

BRITISH ANTARCTIC TERRITORY

NORWEG

Anta

A. : ANDORRA
ALB. : ALBANIA
AUS. : AUSTRIA
B. : BELGIUM
BANGLA. : BANGLADESH
BULG. : BULGARIA
CAM. : CAMBODIA
CZECH. : CZECHOSLOVAKIA
E. GER. : EAST GERMANY
G.B. : GUINEA BISSAU
GUAT. : GUATEMALA
HUNG. : HUNGARY
L. : LUXEMBOURG
LEB. : LEBANON
M. : MONACO
NETH. : NETHERLANDS
S. : SWITZERLAND
S.M. : SAN MARINO
T. : TURKEY (in Europe)
U.A.E. : UNITED ARAB EMIRATES
W. GER. : WEST GERMANY
YUGO. : YUGOSLAVIA

© Wm Collins Sons & Co Ltd C/L bi

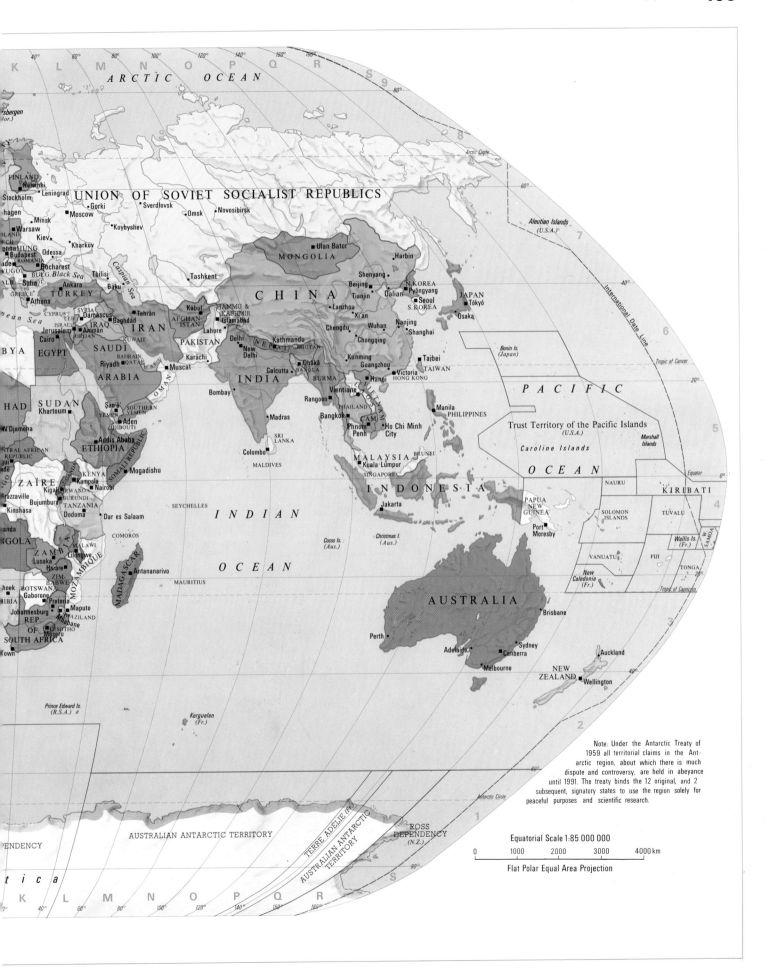

ARCTIC OCEAN

Arctic Circle

FINLAND
Helsinki
Leningrad • Gorki • Sverdlovsk • Omsk • Novosibirsk
Stockholm
hagen • Moscow
• Minsk
Warsaw • Kiev • Kharkov • Kuybyshev

UNION OF SOVIET SOCIALIST REPUBLICS

Aleutian Islands
(U.S.A.)

LAND
CH vienna HUNG
Budapest
YUGO ROMANIA
Bucharest
ALB Sofia BULG
GREECE
Athens
TURKEY
Black Sea
Tbilisi • Ankara • Baku
CYPRUS LEB
SYRIA Damascus
ISRAEL IRAQ
Jerusalem JORDAN Baghdad
Cairo
ean Sea

Odessa

Caspian Sea

Tashkent

• Ulan Bator
MONGOLIA
• Harbin

Shenyang
Beijing • Tianjin • Dalian
N. KOREA
Pyongyang
Seoul
S. KOREA
JAPAN
Tōkyō
Ōsaka

CHINA

Tehran
Kābul
AFGHAN-ISTAN
JAMMU & KASHMIR
Islāmābād
Lahore
Delhi
New Delhi

Lanzhou
Xi'an
Chengdu
Wuhan
Chongqing
Nanjing
Shanghai

International Date Line

60°

40°

20°

Tropic of Cancer

IRAN
BAHRAIN
QATAR
U.A.E.
• Muscat
OMAN
PAKISTAN
Karāchi
NEPAL
Kathmandu
BHUTAN
Dhākā
BANGLA.
Calcutta

Kunming
Guangzhou
Victoria
HONG KONG

Taibei
TAIWAN

Bonin Is.
(Japan)

PACIFIC

IBYA
EGYPT
KUWAIT
Riyadh
SAUDI
ARABIA
San'ā
SOUTHERN
YEMEN
Aden
(DJIBOUTI)

INDIA
BURMA
Hanoi

Bombay
Rangoon
Madras
THAILAND
VIETNAM
Vientiane

HAD
SUDAN
Khartoum
N'Djamena
ETHIOPIA
Addis Ababa
CENTRAL AFRICAN REPUBLIC

Bangkok
CAM.
Phnom Penh
Ho Chi Minh City
Manila
PHILIPPINES

Trust Territory of the Pacific Islands
(U.S.A.)
Caroline Islands

Marshall Islands

OCEAN

SRI LANKA
Colombo
MALDIVES
MALAYSIA
Kuala Lumpur
SINGAPORE
BRUNEI

Equator

NAURU

KIRIBATI

ZAIRE
KENYA
SOMALI REP.
Kampala
UGANDA
Nairobi
RWANDA
Kigali
BURUNDI
Bujumbura
TANZANIA
Dodoma
Dar es Salaam

Mogadishu

SEYCHELLES

INDONESIA

Jakarta

PAPUA NEW GUINEA
Port Moresby

SOLOMON ISLANDS

TUVALU

Wallis Is.
(Fr.)

W. SAMOA

razzaville
Kinshasa
NGOLA

ZAMBIA
Lusaka
Harare
ZIM-BABWE
MALAWI
Lilongwe
MOZAMBIQUE

COMOROS
MADAGASCAR
Antananarivo

Cocos Is.
(Aus.)
Christmas I.
(Aus.)

INDIAN

OCEAN

MAURITIUS

VANUATU

New Caledonia
(Fr.)

FIJI

TONGA

Tropic of Capricorn

hoek
NIBIA
BOTSWANA
Gaborone
Johannesburg
Pretoria
Maputo
SWAZILAND
Mbabane
REP.
OF
SOUTH AFRICA
Maseru
LESOTHO
Town

AUSTRALIA

Brisbane

Perth

Adelaide
Melbourne
Sydney
Canberra

Auckland

NEW ZEALAND
Wellington

40°

Prince Edward Is.
(R.S.A.)

Kerguelen
(Fr.)

Note: Under the Antarctic Treaty of 1959 all territorial claims in the Antarctic region, about which there is much dispute and controversy, are held in abeyance until 1991. The treaty binds the 12 original, and 2 subsequent, signatory states to use the region solely for peaceful purposes and scientific research.

Antarctic Circle

AUSTRALIAN ANTARCTIC TERRITORY

TERRE ADÉLIE (Fr.)
AUSTRALIAN ANTARCTIC TERRITORY

ROSS DEPENDENCY
(N.Z.)

PENDENCY

tica

Equatorial Scale 1:85 000 000

0   1000   2000   3000   4000 km

Flat Polar Equal Area Projection

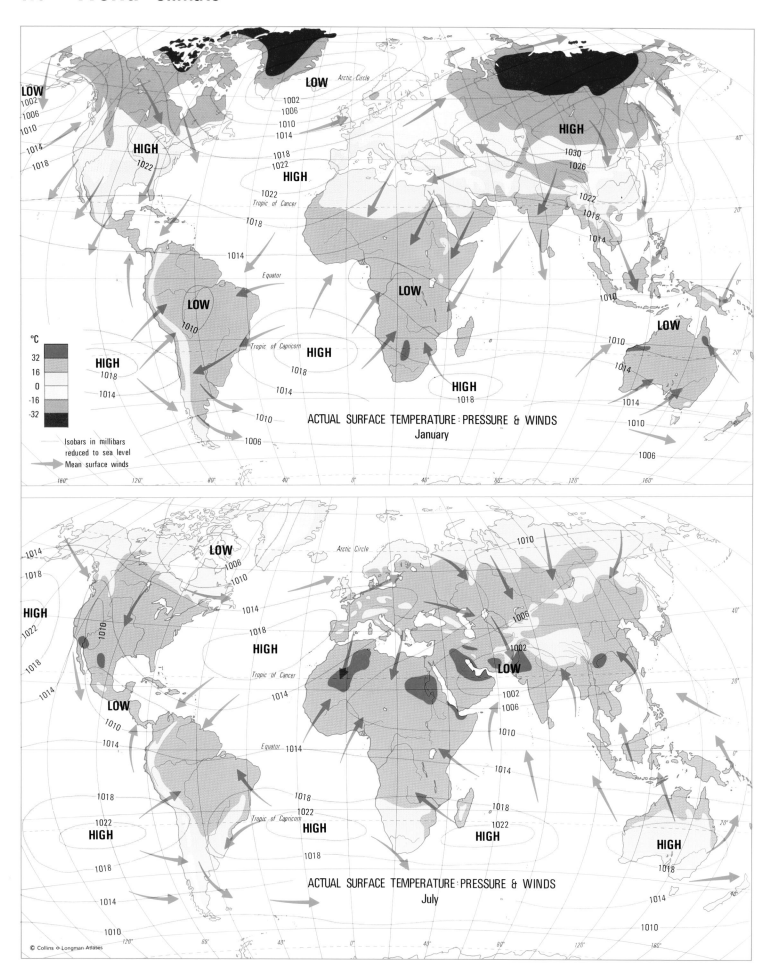

ACTUAL SURFACE TEMPERATURE: PRESSURE & WINDS
January

°C
32
16
0
-16
-32

Isobars in millibars
reduced to sea level
Mean surface winds

ACTUAL SURFACE TEMPERATURE: PRESSURE & WINDS
July

© Collins ◇ Longman Atlases

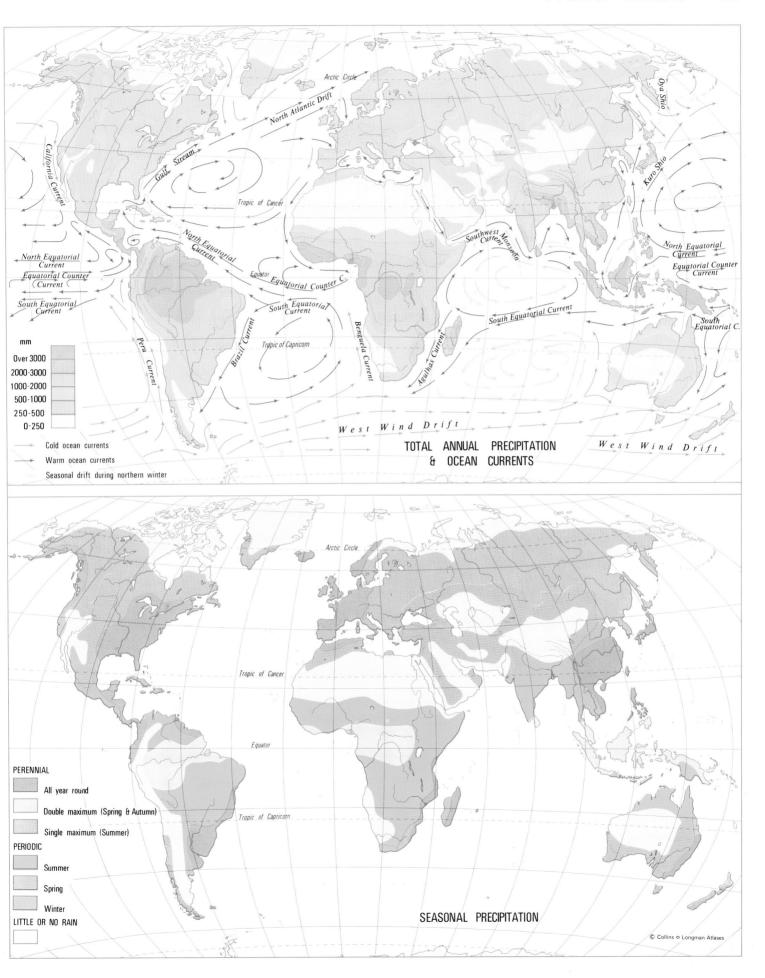

mm

Over 3000
2000-3000
1000-2000
500-1000
250-500
0-250

→ Cold ocean currents
→ Warm ocean currents
→ Seasonal drift during northern winter

TOTAL ANNUAL PRECIPITATION & OCEAN CURRENTS

California Current

North Atlantic Drift

Gulf Stream

Arctic Circle

Tropic of Cancer

North Equatorial Current

North Equatorial Current

Equatorial Counter Current

South Equatorial Current

Equator

Equatorial Counter C.

South Equatorial Current

Peru Current

Brazil Current

Tropic of Capricorn

Benguela Current

Agulhas Current

Southwest Monsoon Current

South Equatorial Current

Oya Shio

Kuro Shio

North Equatorial Current

Equatorial Counter Current

South Equatorial C.

West Wind Drift

West Wind Drift

PERENNIAL

All year round

Double maximum (Spring & Autumn)

Single maximum (Summer)

PERIODIC

Summer

Spring

Winter

LITTLE OR NO RAIN

Arctic Circle

Tropic of Cancer

Equator

Tropic of Capricorn

SEASONAL PRECIPITATION

© Collins ◇ Longman Atlases

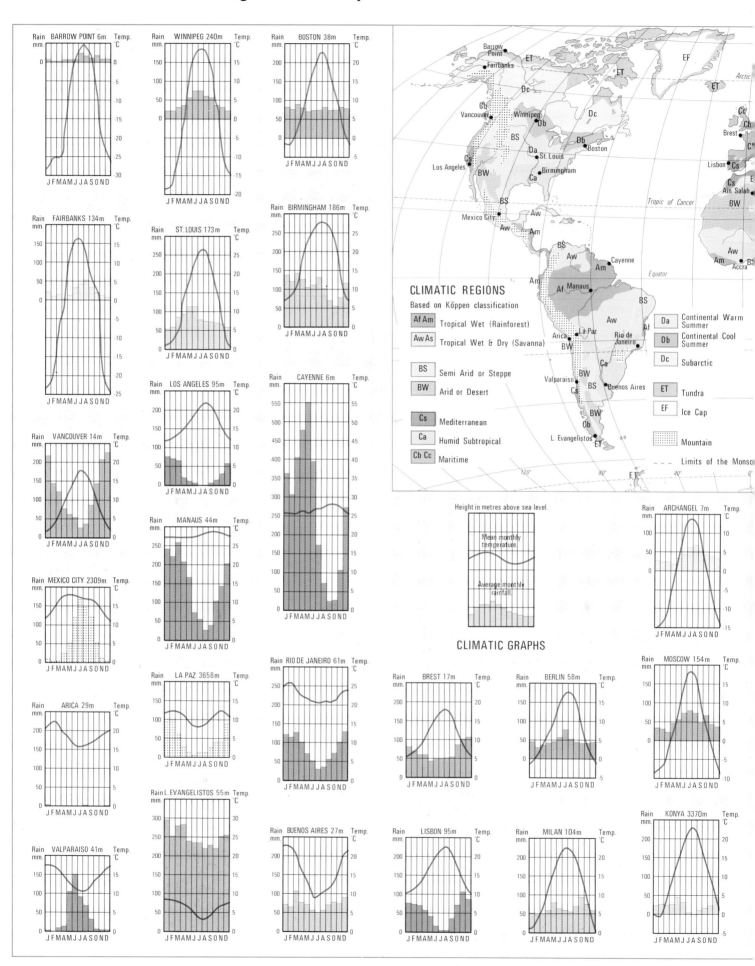

CLIMATIC REGIONS

Based on Köppen classification

| Af Am | Tropical Wet (Rainforest) |
| Aw As | Tropical Wet & Dry (Savanna) |

| BS | Semi Arid or Steppe |
| BW | Arid or Desert |

Cs	Mediterranean
Ca	Humid Subtropical
Cb Cc	Maritime

Da	Continental Warm Summer
Db	Continental Cool Summer
Dc	Subarctic

| ET | Tundra |
| EF | Ice Cap |

Mountain

Limits of the Monso

Height in metres above sea level.

Mean monthly temperature.

Average monthly rainfall.

CLIMATIC GRAPHS

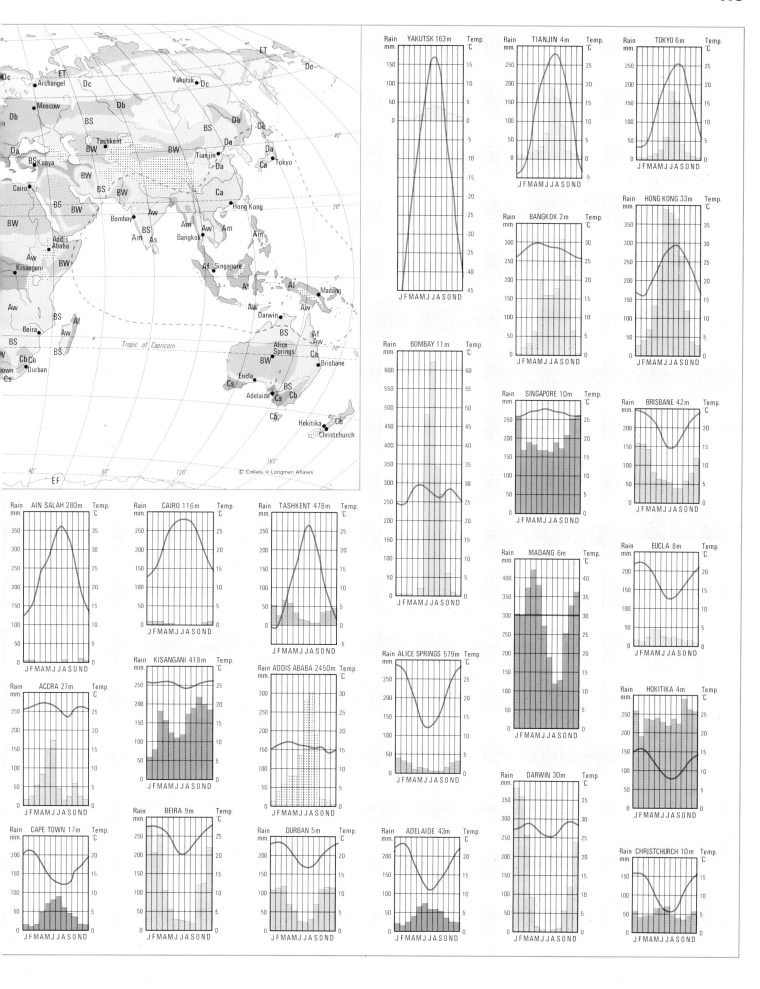

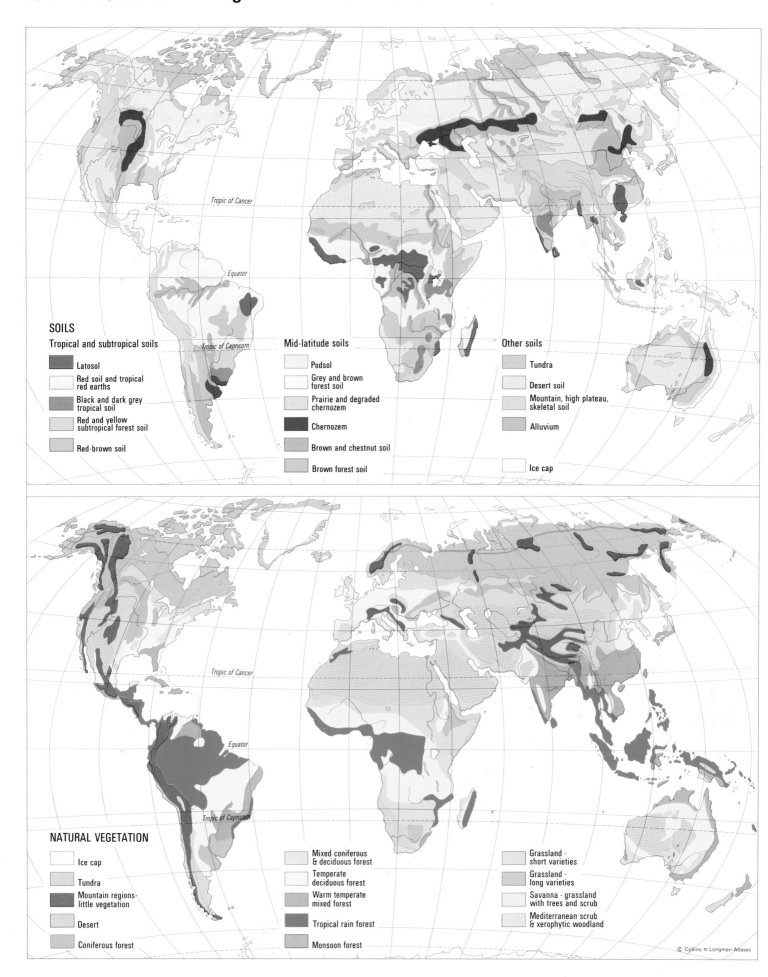

SOILS

Tropical and subtropical soils

- Latosol
- Red soil and tropical red earths
- Black and dark grey tropical soil
- Red and yellow subtropical forest soil
- Red-brown soil

Mid-latitude soils

- Podsol
- Grey and brown forest soil
- Prairie and degraded chernozem
- Chernozem
- Brown and chestnut soil
- Brown forest soil

Other soils

- Tundra
- Desert soil
- Mountain, high plateau, skeletal soil
- Alluvium
- Ice cap

NATURAL VEGETATION

- Ice cap
- Tundra
- Mountain regions- little vegetation
- Desert
- Coniferous forest
- Mixed coniferous & deciduous forest
- Temperate deciduous forest
- Warm temperate mixed forest
- Tropical rain forest
- Monsoon forest
- Grassland - short varieties
- Grassland - long varieties
- Savanna - grassland with trees and scrub
- Mediterranean scrub & xerophytic woodland

Tropic of Cancer

Equator

Tropic of Capricorn

© Collins ○ Longman Atlases

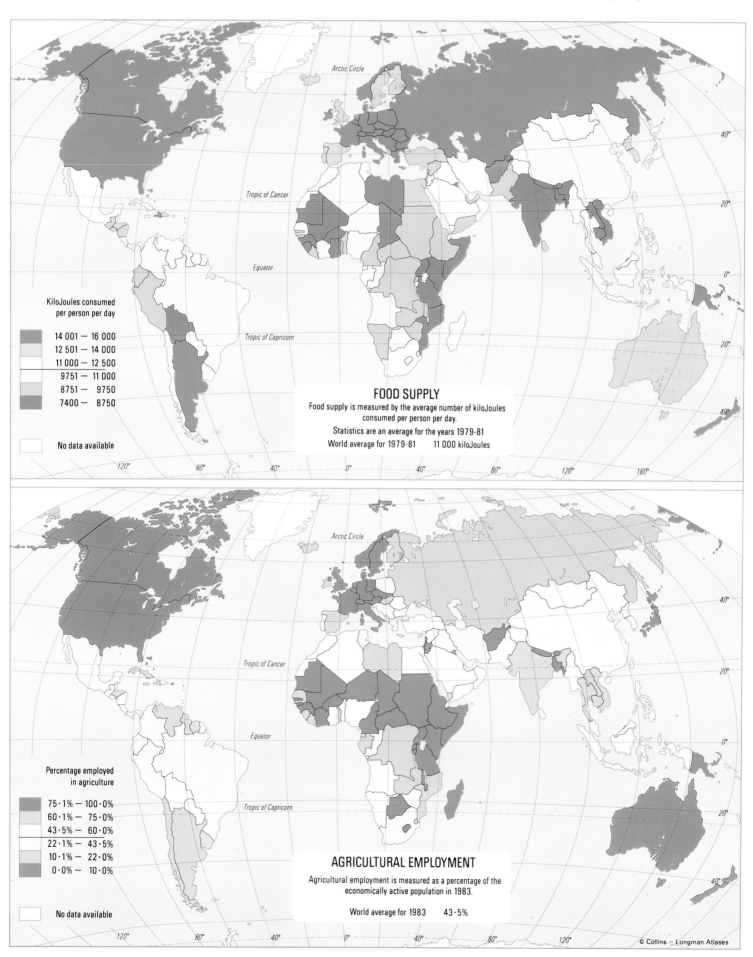

**KiloJoules consumed
per person per day**

14 001 — 16 000
12 501 — 14 000
11 000 — 12 500
9751 — 11 000
8751 — 9750
7400 — 8750

No data available

FOOD SUPPLY

Food supply is measured by the average number of kiloJoules
consumed per person per day.

Statistics are an average for the years 1979-81

World average for 1979-81   11 000 kiloJoules

**Percentage employed
in agriculture**

75·1% — 100·0%
60·1% — 75·0%
43·5% — 60·0%
22·1% — 43·5%
10·1% — 22·0%
0·0% — 10·0%

No data available

AGRICULTURAL EMPLOYMENT

Agricultural employment is measured as a percentage of the
economically active population in 1983.

World average for 1983   43·5%

© Collins – Longman Atlases

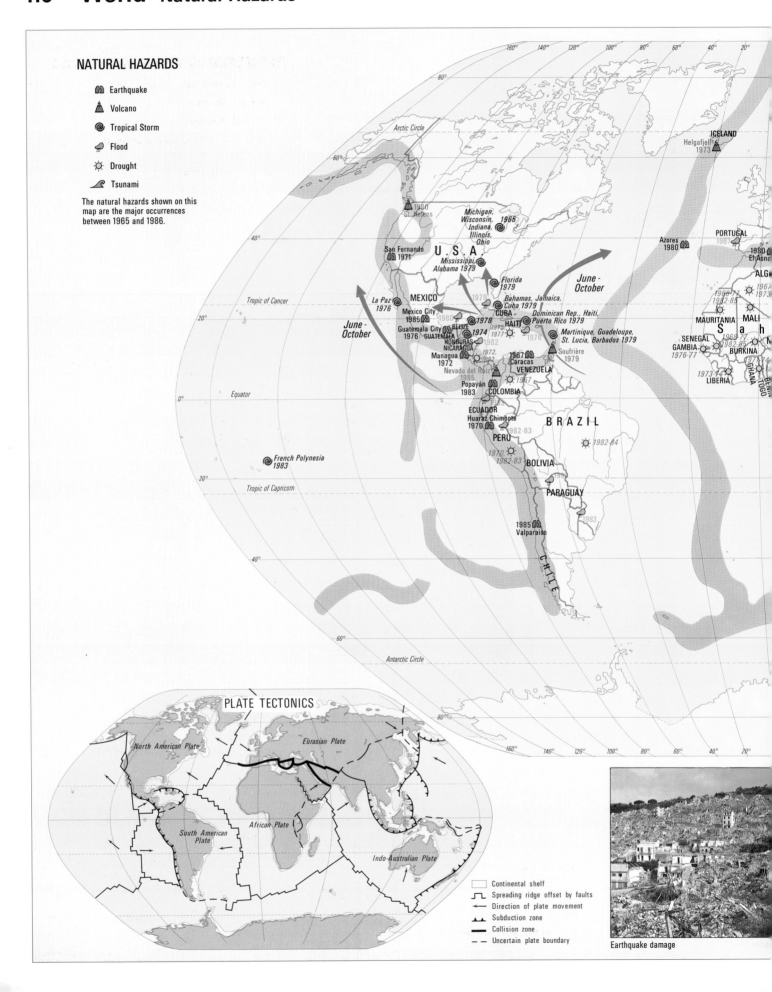

NATURAL HAZARDS

- 🐚 Earthquake
- 🔺 Volcano
- 🌀 Tropical Storm
- 🌧 Flood
- ☀ Drought
- 🌊 Tsunami

The natural hazards shown on this map are the major occurrences between 1965 and 1986.

ICELAND
Helgafjell
1973

PORTUGAL
1981
Azores
1980
1980
El Asna

ALG
1967
1973
1968-77
1982-85

MAURITANIA
1973-74

MALI
Sah

SENEGAL
GAMBIA
1976-77

BURKINA

LIBERIA

GHANA

TOGO

BEN

St. Helens
1980

Michigan,
Wisconsin, 1965
Indiana,
Illinois,
Ohio

U.S.A.

San Fernando
1971

Mississippi,
Alabama 1979

Florida
1979

June -
October

June -
October

La Paz
1976

MEXICO

Mexico City
1985

Guatemala City
1976

GUATEMALA
HONDURAS
NICARAGUA

Managua
1972

BELIZE

CUBA

1980

1978

1974

1982

HAITI

Bahamas, Jamaica,
Cuba 1979

Dominican Rep., Haiti,
Puerto Rico 1979

Martinique, Guadeloupe,
St. Lucia, Barbados 1979

Soufrière
1979

1975
1977

1976

1967
Caracas

VENEZUELA

1967

Nevado del Ruiz
1985

Popayán
1983

COLOMBIA

ECUADOR

Huaraz Chimbote
1970

1982-83

PERU

1970

1982-83

BOLIVIA

B R A Z I L

1982-84

French Polynesia
1983

PARAGUAY

1983

1985
Valparaíso

C H I L E

PLATE TECTONICS

North American Plate

Eurasian Plate

African Plate

South American
Plate

Indo-Australian Plate

- ▭ Continental shelf
- ⊐⊏ Spreading ridge offset by faults
- ← Direction of plate movement
- ⊥⊥ Subduction zone
- ▬ Collision zone
- -- Uncertain plate boundary

Earthquake damage

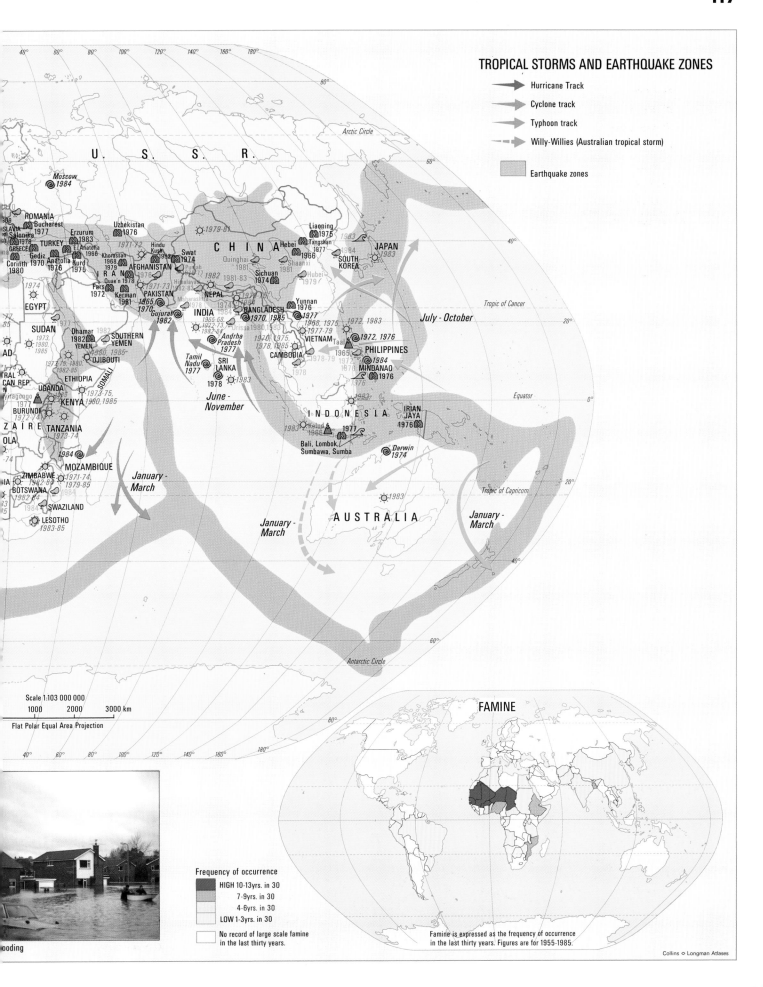

TROPICAL STORMS AND EARTHQUAKE ZONES

Hurricane Track
Cyclone track
Typhoon track
Willy-Willies (Australian tropical storm)
Earthquake zones

FAMINE

Famine is expressed as the frequency of occurrence in the last thirty years. Figures are for 1955-1985.

Frequency of occurrence

HIGH 10-13yrs. in 30
7-9yrs. in 30
4-6yrs. in 30
LOW 1-3yrs. in 30
No record of large scale famine in the last thirty years.

Scale 1:103 000 000
1000 2000 3000 km
Flat Polar Equal Area Projection

Collins ○ Longman Atlases

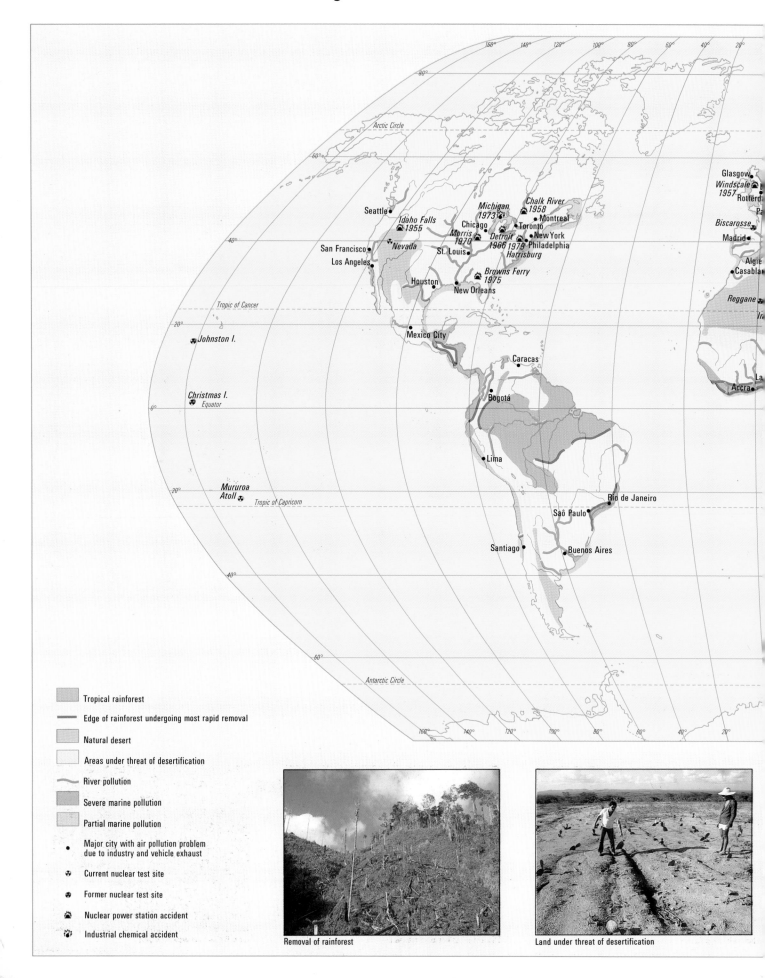

Glasgow
Windscale 1957 Rotterd.
Pa
Biscarosse
Madrid
Algie
Casabla
Reggane
Ir
La
Accra

Seattle
Idaho Falls 1955
Michigan 1973
Chalk River 1958
Chicago
Morris 1970
Detroit 1966 1979
Montreal
Toronto
New York
Philadelphia
San Francisco
Nevada
St. Louis
Harrisburg
Los Angeles
Houston
Browns Ferry 1975
New Orleans
Johnston I.
Mexico City
Caracas
Christmas I.
Equator
Bogotá
Lima
Mururoa Atoll
Tropic of Capricorn
Rio de Janeiro
São Paulo
Santiago
Buenos Aires

Arctic Circle
Tropic of Cancer
Antarctic Circle

Legend:

- ▨ Tropical rainforest
- — Edge of rainforest undergoing most rapid removal
- ▨ Natural desert
- ▢ Areas under threat of desertification
- ⌇ River pollution
- ▨ Severe marine pollution
- ▨ Partial marine pollution
- • Major city with air pollution problem due to industry and vehicle exhaust
- ☢ Current nuclear test site
- ☢ Former nuclear test site
- ⌂ Nuclear power station accident
- ☣ Industrial chemical accident

Removal of rainforest

Land under threat of desertification

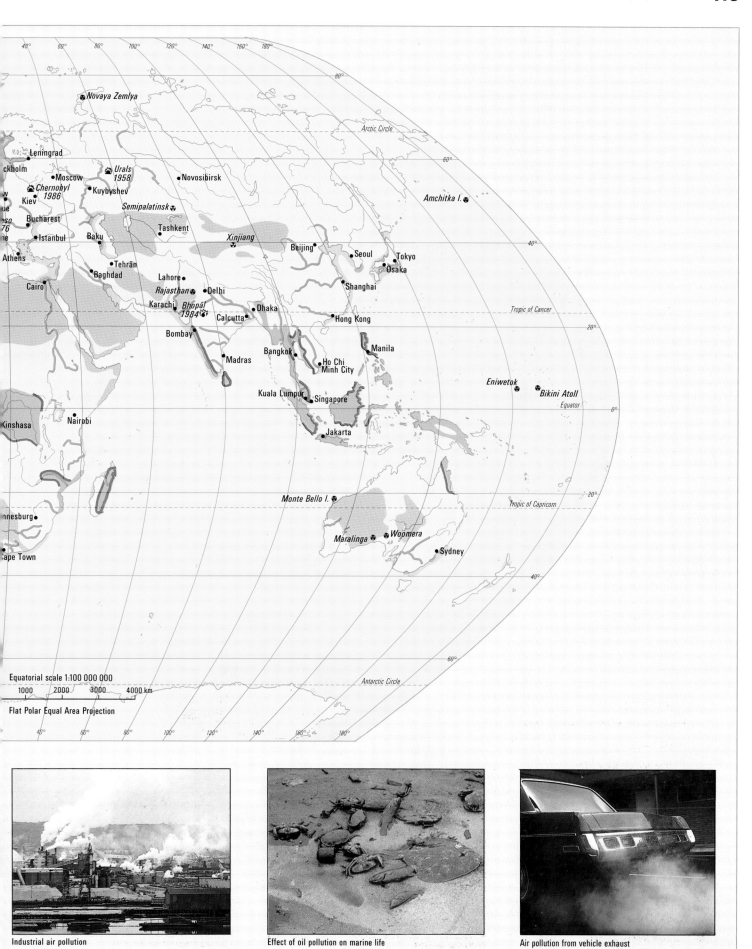

Novaya Zemlya

Leningrad
ckholm
Moscow
Urals
1958
Novosibirsk
Chernobyl
1986
Kuybyshev
Kiev
Semipalatinsk
Bucharest
eso
76
Istanbul
Baku
Tashkent
ne
Xinjiang
Athens
Beijing
Seoul
Tokyo
Tehrān
Osaka
Baghdad
Lahore
Shanghai
Cairo
Rajasthan
Delhi
Karachi
Bhopāl
1984
Dhaka
Calcutta
Hong Kong
Bombay
Manila
Bangkok
Madras
Ho Chi
Minh City
Eniwetok
Kuala Lumpur
Bikini Atoll
Singapore
Kinshasa
Nairobi
Jakarta

Amchitka I.

Arctic Circle

80°
60°
40°
Tropic of Cancer
20°
0°
Equator

Monte Bello I.

Maralinga
Woomera
Sydney

Tropic of Capricorn

nnesburg
ape Town

Equatorial scale 1:100 000 000

1000   2000   3000   4000 km

Flat Polar Equal Area Projection

40°   60°   80°   100°   120°   140°   160°   180°

Antarctic Circle

Industrial air pollution

Effect of oil pollution on marine life

Air pollution from vehicle exhaust

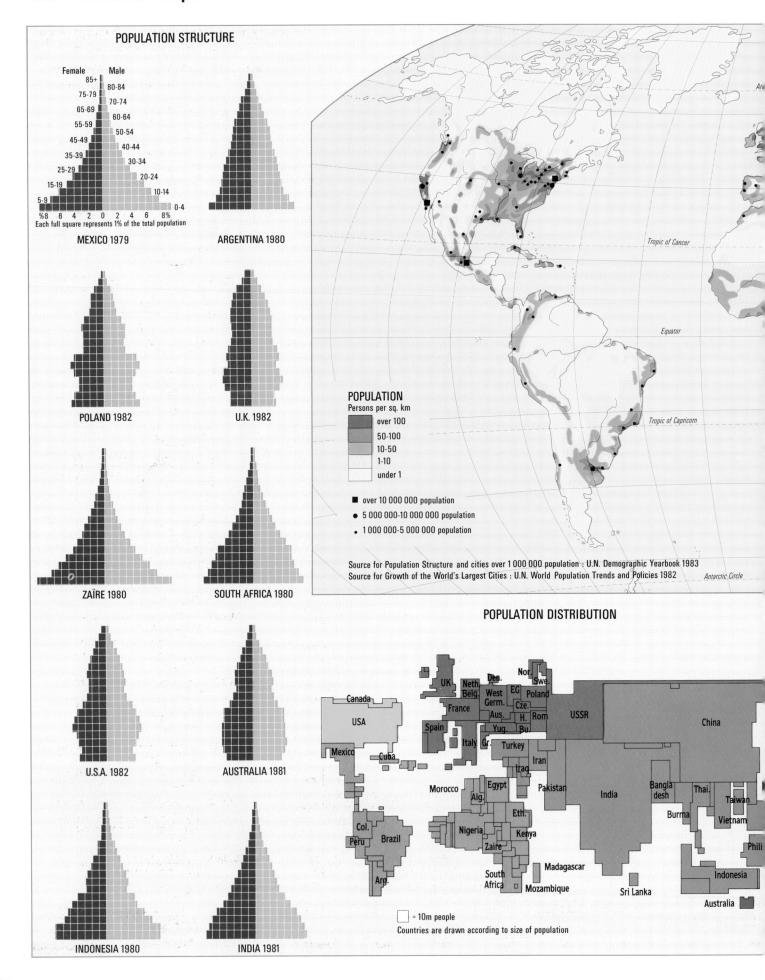

POPULATION STRUCTURE

Female   Male
85+
80-84
75-79
70-74
65-69
60-64
55-59
50-54
45-49
40-44
35-39
30-34
25-29
20-24
15-19
10-14
5-9
0-4
%8 6 4 2 0 2 4 6 8%
Each full square represents 1% of the total population

MEXICO 1979 **ARGENTINA 1980**

POLAND 1982 **U.K. 1982**

ZAÏRE 1980 **SOUTH AFRICA 1980**

U.S.A. 1982 **AUSTRALIA 1981**

INDONESIA 1980 **INDIA 1981**

POPULATION
Persons per sq. km
- over 100
- 50-100
- 10-50
- 1-10
- under 1

■ over 10 000 000 population
● 5 000 000-10 000 000 population
• 1 000 000-5 000 000 population

Source for Population Structure and cities over 1 000 000 population : U.N. Demographic Yearbook 1983
Source for Growth of the World's Largest Cities : U.N. World Population Trends and Policies 1982

Tropic of Cancer
Equator
Tropic of Capricorn
Antarctic Circle

POPULATION DISTRIBUTION

Canada
USA
Mexico
Cuba
Spain
France
UK
Neth.
Belg.
Den.
Nor.
Swe.
West Germ.
EG
Poland
Aus.
Cze.
H.
Bu.
Rom
Yug.
Italy
Gr.
Turkey
Iran
Iraq
USSR
China
Morocco
Alg.
Egypt
Pakistan
India
Bangla desh
Thai.
Taiwan
Burma
Vietnam
Phili
Col.
Peru
Brazil
Nigeria
Kenya
Eth.
Zaire
Madagascar
South Africa
Mozambique
Sri Lanka
Indonesia
Arg.
Australia

☐ = 10m people
Countries are drawn according to size of population

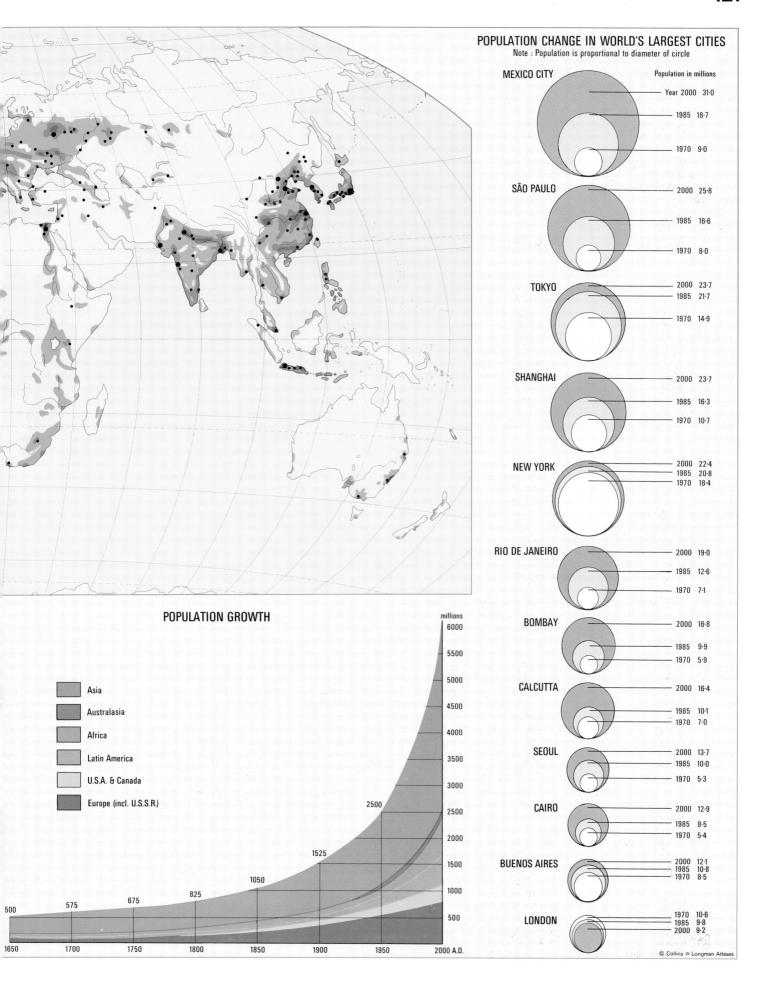

POPULATION CHANGE IN WORLD'S LARGEST CITIES
Note : Population is proportional to diameter of circle

MEXICO CITY   Population in millions

Year 2000	31·0
1985	18·7
1970	9·0

SÃO PAULO

2000	25·8
1985	16·6
1970	8·0

TOKYO

2000	23·7
1985	21·7
1970	14·9

SHANGHAI

2000	23·7
1985	16·3
1970	10·7

NEW YORK

2000	22·4
1985	20·8
1970	18·4

RIO DE JANEIRO

2000	19·0
1985	12·6
1970	7·1

BOMBAY

2000	16·8
1985	9·9
1970	5·9

CALCUTTA

2000	16·4
1985	10·1
1970	7·0

SEOUL

2000	13·7
1985	10·0
1970	5·3

CAIRO

2000	12·9
1985	8·5
1970	5·4

BUENOS AIRES

2000	12·1
1985	10·8
1970	8·5

LONDON

1970	10·6
1985	9·8
2000	9·2

POPULATION GROWTH

millions
- 6000
- 5500
- 5000
- 4500
- 4000
- 3500
- 3000
- 2500
- 2000
- 1500
- 1000
- 500

Asia

Australasia

Africa

Latin America

U.S.A. & Canada

Europe (incl. U.S.S.R.)

500   575   675   825   1050   1525   2500

1650   1700   1750   1800   1850   1900   1950   2000 A.D.

© Collins ◇ Longman Atlases

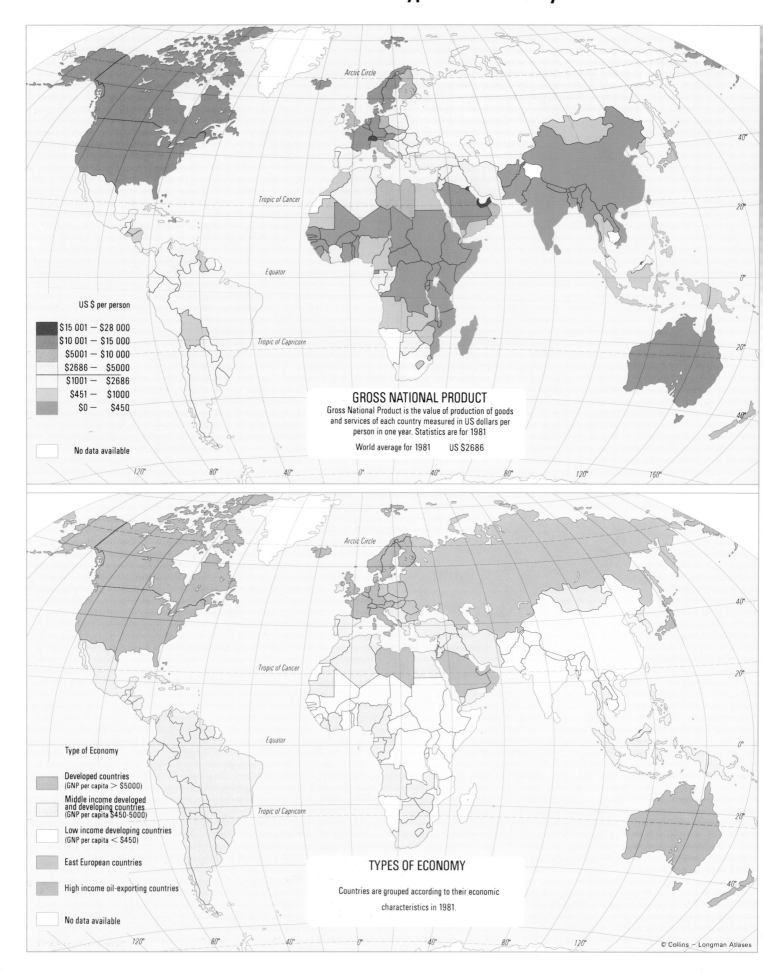

US $ per person

	$15 001 — $28 000
	$10 001 — $15 000
	$5001 — $10 000
	$2686 — $5000
	$1001 — $2686
	$451 — $1000
	$0 — $450

No data available

GROSS NATIONAL PRODUCT

Gross National Product is the value of production of goods and services of each country measured in US dollars per person in one year. Statistics are for 1981

World average for 1981   US $2686

Type of Economy

Developed countries
(GNP per capita > $5000)

Middle income developed
and developing countries
(GNP per capita $450-5000)

Low income developing countries
(GNP per capita < $450)

East European countries

High income oil-exporting countries

No data available

TYPES OF ECONOMY

Countries are grouped according to their economic

characteristics in 1981.

© Collins — Longman Atlases

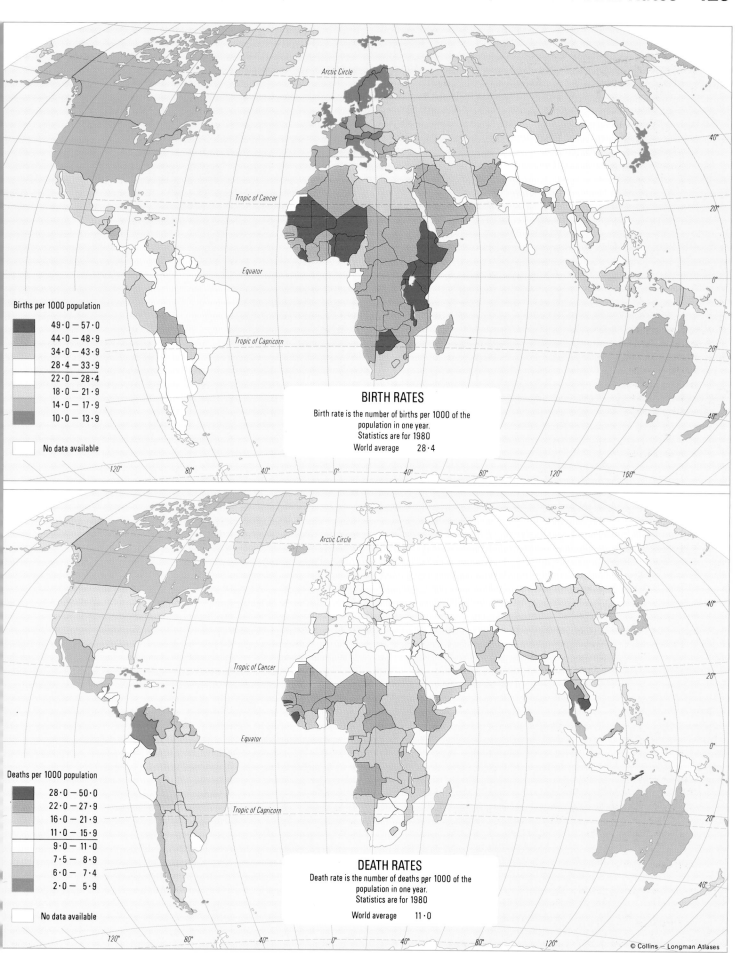

Births per 1000 population

- 49·0 — 57·0
- 44·0 — 48·9
- 34·0 — 43·9
- 28·4 — 33·9
- 22·0 — 28·4
- 18·0 — 21·9
- 14·0 — 17·9
- 10·0 — 13·9

No data available

BIRTH RATES

Birth rate is the number of births per 1000 of the
population in one year.
Statistics are for 1980
World average   28·4

Deaths per 1000 population

- 28·0 — 50·0
- 22·0 — 27·9
- 16·0 — 21·9
- 11·0 — 15·9
- 9·0 — 11·0
- 7·5 — 8·9
- 6·0 — 7·4
- 2·0 — 5·9

No data available

DEATH RATES

Death rate is the number of deaths per 1000 of the
population in one year.
Statistics are for 1980

World average   11·0

© Collins – Longman Atlases

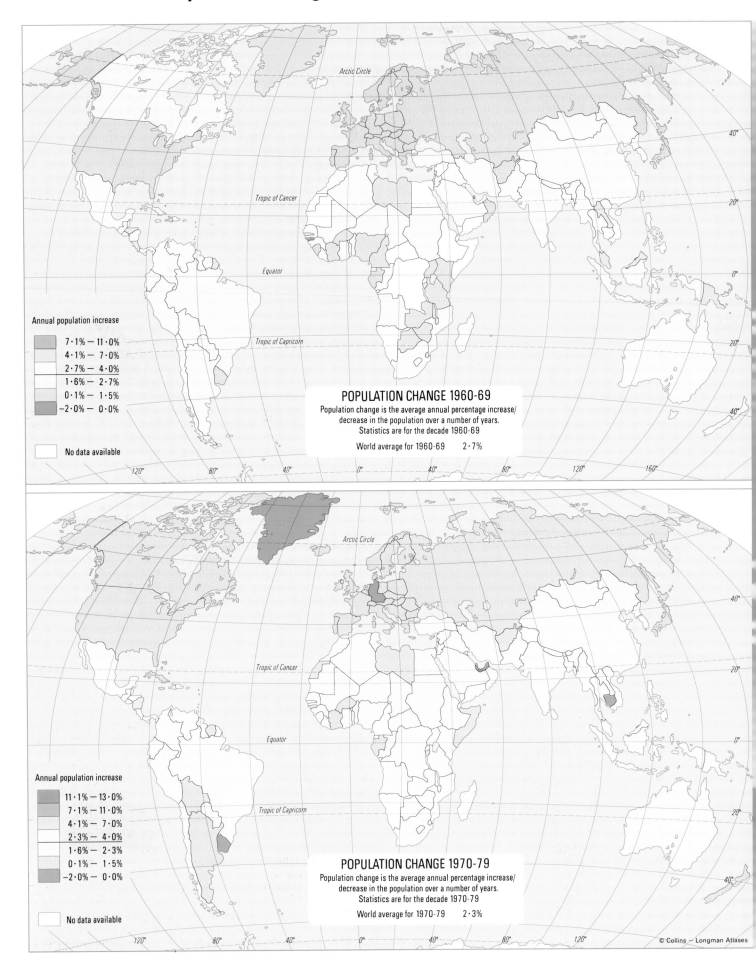

Annual population increase

7·1% — 11·0%
4·1% — 7·0%
2·7% — 4·0%
1·6% — 2·7%
0·1% — 1·5%
−2·0% — 0·0%

No data available

POPULATION CHANGE 1960-69

Population change is the average annual percentage increase/
decrease in the population over a number of years.
Statistics are for the decade 1960-69

World average for 1960-69   2·7%

Annual population increase

11·1% — 13·0%
7·1% — 11·0%
4·1% — 7·0%
2·3% — 4·0%
1·6% — 2·3%
0·1% — 1·5%
−2·0% — 0·0%

No data available

POPULATION CHANGE 1970-79

Population change is the average annual percentage increase/
decrease in the population over a number of years.
Statistics are for the decade 1970-79

World average for 1970-79   2·3%

© Collins — Longman Atlases

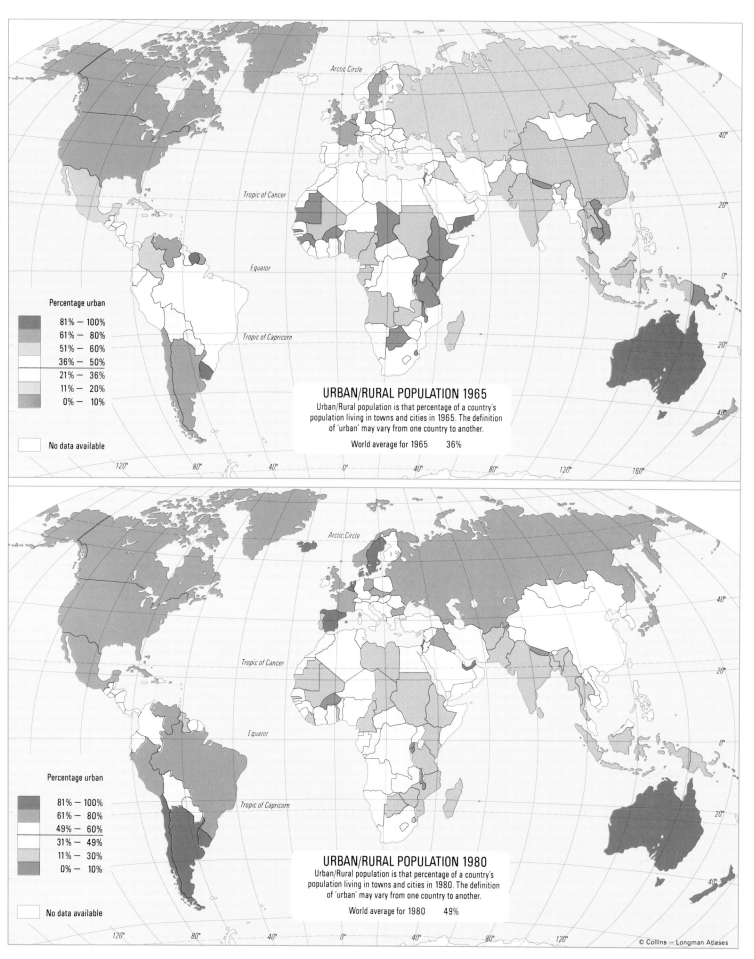

Percentage urban

	81% — 100%
	61% — 80%
	51% — 60%
	36% — 50%
	21% — 36%
	11% — 20%
	0% — 10%

No data available

URBAN/RURAL POPULATION 1965

Urban/Rural population is that percentage of a country's population living in towns and cities in 1965. The definition of 'urban' may vary from one country to another.

World average for 1965   36%

Percentage urban

	81% — 100%
	61% — 80%
	49% — 60%
	31% — 49%
	11% — 30%
	0% — 10%

No data available

URBAN/RURAL POPULATION 1980

Urban/Rural population is that percentage of a country's population living in towns and cities in 1980. The definition of 'urban' may vary from one country to another.

World average for 1980   49%

© Collins — Longman Atlases

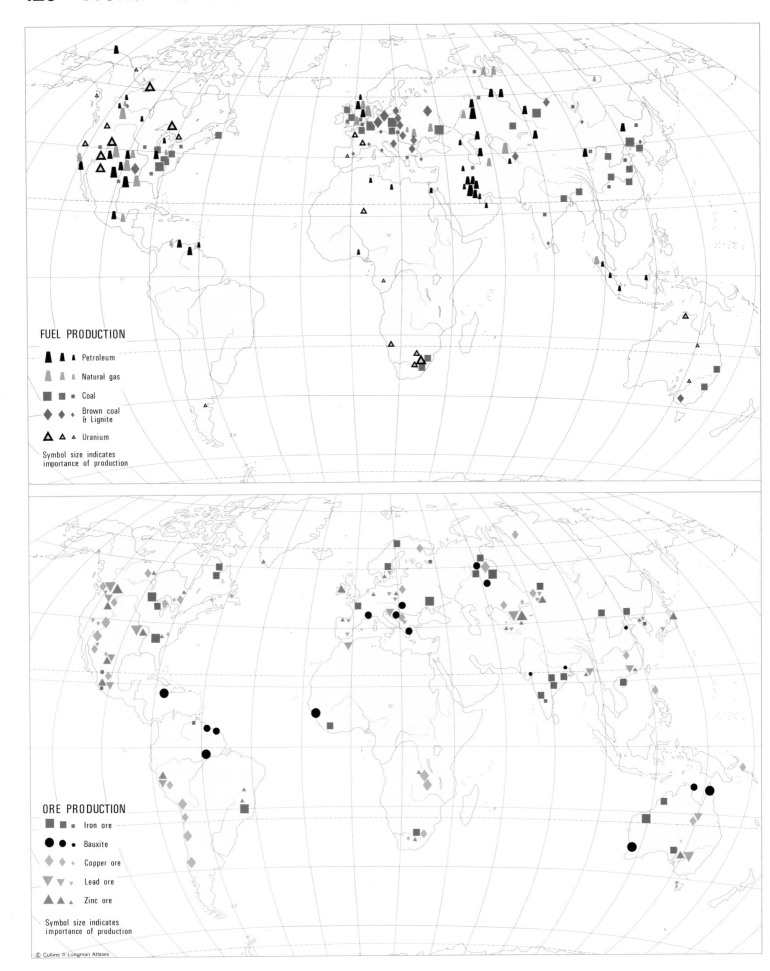

FUEL PRODUCTION

▲ ▲ ▲ Petroleum

▲ ▲ ▲ Natural gas

■ ■ ■ Coal

◆ ◆ ◆ Brown coal & Lignite

△ △ △ Uranium

Symbol size indicates importance of production

ORE PRODUCTION

■ ■ ■ Iron ore

● ● ● Bauxite

◆ ◆ ◆ Copper ore

▼ ▼ ▼ Lead ore

▲ ▲ ▲ Zinc ore

Symbol size indicates importance of production

© Collins ◊ Longman Atlases

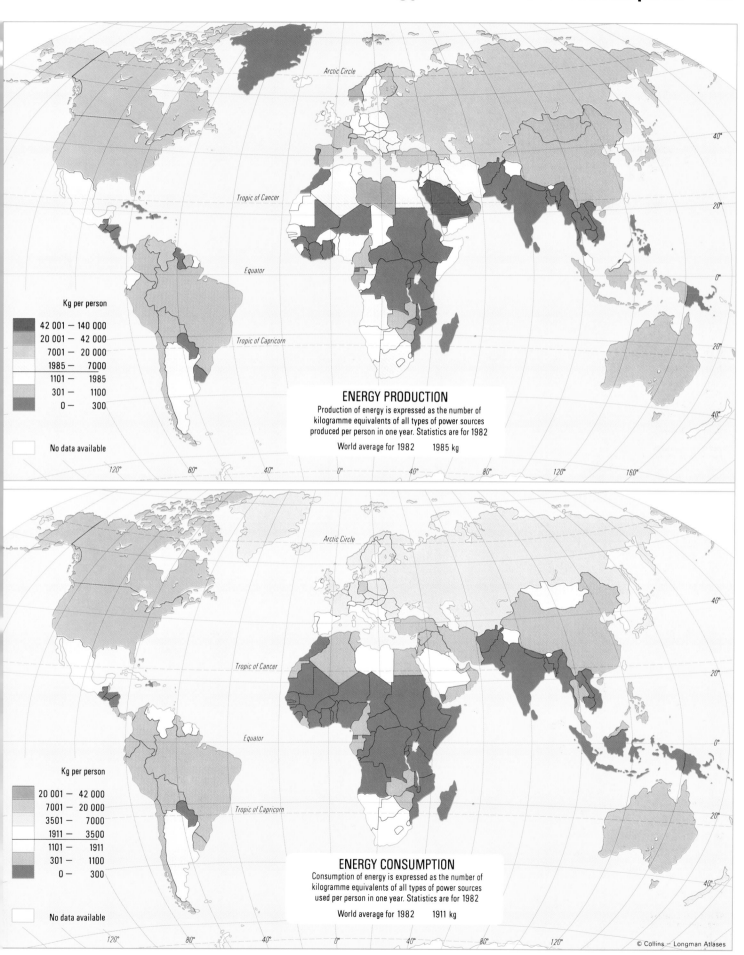

Kg per person

42 001 — 140 000
20 001 — 42 000
7001 — 20 000
1985 — 7000
1101 — 1985
301 — 1100
0 — 300

No data available

ENERGY PRODUCTION

Production of energy is expressed as the number of
kilogramme equivalents of all types of power sources
produced per person in one year. Statistics are for 1982

World average for 1982   1985 kg

Kg per person

20 001 — 42 000
7001 — 20 000
3501 — 7000
1911 — 3500
1101 — 1911
301 — 1100
0 — 300

No data available

ENERGY CONSUMPTION

Consumption of energy is expressed as the number of
kilogramme equivalents of all types of power sources
used per person in one year. Statistics are for 1982

World average for 1982   1911 kg

© Collins – Longman Atlases

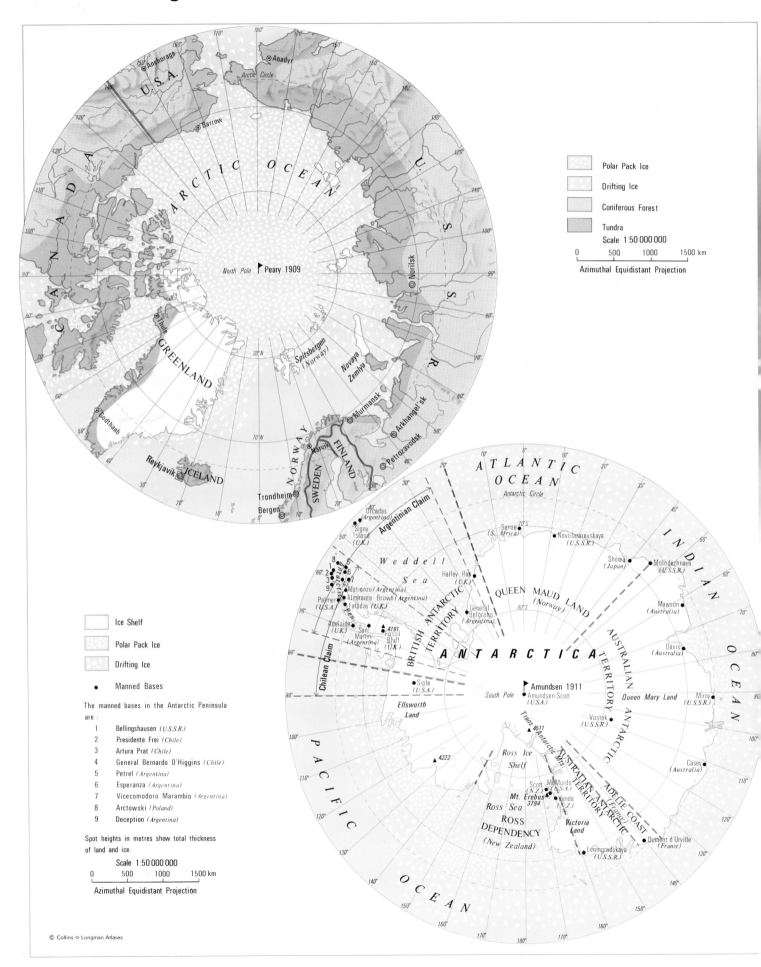

Legend (upper right):
- Polar Pack Ice
- Drifting Ice
- Coniferous Forest
- Tundra

Scale 1:50 000 000

0 500 1000 1500 km

Azimuthal Equidistant Projection

Legend (lower left):
- Ice Shelf
- Polar Pack Ice
- Drifting Ice
- • Manned Bases

The manned bases in the Antarctic Peninsula are:

1 Bellingshausen *(U.S.S.R.)*
2 Presidente Frei *(Chile)*
3 Artura Prat *(Chile)*
4 General Bernardo O'Higgins *(Chile)*
5 Petrel *(Argentina)*
6 Esperanza *(Argentina)*
7 Vicecomodoro Marambio *(Argentina)*
8 Arctowski *(Poland)*
9 Deception *(Argentina)*

Spot heights in metres show total thickness of land and ice.

Scale 1:50 000 000

0 500 1000 1500 km

Azimuthal Equidistant Projection

country	population	area in sq km	population density	exports	imports
EUROPE					
ALBANIA	2 841 000	28 748	99	non-ferrous metal ores	iron and steel
ANDORRA	34 000	453	75		food, instruments
AUSTRIA	7 549 000	83 849	90	machinery (non-electric)	machinery (non-electric), chemicals
BELGIUM	9 856 000	30 513	323	chemicals, motor vehicles, food	crude oil, food, motor vehicles
BULGARIA	8 939 000	110 912	81	transport equipment, machinery	transport equipment, machinery, crude oil
CZECHOSLOVAKIA	15 415 000	127 869	121	machinery (non-electric)	machinery (non-electric), crude oil and products
DENMARK	5 114 000	43 069	119	machinery (non-electric), food	machinery (non-electric), chemicals, crude oil and products
EAST GERMANY	16 699 000	108 178	154	machinery (non-electric)	crude oil and products and metals, machinery and transport equipment, food and other raw materials
FINLAND	4 863 000	337 032	14	paper, machinery	crude oil, machinery (non-electric)
FRANCE	58 652 000	547 026	100	food, chemicals, machinery (non-electric), motor vehicles	crude oil
GREECE	9 840 000	131 944	75	fruit and vegetables, textile yarns and fabrics	crude oil, food, machinery (non-electric), chemicals
HUNGARY	10 690 000	93 030	115	food, machinery (non-electric), checmicals, electrical machinery	machinery, chemicals, crude oil and products
ICELAND	237 000	103 000	2	fish, aluminium	petroleum products, machinery (non-electric)
IRELAND, REP. OF	3 508 000	70 283	50	chemicals, machinery (non-electric)	machinery, transport equipment, petroleum, chemicals
ITALY	56 559 000	301 225	188	machinery (non-electric)	crude oil, food
LIECHTENSTEIN	26 000	157	166	machinery and transport equipment, metal manufactures	
LUXEMBOURG	365 000	2 586	141	chemicals, steel and other metals	machinery, crude oil and products
MALTA	377 000	316	1 193	clothing, machinery	food, petroleum products, textile yarns and fabrics, machinery (non-electric)
MONACO	27 000	1.5	18 000		
NETHERLANDS	14 362 000	40 844	352	chemicals, petroleum products, food	crude oil, food
NORWAY	4 129 000	324 219	13	natural gas, crude oil	machinery (non-electric)
POLAND	36 571 000	312 677	117	machinery	machinery, food, crude oil
PORTUGAL	10 099 000	92 082	110	clothing, textile yarns and fabrics	petroleum, machinery, chemicals, transport equipment, cereals
ROMANIA	22 553 000	237 500	95	machinery and transport equipment, petroleum products, food, chemicals	machinery (non-electric)
SAN MARINO	22 000	61	361		
SPAIN	38 228 000	504 782	76	machinery (non-electric)	crude oil
SWEDEN	8 329 000	449 964	19	machinery, vehicles, paper, timber products, iron and steel	machinery, petroleum, chemical products
SWITZERLAND	6 505 000	41 288	158	machinery (non-electric), motor vehicles, paper	machinery (non-electric), petroleum products, crude oil
U.S.S.R.	272 500 000	22 402 200	12	crude oil and products	machinery
UNITED KINGDOM	55 610 000	244 046	228	machinery (non-electric), chemicals, crude oil	machinery (non-electric), food
WEST GERMANY	61 421 000	248 577	247	machinery (non-electric), vehicles, chemicals	crude oil, food
YUGOSLAVIA	22 855 000	255 804	89	machinery (non-electric), chemicals	chemicals, machinery (non-electric), iron and steel, petroleum and products, crude oil
ASIA					
AFGHANISTAN	17 222 000	647 497	27	natural gas, fruit and nuts, carpets	petroleum products, motor vehicles, textile yarns and fabrics
BAHRAIN	397 000	622	638	petroleum products, crude oil	crude oil
BANGLADESH	94 651 000	143 998	657	jute, jute products, leather	machinery, chemicals, crude oil and products
BHUTAN	1 360 000	47 000	29		food and raw materials, consumer manufactures
BRUNEI	260 000	5 765	45	natural gas, crude oil	machinery (non-electric), food, iron and steel
BURMA	37 553 000	676 552	55	rice, teak	machinery, textile yarns and fabrics, chemicals
CHINA	1 031 890 000	9 596 961	108	crude oil and products, food, textile yarns and fabrics, clothing	machinery, cereals, chemicals, iron and steel
CYPRUS	655 000	9 251	71	fruit and vegetables, clothing	machinery, crude oil, food
HONG KONG	5 313 000	1 045	5 084	clothing, electrical machinery	foodstuffs, textile yarns and fabrics, electrical machinery
INDIA	732 256 000	3 287 590	223	textile yarns and fabrics, foodstuffs	machinery, crude oil, petroleum products, chemicals
INDONESIA	159 434 000	1 904 569	84	crude oil, natural gas	chemicals, machinery (non-electric), crude oil and products, food

country	population	area in sq km	population density	exports	imports

ASIA *continued*

country	population	area in sq km	population density	exports	imports
IRAN	41 635 000	1 648 000	25	crude oil	foodstuffs, chemicals, motor vehicles, iron and steel, machinery (non-electric)
IRAQ	14 654 000	434 924	34	petroleum, dates, skins	machinery, vehicles, sugar, medicines
ISRAEL	4 097 000	20 770	197	crude oil	machinery (non-electric), electrical machinery, food
JAPAN	119 259 000	372 313	316	iron and steel, motor vehicles, electrical machinery, machinery (non-electric)	foodstuffs, crude oil
JORDAN	3 247 000	97 740	33	phosphates, chemicals	foodstuffs, crude oil
KAMPUCHEA (CAMBODIA)	6 888 000	181 035	38	rubber	machinery, chemicals, motor vehicles, iron and steel
KUWAIT	1 672 000	17 818	94	petroleum products, crude oil	foodstuffs, motor vehicles, electrical machinery
LAOS	4 209 000	236 800	18	timber, electricity, coffee	rice, petroleum products, electrical machinery
LEBANON	2 635 000	10 400	253	vegetables and fruit, financial paper and stamps, chemicals	machinery, food, gold
MALAYSIA	14 863 000	329 749	45	timber, crude oil, transistors, tubes etc.	machinery, foodstuffs, crude oil and products
MALDIVES	168 000	298	564	fresh fish, dried salt fish	foodstuffs
MONGOLIA	1 803 000	1 565 000	1	wool, meat, livestock	machinery
NEPAL	15 738 000	140 797	112	jute, goat and kid skins, fruit and vegetables, jute fabrics	manufactured goods, machinery and transport equipment, food, crude oil and products, chemicals
NORTH KOREA	19 185 000	120 538	159	metal and metal ores, raw materials (coal, cement, silk, tobacco), food	machinery and transport equipment, petroleum products, food
OMAN	1 131 000	212 457	5	crude oil	foodstuffs, motor vehicles, machinery (non-electric), petroleum products
PAKISTAN	89 729 000	803 943	113	rice, cotton, cotton cloth	machinery, crude oil, petroleum products
PHILIPPINES	51 956 000	300 000	173	electronic devices, clothing, metal ores	crude oil, machinery (non-electric), chemicals
QATAR	281 000	11 000	26	crude oil	foodstuffs, vehicles, machinery
SAUDI ARABIA	10 421 000	2 149 690	5	crude oil	foodstuffs, machinery (non-electric), electrical machinery, motor vehicles
SINGAPORE	2 502 000	581	4 306	petroleum products, electrical machinery	crude oil, machinery (non-electric), electrical machinery
SOUTH KOREA	39 951 000	98 484	406	clothing, textile yarns and fabrics, electrical machinery	crude oil, machinery (non-electric)
SOUTHERN YEMEN	2 158 000	332 968	6	petroleum products	food, crude oil
SRI LANKA	15 416 000	65 610	235	tea, rubber, clothing, petroleum products	machinery, crude oil, food
SYRIA	9 606 000	185 180	52	cotton, crude oil	crude oil, food, machinery (non-electric)
TAIWAN	18 458 000	35 961	513	clothing, electrical machinery	crude oil, electrical machinery, chemicals, machinery (non-electric)
THAILAND	49 459 000	514 000	96	rice, tapioca	crude oil, chemicals, machinery (non-electric), petroleum products
TURKEY	46 312 000	780 576	59	fruit and vegetables, textile yarns and fabrics	machinery, petroleum, medicines, transport equipment
U.A.E.	1 206 000	83 600	14	crude oil	machinery, foodstuffs, petroleum products
VIETNAM	57 181 000	329 556	174	coal, clothing	food and raw materials, manufactures, machinery and transport equipment
YEMEN	6 232 000	195 000	32	machinery, bakery products, sugar	foodstuffs, machinery, motor vehicles

AUSTRALASIA

country	population	area in sq km	population density	exports	imports
AUSTRALIA	15 369 000	7 686 848	2.1	metal ores, coal	machinery (non-electric), electrical machinery
FIJI	670 000	18 274	37	sugar, petroleum products	food, petroleum products
KIRIBATI	61 000	728	84	copra, fish	food, petroleum products, machinery
NAURU	8 000	21	381	phosphate	food, machinery and transport equipment
NEW CALEDONIA	149 000	19 058	8	ferro-alloys, nickel ore, nickel	machinery, food, petroleum products
NEW ZEALAND	3 203 000	268 676	12	meat, wool	chemicals, machinery (non-electric)
PAPUA NEW GUINEA	3 190 000	461 691	7	copper, coffee, gold	machinery, foodstuffs, petroleum products
SOLOMON ISLANDS	259 000	28 446	9	copra, fish, timber, palm oil	machinery, petroleum products, food
TONGA	104 000	699	149	coconut oil, vanilla beans	food, petroleum products, machinery
TUVALU	8 000	158	51	postage stamps	food, petroleum products
VANUATU	124 000	14 763	8	fish, copra	foodstuffs, petroleum products
WESTERN SAMOA	161 000	2 842	57	coconut oil, copra, taro	petroleum products, food, metal small manufactures

country	population	area in sq km	population density	exports	imports

NORTH AMERICA

country	population	area in sq km	population density	exports	imports
ANTIGUA AND BARBUDA	78 000	442	176	aircraft engines and machinery	foodstuffs, machinery
BAHAMAS	222 000	13 935	16	petroleum products, crude oil	crude oil
BARBADOS	252 000	431	584	sugar, clothing, electrical parts, petroleum products	foodstuffs, crude oil and products, chemicals
BELIZE	156 000	22 965	7	sugar, machinery, dairy products	food, petroleum products, machinery
BERMUDA	55 000	53	1 038	drugs and medicines, electronic supplies	petroleum products, machinery, food
CANADA	24 907 000	9 976 139	3	motor vehicles, machinery	transport equipment, manufactured goods, machinery, petroleum, machinery (non-electric), motor vehicles, crude oil
COSTA RICA	2 435 000	50 700	48	coffee, bananas	machinery (non-electric), chemicals, crude oil and products
CUBA	9 891 000	110 861	89	sugar	foodstuffs, chemicals
DOMINICA	76 000	751	101	bananas, soap	food, chemicals
DOMINICAN REPUBLIC	5 962 000	48 734	122	sugar, gold and alloys	foodstuffs, chemicals, crude oil, machinery
EL SALVADOR	5 232 000	21 041	249	coffee, cotton	machinery, chemicals, foodstuffs, crude oil
GREENLAND	52 000	2 175 600	0	zinc ore, fish and products	machinery, petroleum products, foodstuffs
GRENADA	110 000	344	320	nutmegs, cocoa, bananas	food, machinery and vehicles, petroleum products
GUATEMALA	7 932 000	108 889	73	coffee, bananas	machinery, chemicals, crude oil and products
HAITI	5 201 000	27 750	187	coffee, bauxite, toys and sports goods	foodstuffs, machinery, motor vehicles, petroleum products
HONDURAS	4 092 000	112 088	37	bananas, coffee	machinery (non-electric), chemicals, crude oil and products
JAMAICA	2 258 000	10 991	205	alumina, bauxite	foodstuffs, machinery, chemicals, crude oil and products
MEXICO	75 103 000	1 972 547	38	crude oil	machinery
NICARAGUA	3 058 000	130 000	24	cotton, coffee	machinery, chemicals, foodstuffs, crude oil and products
PANAMA	2 089 000	77 082	27	petroleum products, bananas, shrimps	machinery, chemicals, crude oil
PUERTO RICO	3 350 000	8 897	377	sugar	foodstuffs, machinery
ST KITTS - NEVIS	44 400	266	167	sugar	foodstuffs, machinery
ST LUCIA	125 000	616	203	bananas, cardboard boxes, clothing	food, machinery, petroleum products, chemicals
ST VINCENT	102 000	388	263	bananas	foodstuffs, machinery and vehicles, chemicals
U.S.A.	233 700 000	9 372 614	25	machinery (non-electric), electrical machinery	vehicles, crude oil, electrical machinery

SOUTH AMERICA

country	population	area in sq km	population density	exports	imports
ARGENTINA	29 627 000	2 766 889	11	meat and products, cereals	machinery (non-electric), chemicals, electrical machinery
BOLIVIA	6 082 000	1 098 581	6	tin, natural gas	machinery, vehicles, food
BRAZIL	129 660 000	8 511 965	15	machinery, animal feeding stuffs	machinery, crude oil
CHILE	11 682 000	756 945	15	copper	machinery (non-electric), foodstuffs, crude oil
COLOMBIA	27 515 000	1 138 914	24	coffee	machinery (non-electric), chemicals, vehicles, crude oil and products
ECUADOR	9 251 000	283 561	33	crude oil	machinery, chemicals, motor vehicles
FALKLAND ISLANDS	2 000	12 173	0	wool, postage stamps	metal small manufactures, food
GUIANA	70 000	91 000	1	timber, shellfish	foodstuffs, petroleum products, machinery
GUYANA	918 000	214 969	4	bauxite, sugar	petroleum products, machinery, chemicals, foodstuffs
PARAGUAY	3 473 000	406 752	9	cotton, timber, soyabeans	machinery, crude oil and products
PERU	18 707 000	1 285 216	15	copper, crude oil	machinery, chemicals, cereals
SURINAM	351 000	163 265	2	alumina, bauxite, aluminium	petroleum products, chemicals, machinery
TRINIDAD AND TOBAGO	1 149 000	5 130	224	petroleum products, crude oil	foodstuffs, machinery, crude oil
URUGUAY	2 968 000	176 215	17	wool, beef and veal	machinery, chemicals, crude oil, motor vehicles
VENEZUELA	16 394 000	912 050	18	petroleum products, crude oil	chemicals, machinery (non-electric), food, electrical machinery

AFRICA

country	population	area in sq km	population density	exports	imports
ALGERIA	20 500 000	2 381 741	9	crude oil	machinery (non-electric), food
ANGOLA	8 339 000	1 246 700	7	coffee, diamonds, crude oil	machinery and equipment, food, raw materials
BENIN	3 720 000	112 622	33	cotton, cocoa, palm kernel oil	machinery, textile yarns and fabrics, clothing

country	population	area in sq km	population density	exports	imports
AFRICA *continued*					
BOTSWANA	1 007 000	600 372	2	diamonds, meat and products, copper-nickel matte	foodstuffs, machinery, petroleum products, metals, motor vehicles
BURKINA	6 607 000	274 200	24	cotton, livestock, oil seeds and nuts	machinery, petroleum products, food, motor vehicles, chemicals
BURUNDI	4 421 000	27 834	159	coffee	food, machinery, motor vehicles
CAMEROON	9 165 000	475 442	19	coffee, cocoa, timber products, crude oil	chemicals, machinery (non-electric), petroleum products
CENTRAL AFRICAN REP	2 450 000	622 984	4	coffee, diamonds, timber	motor vehicles, chemicals, food, machinery
CHAD	4 789 000	1 284 000	4	cotton	machinery, petroleum products, chemicals, food
COMOROS	421 000	2 171	194	vanilla, essential oils, cloves	rice
CONGO	1 651 000	342 000	5	crude oil, veneers and plywood	machinery, food, chemicals
DJIBOUTI	330 000	22 000	15	special transactions	food
EGYPT	44 533 000	1 001 449	44	cotton, crude oil, petroleum products	machinery, food, motor vehicles
EQUATORIAL GUINEA	375 000	28 051	13	cocoa, timber	food, beverages and tobacco, crude oil and products, machinery and transport equipment
ETHIOPIA	33 680 000	1 221 900	28	coffee, skins and hides	chemicals, machinery, crude oil, motor vehicles
GABON	1 127 000	267 667	4	crude oil	machinery (non-electric), iron and steel, motor vehicles
GAMBIA	618 000	11 295	55	ground nuts, ground nut oil	foodstuffs, textile yarns and fabrics, machinery
GHANA	12 700 000	238 537	53	cocoa, gold	machinery, chemicals, crude oil and products, motor vehicles
GUINEA	5 177 000	245 857	21	bauxite, alumina	crude oil and products, textiles and clothing, rice
GUINEA BISSAU	863 000	36 125	24	groundnuts, fish	foodstuffs, machinery, petroleum products, textile yarns and fabrics
IVORY COAST	9 161 000	322 463	28	coffee, timber, cocoa	food, crude oil, machinery (non-electric)
KENYA	18 784 000	582 646	32	coffee, petroleum products, tea	machinery, crude oil, chemicals
LESOTHO	1 444 000	30 355	48	wool, diamonds, manufactures	foodstuffs, clothing
LIBERIA	2 057 000	111 369	18	iron ore, rubber	machinery, crude oil, food
LIBYA	3 342 000	1 759 540	2	crude oil	foodstuffs, electrical machinery, machinery (non-electric), motor vehicles
MADAGASCAR	9 400 000	587 041	16	coffee, spices	chemicals, machinery (non-electric), petroleum products
MALAWI	6 429 000	118 484	54	tobacco, tea, sugar	vehicles, petroleum products, chemicals, machinery (non-electric)
MALI	7 528 000	1 240 000	6	cotton, groundnuts, livestock	machinery, vehicles, petroleum products, medicines, chemicals, food
MAURITANIA	1 779 000	1 030 700	2	iron ore, fish	foodstuffs, vehicles, crude oil and products, machinery
MAURITIUS	993 000	2 045	486	sugar, clothing	machinery, food
MOROCCO	22 109 000	446 550	50	phosphates, fruit and vegetables	foodstuffs, crude oil, machinery (non-electric)
MOZAMBIQUE	13 311 000	801 590	17	cashew nuts, sugar	machinery, transport equipment, metals, chemicals
NAMIBIA	1 465 000	824 292	2	diamonds, uranium	
NIGER	5 772 000	1 267 000	5	uranium, livestock	petroleum products, food
NIGERIA	89 022 000	923 768	96	crude oil	vehicles, machinery, food
RWANDA	5 700 000	26 338	216	coffee, tea, metal ores	machinery, petroleum products, motor vehicles
SÃO TOMÉ AND PRÍNCIPE	92 000	964	95	cocoa	food, machinery, textiles, chemicals
SENEGAL	6 316 000	196 192	32	petroleum products, fish, phosphate fertiliser	machinery, food, crude oil, chemicals
SEYCHELLES	64 000	280	230	copra, fish	foodstuffs, petroleum products, machinery
SIERRA LEONE	3 472 000	71 740	48	diamonds, coffee, cocoa	machinery, foodstuffs, textile yarns and fabrics, crude oil
SOMALI REPUBLIC	5 269 000	637 657	8.1	livestock	motor vehicles, machinery, food
SOUTH AFRICA, REPUBLIC OF	30 802 000	1 221 037	25	gold	machinery, chemicals, crude oil and products, motor vehicles
SUDAN	20 362 000	2 505 813	8	cotton, groundnuts, sesame seed, cereals	machinery, food, chemicals, crude oil
SWAZILAND	605 000	17 363	35	sugar, wood pulp, chemicals	machinery and transport equipment, chemicals
TANZANIA	20 378 000	945 087	22	coffee, cotton	machinery, petroleum, manufactured goods
TOGO	2 756 000	56 785	49	phosphates, cocoa, coffee	machinery, crude oil, metal small manufactures, textile yarns and fabrics
TUNISIA	6 886 000	163 610	42	clothing, crude oil, chemicals	machinery, food, crude oil and products
UGANDA	14 625 000	236 036	62	coffee	machinery, motor vehicles, chemicals
WESTERN SAHARA	147 000	266 000	0.6		
ZAÏRE	31 151 000	2 345 409	13	copper, diamonds, coffee	foodstuffs, machinery, chemicals
ZAMBIA	6 242 000	752 614	8	copper	chemicals, crude oil and products
ZIMBABWE	7 740 000	390 580	20	tobacco, gold, nickel, asbestos, copper, meat	machinery, petroleum, chemical products

All the names on the maps in this atlas, except some of those on the special topic maps, are included in the index.

The names are arranged in **alphabetical order.** Where the name has more than one word the separate words are considered as one to decide the position of the name in the index:

Thetford
The Wash
The Weald
Thiers

Where there is more than one place with the same name, the country name is used to decide the order:

London Canada
London U.K.

If both places are in the same country, the county or state name is also used:

Avon *r.* Dorset U.K.
Avon *r.* Glos U.K.

Each entry in the index starts with the name of the place or feature, followed by the name of the country or region in which it is located. This is followed by the number of the most appropriate page on which the name appears, usually the largest scale map. Next comes the alphanumeric reference followed by the latitude and longitude.

Names of physical features such as rivers, capes, mountains etc are followed by a description. The descriptions are usually shortened to one or two letters, these abbreviations are keyed below. Town names are followed by a description only when the name may be confused with that of a physical feature:

Black River *town*

To help to distinguish the different parts of each entry, different styles of type are used:

place name   country name   alphanumeric
                     or   grid reference
              region name

description   page   latitude/
(if any)   number   longitude

Thames   *r.*   U.K.   **13**   H3 51.30N 0.05E

To use the **alphanumeric grid reference** to find a feature on the map, first find the correct page and then look at the letters printed in blue along the top and bottom of the map and the numbers printed in blue at the sides of the map. When you have found the correct letter and number follow the grid boxes up and along until you find the correct grid box in which the feature appears. You must then search the grid box until you find the name of the feature.

The **latitude and longitude reference** gives a more exact description of the position of the feature.

Page 6 of the atlas describes lines of latitude and lines of longitude, and explains how they are numbered and divided into degrees and minutes. Each name in the index has a different latitude and longitude reference, so the feature can be located accurately. The lines of latitude and lines of longitude shown on each map are numbered in degrees. These numbers are printed black along the top, bottom and sides of the map.

The drawing above shows part of the map on page 15 and the lines of latitude and lines of longitude.

The index entry for Wexford is given as follows

Wexford Rep. of Ire. **15 E2** 52.20N 6.25W

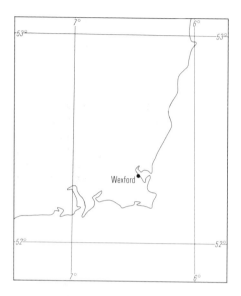

To locate Wexford, first find latitude 52N and estimate 20 minutes north from 52 degrees to find 52.20N, then find longitude 6W and estimate 25 minutes west from 6 degrees to find 6.25W. The symbol for the town of Wexford is where latitude 52.20N and longitude 6.25W meet.

On maps at a smaller scale than the map of Ireland, it is not possible to show every line of latitude and longitude. Only every 5 or 10 degrees of latitude and longitude may be shown. On these maps you must estimate the degrees and minutes to find the exact location of a feature.

Abbreviations

Afghan.	Afghanistan
Bangla.	Bangladesh
b., **B.**	bay, Bay
Beds.	Bedfordshire
Berks.	Berkshire
Bucks.	Buckinghamshire
Cambs.	Cambridgeshire
c., **C.**	cape, Cape
C.A.R.	Central African Republic
Czech.	Czechoslovakia
d.	internal division eg. county, state
Derbys.	Derbyshire
des.	desert
Dom. Rep.	Dominican Republic
D. and G.	Dumfries and Galloway
E. Germany	East Germany
E. Sussex	East Sussex
Equat. Guinea	Equatorial Guinea
est.	estuary
f.	physical feature eg. valley, plain, geographic district
Glos.	Gloucestershire
G.L.	Greater London
G.M.	Greater Manchester
g., **G.**	Gulf
Hants.	Hampshire
H. and W.	Hereford and Worcester
Herts.	Hertfordshire

Humber.	Humberside
i., **I.,** *is.,* **Is.**	island, Island, islands, Islands
I.o.M.	Isle of Man
I.o.W.	Isle of Wight
l., **L.**	lake, Lake
Lancs.	Lancashire
Leics.	Leicestershire
Liech.	Liechtenstein
Lincs.	Lincolnshire
Lux.	Luxembourg
Mersey.	Merseyside
M.G.	Mid Glamorgan
Mt.	Mount
mtn., **Mtn.**	mountain, Mountain
mts., **Mts.**	mountains, Mountains
Neth.	Netherlands
N. Ireland	Northern Ireland
Northants.	Northamptonshire
Northum.	Northumberland
N. Korea	North Korea
N. Yorks.	North Yorkshire
Notts.	Nottinghamshire
Oxon.	Oxfordshire
P.N.G.	Papua New Guinea
pen., **Pen.**	peninsula, Peninsula
Phil.	Philippines
Pt.	Point
r., **R.**	river, River
Rep. of Ire.	Republic of Ireland

R.S.A.	Republic of South Africa
Resr.	Reservoir
Somali Rep.	Somali Republic
Sd.	Sound
S. Yemen	Southern Yemen
S.G.	South Glamorgan
S. Korea	South Korea
S. Yorks.	South Yorkshire
Staffs.	Staffordshire
str., **Str.**	strait, Strait
Strath.	Strathclyde
Switz.	Switzerland
T. and W.	Tyne and Wear
U.A.E.	United Arab Emirates
U.S.S.R.	Union of Soviet Socialist Republics
U.K.	United Kingdom
U.S.A.	United States of America
Warwicks.	Warwickshire
W. Germany	West Germany
W.G.	West Glamorgan
W. Isles	Western Isles
W. Midlands	West Midlands
W. Sahara	Western Sahara
W. Sussex	West Sussex
W. Yorks.	West Yorkshire
Wilts.	Wiltshire
Yugo.	Yugoslavia

Antrim U.K. **15 E4** 54.43N 6.14W
Antrim *d.* U.K. **15 E4** 54.58N 6.20W
Antrim, Mts. of U.K. **15 E5** 55.00N 6.10W
Antsiranana Madagascar **99 G9** 12.19S 49.17E
Antwerp Belgium **39 C3** 51.13N 4.25E
Antwerp *d.* Belgium **39 C3** 51.16N 4.45E
Anvik U.S.A. **80 B4** 62.38N160.12W
Anxi China **66 E5** 40.32N 95.57E
Anyang China **67 I4** 36.04N114.20E
Anzhero-Sudzhensk U.S.S.R. **52 H3** 56.10N 86.10E
Aomori Japan **70 D7** 40.50N140.43E
Aosta Italy **46 C6** 45.43N 7.19E
Apalachee B. U.S.A. **83 J2** 29.30N 84.00W
Aparri Phil. **69 G7** 18.22N121.40E
Apatity U.S.S.R. **50 H4** 67.32N 33.21E
Apeldoorn Neth. **39 D4** 52.13N 5.57E
Apennines *mts.* Italy **46 E6** 42.00N 13.30E
Apia W. Samoa **74 I6** 13.48S171.45W
Apostle Is. U.S.A. **83 H6** 47.00N 90.30W
Appalachian Mts. U.S.A. **83 J3** 39.30N 78.00W
Appingedam Neth. **39 E5** 53.18N 6.52E
Appleby U.K. **12 E6** 54.33N 2.27W
Apsheron Pen. U.S.S.R. **61 H6** 40.28N 50.00E
Apure *r.* Venezuela **88 C8** 7.44N 66.38W
Aqaba Jordan **60 D3** 29.32N 35.00E
Aqaba, G. of Asia **60 D3** 28.45N 34.45E
Aqlat as Suqur Saudi Arabia **60 F2** 25.50N 42.12E
Aquila Mexico **86 D3** 18.30N103.50W
Arabia Asia **107 K6** 25.00N 45.00E
Arabian Desert Egypt **60 C3** 28.15N 31.55E
Arabian Sea Asia **62 B3** 16.00N 65.00E
Aracaju Brazil **88 F6** 10.54S 37.07W
Arad Romania **49 J3** 46.12N 21.19E
Arafura Sea Austa. **69 I2** 9.00S135.00E
Aragon *d.* Spain **43 E4** 42.00N 1.00W
Aragón *r.* Spain **43 E5** 42.20N 1.45W
Araguaia *r.* Brazil **88 E7** 5.30S 48.05W
Araguari Brazil **89 E6** 18.38S 48.13W
Arāk Iran **61 H4** 34.06N 49.44E
Arakan Yoma *mts.* Burma **63 G4** 20.00N 94.00E
Aral Sea U.S.S.R. **52 E2** 45.00N 60.00E
Aralsk U.S.S.R. **52 F2** 46.56N 61.43E
Aranda de Duero Spain **43 D4** 41.40N 3.41W
Aran I. Rep. of Ire. **15 C5** 55.00N 8.32W
Aran Is. Rep. of Ire. **15 B3** 53.07N 9.38W
Aranjuez Spain **43 D4** 40.02N 3.37W
Arapkir Turkey **60 E5** 39.03N 38.29E
Arar, Wadi *r.* Iraq **60 F3** 32.00N 42.30E
Ararat, Mt. Turkey **61 G5** 39.45N 44.15E
Aras *r. see* Araxes *r.* Turkey **60**
Araxes *r.* U.S.S.R. **61 H5** 40.00N 48.28E
Arbatax Italy **46 D3** 39.56N 9.41E
Arbroath U.K. **14 F3** 56.34N 2.35W
Arcachon France **42 D3** 44.40N 1.11W
Arctic Ocean **106 B9**
Arctic Red *r.* Canada **80 E4** 67.26N133.48W
Arda *r.* Greece **47 M4** 41.39N 26.30E
Ardabīl Iran **61 H5** 38.15N 48.18E
Ardara Rep. of Ire. **15 C4** 54.45N 8.28W
Ardèche *r.* France **42 G3** 44.31N 4.40E
Ardennes *mts.* Belgium **39 D2** 50.10N 5.30E
Ardfert Rep. of Ire. **15 B2** 52.19N 9.49W
Ardila *r.* Portugal **43 B3** 38.10N 7.30W
Ardmore Rep. of Ire. **15 D1** 51.58N 7.43W
Ardnamurchan, Pt. of U.K. **14 B3** 56.44N 6.14W
Ardrossan U.K. **14 D2** 55.38N 4.49W
Ards Peninsula U.K. **15 F4** 54.30N 5.30W
Arecibo Puerto Rico **87 K3** 18.29N 66.44W
Arena, Pt. U.S.A. **82 B4** 38.58N123.44W
Arendal Norway **50 B2** 58.27N 8.56E
Arequipa Peru **88 B6** 16.25S 71.32W
Arès France **42 D3** 44.47N 1.08W
Arezzo Italy **46 E5** 43.27N 11.52E
Arfak *mtn.* Indonesia **69 I3** 1.30S133.50E
Arganda Spain **43 D4** 40.19N 3.26W
Argens *r.* France **42 H2** 43.10N 6.45E
Argentan France **42 D5** 48.45N 0.01W
Argentina S. America **89 C4** 35.00S 65.00W
Argentine Basin Atlantic Oc. **106 G3** 40.00S 40.00W
Argenton France **42 E4** 46.36N 1.30E
Argeș *r.* Romania **47 M6** 44.13N 26.22E
Árgos Greece **47 K2** 37.37N 22.45E
Argun *r.* U.S.S.R. **67 J7** 53.30N121.48E
Århus Denmark **38 D4** 56.10N 10.13E
Ariano Italy **46 G4** 41.04N 15.00E
Arica Chile **89 B6** 18.30S 70.20W
Arild Sweden **38 F4** 56.16N 12.32E
Arisaig U.K. **14 C3** 56.55N 5.51W
Ariza Spain **43 D4** 41.19N 2.03W
Arizona *d.* U.S.A. **82 D3** 34.00N112.00W
Arkaig, L. U.K. **14 C3** 56.59N 5.10W
Arkansas *d.* U.S.A. **83 H4** 35.00N 92.00W
Arkansas *r.* U.S.A. **83 H3** 33.50N 91.00W
Arkansas City U.S.A. **83 G4** 37.03N 97.02W
Arkhangel'sk U.S.S.R. **52 D4** 64.32N 41.10E
Arklow Rep. of Ire. **15 E2** 52.47N 6.10W
Arlberg Pass Austria **48 E3** 47.00N 10.05E
Arles France **42 G2** 43.41N 4.38E
Arlon Belgium **39 D1** 49.41N 5.49E
Armagh U.K. **15 E4** 54.21N 6.41W
Armagh *d.* U.K. **15 E4** 54.16N 6.35W
Arma Plateau Saudi Arabia **61 G2** 25.30N 46.30E
Armavir U.S.S.R. **52 D2** 44.59N 41.10E
Armenia Colombia **88 B8** 4.32N 75.40W
Armenia S.S.R. *d.* U.S.S.R. **61 G6** 40.00N 45.00E
Armentières France **39 A2** 50.41N 2.53E
Arnaud *r.* Canada **81 L3** 60.00N 69.45W
Arnauti, C. Cyprus **60 D4** 35.06N 32.17E
Arnborg Denmark **38 B4** 56.02N 8.59E
Arnhem Neth. **39 D4** 52.00N 5.55E
Arnhem Land *f.* Australia **71 C4** 13.00S132.30E
Arno *r.* Italy **46 E5** 43.43N 10.17E
Arnsberg W. Germany **39 G3** 51.24N 8.03E
Ar Ramadi Iraq **60 F4** 33.27N 43.19E
Arran *i.* U.K. **14 C2** 55.35N 5.14W
Arras France **39 A2** 50.17N 2.46E
Arrochar U.K. **14 D3** 56.12N 4.45W
Arrow, Lough Rep. of Ire. **15 C4** 54.03N 8.20W
Ar Rutba Iraq **60 F4** 33.03N 40.18E
Års Denmark **38 C4** 56.50N 9.30E
Árta Greece **47 J3** 39.10N 20.57E
Artois *f.* France **39 A2** 50.16N 2.50E
Artux China **66 B5** 39.40N 75.49E
Artvin Turkey **60 F6** 41.12N 41.48E
Aruba *i.* Neth. Ant. **87 J2** 12.30N 70.00W
Aru Is. Indonesia **69 I2** 6.00S134.30E
Arun *r.* U.K. **8 F2** 50.47N 0.34W
Arunachal Pradesh *d.* India **63 G5** 28.40N 94.60E
Ārup Denmark **38 D3** 55.23N 10.06E
Arusha Tanzania **99 D4** 3.21S 36.40E
Aruwimi *r.* Zaïre **94 E5** 1.20N 23.36E
Arvagh Rep. of Ire. **15 D3** 53.55N 7.36W
Arvidsjaur Sweden **50 D4** 65.37N 19.10E
Arvika Sweden **50 C2** 59.41N 12.38E
Asahi daki *mtn.* Japan **70 E8** 43.42N142.54E
Asahikawa Japan **70 E8** 43.46N142.23E
Asansol India **63 F4** 23.40N 87.00E
Ascension I. Atlantic Oc. **108 I4** 8.00S 14.00W
Aschendorf W. Germany **39 F5** 53.03N 7.20E
Aschersleben E. Germany **48 E5** 51.46N 11.28E
Ascoli Piceno Italy **46 F5** 42.52N 13.36E
Åseda Sweden **50 C2** 57.10N 15.20E
Ashbourne Rep. of Ire. **15 E3** 53.30N 6.24W
Ashburton *r.* Australia **71 A3** 21.15S115.00E
Ashby de la Zouch U.K. **13 F4** 52.45N 1.29W
Asheville U.S.A. **83 J4** 35.35N 82.35W
Ashford U.K. **13 H3** 51.08N 0.53E
Ashikaga Japan **70 D5** 36.21N139.26E
Ashington U.K. **12 F7** 55.11N 1.34W
Ashizuri saki *c.* Japan **70 B3** 32.45N133.05E
Ashkhabad U.S.S.R. **52 E1** 37.58N 58.24E
Ashland Ky. U.S.A. **83 J4** 38.28N 82.40W
Ashland Wisc. U.S.A. **83 H6** 46.34N 90.45W
Ash Sham *des.* Saudi Arabia **60 F3** 28.15N 43.05E
Ash Shama *des.* Saudi Arabia **60 E3** 31.20N 38.00E
Asia **54**
Asinara *i.* Italy **46 D4** 41.04N 8.18E
Asinara, G. of Med. Sea **46 D4** 41.00N 8.32E
'Asīr *f.* Saudi Arabia **101 G3** 19.00N 42.00E
Askeaton Rep. of Ire. **15 C2** 52.35N 8.59W
Askersund Sweden **50 C2** 58.55N 14.55E
Askim Norway **50 B2** 59.33N 11.20E
Asmara Ethiopia **101 F3** 15.20N 38.58E
Assab Ethiopia **101 G3** 13.01N 42.47E
Assam *d.* India **63 G5** 26.30N 93.00E
Assen Neth. **39 E5** 53.00N 6.34E
Assens Denmark **38 C3** 55.14N 9.54E
Åsted Denmark **38 B4** 56.48N 8.59E
Asti Italy **46 D6** 44.54N 8.13E
Astorga Spain **43 B5** 42.30N 6.02W
Astoria U.S.A. **82 B6** 46.12N123.50W
Astrakhan U.S.S.R. **52 E2** 46.22N 48.00E
Åstrup Denmark **38 C3** 55.57N 9.40E
Asturias *d.* Spain **43 B5** 43.30N 6.00W
Asunción Paraguay **89 D5** 25.15S 57.40W
Aswân Egypt **60 D2** 24.05N 32.56E
Aswân High Dam Egypt **60 D1** 23.59N 32.54E
Asyûţ Egypt **60 C2** 27.14N 31.07E
Atacama Desert S. America **89 B6** 20.00S 69.00W
Atafu Pacific Oc. **74 I7** 8.40S172.40W
Atakpamé Togo **103 E2** 7.34N 1.14E
Atar Mauritania **100 A4** 20.32N 13.08W
Atbara Sudan **101 F3** 17.42N 34.00E
Atbara *r.* Sudan **101 F3** 17.47N 34.00E
Atchafalaya B. U.S.A. **83 H2** 29.30N 92.00W
Ath Belgium **39 B2** 50.38N 3.45E
Athabasca Canada **80 G3** 54.44N113.15W
Athabasca *r.* Canada **80 G3** 58.30N111.00W
Athabasca, L. Canada **80 H3** 59.30N109.00W
Athea Rep. of Ire. **15 B2** 52.28N 9.18W
Athenry Rep. of Ire. **15 C3** 53.18N 8.48W
Athens Greece **47 K2** 37.59N 23.42E
Athlone Rep. of Ire. **15 D3** 53.26N 7.57W
Áthos, Mt. Greece **47 L4** 40.09N 24.19E
Atlanta U.S.A. **83 J3** 33.45N 84.23W
Atlantic-Antarctic Ridge Atlantic Oc. **106 I2** 53.00S 0.00
Atlantic City U.S.A. **83 L4** 39.23N 74.27W
Atlantic-Indian-Antarctic Basin Atl. Oc. / Ind. Oc. **106 I1** 61.00S 0.00
Atlantic Ocean **106 F6**
Atlas Mts. Africa **94 B8** 33.00N 4.00W
Atouguia Portugal **43 A3** 39.20N 9.20W
Ätran *r.* Sweden **50 C2** 56.54N 12.30E
Atrek *r.* Asia **101 H5** 37.23N 54.00E
Atsugi Japan **70 D4** 35.27N139.22E
Aţ Ţā'if Saudi Arabia **101 G4** 21.15N 40.21E
Attleborough U.K. **13 I4** 52.33N 1.02E
Attopeu Laos **68 D6** 14.51N106.56E
Atui I. Cook Is. **75 K5** 20.00S158.07W
Aubagne France **42 G2** 43.17N 5.35E
Aube *r.* France **42 F5** 48.30N 3.37E
Aubigny-sur-Nère France **42 F4** 47.29N 2.26E
Aubin France **42 F3** 44.32N 2.14E
Auch France **42 E2** 43.40N 0.36E
Auchterarder U.K. **14 E3** 56.18N 3.42W
Auckland New Zealand **71 G2** 36.52S174.45E
Auckland Is. Pacific Oc. **74 G2** 50.35S166.00E
Aude *r.* France **42 F2** 43.13N 2.20E
Augrabies Falls *f.* R.S.A. **99 C2** 28.45S 20.00E
Augsburg W. Germany **48 E4** 48.21N 10.54E
Augusta Ga. U.S.A. **83 J3** 33.29N 82.00W
Augusta Maine U.S.A. **83 M5** 44.20N 69.50W
Auki Solomon Is. **71 F5** 8.45S160.46E
Aulne *r.* France **42 B5** 48.30N 4.11W
Aumale France **42 E5** 49.46N 1.45E
Aurangābād India **63 D3** 19.52N 75.22E
Aurich W. Germany **39 F5** 53.28N 7.29E
Aurillac France **42 F3** 44.56N 2.26E
Austin U.S.A. **82 G3** 30.18N 97.47W
Australasia **71**
Australia Austa. **71 B3** 25.00S135.00E
Austral Ridge Pacific Oc. **75 L5** 24.00S148.00W
Austria Europe **48 F3** 47.30N 14.00E
Autun France **42 G4** 46.58N 4.18E
Auxerre France **42 F4** 47.48N 3.35E
Auzances France **42 F4** 46.02N 2.29E
Avallon France **42 F4** 47.30N 3.54E
Avanos Turkey **60 D5** 38.44N 34.51E
Avarua Rarotonga Cook Is. **75 K5** 21.12S159.46W
Aveiro Portugal **43 A4** 40.40N 8.35W
Avellino Italy **46 G4** 40.55N 14.46E
Avesnes France **39 B2** 50.08N 3.57E
Avesta Sweden **50 D3** 60.09N 16.10E
Aveyron *r.* France **42 E3** 44.09N 1.10E
Avezzano Italy **46 F5** 42.03N 13.26E
Aviemore U.K. **14 E4** 57.11N 3.51W
Avignon France **42 G2** 43.56N 4.48E
Ávila Spain **43 C4** 40.39N 4.42W
Avon *d.* U.K. **13 E3** 51.35N 2.40W
Avon *r.* Avon U.K. **8 E2** 51.28N 2.45W
Avon *r.* Dorset U.K. **13 F2** 50.43N 1.45W
Avon *r.* Glos. U.K. **13 E4** 52.00N 2.10W
Avonmouth U.K. **13 E3** 51.31N 2.41W
Avranches France **42 D5** 48.42N 1.21W
Awa shima *i.* Japan **70 D6** 38.30N139.20E
Awaso Ghana **102 D2** 6.20N 2.22W
Awe, Loch U.K. **14 C3** 56.18N 5.24W
Axel Heiberg I. Canada **81 I5** 79.30N 90.00W
Axim Ghana **102 D1** 4.53N 2.14W
Axiós *r.* Greece **32 J3** 40.31N 22.43E
Axminster U.K. **13 E2** 50.48N 2.59W
Ayaguz U.S.S.R. **66 C6** 47.59N 80.27E
Ayan U.S.S.R. **53 L3** 56.29N138.00E
Aydin Turkey **60 B5** 37.52N 27.50E
Áyios Evstrátios *i.* Greece **47 L3** 39.30N 25.00E
Aylesbury U.K. **13 G3** 51.48N 0.49W
Aylsham U.K. **12 I4** 52.48N 1.42E
Ayr U.K. **14 D2** 55.28N 4.37W
Ayr *r.* U.K. **14 D2** 55.28N 4.38W
Ayre, Pt. of U.K. **12 C6** 54.25N 4.21W
Ayutthaya Thailand **68 C6** 14.25N100.30E
Ayvalik Turkey **47 M3** 39.19N 26.42E
Azare Nigeria **103 G3** 11.40N 10.08E
Azbine *mts. see* Aïr *mts.* Niger **100**
Azerbaijan S.S.R. *d.* U.S.S.R. **61 G6** 40.10N 47.50E
Azores *is.* Atlantic Oc. **106 H6** 39.00N 30.00W
Azov, Sea of U.S.S.R. **52 D2** 46.00N 36.30E
Azua Dom. Rep. **87 J3** 18.29N 70.44W
Azuaga Spain **43 C3** 38.16N 5.40W
Azuero Pen. Panama **87 H1** 7.30N 80.30W
Azul Argentina **89 D4** 36.46S 59.50W

B

Ba'albek Lebanon **60 E4** 34.00N 36.12E
Baarle-Hertog Neth. **39 C3** 51.26N 4.56E
Babar Is. Indonesia **69 H2** 8.00S129.30E
Bab el Mandeb *str.* Asia **101 G3** 13.00N 43.10E
Babia Gora *mtn.* Czech. / Poland **49 I4** 49.38N 19.38E
Babo Indonesia **69 I3** 2.33S133.25E
Baboua C.A.R. **103 G2** 5.49N 14.51E
Babuyan Is. Phil. **69 G7** 19.20N121.30E
Babylon *ruins* Iraq **61 G4** 32.33N 44.25E
Bacan *i.* Indonesia **69 H3** 0.30S127.30E
Bacău Romania **49 M3** 46.32N 26.59E
Bac Can Vietnam **68 D8** 22.08N105.49E
Baccarat France **42 H5** 48.27N 6.45E
Back *r.* Canada **81 I4** 66.37N 96.00W
Bac Ninh Vietnam **68 D8** 21.10N106.04E
Bacolod Phil. **69 G6** 10.38N122.58E
Badajoz Spain **43 B3** 38.53N 6.58W
Badalona Spain **43 G4** 41.27N 2.15E
Bad Bramstedt W. Germany **38 C1** 53.56N 9.59E
Bad Doberan E. Germany **38 E2** 54.06N 11.57E
Baden-Baden W. Germany **48 D4** 48.45N 8.15E
Badgastein Austria **48 F3** 47.07N 13.09E
Bad Ischl Austria **48 F3** 47.43N 13.38E
Bad Kreuznach W. Germany **39 F1** 49.51N 7.52E
Bad Schwartau W. Germany **38 D1** 53.56N 10.43E
Bad Segeberg W. Germany **38 D1** 53.58N 10.19E
Bad Sülze E. Germany **38 F2** 54.07N 12.41E
Baffin *d.* Canada **80 J4** 66.00N 72.00W
Baffin B. Canada **81 L5** 74.00N 70.00W
Baffin I. Canada **81 K5** 68.50N 70.00W
Bafia Cameroon **103 G1** 4.39N 11.14E
Bafing *r.* Mali **102 B3** 14.48N 12.10W
Bafoulabé Mali **102 B3** 13.49N 10.50W
Bafra Turkey **60 D6** 41.34N 35.56E
Baggy Pt. U.K. **13 C3** 51.09N 4.16W
Baghdād Iraq **61 G4** 33.20N 44.26E
Baghlān Afghan. **63 C6** 36.11N 68.44E
Bagoé *r.* Mali **102 C3** 12.34N 6.30W
Baguio Phil. **69 G7** 16.25N120.37E
Bahamas C. America **87 I4** 23.30N 75.00W
Bahao Kalat Iran **61 K2** 25.42N 61.28E
Bahāwalpur Pakistan **63 C5** 29.24N 71.47E
Bahía Blanca Argentina **89 C4** 38.45S 62.15W
Bahrain Asia **61 H2** 26.00N 50.35E
Bahr Aouk *r.* C.A.R. **94 D5** 8.50N 18.50E
Bahr el Arab *r.* Sudan **94 E5** 9.12N 29.28E
Bahr el Ghazal *r.* Chad **103 H3** 12.26N 15.25E
Bahr el Ghazal *r.* Sudan **101 F2** 9.30N 31.30E
Bahr el Jebel *r.* Sudan **101 F2** 9.30N 30.20E
Baia-Mare Romania **49 K3** 47.40N 23.35E
Baicheng China **67 J6** 45.40N122.52E
Baie Comeau Canada **81 L2** 49.12N 68.10W
Baikal, L. U.S.S.R. **53 I3** 53.30N108.00E
Bailleul France **39 A2** 50.44N 2.44E
Baimuru P.N.G. **69 K2** 7.30S144.49E
Baing Indonesia **69 G1** 10.15S120.34E
Baise *r.* France **42 E3** 44.15N 0.20E
Baja California Norte *d.* Mexico **86 B5** 30.00N115.00W
Baja California Sur *d.* Mexico **86 B5** 26.00N112.00W
Bakel Senegal **102 B3** 14.54N 12.26W
Baker Mont. U.S.A. **82 F6** 46.23N104.16W
Baker Oreg. U.S.A. **82 C5** 44.46N117.50W
Baker, Mt. U.S.A. **82 B6** 48.48N121.10W
Bakersfield U.S.A. **82 C4** 35.25N119.00W
Baku U.S.S.R. **61 H6** 40.22N 49.53E
Bala U.K. **12 D4** 52.55N 3.37W
Balabac Str. Malaysia / Phil. **68 F5** 7.30N117.00E
Balakovo U.S.S.R. **52 D3** 52.04N 47.46E
Balasore India **63 F4** 21.31N 86.59E
Balaton *l.* Hungary **49 H3** 46.55N 17.50E
Balboa Panama **87 I1** 8.37N 79.33W
Balbriggan Rep. of Ire. **15 E3** 53.36N 6.12W
Balchik Bulgaria **47 N5** 43.24N 28.10E
Balearic Is. Spain **43 F3** 39.30N 2.30E
Bali *i.* Indonesia **68 E2** 8.30S115.05E
Balikesir Turkey **47 M3** 39.38N 27.51E
Balikpapan Indonesia **68 F3** 1.15S116.50E
Balkan Mts. Bulgaria **47 K5** 42.50N 24.30E
Balkhash U.S.S.R. **66 B6** 46.51N 75.00E
Balkhash, L. U.S.S.R. **66 B6** 46.40N 75.00E
Ballachulish U.K. **14 C3** 56.41N 5.08N
Ballantrae U.K. **14 D2** 55.07N 4.59W
Ballarat Australia **71 D2** 37.36S143.58E
Ballater U.K. **14 E4** 57.03N 3.04W
Ballenas B. Mexico **86 B5** 26.40N113.30W
Balleny Is. Antarctica **74 G1** 66.35S162.50E
Ballina Rep. of Ire. **15 B4** 54.08N 9.10W
Ballinasloe Rep. of Ire. **15 C3** 53.20N 8.15W
Ballingeary Rep. of Ire. **15 B1** 51.50N 9.17W
Ball's Pyramid *i.* Pacific Oc. **74 F4** 31.45S159.15E
Ballybay *town* Rep. of Ire. **15 E4** 54.07N 6.53W
Ballycastle U.K. **15 E5** 55.12N 6.15W
Ballyclare U.K. **15 E4** 54.46N 6.00W
Ballyconnell Rep. of Ire. **15 D4** 54.07N 7.38W
Ballydehob Rep. of Ire. **15 B1** 51.34N 9.28W
Ballydonegan Rep. of Ire. **15 A1** 51.38N 10.03W
Ballygar Rep. of Ire. **15 C3** 53.31N 8.20W
Ballygawley U.K. **15 D4** 54.28N 7.03W
Ballykelly U.K. **15 E5** 55.03N 7.01W
Ballymena U.K. **15 E4** 54.52N 6.17W
Ballymoney U.K. **15 E5** 55.05N 6.31W
Ballyquintin Pt. U.K. **15 F4** 54.20N 5.30W
Ballyragget Rep. of Ire. **15 D2** 52.47N 7.20W
Ballyshannon Rep. of Ire. **15 C4** 54.30N 8.11W
Ballyvaughan Rep. of Ire. **15 B3** 53.07N 9.10W
Ballyvourney Rep. of Ire. **15 B1** 51.57N 9.10W
Balsas *r.* Mexico **86 D3** 18.10N102.05W
Baltic Sea Europe **50 D1** 56.30N 19.00E
Baltic Shield *f.* Europe **107 K8** 63.00N 30.00E
Baltimore U.S.A. **83 K4** 39.18N 76.38W
Baluchistan *f.* Pakistan **62 B5** 28.00N 66.00E
Bām Iran **61 J3** 29.07N 58.20E
Bamako Mali **102 C3** 12.40N 7.59W
Bamba Mali **102 D4** 17.05N 1.23W
Bamberg W. Germany **48 E4** 49.54N 10.53E
Bam Co *l.* China **63 G5** 31.30N 91.10E
Bamenda Cameroon **103 G2** 5.55N 10.09E
Bamenda Highlands Cameroon **103 G2** 6.20N 10.20E
Bampton U.K. **13 D2** 50.59N 3.30W
Bampūr Iran **61 K2** 27.13N 60.29E
Bampūr *r.* Iran **61 J2** 27.18N 59.02E
Banaba *i.* Kiribati **74 H7** 0.52S169.35E
Banagher Rep. of Ire. **15 C3** 53.11N 8.01W
Banbridge U.K. **15 E4** 54.20N 6.18W
Banbury U.K. **13 F4** 52.03N 1.20W
Banchory U.K. **14 F4** 57.04N 2.28W
Banda *i.* Indonesia **69 H3** 4.30S129.55E
Banda Aceh Indonesia **68 B5** 5.35N 95.20E
Bandama *r.* Ivory Coast **102 D2** 5.10N 4.59W
Bandar 'Abbās Iran **61 J2** 27.10N 56.15E
Bandar Dilam Iran **61 H3** 30.05N 50.11E
Bandar-e Anzalī Iran **61 H5** 37.26N 49.29E
Bandar-e Khomeyni Iran **61 H3** 30.26N 49.03E
Bandar-e-Lengeh Iran **61 I2** 26.34N 54.53E
Bandar-e Torkeman Iran **101 H5** 36.55N 54.05E
Bandar Rig Iran **61 H3** 29.30N 50.40E
Bandar Seri Begawan Brunei **68 E5** 4.56N114.58E
Banda Sea Indonesia **69 H2** 5.00S128.00E
Bandeira *mtn.* Brazil **89 E5** 20.25S 41.45W
Bandirma Turkey **47 N4** 40.22N 28.00E
Bandon Rep. of Ire. **15 C1** 51.45N 8.45W
Bandon *r.* Rep. of Ire. **15 C1** 51.43N 8.38W
Bandundu Zaïre **99 B4** 3.20S 17.24E
Bandung Indonesia **68 D2** 6.57S107.34E
Banes Cuba **87 I4** 20.59N 75.24W
Banff Canada **80 G3** 51.10N115.34W
Banff U.K. **14 F4** 57.40N 2.31W
Bangalore India **63 D2** 12.58N 77.35E
Bangassou C.A.R. **101 E2** 4.41N 22.48E
Banggai Is. Indonesia **69 G3** 1.30S123.10E
Bangka *i.* Indonesia **68 D3** 2.20S106.10E
Bangkok Thailand **68 C6** 13.45N100.35E
Bangladesh Asia **63 F4** 24.00N 90.00E
Bangor Rep. of Ire. **15 B4** 54.09N 9.46W
Bangor Down U.K. **15 F4** 54.40N 5.41W
Bangor Gwynedd U.K. **12 C5** 53.13N 4.09W
Bangor U.S.A. **83 M5** 44.49N 68.47W
Bangui C.A.R. **100 D2** 4.23N 18.37E
Bangweulu, L. Zambia **99 C3** 11.15S 29.45E
Ban Hat Yai Thailand **68 C5** 7.00N100.28E
Ban Houei Sai Laos **63 C8** 20.21N100.26E
Bani *r.* Mali **102 D3** 14.30N 4.15W
Banjak Is. Indonesia **68 B4** 2.15N 97.10E
Banja Luka Yugo. **47 H6** 44.47N 17.10E
Banjarmasin Indonesia **68 E3** 3.22S114.36E
Banjul Gambia **102 A3** 13.28N 16.39W
Banks I. Australia **69 K1** 10.15S142.15E
Banks I. Canada **80 F5** 73.00N122.00W
Ban Me Thuot Vietnam **68 D6** 12.41N108.02E

Bann *r.* U.K. 15 E5 55.10N 6.46W
Bannockburn U.K. 14 E3 56.06N 3.56W
Banská Bystrica Czech. 49 I4 48.44N 19.07E
Bantry Rep. of Ire. 15 B1 51.41N 9.27W
Bantry B. Rep. of Ire. 15 B1 51.40N 9.40W
Banyo Cameroon 103 G2 6.47N 11.50E
Banyuwangi Indonesia 68 E2 8.12S114.22E
Baoding China 67 I5 38.54N115.26E
Baoji China 66 G4 34.23N107.16E
Baoshan China 66 F2 25.07N 99.08E
Baotou China 67 H5 40.38N109.59E
Baoulé *r.* Mali 102 B3 13.47N 10.45W
Bapaume France 39 A2 50.07N 2.51E
Bar Albania 47 I5 42.05N 19.06E
Bar U.S.S.R. 49 M4 49.05N 27.40E
Baracoa Cuba 87 J4 20.23N 74.31W
Barahona Dom. Rep. 87 J3 18.13N 71.07W
Baranof I. U.S.A. 80 E3 57.05N135.00W
Baranovichi U.S.S.R. 49 M6 53.09N 26.00E
Barbados Lesser Antilles 87 M2 13.20N 59.40W
Barbastro Spain 43 F5 42.02N 0.07E
Barbezieux France 42 D3 45.28N 0.09W
Barbuda *i.* Leeward Is. 87 L3 17.41N 61.48W
Barcellona Italy 46 G3 38.10N 15.13E
Barcelona Spain 43 G4 41.25N 2.10E
Barcelona Venezuela 88 C9 10.08N 64.43W
Bardai Chad 100 D4 21.21N 16.56E
Bardejov Czech. 49 J4 49.18N 21.16E
Bardera Somali Rep. 101 G2 2.18N 42.18E
Bardsey *i.* U.K. 12 C4 52.47N 4.50W
Bardu Norway 50 D5 68.54N 18.20E
Bareilly India 63 E5 28.20N 79.24E
Barents Sea Arctic Oc. 52 D4 73.00N 40.00E
Bari Italy 47 H4 41.08N 16.52E
Barisan Range *mts.* Indonesia 68 C3 3.30S102.30E
Barito *r.* Indonesia 68 E3 3.35S114.35E
Bariz Kuh, Jebel *mts.* Iran 61 J3 28.40N 58.10E
Barking U.K. 13 H3 51.32N 0.10E
Barkly Tableland *f.* Australia 71 C4 19.00S136.40E
Bar-le-Duc France 42 G5 48.46N 5.10E
Barletta Italy 46 H4 41.20N 16.15E
Barmouth U.K. 12 C4 52.45N 4.02W
Barnard Castle U.K. 12 F6 54.32N 1.56W
Barnaul U.S.S.R. 52 G3 53.21N 83.15E
Barnet U.K. 13 G3 51.39N 0.15W
Barneveld Neth. 39 D4 52.10N 5.39E
Barnsley U.K. 12 F5 53.33N 1.29W
Barnstaple U.K. 13 C3 51.05N 4.03W
Baro Nigeria 103 F2 8.37N 6.19E
Barquisimeto Venezuela 88 C9 10.03N 69.18W
Barra *i.* U.K. 14 A3 56.59N 7.28W
Barra, Sound of U.K. 14 A4 57.03N 7.25W
Barra Head U.K. 8 C5 56.48N 7.40W
Barrancas Venezuela 88 C8 8.55N 62.05W
Barranquilla Colombia 88 B9 11.00N 74.50W
Barreiro Portugal 43 A3 38.40N 9.05W
Barrhead U.K. 14 D2 55.48N 4.22W
Barrow *r.* Rep. of Ire. 15 D2 52.17N 7.00W
Barrow U.S.A. 80 C5 71.16N156.50W
Barrow, Pt. U.S.A. 76 E9 71.30N156.00W
Barrow-in-Furness U.K. 12 D6 54.08N 3.15W
Barry U.K. 13 D3 51.23N 3.19W
Barstow U.S.A. 82 C3 34.55N117.01W
Bar-sur-Aube France 42 G5 48.14N 4.43E
Barth E. Germany 38 F2 54.22N 12.43E
Bartin Turkey 60 D6 41.37N 32.20E
Barton-upon-Humber U.K. 12 G5 53.42N 0.26W
Basel Switz. 48 C3 47.33N 7.36E
Bashi Channel Phil. / Taiwan 67 J2 21.40N121.20E
Basilan Phil. 69 G5 6.40N121.59E
Basilan *i.* Phil. 69 G5 6.40N122.10E
Basildon U.K. 13 H3 51.34N 0.25E
Basingstoke U.K. 13 F3 51.15N 1.05W
Basra Iraq 61 G3 30.33N 47.50E
Bassein Burma 63 G3 16.45N 94.30E
Basse-Terre Guadeloupe 87 L3 16.00N 61.43W
Bass Str. Australia 71 D2 39.45S146.00E
Bastak Iran 61 I2 27.15N 54.26E
Bastelica France 42 I2 42.00N 9.03E
Bastia France 42 I2 42.41N 9.26E
Bastogne Belgium 39 D2 50.00N 5.43E
Bata Equat. Guinea 103 F1 1.51N 9.49E
Batabanó, G. of Cuba 87 H4 23.15N 82.30W
Batang China 66 F3 30.02N 99.01E
Batangas Phil. 69 G6 13.46N121.01E
Batan Is. Phil. 69 G8 20.50N121.55E
Bath U.K. 13 E3 51.22N 2.22W
Batha, Wadi *r.* Oman 61 J1 22.01N 59.39E
Bathgate U.K. 14 E2 55.54N 3.38W
Bathurst Canada 81 L2 47.37N 65.40W
Bathurst, C. Canada 80 F5 70.30N128.00W
Bathurst I. Australia 71 C4 11.45S130.15E
Bathurst I. Canada 81 H5 76.00N100.00W
Bathurst Inlet *town* Canada 80 H4 66.48N108.00W
Batinah *f.* Oman 61 J2 24.25N 56.50E
Batley U.K. 12 F5 53.44N 1.39W
Batna Algeria 100 C5 35.34N 6.11E
Baton Rouge U.S.A. 83 H3 30.30N 91.10W
Batouri Cameroon 103 G1 4.26N 14.27E
Battambang Cambodia 68 C6 13.06N103.13E
Batticaloa Sri Lanka 63 E1 7.43N 81.42E
Battle U.K. 13 H2 50.55N 0.28E
Battle Harbour Canada 81 M3 52.16N 55.36W
Batu Is. Indonesia 68 B3 0.30S 98.20E
Batumi U.S.S.R. 60 F6 41.37N 41.36E
Batu Pahat Malaysia 68 C4 1.50N102.48E
Baturaja Indonesia 68 C3 4.10S104.10E
Baubau Indonesia 69 G2 5.30S122.37E
Bauchi Nigeria 103 F3 10.16N 9.50E
Bauchi *d.* Nigeria 103 F3 10.40N 10.00E
Baugé France 42 D4 47.33N 0.06W
Bauld, C. Canada 81 M3 51.30N 55.45W
Bauru Brazil 89 E5 22.19S 49.07W
Bautzen E. Germany 48 G5 51.11N 14.29E
Bavay France 39 B2 50.18N 3.48E
Bawean *i.* Indonesia 68 E2 5.50S112.35E
Bawiti Egypt 60 C3 28.21N 28.51E
Bayamo Cuba 87 I4 20.23N 76.39W
Bayamón Puerto Rico 87 K3 18.24N 66.10W
Bayan Har Shan *mts.* China 66 F4 34.00N 97.20E
Bayburt Turkey 60 F6 40.15N 40.16E
Bay City U.S.A. 83 J5 43.35N 83.52W
Baydaratskaya B. U.S.S.R. 52 F4 70.00N 66.00E
Bayeux France 42 D5 49.16N 0.42W
Bay Is. Honduras 87 G3 16.10N 86.30W
Bayombong Phil. 69 G7 16.27N121.10E
Bayonne France 42 D2 43.30N 1.28W
Bayreuth W. Germany 48 E4 49.56N 11.35E
Baza Spain 43 D2 37.30N 2.45W
Bazaliya U.S.S.R. 49 M4 49.42N 26.29E
Bazman Kuh *mtn.* Iran 61 J3 28.06N 60.00E
Beachy Hd. U.K. 13 H2 50.43N 0.14E
Beaufort Sea N. America 80 D5 72.00N141.00W
Beauly U.K. 14 D4 57.29N 4.28W
Beauly *r.* U.K. 14 D4 57.29N 4.27W
Beaumaris U.K. 12 C5 53.16N 4.07W
Beaumont Belgium 39 C2 50.14N 4.16E
Beaumont U.S.A. 83 H3 30.04N 94.06W
Beaune France 42 G4 47.02N 4.50E
Beauvais France 42 F5 49.26N 2.05E
Beāwar India 63 D5 26.02N 74.20E
Bebington U.K. 12 E5 53.20N 2.59W
Beccles U.K. 13 I4 52.28N 1.33E
Béchar Algeria 100 B5 31.35N 2.17W
Beckum W. Germany 39 G3 51.45N 8.02E
Bédarieux France 42 F2 43.35N 3.10E
Bedford U.K. 13 G4 52.08N 0.29W
Bedford Levels *f.* U.K. 13 G4 52.35N 0.00W
Bedfordshire *d.* U.K. 13 G4 52.04N 0.28W
Bedlington U.K. 12 F7 55.08N 1.34W
Beersheba Israel 60 D3 31.15N 34.47E
Beeston U.K. 12 F4 52.55N 1.13W
Beeville U.S.A. 82 G2 28.25N 97.47W
Beg, Lough U.K. 15 E4 54.47N 6.30W
Begna *r.* Norway 50 B3 60.06N 10.15E
Behbehān Iran 61 H3 30.35N 50.17E
Bei'an China 67 K6 48.17N126.33E
Beida Libya 101 E5 32.50N 21.50E
Beihai China 67 H2 21.29N109.10E
Beijing China 67 I5 39.55N116.25E
Beilen Neth. 39 E4 52.51N 6.31E
Beinn Dearg *mtn.* U.K. 14 D4 57.49N 4.55W
Beira Mozambique 99 D3 19.49S 34.52E
Beirut Lebanon 60 D4 33.52N 35.30E
Beitbridge Zimbabwe 99 C2 22.10S 29.59E
Beja Portugal 43 B3 38.01N 7.52W
Bejaïa Algeria 100 C5 36.45N 5.05E
Béjar Spain 43 C4 40.24N 5.45W
Békéscsaba Hungary 49 J3 46.41N 21.06E
Bela Pakistan 62 C5 26.12N 66.20E
Belalcázar Spain 43 C3 38.35N 5.10W
Belang Indonesia 69 G4 0.58N124.56E
Belau Pacific Oc. 69 I5 7.00N134.25E
Belaya *r.* U.S.S.R. 52 E3 55.40N 52.30E
Belaya Tserkov U.S.S.R. 49 O4 49.49N 30.10E
Belcher Is. Canada 81 K3 56.00N 79.00W
Belcoo U.K. 15 D4 54.18N 7.53W
Belém Brazil 88 E7 1.27S 48.29W
Belen U.S.A. 82 E3 34.39N106.48W
Belfast U.K. 15 F4 54.36N 5.57W
Belfast Lough U.K. 15 F4 54.42N 5.45W
Belfort France 42 H4 47.38N 6.52E
Belgaum India 63 D3 15.54N 74.36E
Belgium Europe 39 C2 51.00N 4.30E
Belgorod U.S.S.R. 52 D2 50.38N 36.36E
Belgorod-Dnestrovskiy U.S.S.R. 49 O3 46.10N 30.19E
Belgrade Yugo. 47 J6 44.49N 20.28E
Belikh *r.* Syria 60 E4 35.58N 39.05E
Belitung *i.* Indonesia 68 D3 3.00S108.00E
Belize Belize 87 G3 17.29N 88.20W
Belize C. America 87 G3 17.00N 88.30W
Bellac France 42 E4 46.07N 1.04E
Bellary India 63 D3 15.11N 76.54E
Belle Île France 42 C4 47.20N 3.10W
Belle Isle Str. Canada 81 M3 50.45N 58.00W
Bellingham U.K. 12 E7 55.09N 2.16W
Bellingham U.S.A. 82 B6 48.45N122.29W
Bellingshausen Sea Antarctica 106 E1 70.00S 84.00W
Belmopan Belize 87 G3 17.25N 88.46W
Belmullet Rep. of Ire. 15 A4 54.13N 10.00W
Belo Horizonte Brazil 89 E6 19.45S 43.53W
Belper U.K. 12 F5 53.01N 1.29W
Beltsy U.S.S.R. 49 M3 47.45N 27.59E
Belukha, Mt. U.S.S.R. 66 D6 49.46N 86.40E
Belzec Poland 49 K5 50.24N 23.26E
Bemidji U.S.A. 83 H6 47.29N 94.52W
Benavente Spain 43 C5 42.00N 5.40W
Benbecula *i.* U.K. 14 A4 57.26N 7.18W
Ben Cruachan *mtn.* U.K. 14 C3 56.26N 5.18W
Bend U.S.A. 82 B5 44.04N121.20W
Bendel *d.* Nigeria 103 F2 6.10N 6.00E
Bendigo Australia 71 D2 36.48S144.21E
Benevento Italy 46 G4 41.07N 14.46E
Bengal, B. of Indian Oc. 63 F3 17.00N 89.00E
Bengbu China 67 I4 32.56N117.27E
Benghazi Libya 100 E5 32.07N 20.05E
Bengkulu Indonesia 68 C3 3.46S102.16E
Benguela Angola 99 B3 12.34S 13.24E
Ben Hope *mtn.* U.K. 14 D5 58.24N 4.36W
Beni *r.* Bolivia 88 C6 10.30S 66.00W
Benicarló Spain 43 F4 40.25N 0.25E
Benidorm Spain 43 E3 38.33N 0.09W
Beni-Mellal Morocco 100 B5 32.21N 6.21W
Benin Africa 103 E2 9.00N 2.30E
Benin, Bight of Africa 103 E2 5.30N 3.00E
Benin City Nigeria 103 F2 6.19N 5.41E
Beni Suef Egypt 60 C3 29.05N 31.05E
Ben Lawers *mtn.* U.K. 14 D3 56.33N 4.14W
Ben Lomond *mtn.* U.K. 14 D3 56.12N 4.38W
Ben Macdhui *mtn.* U.K. 14 E4 57.04N 3.40W
Ben More *mtn.* Central U.K. 14 D3 56.23N 4.31W
Ben More *mtn.* Strath. U.K. 14 B3 56.26N 6.02W
Ben More Assynt *mtn.* U.K. 14 D5 58.07N 4.52W
Ben Nevis *mtn.* U.K. 14 D3 56.48N 5.00W
Benue *d.* Nigeria 103 F2 7.20N 8.00E
Benue *r.* Nigeria 103 F2 7.52N 6.45E
Ben Wyvis *mtn.* U.K. 14 D4 57.40N 4.35W
Benxi China 67 J5 41.21N123.45E
Beppu Japan 70 A3 33.18N131.30E
Berat Albania 47 I4 40.42N 19.59E
Berau, Teluk *b.* Indonesia 69 I3 2.20S133.00E
Berbera Somali Rep. 101 G3 10.28N 45.02E
Berbérati C.A.R. 103 H1 4.19N 15.51E
Berchem Belgium 39 B2 50.48N 3.32E
Berdichev U.S.S.R. 49 N4 49.54N 28.39E
Berezina *r.* U.S.S.R. 49 O6 52.33N 30.14E
Berezniki U.S.S.R. 52 E3 59.26N 56.49E
Bergama Turkey 47 M3 39.08N 27.10E
Bergamo Italy 46 D6 45.42N 9.40E
Bergen E. Germany 38 G2 54.27N 13.27E
Bergen Norway 50 A3 60.23N 5.20E
Bergen op Zoom Neth. 39 C3 51.30N 4.17E
Bergerac France 42 E3 44.50N 0.29E
Bergheim W. Germany 39 E2 50.58N 6.39E
Bergisch Gladbach W. Germany 39 F2 50.59N 7.10E
Berhampore India 63 F4 24.06N 88.18E
Berhampur India 63 F3 19.21N 84.51E
Bering Sea N. America / Asia 80 A4 60.00N170.00W
Bering Str. U.S.S.R. / U.S.A. 80 B4 65.00N170.00W
Berkel *r.* Neth. 39 E4 52.10N 6.12E
Berkshire *d.* U.K. 13 F3 51.25N 1.03W
Berkshire Downs *hills* U.K. 13 F3 51.32N 1.36W
Berlin E. Germany 48 F6 52.32N 13.25E
Bermejo *r.* Argentina 89 D5 26.47S 58.30W
Bermuda *i.* Atlantic Oc. 76 N5 32.18N 65.00W
Bernburg E. Germany 48 E5 51.48N 11.44E
Berne Switz. 48 C3 46.57N 7.26E
Bernina *mtn.* Italy / Switz. 46 D7 46.22N 9.57E
Bernkastel W. Germany 39 F1 49.55N 7.05E
Berry Head U.K. 13 D2 50.23N 3.29W
Bershad U.S.S.R. 49 N4 48.20N 29.30E
Bertnaghboy Bay Rep. of Ire. 15 B3 53.23N 9.55W
Bertoua Cameroon 103 G1 4.34N 13.42E
Berwick-upon-Tweed U.K. 12 E7 55.46N 2.00W
Besançon France 42 H4 47.14N 6.02E
Bessarabia *f.* U.S.S.R. 49 N3 46.30N 28.40E
Betanzos Spain 43 A5 43.17N 8.13W
Bétaré Oya Cameroon 103 G2 5.34N 14.09E
Béthune France 39 A2 50.32N 2.38E
Beverley U.K. 12 G5 53.52N 0.26W
Beverwijk Neth. 39 C4 52.29N 4.40E
Bewcastle Fells *hills* U.K. 12 E7 55.05N 2.40W
Bexhill U.K. 13 H2 50.50N 0.27E
Bexley U.K. 13 H3 51.25N 0.05E
Beyla Guinea 102 C2 8.42N 8.39W
Beysehir L. Turkey 60 C5 37.47N 31.30E
Béziers France 42 F2 43.21N 3.13E
Bhāgalpur India 63 F4 25.14N 86.59E
Bhamo Burma 63 H4 24.15N 97.15E
Bhātpāra India 66 D2 22.51N 88.31E
Bhavnagar India 63 D4 21.46N 72.14E
Bhima *r.* India 63 D3 16.30N 77.10E
Bhopāl India 63 D4 23.17N 77.28E
Bhubaneswar India 63 F4 20.15N 85.50E
Bhuj India 63 C4 23.12N 69.54E
Bhutan Asia 63 F5 27.25N 89.50E
Biak Indonesia 69 J3 1.10S136.05E
Biak *i.* Indonesia 69 J3 0.55S136.00E
Białogard Poland 48 G7 54.00N 16.00E
Białystok Poland 49 K6 53.09N 23.10E
Biarritz France 42 D2 43.29N 1.33W
Bicester U.K. 13 F3 51.54N 1.08W
Bida Nigeria 103 F2 9.06N 5.59E
Bideford U.K. 13 C3 51.01N 4.12W
Biel Switz. 48 C3 47.09N 7.16E
Bielefeld W. Germany 48 D6 52.02N 8.32E
Bielsko-Biała Poland 49 I4 49.49N 19.02E
Bié Plateau *f.* Africa 94 D3 13.00S 16.00E
Bigbury Bay U.K. 13 D2 50.15N 3.53W
Biggar U.K. 14 E2 55.38N 3.30W
Bighorn *r.* U.S.A. 82 E6 46.05N107.20W
Bighorn Mts. U.S.A. 82 E5 44.00N107.30W
Bignona Senegal 102 A3 12.48N 16.18W
Big Snowy Mtn. U.S.A. 82 E6 46.46N109.31W
Big Spring *town* U.S.A. 82 F3 32.15N101.30W
Bihać Yugo. 46 G6 44.49N 15.53E
Bīhar India 63 F4 25.13N 85.31E
Bīhar *d.* India 63 F4 24.15N 86.00E
Bihor *mtn.* Romania 49 K3 46.26N 22.43E
Bijagos Archipelago *is.* Guinea Bissau 102 A3 11.30N 16.00W
Bijāpur India 63 D3 16.52N 75.47E
Bijār Iran 61 G4 35.52N 47.39E
Bijāwar India 63 E4 24.36N 79.30E
Bīkaner India 63 D5 28.01N 73.22E
Bikin U.S.S.R. 67 L6 46.52N134.15E
Bikini *i.* Pacific Oc. 74 G9 11.35N165.23E
Bilāspur India 63 E4 22.03N 82.12E
Bilauktaung Range *mts.* Asia 68 B6 13.20N 99.30E
Bilbao Spain 43 D5 43.15N 2.56W
Bilecik Turkey 60 C6 40.10N 29.59E
Billingham U.K. 12 F6 54.38N 1.17W
Billings U.S.A. 82 E6 45.47N108.30W
Bill of Portland *c.* U.K. 13 E2 50.32N 2.28W
Biloxi U.S.A. 83 I3 30.30N 88.53W
Binaija *mtn.* Indonesia 69 H3 3.10S129.30E
Binche Belgium 39 C2 50.25N 4.10E
Binderup Denmark 38 C4 56.46N 9.35E
Bingen W. Germany 39 F1 49.58N 7.55E
Bingerville Ivory Coast 102 D2 5.20N 3.53W
Bingham U.K. 12 G4 52.57N 0.52W
Binghamton U.S.A. 83 K5 42.06N 75.55W
Bingkor Malaysia 68 F5 5.26N116.15E
Bingol Daglari *mtn.* Turkey 60 F5 39.21N 41.22E
Binh Dinh Vietnam 68 D6 13.55N109.07E
Binjai Indonesia 68 B4 3.37N 98.25E
Bintan *i.* Indonesia 68 C4 1.10N104.30E
Bintulu Malaysia 68 E4 3.12N113.01E
Bioko *i.* Equat. Guinea 94 C5 3.25N 8.45E
Birecik Turkey 60 E5 37.03N 37.59E
Birhan *mtn.* Ethiopia 101 F3 11.00N 37.50E
Bīrjand Iran 62 A6 32.54N 59.10E
Birkenfeld W. Germany 39 F1 49.39N 7.10E
Birkenhead U.K. 12 D5 53.24N 3.01W
Birket Qârûn *l.* Egypt 60 C3 29.30N 30.40E
Bîrlad Romania 49 M3 46.14N 27.40E
Birmingham U.K. 13 F4 52.30N 1.55W
Birmingham U.S.A. 83 I3 33.30N 86.55W
Birnin Kebbi Nigeria 103 E3 12.30N 4.11E
Birni N'Konni Niger 103 F3 13.49N 5.19E
Birobidzhan U.S.S.R. 67 L6 48.49N132.54E
Birq, Wadi *r.* Saudi Arabia 61 G2 24.08N 47.35E
Birr Rep. of Ire. 15 D3 53.06N 7.56W
Biscay, B. of France 42 C3 45.30N 4.00W
Bishop Auckland U.K. 12 F6 54.40N 1.40W
Bishop's Stortford U.K. 13 H3 51.53N 0.10E
Bisitun Iran 61 G4 34.22N 47.29E
Biskra Algeria 100 C5 34.48N 5.40E
Bismarck U.S.A. 82 F6 46.50N100.48W
Bismarck Range *mts.* P.N.G. 69 L2 6.00S145.00E
Bismarck Sea Pacific Oc. 69 L3 4.00S146.30E
Bissau Guinea Bissau 102 A3 11.52N 15.39W
Bistrița Romania 49 L3 47.08N 24.30E
Bistrița *r.* Romania 49 M3 46.30N 26.54E
Bitburg W. Germany 39 E1 49.58N 6.31E
Bitlis Turkey 60 F5 38.23N 42.04E
Bitola Yugo. 47 J4 41.02N 21.21E
Bitterfontein R.S.A. 99 B1 31.03S 18.16E
Bitterroot Range U.S.A. 82 D6 47.06N115.10W
Biu Nigeria 103 G3 10.36N 12.11E
Biwa ko *l.* Japan 70 C4 35.20N136.10E
Biysk U.S.S.R. 52 H3 52.35N 85.16E
Bizerta Tunisia 100 C5 37.17N 9.51E
Bjärred Sweden 38 F3 55.43N 12.59E
Bjerringbro Denmark 38 C4 56.23N 9.39E
Black *r.* U.S.A. 83 H4 35.30N 91.20W
Black *r.* Vietnam 68 D8 21.20N105.45E
Blackburn U.K. 12 E5 53.44N 2.30W
Black Forest *f.* W. Germany 48 D4 48.00N 7.45E
Black Mtn. U.K. 13 D3 51.52N 3.52W
Black Mts. U.K. 13 D3 51.56N 3.10W
Blackpool U.K. 12 D5 53.48N 3.03W
Black River *town* Jamaica 87 I3 18.02N 77.52W
Black Rock Desert U.S.A. 82 C5 41.10N118.45W
Black Sea Europe 33 L3 44.00N 30.00E
Blacksod B. Rep. of Ire. 15 A4 54.04N 10.00W
Black Volta *r.* Ghana / Burkina 102 D2 8.14N 2.11W
Blackwater *r.* Rep. of Ire. 15 D1 51.58N 7.52W
Blackwater *r.* U.K. 8 C4 54.28N 6.37W
Blaenau Ffestiniog U.K. 12 D5 53.00N 3.52W
Blagoevgrad Bulgaria 47 K5 42.02N 23.04E
Blagoveshchensk U.S.S.R. 67 K7 50.19N127.30E
Blair Atholl U.K. 14 E3 56.48N 3.50W
Blairgowrie U.K. 14 E3 56.37N 3.21W
Blanc, Cap *c.* Mauritania 100 A4 20.44N 17.05W
Blanc, Mont *mtn.* Europe 42 H3 45.50N 6.52E
Blanca, Bahía *b.* Argentina 89 C4 39.15S 61.00W
Blanca, Sierra *mtn.* U.S.A. 82 E3 33.23N105.49W
Blanco, C. Costa Rica 87 G1 9.36N 85.06W
Blanco, C. U.S.A. 82 B5 42.50N124.29W
Blandford Forum U.K. 13 E2 50.52N 2.11W
Blankenberge Belgium 39 B3 51.18N 3.08E
Blantyre Malawi 99 D3 15.46S 35.00E
Blarney Rep. of Ire. 15 C1 51.56N 8.34W
Blavet *r.* France 42 C4 47.43N 3.18W
Blaye France 42 D3 45.08N 0.40W
Bletchley U.K. 13 G3 51.59N 0.42W
Blida Algeria 100 C5 36.30N 2.50E
Blitar Indonesia 68 E2 8.06S112.12E
Blitta Togo 103 E2 8.23N 1.06E
Bloemfontein R.S.A. 99 C2 29.07S 26.14E
Blois France 42 E4 47.36N 1.20E
Bloody Foreland *c.* Rep. of Ire. 15 C5 55.09N 8.17W
Bluefield U.S.A. 83 J4 37.14N 81.17W
Bluefields Nicaragua 87 H2 12.00N 83.49W
Blue Mts. U.S.A. 82 C6 45.00N118.00W
Blue Nile *r.* Sudan 101 F3 15.45N 32.25E
Blue Stack Mts. Rep. of Ire. 15 C4 54.44N 8.09W
Blyth U.K. 12 F7 55.07N 1.29W
Bo Sierra Leone 102 B2 7.58N 11.45W
Boa Vista Brazil 88 C8 2.51N 60.43W
Bobo-Dioulasso Burkina 102 D3 11.11N 4.18W
Bobruysk U.S.S.R. 49 N6 53.08N 29.10E
Bocholt W. Germany 39 E3 51.49N 6.37E
Bochum W. Germany 39 F3 51.28N 7.11E
Bodélé Depression *f.* Chad 100 D3 16.50N 17.10E
Boden Sweden 50 E4 65.50N 21.44E
Bodmin U.K. 13 C2 50.29N 4.41W
Bodmin Moor U.K. 13 C2 50.35N 4.35W
Bodö Norway 50 C4 67.18N 14.26E
Boffa Guinea 102 B3 10.12N 14.02W
Bogense Denmark 38 D3 55.34N 10.07E
Boggeragh Mts. Rep. of Ire. 15 C2 52.04N 8.50W
Bogia P.N.G. 69 L3 4.16S145.00E
Bognor Regis U.K. 13 G2 50.48N 0.40W
Bog of Allen *f.* Rep. of Ire. 15 D3 53.17N 7.00W
Bogor Indonesia 68 D2 6.34S106.45E
Bogotá Colombia 88 B8 4.38N 74.05W
Bogué Mauritania 102 B4 16.40N 14.10W
Bohain France 39 B1 49.59N 3.28E
Bohemian Forest *mts.* W. Germany / Czech. 48 F4 49.20N 13.10E
Bohol *i.* Phil. 69 G5 9.45N124.10E
Boise U.S.A. 82 C5 43.38N116.12W
Bojeador, C. Phil. 69 G7 18.30N120.50E
Boké Guinea 102 B3 10.57N 14.13W

Colne *r.* U.K. 13 H3 51.51N 0.58E
Colnett, C. Mexico 86 A6 31.00N116.20W
Cologne W. Germany 39 E2 50.56N 6.57E
Colombia S. America 88 B8 5.00N 75.00W
Colombo Sri Lanka 63 E1 6.55N 79.52E
Colón Panama 87 I1 9.21N 79.54W
Colonsay *i.* U.K. 14 B3 56.04N 6.13W
Colorado *r.* Argentina 89 C4 39.50S 62.02W
Colorado *r.* Ariz. N. America 82 D3 32.00N114.58W
Colorado *d.* U.S.A. 82 E4 39.00N106.00W
Colorado *r.* Tex. U.S.A. 83 G2 28.30N 96.00W
Colorado Plateau *f.* U.S.A. 82 D4 35.45N112.00W
Colorado Springs *town* U.S.A. 82 F4 38.50N104.40W
Columbia U.S.A. 83 J3 34.00N 81.00W
Columbia *r.* U.S.A. 82 B6 46.10N123.30W
Columbretes, Islas *is.* Spain 43 F3 39.50N 0.40E
Columbus Ga. U.S.A. 83 J3 32.28N 84.59W
Columbus Ohio U.S.A. 83 J4 39.59N 83.03W
Colville *r.* U.S.A. 80 C5 70.06N151.30W
Colwyn Bay *town* U.K. 12 D5 53.18N 3.43W
Comayagua Honduras 87 G2 14.30N 87.39W
Comeragh Mts. Rep. of Ire. 15 D2 52.15N 7.35W
Comilla Bangla. 63 G4 23.28N 91.10E
Como Italy 46 D6 45.48N 9.04E
Como, L. Italy 46 D7 46.05N 9.17E
Comodoro Rivadavia Argentina 89 C3 45.50S 67.30W
Comorin, C. India 63 D2 8.04N 77.35E
Comoros Africa 99 E3 12.15S 44.00E
Conakry Guinea 102 B2 9.30N 13.43W
Concarneau France 42 C4 47.53N 3.55W
Concepción Chile 89 B4 36.50S 73.03W
Concepción Paraguay 89 D5 23.22S 57.26W
Conception, Pt. U.S.A. 82 B3 34.27N120.26W
Conchos *r.* Mexico 86 D5 29.34N104.30W
Concord U.S.A. 83 L5 43.13N 71.34W
Concordia Argentina 89 D4 31.25S 58.00W
Condom France 42 E3 43.58N 0.22E
Confolens France 42 E3 46.01N 0.40E
Congleton U.K. 12 E5 53.09N 2.14W
Congo Africa 99 B4 1.00S 16.00E
Coningsby U.K. 12 G5 53.06N 0.10W
Coniston U.K. 12 D6 54.22N 3.03W
Conn, Lough Rep. of Ire. 15 B4 54.01N 9.15W
Connah's Quay U.K. 12 D5 53.12N 3.02W
Connecticut *d.* U.S.A. 83 L5 41.30N 73.00W
Connemara *f.* Rep. of Ire. 15 B3 53.30N 9.50W
Conon *r.* U.K. 14 D4 57.33N 4.28W
Consett U.K. 12 F6 54.52N 1.50W
Con Son Is. Vietnam 68 D5 8.30N106.30E
Constance, L. Europe 48 D3 47.40N 9.30E
Constanţa Romania 47 N6 44.10N 28.31E
Constantina Spain 43 C2 37.54N 5.36W
Constantine Algeria 100 C5 36.22N 6.38E
Conwy U.K. 12 D5 53.18N 3.48W
Conwy *r.* U.K. 12 D5 53.18N 3.48W
Cook, Mt. New Zealand 71 G1 43.36S170.09E
Cook Is. Pacific Oc. 74 J6 15.00S160.00W
Cookstown U.K. 15 E4 54.39N 6.46W
Cook Str. New Zealand 71 G1 41.15S174.30E
Cooktown Australia 71 D4 15.29S145.15E
Cootehill Rep. of Ire. 15 D4 54.05N 7.05W
Copán *ruins* Honduras 87 G2 14.52N 89.10W
Copenhagen Denmark 38 F3 55.43N 12.34E
Copenhagen *d.* Denmark 38 F3 55.40N 12.10E
Copiapó Chile 89 B5 27.20S 70.23W
Coppermine *r.* Canada 80 G4 67.54N115.10W
Coppermine *town* Canada 80 G4 67.49N115.12W
Coquet *r.* U.K. 12 F7 55.21N 1.34W
Coquimbo Chile 89 B5 30.00S 71.25W
Corabia Romania 47 L5 43.45N 24.29E
Coral Sea Pacific Oc. 71 E4 13.00S148.00E
Corbeil France 42 F5 48.37N 2.29E
Corby U.K. 13 G4 52.29N 0.41W
Córdoba Argentina 89 C4 31.25S 64.11W
Córdoba Mexico 86 E3 18.55N 96.55W
Córdoba Spain 43 C2 37.53N 4.46W
Corfu Greece 47 I3 39.37N 19.50E
Corfu *i.* Greece 47 I3 39.35N 19.50E
Corigliano Italy 47 H3 39.36N 16.31E
Corinth Greece 47 K2 37.56N 22.55E
Corinth, G. of Greece 47 K3 38.15N 22.30E
Corinto Nicaragua 87 G2 12.29N 87.14W
Cork Rep. of Ire. 15 C1 51.54N 8.28W
Cork *d.* Rep. of Ire. 15 C1 52.00N 8.40W
Cork Harbour *est.* Rep. of Ire. 15 C1 51.50N 8.17W
Corner Brook *town* Canada 81 M2 48.58N 57.58W
Corno, Monte *mtn.* Italy 46 F5 42.29N 13.33E
Cornwall *d.* U.K. 13 C2 50.26N 4.40W
Cornwallis I. Canada 81 I5 75.00N 95.00W
Coronation G. Canada 80 G4 68.00N112.00W
Corozal Belize 87 G3 18.23N 88.23W
Corpus Christi U.S.A. 83 G2 27.47N 97.26W
Corrib, Lough Rep. of Ire. 15 B3 53.26N 9.14W
Corrientes Argentina 89 D5 27.30S 58.48W
Corse, Cap *c.* France 42 I2 43.00N 9.21E
Corsham U.K. 13 E3 51.27N 2.10W
Corsica *i.* France 42 I2 42.00N 9.10E
Corte France 42 I2 42.18N 9.08E
Cortegana Spain 43 B2 37.55N 6.49W
Coruche Portugal 43 A3 38.58N 8.31W
Çorum Turkey 60 D6 40.31N 34.57E
Corumbá Brazil 89 D6 19.00S 57.25W
Corwen U.K. 12 D4 52.58N 3.23W
Cosenza Italy 46 H3 39.17N 16.14E
Cosne France 42 F4 47.25N 2.55E
Costa Brava *f.* Spain 43 G4 41.30N 3.00E
Costa del Sol *f.* Spain 43 C2 36.30N 4.00W
Costa Rica C. America 87 H2 10.00N 84.00W
Cotabato Phil. 69 G5 7.14N124.15E
Côte d'Azur *f.* France 42 H2 43.20N 6.45E
Cotonou Benin 103 E2 6.24N 2.31E
Cotopaxi *mtn.* Ecuador 88 B7 0.40S 78.30W
Cotswold Hills U.K. 13 E3 51.50N 2.00W
Cottbus E. Germany 48 G5 51.43N 14.21E
Coucy France 39 B1 49.32N 3.20E
Coulagh B. Rep. of Ire. 15 A1 51.40N 10.05W
Council Bluffs U.S.A. 83 G5 41.14N 95.54W
Coupar Angus U.K. 14 E3 56.33N 3.18W
Courtrai Belgium 39 B2 50.49N 3.17E
Coutances France 42 D5 49.03N 1.29W
Couvin Belgium 39 C2 50.03N 4.30E
Coventry U.K. 13 F4 52.25N 1.31W
Covilhã Portugal 43 B4 40.17N 7.30W
Cowdenbeath U.K. 14 E3 56.08N 3.22W
Cowes U.K. 13 F2 50.46N 1.20W
Cox's Bāzār Bangla. 63 G4 21.25N 91.59E
Cozumel I. Mexico 87 G4 20.30N 87.00W
Cracow Poland 49 I5 50.03N 19.55E
Craigavon U.K. 15 E4 54.28N 6.25W
Craignure U.K. 14 C3 56.28N 5.43W
Crail U.K. 14 F3 56.16N 2.39W
Crailsheim W. Germany 48 E4 49.09N 10.06E
Craiova Romania 47 K6 44.18N 23.46E
Cranbrook Canada 80 G2 49.29N115.48W
Crati *r.* Italy 47 H3 39.43N 16.29E
Craughwell Rep. of Ire. 15 C3 53.13N 8.45W
Crawley U.K. 13 G3 51.07N 0.10W
Cree L. Canada 80 H3 57.20N108.30W
Creil France 42 F5 49.16N 2.29E
Cremona Italy 46 E6 45.08N 10.03E
Cres *i.* Yugo. 46 G6 44.50N 14.20E
Crescent City U.S.A. 82 B5 41.46N124.13W
Crest France 42 G3 44.44N 5.02E
Creston U.S.A. 83 H5 41.04N 94.20W
Crete *i.* Greece 47 L1 35.15N 25.00E
Crete, Sea of Med. Sea 47 L1 36.00N 25.00E
Creus, Cabo *c.* Spain 43 G5 42.20N 3.19E
Creuse *r.* France 42 E4 47.00N 0.35E
Crewe U.K. 12 E5 53.06N 2.28W
Crianlarich U.K. 14 D3 56.26N 4.40W
Criccieth U.K. 12 C4 52.56N 4.16W
Crieff U.K. 14 E3 56.23N 3.52W
Crimea *pen.* U.S.S.R. 52 C2 45.30N 34.00E
Crinan U.K. 14 C3 56.05N 5.35W
Cristóbal Colón *mtn.* Colombia 88 B9 10.53N 73.48W
Crna *r.* Yugo. 47 J4 41.33N 21.58E
Croaghnameal *mtn.* Rep. of Ire. 15 D4 54.40N 7.57W
Cromarty U.K. 14 D4 57.40N 4.01W
Cromarty Firth *est.* U.K. 14 D4 57.41N 4.10W
Cromer U.K. 12 I4 52.56N 1.40E
Crooked I. Bahamas 87 J4 22.45N 74.00W
Crookhaven Rep. of Ire. 15 B1 51.28N 9.45W
Croom Rep. of Ire. 15 C2 52.30N 8.42W
Crosby U.K. 12 C6 54.10N 4.32W
Cross Fell *mtn.* U.K. 12 E6 54.43N 2.28W
Cross River *d.* Nigeria 103 F2 5.45N 8.25E
Crotone Italy 47 H3 39.05N 17.06E
Crowsnest Pass Canada 80 G2 49.40N114.41W
Croyde U.K. 13 C3 51.09N 4.12W
Croydon U.K. 13 H3 51.20N 0.05E
Crozet Is. Indian Oc. 107 L2 46.27S 52.00E
Cruz, Cabo *c.* Cuba 87 I3 19.52N 77.44W
Csurgó Hungary 49 H3 46.16N 17.06E
Cuando *r.* Africa 99 C3 18.30S 23.30E
Cuango *r. see* Kwango *r.* Angola 99
Cuanza *r.* Angola 99 B4 9.22S 13.09E
Cuba C. America 87 H4 22.00N 79.00W
Cubango *r. see* Okavango *r.* Angola 99
Cuckfield U.K. 13 G3 51.01N 0.10W
Cúcuta Colombia 88 B8 7.55N 72.31W
Cuddalore India 63 E2 11.43N 79.46E
Cuenca Ecuador 88 B7 2.54S 79.00W
Cuenca Spain 43 D4 40.04N 2.07W
Cuenca, Serranía de *mts.* Spain 43 E4 40.25N 2.00W
Cuernavaca Mexico 86 E3 18.57N 99.15W
Cuiabá Brazil 88 D6 15.32S 56.05W
Cuiabá *r.* Brazil 88 D6 17.00S 56.35W
Cuillin Hills U.K. 14 B4 57.12N 6.13W
Cuito *r.* Angola 99 C3 18.01S 20.46E
Culemborg Neth. 39 D3 51.57N 5.14E
Culiacán Mexico 86 C4 24.50N107.23W
Cullen U.K. 14 F4 57.42N 2.50W
Cullera Spain 43 E3 39.10N 0.15W
Cullin Sound U.K. 14 B4 57.05N 6.20W
Culloden Moor *f.* U.K. 14 E4 57.30N 3.59W
Cumaná Venezuela 88 C9 10.29N 64.12W
Cumberland U.S.A. 83 K4 39.40N 78.47W
Cumberland *r.* U.S.A. 83 I4 37.16N 88.25W
Cumberland, L. U.S.A. 83 I4 37.00N 85.00W
Cumberland Sd. Canada 81 L4 65.00N 65.30W
Cumbernauld U.K. 14 D2 55.57N 4.00W
Cumbria *d.* U.K. 12 E6 54.30N 3.00W
Cumbrian Mts. U.K. 12 D6 54.32N 3.05W
Cumnock U.K. 14 D2 55.27N 4.15W
Cunene *r.* Angola 99 B3 17.15S 11.50E
Cuneo Italy 46 C6 44.22N 7.32E
Cupar U.K. 14 E3 56.19N 3.01W
Curaçao *i.* Neth. Antilles 87 K2 12.15N 69.00W
Curicó Chile 89 B4 35.00S 71.15W
Curitiba Brazil 89 E5 25.24S 49.16W
Currane, Lough Rep. of Ire. 15 A1 51.49N 10.08W
Cushendall U.K. 15 E5 55.06N 6.05W
Cuttack India 63 F4 20.26N 85.56E
Cuxhaven W. Germany 48 D6 53.52N 8.42E
Cuzco Peru 88 B6 13.32S 72.10W
Čvrsnica *mtn.* Yugo. 47 H5 43.35N 17.33E
Cwmbran U.K. 13 D3 51.39N 3.01W
Cyclades *is.* Greece 47 L2 37.00N 25.00E
Cyprus Asia 60 D4 35.00N 33.00E
Cyrenaica *f.* Libya 101 E5 31.00N 22.10E
Czechoslovakia Europe 48 G4 49.30N 15.00E
Czeremcha Poland 49 K6 52.32N 23.15E
Częstochowa Poland 49 I5 50.49N 19.07E

D

Dabakala Ivory Coast 102 D2 8.19N 4.24W
Dabola Guinea 102 B3 10.48N 11.02W
Dachau W. Germany 48 E4 48.15N 11.26E
Daet Phil. 69 G6 14.07N122.58E
Dagana Senegal 102 A4 16.28N 15.35W
Dagupan Phil. 69 G7 16.02N120.21E
Da Hinggan Ling *mts.* China 67 J6 50.00N122.10E
Dahme W. Germany 38 E2 54.12N 11.04E
Dajing China 67 J3 28.24N121.08E
Dakar Senegal 102 A3 14.38N 17.27W
Dakhla W. Sahara 100 A4 23.43N 15.57W
Dakhla Oasis Egypt 60 C2 25.30N 29.00E
Dal *r.* Sweden 50 D3 60.38N 17.05E
Da Lat Vietnam 68 D6 11.56N108.25E
Dalbeattie U.K. 14 E1 54.54N 3.50W
Dali China 66 F2 25.42N100.11E
Dalkeith U.K. 14 E2 55.54N 3.04W
Dallas U.S.A. 83 G3 32.47N 96.48W
Dalmally U.K. 14 D3 56.24N 4.59W
Dalmatia *f.* Yugo. 47 H5 43.30N 17.00E
Dalmellington U.K. 14 D2 55.18N 4.23W
Dalnerechensk U.S.S.R. 67 L6 45.55N133.45E
Daloa Ivory Coast 102 C2 6.56N 6.28W
Daltonganj India 63 F4 24.02N 84.07E
Dalwhinnie U.K. 14 D3 56.55N 4.15W
Damā, Wādī *r.* Saudi Arabia 60 D2 27.04N 35.48E
Damān India 63 D4 20.25N 72.58E
Damanhûr Egypt 60 C3 31.03N 30.28E
Damar *i.* Indonesia 69 H2 7.10S128.30E
Damascus Syria 60 E4 33.30N 36.19E
Damaturu Nigeria 103 G3 11.49N 11.50E
Dammam Saudi Arabia 61 H2 26.23N 50.08E
Dampier Str. Pacific Oc. 69 I3 0.30S130.50E
Danakil *f.* Ethiopia 101 G3 13.00N 41.00E
Da Nang Vietnam 68 D7 16.04N108.14E
Dandong China 67 J5 40.06N124.25E
Danger Is. Cook Is. 74 J6 10.53S165.49W
Danlí Honduras 87 G2 14.02N 86.30W
Danube *r.* Europe 49 N2 45.26N 29.38E
Danube, Mouths of the *f.* Romania 49 N2 45.05N 29.45E
Danville U.S.A. 83 K4 36.34N 79.25W
Da Qaidam China 66 E4 37.44N 95.08E
Darabani Romania 49 M4 48.11N 26.35E
Dārān Iran 61 H4 33.00N 50.27E
Darbhanga India 63 F5 26.10N 85.54E
Dardanelles *str.* Turkey 47 M4 40.15N 26.30E
Dar es Salaam Tanzania 99 D4 6.51S 39.18E
Darfur *mts.* Sudan 101 E3 12.30N 24.00E
Darhan Suma Mongolia 66 G6 49.34N106.23E
Darien, G. of Colombia 88 B8 9.20N 77.00W
Darjeeling India 63 F5 27.02N 88.20E
Darling *r.* Australia 71 D2 34.05S141.57E
Darlington U.K. 12 F6 54.33N 1.33W
Darmstadt W. Germany 48 D4 49.52N 8.30E
Darss *pen.* E. Germany 38 F2 54.26N 12.30E
Dart *r.* U.K. 13 D2 50.24N 3.38W
Dartmoor Forest *hills* U.K. 13 D2 50.33N 3.55W
Dartmouth U.K. 13 D2 50.21N 3.35W
Dartry Mts. Rep. of Ire. 15 C4 54.21N 8.25W
Daru P.N.G. 69 K2 9.05S143.10E
Darvel B. Malaysia 68 F4 4.40N118.30E
Darwen U.K. 12 E5 53.41N 2.29W
Darwin Australia 71 C4 12.23S130.44E
Dasht *r.* Pakistan 62 B4 25.07N 61.45E
Dasht-e Kavīr *des.* Iran 101 H5 34.40N 55.00E
Dasht-e Lūt *des.* Iran 101 H5 31.30N 58.00E
Dashtiari Iran 61 K2 25.29N 61.15E
Dasht-i-Margo *des.* Afghan. 62 B5 30.45N 63.00E
Dassow E. Germany 38 E1 53.54N 11.00E
Datong China 67 H5 40.12N113.12E
Datu, Tanjung *c.* Malaysia 68 D4 2.00N109.30E
Datu Piang Phil. 69 G5 7.02N124.30E
Daugavpils U.S.S.R. 50 F1 55.52N 26.31E
Daulatabad Iran 61 J3 28.19N 56.40E
Daun W. Germany 39 E2 50.11N 6.50E
Dauphin Canada 81 H3 51.09N100.05W
Dauphiné, Alpes du *mts.* France 42 G3 44.35N 5.45E
Dāvangere India 63 D3 14.30N 75.52E
Davao Phil. 69 H5 7.05N125.38E
Davao G. Phil. 69 H5 6.30N126.00E
Davenport U.S.A. 83 H5 41.40N 90.36W
Daventry U.K. 13 F4 52.17N 1.11W
David Panama 87 H1 8.26N 82.26W
Davis Str. N. America 81 M4 66.00N 58.00W
Davos Switz. 48 D3 46.47N 9.50E
Dawlish U.K. 13 D2 50.36N 3.27W
Dawna Range *mts.* Asia 68 B7 16.10N 98.30E
Dawson Canada 80 E4 64.04N139.24W
Dawson Creek *town* Canada 80 F3 55.44N120.15W
Dax France 42 D2 43.43N 1.03W
Dayton U.S.A. 83 J4 39.45N 84.10W
Daytona Beach *town* U.S.A. 83 J2 29.11N 81.01W
De Aar R.S.A. 99 C1 30.39S 24.00E
Dead Sea Jordan 60 D3 31.25N 35.30E
Deal U.K. 13 I3 51.13N 1.25E
Death Valley *f.* U.S.A. 82 C4 36.00N116.45W
Deauville France 42 E5 49.21N 0.04E
Debrecen Hungary 49 J3 47.30N 21.37E
Decatur U.S.A. 83 I4 39.44N 88.57W
Deccan *f.* India 63 D3 18.30N 77.30E
Děčín Czech. 48 G5 50.48N 14.15E
Dee *r.* D. and G. U.K. 14 D1 54.50N 4.05W
Dee *r.* Grampian U.K. 14 F4 57.07N 2.04W
Dee *r.* Wales U.K. 12 D5 53.13N 3.05W
Dehra Dūn India 63 E5 30.19N 78.00E
Deinze Belgium 39 B2 50.59N 3.32E
Deir-ez-Zor Syria 60 F4 35.20N 40.08E
Dej Romania 49 K3 47.08N 23.55E
Delano U.S.A. 82 C4 35.45N119.16W
Delaware *d.* U.S.A 83 K4 39.00N 75.30W
Delaware B. U.S.A. 83 K4 39.00N 75.05W
Delft Neth. 39 C4 52.01N 4.23E
Delfzijl Neth. 39 E5 53.20N 6.56E
Delhi India 63 D5 28.40N 77.14E
Delicias Mexico 86 C5 28.10N105.30W
Delmenhorst W. Germany 48 D6 53.03N 8.37E
De Long Str. U.S.S.R. 53 O4 70.00N178.00E
Del Rio U.S.A. 82 F2 29.23N100.56W
Delta U.S.A. 82 D4 39.22N112.35W
Demavend *mtn.* Iran 101 H5 35.47N 52.04E
Demer *r.* Belgium 39 D2 50.59N 4.42E
Demmin E. Germany 38 G1 53.55N 13.03E
Denbigh U.K. 12 D5 53.11N 3.25W
Den Burg Neth. 39 C5 53.03N 4.47E
Dendermonde Belgium 39 C3 51.01N 4.07E
Dendre *r.* Belgium 39 C3 51.01N 4.07E
Den Helder Neth. 39 C4 52.58N 4.46E
Denia Spain 43 F3 38.51N 0.07E
Denizli Turkey 60 C5 37.46N 29.05E
Denmark Europe 38 B3 55.00N 10.00E
Denmark Str. Greenland/Iceland 76 R8 66.00N 25.00W
Den Oever Neth. 39 C4 52.56N 5.01E
Denpasar Indonesia 68 F2 8.40S115.14E
Denver U.S.A. 82 F4 39.45N104.58W
Deo *r.* Cameroon 103 G2 8.33N 12.45E
Deogarh India 63 F4 21.22N 84.45E
Dêqên China 66 F3 28.45N 98.58E
Dera Ghāzi Khān Pakistan 63 C5 30.05N 70.44E
Dera Ismāil Khān Pakistan 63 C5 31.51N 70.56E
Derbent U.S.S.R. 61 H6 42.03N 48.18E
Derby U.K. 12 F4 52.55N 1.28W
Derbyshire *d.* U.K. 12 F4 52.55N 1.28W
Derg, Lough Donegal Rep. of Ire. 15 D4 54.37N 7.55W
Derg, Lough Tipperary Rep. of Ire. 15 C2 52.57N 8.18W
Derna Libya 101 E5 32.45N 22.39E
Derrynasaggart Mts. Rep. of Ire. 15 B1 51.58N 9.15W
Derryveagh Mts. Rep. of Ire. 15 C4 55.00N 8.10W
Derwent *r.* Cumria U.K. 12 D6 54.38N 3.34W
Derwent *r.* Derbys U.K. 12 F4 52.52N 1.19W
Derwent *r.* N. Yorks. U.K. 12 G5 53.44N 0.57W
Desappointement, Îles du *is.* Pacific Oc. 75 L6 14.02S141.24W
Deseado Argentina 89 C3 47.44S 65.56W
Des Moines U.S.A. 83 H5 41.35N 93.35W
Desna *r.* U.S.S.R. 49 O5 50.32N 30.37E
Dessau E. Germany 48 F5 51.51N 12.15E
Dessye Ethiopia 101 F3 11.05N 39.40E
Detroit U.S.A. 83 J5 42.23N 83.05W
Deurne Belgium 39 C3 51.13N 4.26E
Deva Romania 49 K2 45.54N 22.55E
Deventer Neth. 39 E4 52.15N 6.10E
Deveron *r.* U.K. 14 F4 57.40N 2.30W
Devil's Bridge U.K. 13 D4 52.23N 3.50W
Devils Lake *town* U.S.A. 82 G6 48.08N 98.50W
Devizes U.K. 13 F3 51.22N 2.00W
Devon *d.* U.K. 13 D2 50.50N 3.40W
Devon I. Canada 81 J5 75.00N 86.00W
Devonport Australia 71 D1 41.09S146.16E
Devrez *r.* Turkey 60 D6 41.07N 34.25E
Dewsbury U.K. 12 F5 53.42N 1.37W
Dezfūl Iran 61 H4 32.24N 48.27E
Dezhou China 67 I4 37.29N116.11E
Dhahran Saudi Arabia 61 H2 26.18N 50.08E
Dhaka Bangla. 63 G4 23.42N 90.22E
Dhānbād India 63 F4 23.47N 86.32E
Dhaulāgiri *mtn.* Nepal 63 E5 28.39N 83.28E
Dhulia India 63 D4 20.52N 74.50E
Dibbagh, Jebel *mtn.* Saudi Arabia 60 D2 27.51N 35.43E
Dibrugarh India 63 G5 27.29N 94.56E
Dickinson U.S.A. 82 F6 46.54N102.48W
Didcot U.K. 13 F3 51.36N 1.14W
Die France 42 G3 44.45N 5.23E
Diekirch Lux. 39 E1 49.52N 6.10E
Dien Bien Phu Vietnam 68 C8 21.23N103.02E
Dieppe France 42 E5 49.55N 1.05E
Dieren Neth. 39 E4 52.03N 6.06E
Diest Belgium 39 D2 50.59N 5.03E
Dieuze France 42 H5 48.49N 6.43E
Digne France 42 H3 44.05N 6.14E
Digoel *r.* Indonesia 69 J2 7.10S139.08E
Dijle *r.* Belgium 39 C3 51.02N 4.25E
Dijon France 42 G4 47.20N 5.02E
Dikili Turkey 47 M3 39.05N 26.52E
Dikwa Nigeria 103 G3 12.01N 13.55E
Dili Indonesia 69 H2 8.35S125.35E
Dillon U.S.A. 82 D6 45.14N112.38W
Dimbokro Ivory Coast 102 D2 6.43N 4.46W
Dîmboviţa *r.* Romania 49 M2 44.13N 26.22E
Dimitrovgrad Bulgaria 47 L5 42.01N 25.34E
Dimitrovo Bulgaria 47 K5 42.35N 23.03E
Dinagat *i.* Phil. 69 H6 10.15N125.30E
Dinan France 42 C5 48.27N 2.02W
Dinant Belgium 39 C2 50.16N 4.55E
Dinaric Alps *mts.* Yugo. 47 H6 44.00N 16.30E
Dindigul India 63 D2 10.23N 78.00E
Dingle Rep. of Ire. 15 A2 52.08N 10.19W
Dingle B. Rep. of Ire. 15 A2 52.05N 10.12W
Dingwall U.K. 14 D4 57.35N 4.26W
Diourbel Senegal 102 A3 14.30N 16.10W
Dipolog Phil. 69 G5 8.34N123.28E
Diredawa Ethiopia 101 G2 9.35N 41.50E
Disappointment, L. Australia 71 B3 23.30S122.55E
Disko Is. Greenland 81 M4 69.45N 53.00W
Disna *r.* U.S.S.R. 50 G1 55.30N 28.20E
Diss U.K. 13 I4 52.23N 1.06E
District of Columbia *d.* U.S.A. 83 K4 38.55N 77.00W
Distrito Federal *d.* Mexico 86 E3 19.20N 99.10W
Diu India 63 C4 20.41N 70.59E
Divrigi Turkey 60 E5 39.23N 38.06E

E

Gelderland d. Neth. **39 E4** 52.05N 6.00E
Geldern W. Germany **39 E3** 51.31N 6.19E
Geleen Neth. **39 D2** 50.58N 5.51E
Gelligaer U.K. **13 D3** 51.40N 3.19W
Gelsenkirchen W. Germany **39 F3** 51.30N 7.05E
Gemas Malaysia **68 C4** 2.35N102.35E
Gembloux Belgium **39 C2** 50.34N 4.42E
Gemlik Turkey **60 C6** 40.26N 29.10E
Genarp Sweden **38 G3** 55.37N 13.26E
Geneina Sudan **101 E3** 13.27N 22.30E
General Santos Phil. **69 H5** 6.05N125.15E
Geneva Switz. **48 C3** 46.13N 6.09E
Geneva, L. Switz. **48 C3** 46.30N 6.30E
Genil r. Spain **43 C2** 37.42N 5.20W
Genoa Italy **46 D6** 44.24N 8.54E
Genoa, G. of Italy **46 D6** 44.12N 8.55E
Gent Belgium **39 B3** 51.02N 3.42E
George r. Canada **81 L3** 58.30N 66.00W
Georgetown Cayman Is. **87 H3** 19.20N 81.23W
Georgetown Guyana **88 D8** 6.46N 58.10W
George Town Malaysia **68 C5** 5.30N100.16E
Georgia d. U.S.A. **83 J3** 33.00N 83.00W
Georgian B. Canada **81 J2** 45.15N 80.45W
Georgia S.S.R. d. U.S.S.R. **52 D2** 42.30N 43.00E
Gera E. Germany **48 F5** 50.51N 12.11E
Geraardsbergen Belgium **39 B2** 50.47N 3.53E
Geraldton Australia **71 A3** 28.49S114.36E
Gerlachovka mtn. Czech. **32 J4** 49.10N 20.10E
Getafe Spain **43 D4** 40.18N 3.44W
Gete r. Belgium **39 D2** 50.58N 5.07E
Geyve Turkey **60 C6** 40.32N 30.18E
Gezira f. Sudan **101 F3** 14.30N 33.00E
Ghadames Libya **100 C5** 30.10N 9.30E
Ghāghra r. India **63 F4** 25.45N 84.50E
Ghana Africa **103 D2** 8.00N 1.00W
Ghardaïa Algeria **100 C5** 32.20N 3.40E
Ghāt Libya **100 D4** 24.59N 10.11E
Ghaznī Afghan. **62 C6** 33.33N 68.28E
Gheorghe-Gheorghiu-Dej Romania **49 M3** 46.14N 26.44E
Gia Dinh Vietnam **68 D6** 10.48N106.43E
Gialo Libya **101 E4** 29.00N 21.30E
Giant's Causeway U.K. **14 B2** 55.14N 6.31W
Gibraltar Europe **43 C2** 36.07N 5.22W
Gibraltar, Str. of Africa/Europe **43 C1** 36.00N 5.25W
Gibraltar Pt. U.K. **12 H5** 53.06N 0.21E
Giessen W. Germany **48 D5** 50.35N 8.42E
Gieten Neth. **39 E5** 53.01N 6.45E
Gifu Japan **70 C4** 35.27N136.50E
Gigha i. U.K. **14 C2** 55.40N 5.45W
Giglio i. Italy **46 E5** 42.21N 10.53E
Gijón Spain **43 C5** 43.32N 5.40W
Gila r. U.S.A. **82 D3** 32.45N114.30W
Gilbert Is. Kiribati **74 H7** 2.00S175.00E
Gilehdar Iran **61 I2** 27.36N 52.42E
Gilgit Jammu & Kashmir **63 D6** 35.54N 74.20E
Gill, Lough Rep. of Ire. **15 C4** 54.15N 8.25W
Gilleleje Denmark **38 F4** 56.07N 12.19E
Gillingham U.K. **13 H3** 51.24N 0.33E
Gimbala, Jebel mtn. Sudan **101 E3** 13.00N 24.20E
Girdle Ness c. U.K. **14 F4** 57.09N 2.02W
Giresun Turkey **60 E6** 40.55N 38.25E
Girona Spain **43 G4** 41.59N 2.49E
Gironde r. France **42 D3** 45.35N 1.00W
Girvan U.K. **14 D2** 55.15N 4.51W
Giurgiu Romania **49 L1** 43.52N 25.58E
Givet France **42 G6** 50.08N 4.49E
Gizhiga U.S.S.R. **53 N3** 62.00N160.34E
Gizhiga G. U.S.S.R. **53 N3** 61.00N158.00E
Gjövik Norway **50 B3** 60.47N 10.41E
Glacier Peak mtn. U.S.A. **82 B6** 48.07N121.06W
Gladstone Australia **71 E3** 23.52S151.16E
Glåma r. Norway **50 B2** 59.15N 10.55E
Glan r. W. Germany **39 F1** 49.46N 7.43E
Glanaman U.K. **13 D3** 51.48N 3.53W
Glandorf W. Germany **39 G4** 52.05N 8.00E
Glasgow U.K. **14 D2** 55.52N 4.15W
Glasgow U.S.A. **82 E6** 48.12N106.37W
Glastonbury U.K. **13 E3** 51.09N 2.43W
Glen Affric f. U.K. **14 D4** 57.18N 4.55W
Glénans, Îles de is. France **42 B4** 47.43N 3.57W
Glenarm U.K. **15 F4** 54.58N 5.59W
Glen Coe f. U.K. **14 D3** 56.40N 4.55W
Glendive U.S.A. **82 F6** 47.08N104.42W
Glengarriff Rep. of Ire. **15 B1** 51.46N 9.33W
Glen Garry f. U.K. **14 C4** 57.03N 5.05W
Glen Hd. Rep. of Ire. **15 C4** 54.44N 8.46W
Glen Mòr f. U.K. **14 D4** 57.15N 4.30W
Glen Moriston f. U.K. **14 D4** 57.10N 4.50W
Glenrothes U.K. **14 E3** 56.12N 3.10W
Glenshee f. U.K. **14 E3** 56.50N 3.28W
Glen Spean f. U.K. **14 D3** 56.57N 4.35W
Glittertind mtn. Norway **50 B3** 61.30N 8.20E
Gliwice Poland **49 I5** 50.17N 18.40E
Głogów Poland **48 H5** 51.40N 16.06E
Gloucester U.K. **13 E3** 51.52N 2.15W
Gloucestershire d. U.K. **13 E3** 51.45N 2.00W
Gmünd Austria **48 G4** 48.47N 14.59E
Gniezno Poland **49 H6** 52.32N 17.32E
Gnoien E. Germany **38 F1** 53.58N 12.47E
Goa d. India **63 D3** 15.30N 74.00E
Goat Fell mtn. U.K. **14 C2** 55.37N 5.12W
Gobabis Namibia **99 B2** 22.30S 18.58E
Gobi des. Asia **66 F5** 43.30N103.30E
Godalming U.K. **13 G3** 51.10N 0.39W
Godāvari r. India **63 E3** 16.40N 82.15E
Godhavn Greenland **81 M4** 69.20N 53.30W
Godhra India **63 D4** 22.49N 73.40E
Godthåb Greenland **81 M4** 64.10N 51.40W
Gogra r. see Ghāghra India **63**
Goiânia Brazil **88 E6** 16.43S 49.18W
Göksun Turkey **60 E5** 38.03N 36.30E
Gol Norway **50 B3** 60.43N 8.55E
Golden Rep. of Ire. **15 D2** 52.30N 7.59W
Golden Vale f. Rep. of Ire. **15 C2** 52.32N 8.10W
Golfito Costa Rica **87 H1** 8.42N 83.10W
Golling Austria **48 F3** 47.36N 13.10E
Golovanevsk U.S.S.R. **49 O4** 48.25N 30.30E
Golspie U.K. **14 E4** 57.58N 3.58W
Gombe Nigeria **103 G3** 10.17N 11.20E
Gomel U.S.S.R. **49 O6** 52.25N 31.00E
Gómez Palacio Mexico **86 D5** 25.39N103.30W
Gonaïves Haiti **87 J3** 19.29N 72.42W
Gonâve, G. of Haiti **87 J3** 19.20N 73.00W
Gonâve I. Haiti **87 J3** 18.50N 73.00W
Gondar Ethiopia **101 F3** 12.39N 37.29E
Gongga Shan mtn. China **66 F3** 29.30N101.30E
Gongola d. Nigeria **103 G2** 8.40N 11.30E
Gongola r. Nigeria **103 G2** 9.30N 12.06E
Good Hope, C. of R.S.A. **99 B1** 34.20S 18.25E
Goole U.K. **12 G5** 53.44N 0.52W
Goose L. U.S.A. **82 B5** 41.55N120.25W
Göppingen W. Germany **48 D4** 48.43N 9.39E
Gorakhpur India **63 E5** 26.45N 83.23E
Gori U.S.S.R. **61 G6** 41.59N 44.05E
Gorinchem Neth. **39 C3** 51.50N 4.59E
Gorizia Italy **46 F6** 45.58N 13.37E
Gorki U.S.S.R. **52 D3** 56.20N 44.00E
Gorki Resr. U.S.S.R. **33 N6** 56.49N 43.00E
Görlitz E. Germany **48 G5** 51.09N 15.00E
Gorlovka U.S.S.R. **52 D2** 48.17N 38.05E
Gorodok U.S.S.R. **49 K4** 49.48N 23.39E
Goroka P.N.G. **69 L2** 6.02S145.22E
Gorontalo Indonesia **69 G4** 0.33N123.05E
Gort Rep. of Ire. **15 C3** 53.03N 8.50W
Gorzów Wielkopolski Poland **48 G6** 52.42N 15.12E
Goslar W. Germany **48 E5** 51.54N 10.25E
Gospić Yugo. **46 G6** 44.34N 15.23E
Gosport U.K. **13 F2** 50.48N 1.05W
Göta r. Sweden **32 H6** 57.42N 11.52E
Göta Canal Sweden **50 B2** 57.50N 11.50E
Göteborg Sweden **50 B2** 57.45N 12.00E
Gotha E. Germany **48 E5** 50.57N 10.43E
Gotland i. Sweden **50 D2** 57.30N 18.30E
Göttingen W. Germany **48 D5** 51.32N 9.57E
Gottwaldov Czech. **49 H4** 49.13N 17.41E
Gouda Neth. **39 C4** 52.01N 4.43E
Gough I. Atlantic Oc. **108 I2** 41.00S 10.00W
Goulburn Australia **71 D2** 34.47S149.43E
Goundam Mali **102 D4** 16.27N 3.39W
Gourdon France **42 E3** 44.45N 1.22E
Gouré Niger **103 G3** 13.59N 10.15E
Gourma-Rharous Mali **103 D4** 16.58N 1.50W
Gournay France **42 E5** 49.29N 1.44E
Governador Valadares Brazil **89 E6** 18.51S 42.00W
Gower pen. U.K. **13 C3** 51.35N 4.10W
Gozo i. Malta **46 G2** 36.03N 14.16E
Gracias á Dios, Cabo c. Honduras/Nicaragua **87 H2** 15.00N 83.10W
Grafton U.S.A. **83 G6** 48.28N 97.25W
Grahamstown R.S.A. **99 C1** 33.19S 26.32E
Graiguenamanagh Rep. of Ire. **15 E2** 52.32N 6.59W
Gram Denmark **38 C3** 55.17N 9.04E
Grampian d. U.K. **14 F4** 57.22N 2.35W
Grampian Mts. U.K. **14 D3** 56.55N 4.00W
Granada Nicaragua **87 G2** 11.58N 85.59W
Granada Spain **43 D2** 37.10N 3.35W
Gran Canaria i. Canary Is. **100 A4** 28.00N 15.30W
Gran Chaco f. S. America **89 C5** 23.30S 60.00W
Grand Bahama I. Bahamas **87 I5** 26.35N 78.00W
Grand Bassam Ivory Coast **102 D2** 5.14N 3.45W
Grand Canyon f. U.S.A. **82 D4** 36.15N113.00W
Grand Canyon town U.S.A. **82 D4** 36.04N112.07W
Grand Cayman i. Cayman Is. **87 H3** 19.20N 81.30W
Grande, Bahía b. Argentina **89 C2** 50.45S 68.00W
Grande Prairie town Canada **80 G3** 55.10N118.52W
Grand Falls town Canada **81 M2** 48.57N 55.40W
Grand Forks U.S.A. **83 G6** 47.57N 97.05W
Grand Island town U.S.A. **82 G5** 40.56N 98.21W
Grand Junction U.S.A. **82 E4** 39.04N108.33W
Grand Marais U.S.A. **83 H6** 47.55N 90.15W
Grândola Portugal **43 A3** 38.10N 8.34W
Grand Rapids town U.S.A. **83 I5** 42.57N 85.40W
Grand Teton mtn. U.S.A. **82 D5** 43.45N110.50W
Grangemouth U.K. **14 E3** 56.01N 3.44W
Granite Peak mtn. U.S.A. **82 E6** 45.10N109.50W
Grankulla Finland **50 F3** 60.12N 24.45E
Granollers Spain **43 G4** 41.37N 2.18E
Gran Paradiso mtn. Italy **46 C6** 45.31N 7.15E
Grantham U.K. **12 G4** 52.55N 0.39W
Grantown-on-Spey U.K. **14 E4** 57.19N 3.38W
Grants Pass town U.S.A. **82 B5** 42.26N123.20W
Granville France **42 D5** 48.50N 1.35W
Grasse France **42 H2** 43.40N 6.56E
Gråsten Denmark **38 C2** 54.56N 9.37E
Grave Neth. **39 D3** 51.45N 5.45E
Grave, Pointe de c. France **42 D3** 45.35N 1.04W
Gravesend U.K. **13 H3** 51.27N 0.24E
Gray France **42 G4** 47.27N 5.35E
Grays U.K. **13 H3** 51.29N 0.20E
Graz Austria **48 G3** 47.05N 15.22E
Great Abaco I. Bahamas **87 I5** 26.30N 77.00W
Great Artesian Basin f. Australia **71 D3** 26.30S143.02E
Great Australian Bight Australia **71 B2** 33.20S130.00E
Great Barrier Reef f. Australia **71 D4** 16.30S146.30E
Great Basin f. U.S.A. **82 C5** 39.00N115.30W
Great Bear L. Canada **80 F4** 66.00N120.00W
Great Bend town U.S.A. **82 G4** 38.22N 98.47W
Great Bitter L. Egypt **60 D3** 30.20N 32.50E
Great Blasket I. Rep. of Ire. **15 A2** 52.05N 10.32W
Great Coco i. Burma **68 A6** 14.10N 93.25E
Great Dividing Range mts. Australia **71 D2** 33.00S151.00E
Great Driffield U.K. **12 G6** 54.01N 0.24W
Greater Antilles is. C. America **87 I3** 17.00N 70.00W
Greater London d. U.K. **13 G3** 51.31N 0.06W
Greater Manchester d. U.K. **12 E5** 53.30N 2.18W
Great Exuma i. Bahamas **87 I4** 23.00N 76.00W
Great Falls town U.S.A. **82 D6** 47.30N111.16W
Great Fish r. Namibia **94 D2** 28.07S 17.10E
Great Inagua I. Bahamas **87 J4** 21.00N 73.20W
Great Irgiz r. U.S.S.R. **33 O5** 52.00N 48.00E
Great Karoo f. R.S.A. **99 C1** 32.50S 22.30E
Great Lakes N. America **106 E7** 47.00N 83.00W
Great Malvern U.K. **13 E4** 52.05N 2.21W
Great Nicobar i. India **63 G1** 7.00N 93.50E
Great Ouse r. U.K. **12 H4** 52.47N 0.23E
Great Plains f. N. America **76 J6** 45.00N107.00W
Great Rift Valley f. Africa **94 F4** 7.00S 33.00E
Great St. Bernard Pass Italy/Switz. **48 C2** 45.52N 7.11E
Great Salt L. U.S.A. **82 D5** 41.10N112.40W
Great Sandy Desert Australia **71 B3** 22.00S125.00E
Great Sandy Desert Saudi Arabia **60 F3** 28.40N 41.30E
Great Slave L. Canada **80 G4** 61.30N114.20W
Great Victoria Desert Australia **71 B3** 29.00S127.30E
Great Whale r. Canada **81 K3** 55.28N 77.45W
Great Whernside mtn. U.K. **12 F6** 54.09N 1.59W
Great Yarmouth U.K. **13 I4** 52.40N 1.45E
Great Zab r. Iraq **61 F4** 35.57N 43.20E
Gréboun, Mt. Niger **94 C7** 20.01N 8.35E
Gredos, Sierra de mts. Spain **43 C4** 40.18N 5.20W
Gredstedbro Denmark **38 B3** 55.24N 8.43E
Greece Europe **47 J3** 39.00N 22.00E
Greeley U.S.A. **82 F5** 40.26N104.43W
Green r. U.S.A. **82 E4** 38.20N109.53W
Green Bay town U.S.A. **83 I5** 44.32N 88.00W
Greenland N. America **81 N5** 68.00N 45.00W
Greenlaw U.K. **14 F2** 55.43N 2.22W
Greenock U.K. **14 D2** 55.57N 4.45W
Greenore Pt. Rep. of Ire. **15 E2** 52.14N 6.20W
Greensboro U.S.A. **83 K4** 36.03N 79.50W
Greenville Liberia **102 C2** 5.01N 9.03W
Greenville Miss. U.S.A. **83 H3** 33.23N 91.03W
Greenville S.C. U.S.A. **83 J3** 34.52N 82.25W
Greifswald E. Germany **48 F7** 54.06N 13.24E
Grenå Denmark **38 D4** 56.25N 10.53E
Grenada i. Windward Is. **87 L2** 12.15N 61.45W
Grenade France **42 E2** 43.47N 1.10E
Grenen c. Denmark **38 D5** 57.45N 10.35E
Grenoble France **42 G3** 45.11N 5.43E
Gretna U.K. **14 E2** 55.01N 3.05W
Grevesmühlen E. Germany **38 E1** 53.51N 11.12E
Grey Range mts. Australia **71 D3** 28.30S142.15E
Greystones Rep. of Ire. **15 E3** 53.09N 6.05W
Grimmen E. Germany **38 G2** 54.08N 13.07E
Grimsby U.K. **12 G5** 53.35N 0.05W
Grimstrup Denmark **38 B3** 55.32N 8.40E
Grimsvötn mtn. Iceland **50 J7** 64.30N 17.10W
Grindsted Denmark **38 B3** 55.45N 8.57E
Grodno U.S.S.R. **49 K6** 53.40N 23.50E
Grodzisk Poland **48 H6** 52.14N 16.22E
Grodzyanka U.S.S.R. **49 N6** 53.30N 28.41E
Groenlo Neth. **39 E4** 52.02N 6.36E
Groix, Île de France **42 C4** 47.38N 3.26W
Groningen Neth. **39 E5** 53.13N 6.35E
Groningen d. Neth. **39 E5** 53.15N 6.45E
Groote Eylandt i. Australia **71 C4** 14.00S136.30E
Grootfontein Namibia **99 B3** 19.32S 18.05E
Grossenbrode W. Germany **48 E7** 54.23N 11.07E
Grosseto Italy **46 E5** 42.46N 11.08E
Gross Glockner mtn. Austria **48 F3** 47.05N 12.50E
Grote Nete r. Belgium **39 C3** 51.07N 4.20E
Groznyy U.S.S.R. **52 D2** 43.21N 45.42E
Grudziądz Poland **49 I6** 53.29N 18.45E
Guadalajara Mexico **86 D4** 20.30N103.20W
Guadalajara Spain **43 D4** 40.37N 3.10W
Guadalcanal i. Solomon Is. **71 E5** 9.30S160.00E
Guadalete r. Spain **43 B2** 36.37N 6.15W
Guadalmena r. Spain **43 D3** 38.00N 3.50W
Guadalquivir r. Spain **43 B2** 36.50N 6.20W
Guadalupe Mexico **86 D5** 25.41N100.15W
Guadalupe, Sierra de mts. Spain **43 C3** 39.30N 5.25W
Guadalupe I. Mexico **82 C2** 29.00N118.25W
Guadarrama r. Spain **43 C3** 39.55N 4.10W
Guadarrama, Sierra de mts. Spain **43 D4** 41.00N 3.50W
Guadeloupe i. Leeward Is. **87 L3** 16.20N 61.40W
Guadiana r. Portugal **43 B2** 37.10N 7.36W
Guadix Spain **43 D2** 37.19N 3.08W
Guajará Mirim Brazil **88 C6** 10.50S 65.21W
Guam i. Mariana Is. **74 E9** 13.30N144.40E
Guanajuato Mexico **86 D4** 21.00N101.16W
Guanajuato d. Mexico **86 D4** 21.00N101.00W
Guane Cuba **87 H4** 22.13N 84.07W
Guangdong d. China **67 H2** 23.00N113.00E
Guanghua China **67 H4** 32.30N111.50E
Guangxi Zhuangzu d. China **67 H2** 23.50N109.00E
Guangzhou China **67 H2** 23.20N113.30E
Guantánamo Cuba **87 I4** 20.09N 75.14W
Guaporé r. Brazil **88 C6** 12.00S 65.15W
Guarda Portugal **43 B4** 40.32N 7.17W
Guardafui, C. Somali Rep. **101 H3** 12.00N 51.30E
Guardo Spain **43 C5** 42.47N 4.50W
Guatemala C. America **86 F3** 15.40N 90.00W
Guatemala City Guatemala **86 F2** 14.38N 90.22W
Guatemala Trench Pacific Oc. **75 Q9** 15.00N 93.00W
Guaviare r. Colombia **88 C8** 4.00N 67.46W
Guayaquil Ecuador **88 B7** 2.13S 79.54W
Guayaquil, G. of Ecuador **88 A7** 2.30S 80.00W
Guaymas Mexico **86 B5** 27.59N110.54W
Gubin Poland **48 G5** 51.59N 14.42E
Guecho Spain **43 D5** 43.21N 3.01W
Guéret France **42 E4** 46.10N 1.52E
Guernsey i. U.K. **13 E1** 49.27N 2.35W
Guerrero d. Mexico **86 D3** 18.00N100.00W
Guiana S. America **88 D8** 4.00N 53.00W
Guiana Highlands S. America **88 C8** 4.00N 60.00W
Guildford U.K. **13 G3** 51.14N 0.35W
Guilin China **67 H2** 25.21N110.11E
Guinea Africa **102 B3** 10.30N 11.30W
Guinea, G. of Africa **103 E1** 3.00N 3.00E
Guinea Bissau Africa **102 A3** 11.30N 15.00W
Güines Cuba **87 H4** 22.50N 82.02W
Guingamp France **42 C5** 48.34N 3.09W
Guiping China **67 H2** 23.20N110.04E
Güiria Venezuela **88 C9** 10.37N 62.21W
Guise France **39 B1** 49.54N 3.39E
Guiuan Phil. **69 H6** 11.02N125.44E
Guiyang China **66 G3** 26.35N106.40E
Guizhou d. China **66 G3** 27.00N106.30E
Gujarat d. India **63 C4** 22.45N 71.30E
Gujrānwāla Pakistan **63 D6** 32.06N 74.11E
Gujrāt Pakistan **63 D6** 32.35N 74.06E
Gulbarga India **63 D3** 17.22N 76.47E
Gulpaigan Iran **61 H4** 33.23N 50.18E
Gulu Uganda **99 D5** 2.46N 32.21E
Gümüşhane Turkey **60 E6** 40.26N 39.26E
Guntersville L. U.S.A. **83 I3** 34.35N 86.00W
Guntūr India **63 E3** 16.20N 80.27E
Gürün Turkey **60 E5** 38.44N 37.15E
Guryev U.S.S.R. **52 E2** 47.00N 52.00E
Gusau Nigeria **103 F3** 12.12N 6.40E
Güstrow E. Germany **48 F6** 53.48N 12.11E
Gütersloh W. Germany **48 D5** 51.54N 8.22E
Guyana S. America **88 D8** 5.00N 59.00W
Gwādar Pakistan **62 B4** 25.09N 62.21E
Gwalior India **63 E5** 26.12N 78.09E
Gwatar Iran **61 K2** 25.10N 61.31E
Gweebarra Bay Rep. of Ire. **15 C4** 54.52N 8.30W
Gwent d. U.K. **13 E3** 51.44N 3.00W
Gweru Zimbabwe **99 C3** 19.25S 29.50E
Gwynedd d. U.K. **12 C5** 53.00N 4.00W
Gyangzê China **63 F5** 29.00N 89.40E
Gydanskiy Pen. U.S.S.R. **52 G4** 70.00N 78.30E
Gyöngyös Hungary **49 I3** 47.47N 19.56E
Györ Hungary **49 H3** 47.41N 17.40E

H

Ha'apai Group is. Tonga **74 I6** 19.50S174.30W
Haapajärvi Finland **50 F3** 63.45N 25.20E
Haapamäki Finland **50 F3** 62.15N 24.25E
Haapsalu U.S.S.R. **50 E2** 58.58N 23.32E
Haarlem Neth. **39 C4** 52.22N 4.38E
Hachinohe Japan **70 E7** 40.30N141.30E
Haddington U.K. **14 F2** 55.57N 2.47W
Hadejia Nigeria **103 F3** 12.30N 10.03E
Hadejia r. Nigeria **103 G3** 12.47N 10.44E
Haderslev Denmark **38 C3** 55.15N 9.30E
Hadhramaut f. S. Yemen **101 G3** 16.30N 49.30E
Hadsten Denmark **38 D4** 56.19N 10.04E
Hadsund Denmark **38 D4** 56.43N 10.09E
Haeju N. Korea **67 J5** 38.04N125.40E
Hafar Saudi Arabia **61 G3** 28.28N 46.00E
Hafnarfjördhur town Iceland **50 I7** 64.04N 21.58W
Haft Kel Iran **61 H3** 31.28N 49.35E
Hagen W. Germany **39 F3** 51.22N 7.27E
Hagested Denmark **38 E3** 55.46N 11.37E
Hagi Japan **70 A4** 34.25N131.22E
Ha Giang Vietnam **68 C8** 22.50N104.58E
Hags Head Rep. of Ire. **15 B2** 52.56N 9.29W
Hai Duong Vietnam **68 D8** 20.56N106.21E
Haifa Israel **60 D4** 32.49N 34.59E
Haikou China **67 H2** 20.05N110.25E
Ḥā'il Saudi Arabia **60 F2** 27.31N 41.45E
Hailar China **67 I6** 49.15N119.41E
Hailsham U.K. **13 H2** 50.52N 0.16E
Hailun China **67 K6** 47.29N126.58E
Hailuoto i. Finland **50 F4** 65.00N 24.50E
Hainan i. China **67 H1** 18.30N109.40E
Hainaut d. Belgium **39 B2** 50.30N 3.45E
Haines U.S.A. **80 E3** 59.11N135.23W
Haiphong Vietnam **68 D8** 20.58N106.41E
Haiti C. America **87 J3** 19.00N 73.00W
Hajiki saki c. Japan **70 D6** 38.25N138.32E
Hakari Turkey **61 F5** 37.36N 43.45E
Hakodate Japan **70 D7** 41.46N140.44E
Halberstadt E. Germany **48 E5** 51.54N 11.04E
Halden Norway **50 B2** 59.08N 11.13E
Halifax Canada **81 L2** 44.38N 63.35W
Halifax U.K. **12 F5** 53.43N 1.51W
Halkett, C. U.S.A. **80 C5** 71.00N152.00W
Halkirk U.K. **14 E5** 58.30N 3.30W
Halladale r. U.K. **14 E5** 58.32N 3.53W
Halle Belgium **39 C2** 50.45N 4.14E
Halle E. Germany **48 E5** 51.28N 11.58E
Hall Is. Pacific Oc. **74 F8** 8.37N152.00E
Hallsberg Sweden **50 C2** 59.05N 15.07E
Hall's Creek town Australia **71 B4** 18.17S127.44E
Hallstavik Sweden **50 D3** 60.06N 18.42E
Halmahera i. Indonesia **69 H4** 0.45N128.00E
Halmstad Sweden **50 C2** 56.41N 12.55E
Hälsingborg Sweden **50 C2** 56.05N 12.45E
Haltern W. Germany **39 F3** 51.45N 7.10E
Haltia Tunturi mtn. Finland **50 E5** 69.20N 21.10E
Haltwhistle U.K. **12 E6** 54.58N 2.28W
Hama Syria **60 E4** 35.09N 36.44E
Hamadān Iran **61 H4** 34.47N 48.33E
Hamamatsu Japan **70 C4** 34.42N137.42E
Hamar Norway **50 B3** 60.47N 10.55E
Hamata, Gebel mtn. Egypt **60 D2** 24.11N 35.01E
Hamborn W. Germany **39 E3** 51.29N 6.46E
Hamburg W. Germany **48 E6** 53.33N 10.00E
Hamdh, Wadi r. Saudi Arabia **60 E2** 25.49N 36.37E
Hämeenlinna Finland **50 F3** 61.00N 24.25E
Hameln W. Germany **48 D6** 52.06N 9.21E

Little Andaman *i.* India **63 G2** 10.50N 92.38E
Little Cayman *i.* Cayman Is. **87 H3** 19.40N 80.00W
Little Coco *i.* Burma **68 A6** 13.50N 93.10E
Littlehampton U.K. **13 G2** 50.49N 0.32W
Little Inagua *i.* Bahamas **87 J4** 21.30N 73.00W
Little Ouse *r.* U.K. **13 H4** 52.34N 0.20E
Little Rock *town* U.S.A. **83 H3** 34.42N 92.17W
Little St. Bernard Pass France / Italy **46 C6** 45.40N 6.53E
Little Zab *r.* Iraq **61 F4** 35.15N 43.27E
Liuzhou China **67 H2** 24.17N 109.15E
Livermore, Mt. U.S.A. **82 F3** 30.39N 104.11W
Liverpool Canada **81 L2** 44.03N 64.43W
Liverpool U.K. **12 D5** 53.25N 3.00W
Liverpool B. U.K. **12 D5** 53.30N 3.10W
Livingston U.K. **14 E2** 55.54N 3.31W
Livingstone *see* Maramba Zambia **99**
Lizard U.K. **13 B1** 49.58N 5.11W
Lizard Pt. U.K. **13 B1** 49.57N 5.15W
Ljubljana Yugo. **46 G1** 46.04N 14.28E
Ljungan *r.* Sweden **50 D3** 62.20N 17.19E
Ljungby Sweden **50 C2** 56.49N 13.55E
Ljusdal Sweden **50 D3** 61.49N 16.09E
Ljusnan *r.* Sweden **50 D3** 61.15N 17.08E
Ljusnarsberg Sweden **50 C2** 59.48N 14.57E
Llandeilo U.K. **13 D3** 51.54N 3.59W
Llandovery U.K. **13 D3** 52.00N 3.47W
Llandrindod Wells U.K. **13 D4** 52.15N 3.23W
Llandudno U.K. **12 D5** 53.20N 3.48W
Llanelli U.K. **13 C3** 51.41N 4.09W
Llanes Spain **43 C5** 43.25N 4.45W
Llangadfan U.K. **13 D4** 52.43N 3.29W
Llangollen U.K. **12 D4** 52.58N 3.11W
Llanidloes U.K. **13 D4** 52.37N 3.31W
Llanos *f.* Colombia / Venezuela **88 B8** 5.30N 72.00W
Llanwrtyd Wells U.K. **13 D4** 52.04N 3.35W
Lleida Spain **43 F4** 41.37N 0.38E
Llerena Spain **43 B3** 38.14N 6.00W
Lloydminster Canada **80 H3** 53.18N 110.00W
Lobito Angola **99 B3** 12.20S 13.34E
Locarno Switz. **48 D3** 46.10N 8.48E
Lochboisdale *town* U.K. **14 A4** 57.09N 7.19W
Lochem Neth. **39 E4** 52.10N 6.25E
Loches France **42 E4** 47.08N 1.00E
Lochgilphead U.K. **14 C3** 56.02N 5.26W
Lochinver U.K. **14 C5** 58.09N 5.13W
Lochmaddy *town* U.K. **14 A4** 57.36N 7.10W
Lochnagar *mtn.* U.K. **14 E3** 56.57N 3.15W
Lochranza *town* U.K. **14 C2** 55.42N 5.18W
Lochy, L. U.K. **14 D3** 56.58N 4.57W
Lockerbie U.K. **14 E2** 55.07N 3.21W
Loc Ninh Vietnam **68 D6** 11.55N 106.35E
Łódź Poland **49 I5** 51.49N 19.28E
Lofoten *is.* Norway **50 C5** 68.15N 13.50E
Logan, Mt. Canada **80 D4** 60.45N 140.00W
Logone *r.* Cameroon / Chad **103 H3** 12.10N 15.00E
Logroño Spain **43 D5** 42.28N 2.26W
Lögstör Denmark **38 C4** 56.58N 9.16E
Lögumkloster Denmark **38 B3** 55.04N 8.50E
Loimaa Finland **50 E3** 60.50N 23.05E
Loir *r.* France **42 D4** 47.29N 0.32W
Loire *r.* France **42 D4** 47.18N 2.00W
Loja Ecuador **88 B7** 3.59S 79.16W
Loja Spain **43 C2** 37.10N 4.09W
Lokeren Belgium **39 B3** 51.06N 3.59E
Lökken Denmark **38 C5** 57.22N 9.43E
Lokoja Nigeria **103 F2** 7.49N 6.44E
Lolland *i.* Denmark **38 E2** 54.50N 11.30E
Lom Bulgaria **47 K5** 43.49N 23.13E
Lombok *i.* Indonesia **68 F2** 8.30S 116.20E
Lomé Togo **103 E2** 6.10N 1.21E
Lomié Cameroon **103 G1** 3.09N 13.35E
Lomond, Loch U.K. **14 D3** 56.07N 4.36W
Łomża Poland **49 K6** 53.11N 22.04E
London Canada **81 J2** 42.58N 81.15W
London U.K. **13 G3** 51.32N 0.06W
Londonderry U.K. **15 D5** 55.00N 7.21W
Londonderry *d.* U.K. **15 D4** 55.00N 7.00W
Londonderry, C. Australia **71 B4** 13.58S 126.55E
Londrina Brazil **89 D5** 23.30S 51.13W
Long Beach *town* U.S.A. **82 C3** 33.57N 118.15W
Long Eaton U.K. **12 F4** 52.54N 1.16W
Longford Rep. of Ire. **15 D3** 53.44N 7.48W
Longford *d.* Rep. of Ire. **15 D3** 53.42N 7.45W
Long I. Bahamas **87 J4** 23.00N 75.00W
Long I. U.S.A. **83 L5** 40.50N 73.00W
Longlac *town* Canada **81 J2** 49.47N 86.34W
Longniddry U.K. **14 F2** 55.58N 2.53W
Longs Peak U.S.A. **82 E5** 40.16N 105.37W
Longtown U.K. **12 E7** 55.01N 2.58W
Longwy France **39 D1** 49.32N 5.46E
Longxi China **66 G4** 35.00N 105.00E
Long Xuyen Vietnam **68 D6** 10.23N 105.25E
Löningen W. Germany **39 F4** 52.44N 7.46E
Looe U.K. **13 C2** 50.21N 4.28W
Lookout, C. U.S.A. **83 K3** 34.34N 76.34W
Loop Head Rep. of Ire. **15 B2** 52.33N 9.56W
Lop Buri Thailand **68 C6** 14.49N 100.37E
Lopez, C. Gabon **99 A4** 0.36S 8.45E
Lop Nur *l.* China **66 E5** 40.30N 90.30E
Lopphavet *est.* Norway **50 E5** 70.30N 21.00E
Loralai Pakistan **63 C5** 30.20N 68.41E
Lorca Spain **43 E2** 37.40N 1.41W
Lord Howe I. Pacific Oc. **71 E2** 31.33S 159.06E
Lordsburg U.S.A. **82 E3** 32.22N 108.43W
Lorengau P.N.G. **69 L3** 2.01S 147.15E
Lorient France **42 C4** 47.45N 3.21W
Los Angeles U.S.A. **82 C3** 34.00N 118.17W
Los Blancos Spain **43 E2** 37.37N 0.48W
Los Canarreos, Archipiélago de Cuba **87 H4** 21.40N 82.30W
Lošinj *i.* Yugo. **46 G6** 44.36N 14.20E
Los Mochis Mexico **86 C5** 25.45N 108.57W
Los Roques *is.* Venezuela **87 K2** 12.00N 67.00W
Lossiemouth U.K. **14 E4** 57.43N 3.18W
Lot *r.* France **42 E3** 44.17N 0.22E
Lothian *d.* U.K. **14 E2** 55.50N 3.00W
Lötschberg Tunnel Switz. **42 H4** 46.25N 7.53E
Lotta *r.* U.S.S.R. **50 H5** 68.36N 31.06E
Loudéac France **42 C5** 48.11N 2.45W
Louga Senegal **102 A4** 15.37N 16.13W
Loughborough U.K. **12 F4** 52.46N 1.11W
Loughrea Rep. of Ire. **15 C3** 53.11N 8.36W
Loughros More Bay Rep. of Ire. **15 C4** 54.48N 8.40W
Louisburgh Rep. of Ire. **15 B3** 53.47N 9.50W
Louisiana *d.* U.S.A. **83 H3** 31.00N 92.30W
Louisville U.S.A. **83 I4** 38.13N 85.45W
Lourdes France **42 D2** 43.06N 0.02W
Louth *d.* Rep. of Ire. **15 E3** 53.55N 6.30W
Louth U.K. **12 H5** 53.20N 0.01E
Louvain Belgium **39 C2** 50.53N 4.45E
Lovech Bulgaria **47 L5** 43.08N 24.44E
Lower California *f.* Mexico **76 I4** 30.00N 116.00W
Lower Egypt *f.* Egypt **60 C3** 30.30N 31.00E
Lower Lough Erne U.K. **15 D4** 54.28N 7.48W
Lower Tunguska *r.* U.S.S.R. **53 H4** 65.50N 88.00E
Lowestoft U.K. **13 I4** 52.29N 1.44E
Łowicz Poland **49 I6** 52.06N 19.55E
Loyalty Is. N. Cal. **74 G5** 21.00S 167.00E
Lualaba *r.* Zaïre **99 C5** 0.18N 25.30E
Luanda Angola **99 B4** 8.50S 13.20E
Luang Prabang Laos **68 C7** 19.53N 102.10E
Luangwa *r.* Zambia **94 F3** 15.32S 30.28E
Luapula *r.* Zambia **99 C4** 9.25S 28.36E
Luarca Spain **43 B5** 43.33N 6.31W
Lubango Angola **99 B3** 14.55S 13.30E
Lubbock U.S.A. **82 F3** 33.35N 101.53W
Lübeck W. Germany **48 E6** 53.52N 10.40E
Lubeck Bay E. Germany **48 E7** 54.05N 11.00E
Lubilash *r.* Zaïre **94 E4** 4.59S 23.25E
Lublin Poland **49 K5** 51.18N 22.31E
Lubumbashi Zaïre **99 C3** 11.41S 27.29E
Luce B. U.K. **14 D1** 54.45N 4.47W
Lucena Phil. **69 G6** 13.56N 121.37E
Lucena Spain **43 C2** 37.25N 4.29W
Lučenec Czech. **49 I4** 48.20N 19.40E
Lucero Mexico **86 C6** 30.50N 106.30W
Luckenwalde E. Germany **48 F6** 52.05N 13.11E
Lucknow India **63 E5** 26.50N 80.54E
Lüda China **67 J5** 38.53N 121.37E
Lüdenscheid W. Germany **39 F3** 51.13N 7.36E
Lüderitz Namibia **99 B2** 26.38S 15.10E
Ludhiāna India **63 D5** 30.56N 75.52E
Lüdinghausen W. Germany **39 F3** 51.46N 7.27E
Ludlow U.K. **13 E4** 52.22N 2.42W
Ludvika Sweden **50 C3** 60.08N 15.14E
Ludwigshafen W. Germany **48 D4** 49.29N 8.27E
Lufkin U.S.A. **83 H3** 31.21N 94.47W
Luga *r.* U.S.S.R. **50 G2** 59.40N 28.15E
Lugano Switz. **48 D3** 46.01N 8.57E
Lugnaquilla Mtn. Rep. of Ire. **15 E2** 52.59N 6.30W
Lugo Spain **43 B5** 43.00N 7.33W
Lugoj Romania **49 J2** 45.42N 21.56E
Luiro *r.* Finland **50 F4** 67.22N 27.30E
Lukenie *r.* Zaïre **94 D4** 2.43S 18.12E
Lule *r.* Sweden **50 E4** 65.40N 21.48E
Luleå Sweden **50 E4** 65.35N 22.10E
Lüleburgaz Turkey **47 M4** 41.25N 27.23E
Lulua *r.* Zaïre **99 C4** 5.03S 21.07E
Lund Sweden **50 C1** 55.42N 13.10E
Lundy *i.* U.K. **13 C3** 51.10N 4.41W
Lune *r.* U.K. **12 E6** 54.04N 2.51W
Lüneburg W. Germany **48 E6** 53.15N 10.24E
Luninets U.S.S.R. **49 M6** 52.18N 26.50E
Luoyang China **67 H4** 34.48N 112.25E
Lure France **42 H4** 47.42N 6.30E
Lurgan U.K. **15 E4** 54.28N 6.21W
Lusaka Zambia **99 C3** 15.26S 28.20E
Lusk U.S.A. **82 F5** 42.47N 104.26W
Lütjenburg W. Germany **38 D2** 54.18N 10.37E
Luton U.K. **13 G3** 51.53N 0.25W
Lutsk U.S.S.R. **49 L5** 50.42N 25.15E
Lutterworth U.K. **13 F4** 52.27N 1.13W
Luvua *r.* Zaïre **99 C4** 6.45S 27.00E
Luxembourg *d.* Belgium **39 D1** 49.58N 5.30E
Luxembourg Europe **39 E1** 49.50N 6.15E
Luxembourg *town* Lux. **39 E1** 49.37N 6.08E
Luxor Egypt **60 D2** 24.41N 32.24E
Luzern Switz. **48 D3** 47.03N 8.17E
Luzhou China **63 G3** 28.25N 105.20E
Luzon *i.* Phil. **69 G7** 17.50N 121.00E
Luzon Str. Pacific Oc. **69 G8** 20.20N 122.00E
Lvov U.S.S.R. **49 L4** 49.50N 24.00E
Lybster U.K. **14 E5** 58.17N 3.21W
Lycksele Sweden **50 D4** 64.34N 18.40E
Lyell, Mt. U.S.A. **82 C4** 37.45N 119.18W
Lyme B. U.K. **13 E2** 50.40N 2.55W
Lyme Regis U.K. **13 E2** 50.44N 2.56W
Lymington U.K. **13 F2** 50.46N 1.32W
Lyna *r.* Poland **49 J7** 54.37N 21.14E
Lynn Lake *town* Canada **81 H3** 56.51N 101.01W
Lynton U.K. **13 D3** 51.14N 3.50W
Lyon France **42 G3** 45.46N 4.50E
Lysekil Sweden **50 B2** 58.16N 11.26E
Lytham St. Anne's U.K. **12 D5** 53.47N 3.01W

M

Maamakeogh *mtn.* Rep. of Ire. **15 B4** 54.17N 9.30W
Maamturk Mts. Rep. of Ire. **15 B3** 53.32N 9.42W
Ma'ān Jordan **60 D3** 30.11N 35.43E
Maas *r.* Neth. **39 C3** 51.44N 4.42E
Maaseik Belgium **39 D3** 51.08N 5.48E
Maastricht Neth. **39 D2** 50.51N 5.42E
Mablethorpe U.K. **12 H5** 53.19N 0.18E
Macapá Brazil **88 D8** 0.01N 51.01W
Macau Asia **67 H2** 22.13N 113.36E
Macclesfield U.K. **12 E5** 53.15N 2.09W
Macdonnell Ranges *mts.* Australia **71 C3** 23.30S 132.00E
Macduff U.K. **14 F4** 57.40N 2.30W
Maceió Brazil **88 F7** 9.34S 35.47W
Macenta Guinea **102 C2** 8.31N 9.32W
Macerata Italy **46 F5** 43.18N 13.30E
Macgillycuddy's Reeks *mts.* Rep. of Ire. **15 B2** 52.00N 9.45W
Machilipatnam India **63 E3** 16.13N 81.12E
Machrihanish U.K. **14 C2** 55.24N 5.45W
Machynlleth U.K. **13 D4** 52.35N 3.50W
Mackay Australia **71 D3** 21.10S 149.10E
Mackay, L. Australia **71 B3** 22.30S 128.58E
Mackenzie *r.* Canada **80 E4** 69.20N 134.00W
Mackenzie King I. Canada **80 G5** 77.30N 112.00W
Mackenzie Mts. Canada **80 E4** 64.00N 130.00W
Macomer Italy **46 D4** 40.16N 8.45E
Mâcon France **42 G4** 46.18N 4.50E
Macon U.S.A. **83 J3** 32.47N 83.37W
Macquarie I. Pacific Oc. **74 F2** 54.29S 158.58E
Macroom Rep. of Ire. **15 C1** 51.53N 8.59W
Madagascar Africa **99 G7** 20.00S 46.30E
Madang P.N.G. **69 L2** 5.14S 145.45E
Madeira *i.* Atlantic Oc. **100 A5** 32.45N 17.00W
Madeira *r.* Brazil **88 D7** 3.50S 58.30W
Madhya Pradesh *d.* India **63 E4** 23.00N 79.30E
Madison Fla. U.S.A. **83 J3** 30.29N 83.39W
Madison Wisc. U.S.A. **83 I5** 43.04N 89.22W
Madiun Indonesia **68 E2** 7.37S 111.33E
Madras India **63 E2** 13.05N 80.18E
Madre, Sierre *mts.* C. America **76 K3** 15.00N 92.00W
Madre de Dios *r.* Bolivia **88 C6** 11.00S 66.30W
Madre del Sur, Sierra *mts.* Mexico **86 D3** 17.00N 100.00W
Madre Lagoon Mexico **86 E5** 25.00N 97.30W
Madre Occidental, Sierra *mts.* Mexico **86 C5** 24.00N 103.00W
Madre Oriental, Sierra *mts.* Mexico **86 D5** 24.00N 99.00W
Madrid Spain **43 D4** 40.25N 3.43W
Madura *i.* Indonesia **68 E2** 7.00S 113.30E
Madurai India **63 E2** 9.55N 78.07E
Maebashi Japan **70 D5** 36.30N 139.04E
Maestra, Sierra *mts.* Cuba **87 I4** 20.10N 76.30W
Mafia I. Tanzania **99 D4** 7.50S 39.50E
Mafraq Jordan **60 E4** 32.20N 36.12E
Magadan U.S.S.R. **53 M3** 59.38N 150.50E
Magalluf Spain **43 G3** 39.30N 2.31E
Magangué Colombia **88 B8** 9.14N 74.46W
Magas Iran **61 K2** 27.08N 61.36E
Magburaka Sierra Leone **102 B2** 8.44N 11.57W
Magdalena *r.* Colombia **88 B9** 10.56N 74.58W
Magdalena Mexico **86 B6** 30.38N 110.59W
Magdeburg E. Germany **48 E6** 52.08N 11.36E
Magelang Indonesia **68 E2** 7.28S 110.11E
Magellan's Str. Chile **89 B2** 53.00S 71.00W
Mageröya *i.* Norway **50 F5** 71.00N 25.50E
Maggiore, L. Italy **46 D6** 45.57N 8.37E
Maghera U.K. **14 B1** 54.51N 6.42W
Magherafelt U.K. **15 E4** 54.44N 6.38W
Magnitogorsk U.S.S.R. **52 E3** 53.28N 59.06E
Magwe Burma **63 G4** 20.10N 95.00E
Mahābād Iran **61 G5** 36.44N 45.44E
Mahajanga Madagascar **99 G8** 15.40S 46.20E
Maḩallāt Iran **61 H4** 33.54N 50.28E
Mahānadi *r.* India **63 F4** 20.17N 86.43E
Mahārāshtra *d.* India **63 D4** 20.00N 77.00E
Mahón Spain **43 H3** 39.55N 4.18E
Maidenhead U.K. **13 G3** 51.32N 0.44W
Maidstone U.K. **13 H3** 51.17N 0.32E
Maiduguri Nigeria **103 G3** 11.53N 13.16E
Maimana Afghan. **62 B6** 35.54N 64.43E
Main *r.* W. Germany **48 D5** 50.00N 8.19E
Mai Ndombe *l.* Zaïre **99 B4** 2.00S 18.20E
Maine *d.* U.S.A. **83 M6** 45.00N 69.00W
Mainland *i.* Shetland Is. U.K. **14 G7** 60.15N 1.22W
Mainland *i.* Orkney Is. U.K. **14 E6** 59.00N 3.10W
Mainz W. Germany **48 D5** 50.00N 8.16E
Maitland Australia **71 E2** 32.33S 151.33E
Maizuru Japan **70 C4** 35.30N 135.20E
Majene Indonesia **68 F3** 3.33S 118.59E
Majma'a Saudi Arabia **61 G2** 25.52N 45.25E
Majorca *i.* Spain **43 G3** 39.35N 3.00E
Majuro *i.* Pacific Oc. **74 H8** 7.09N 171.12E
Makale Indonesia **68 F3** 3.06S 119.53E
Makarikari Salt Pan *f.* Botswana **99 C2** 20.50S 25.45E
Makassar Str. Indonesia **68 F3** 3.00S 118.00E
Makeni Sierra Leone **102 B2** 8.57N 12.02W
Makeyevka U.S.S.R. **52 D2** 47.55N 38.05E
Makhachkala U.S.S.R. **52 D2** 42.59N 47.30E
Makran *f.* Asia **61 J2** 25.49N 60.00E
Makurdi Nigeria **103 F2** 7.44N 8.35E
Malabo Equat. Guinea **103 F1** 3.45N 8.48E
Malacca, Str. of Indian Oc. **68 B4** 3.00N 100.30E
Málaga Spain **43 C2** 36.43N 4.25W
Malaita Solomon Is. **71 F5** 9.00S 161.00E
Malakāl Sudan **101 F2** 9.31N 31.40E
Malakand Pakistan **63 C6** 34.34N 71.57E
Malang Indonesia **68 E2** 7.59S 112.45E
Malange Angola **99 B4** 9.36S 16.21E
Mälaren *l.* Sweden **50 D2** 59.30N 17.00E
Malatya Turkey **60 E5** 38.22N 38.18E
Malaŵi Africa **99 D3** 13.00S 34.00E
Malaŵi, L. Africa **99 D3** 12.00S 34.30E
Malāyer Iran **61 H4** 34.19N 48.51E
Malay Peninsula Asia **54 M3** 4.00N 102.00E
Malaysia Asia **68 C5** 5.00N 110.00E
Malbork Poland **49 I7** 54.02N 19.01E
Malden I. Kiribati **75 K7** 4.03S 154.49W
Maldives Indian Oc. **63 D1** 6.20N 73.00E
Maldon U.K. **13 H3** 51.44N 0.40E
Maléa, C. Greece **47 K2** 36.27N 23.11E
Mālegaon India **63 D4** 20.32N 74.38E
Malekula *i.* Vanuatu **74 G6** 16.15S 167.30E
Mali Africa **100 B3** 17.30N 2.30E
Malili Indonesia **69 G3** 2.38S 121.06E
Malin U.S.S.R. **49 N5** 50.48N 29.08E
Malines Belgium **39 C3** 51.01N 4.28E
Malin Head Rep. of Ire. **15 D5** 55.23N 7.24W
Malin More Rep. of Ire. **15 C4** 54.41N 8.49W
Mallaig U.K. **14 C4** 57.00N 5.50W
Mallawī Egypt **60 C2** 27.44N 30.50E
Mallorca *i. see* Majorca *i.* Spain **43**
Mallow Rep. of Ire. **15 C2** 52.08N 8.39W
Malmédy Belgium **39 E2** 50.25N 6.02E
Malmö Sweden **50 C1** 55.35N 13.00E
Malorita U.S.S.R. **49 L5** 51.50N 24.08E
Målöy Norway **50 A3** 61.57N 5.06E
Malta Europe **46 G1** 35.55N 14.25E
Malta Channel Med. Sea **46 G2** 36.20N 14.45E
Maltby U.K. **12 F5** 53.27N 1.13W
Malton U.K. **12 G6** 54.09N 0.47W
Maluku *d.* Indonesia **69 H3** 4.00S 129.00E
Mamaia Romania **49 N2** 44.15N 28.37E
Mamberamo *r.* Indonesia **69 J3** 1.45S 137.25E
Mambéré *r.* C.A.R. **103 H1** 3.30N 16.08E
Mamfe Cameroon **103 F2** 5.46N 9.18E
Mamore *r.* Bolivia **88 C6** 12.00S 65.15W
Mamou Guinea **102 B3** 10.24N 12.05W
Mamuju Indonesia **68 F3** 2.41S 118.55E
Man Ivory Coast **102 C2** 7.31N 7.37W
Man, Isle of U.K. **12 C6** 54.15N 4.30W
Manacor Spain **43 G3** 39.32N 3.12E
Manado Indonesia **69 G4** 1.30N 124.58E
Managua Nicaragua **87 G2** 12.06N 86.18W
Managua, L. Nicaragua **87 G2** 12.10N 86.30W
Manama Bahrain **61 H2** 26.12N 50.36E
Manaus Brazil **88 D7** 3.06S 60.00W
Manchester U.K. **12 E5** 53.30N 2.15W
Manchester U.S.A. **83 L5** 42.59N 71.28W
Manchuria *f.* China **67 J6** 46.00N 125.00E
Manchurian Plain *f.* Asia **54 O7** 42.00N 122.00E
Mand *r.* Iran **61 H3** 28.09N 51.16E
Mandal Norway **50 A2** 58.02N 7.30E
Mandala Peak Indonesia **69 K2** 4.45S 140.15E
Mandalay Burma **63 H4** 21.57N 96.04E
Mandalgovi Mongolia **66 G6** 45.40N 106.10E
Mandara Mts. Nigeria / Cameroon **103 G3** 10.30N 13.30E
Manfredonia Italy **46 G4** 41.38N 15.54E
Mangaia I. Cook Is. **75 K5** 21.56S 157.56W
Mangalia Romania **49 N1** 43.50N 28.35E
Mangalore India **63 D2** 12.54N 74.51E
Mangareva *i.* Pacific Oc. **75 M5** 23.07S 134.57W
Mangnai China **66 E4** 37.52N 91.26E
Mango Togo **103 E3** 10.23N 0.30E
Mangoky *r.* Madagascar **99 F7** 21.20S 43.30E
Mangyshlak Pen. U.S.S.R. **52 E2** 44.00N 52.30E
Manicouagane *r.* Canada **81 L2** 49.00N 68.13W
Maniitsoq *see* Sukkertoppen Greenland **81**
Manila Phil. **69 G6** 14.36N 120.59E
Manipur *d.* India **63 G4** 25.00N 93.40E
Manisa Turkey **47 M3** 38.37N 27.28E
Manistique U.S.A. **83 I6** 45.58N 86.07W
Manitoba *d.* Canada **81 I3** 54.00N 96.00W
Manitoba, L. Canada **81 I3** 51.35N 99.00W
Manizales Colombia **88 B8** 5.03N 75.32W
Manjīl Iran **61 H5** 36.44N 49.29E
Mankono Ivory Coast **102 C2** 8.01N 6.09W
Mannar, G. of India / Sri Lanka **63 E2** 8.20N 79.00E
Mannheim W. Germany **48 D4** 49.30N 8.28E
Mannin Bay Rep. of Ire. **15 A3** 53.30N 10.10W
Mannu *r.* Italy **46 D3** 39.16N 9.00E
Manokwari Indonesia **69 I3** 0.53S 134.05E
Manorhamilton Rep. of Ire. **15 C4** 54.18N 8.14W
Manosque France **42 G2** 43.50N 5.47E
Manresa Spain **43 F4** 41.43N 1.50E
Mansel I. Canada **81 J4** 62.00N 80.00W
Mansfield U.K. **12 F5** 53.08N 1.12W
Mansfield U.S.A. **83 J5** 40.46N 82.31W
Mänttä Finland **50 F3** 62.00N 24.40E
Mantua Italy **46 E6** 45.09N 10.47E
Manua Is. Samoa **74 J6** 14.13S 169.35W
Manus *i.* P.N.G. **69 L3** 2.00S 147.00E
Manzala, L. Egypt **60 C3** 31.20N 32.00E
Manzanares Spain **43 D3** 39.00N 3.23W
Manzanillo Cuba **87 I4** 20.21N 77.21W
Manzhouli China **67 I6** 49.36N 117.28E
Maoke Range *mts.* Indonesia **69 J3** 4.00S 137.30E
Maoming China **67 H2** 21.50N 110.56E
Mapia Is. Indonesia **69 I4** 1.00N 134.15E
Mappi Indonesia **69 J2** 7.06S 139.23E
Maprik P.N.G. **69 K3** 3.38S 143.02E
Maputo Mozambique **99 D2** 25.58S 32.35E
Ma'qala Saudi Arabia **61 G2** 26.29N 47.20E
Maracaibo Venezuela **88 B9** 10.44N 71.37W
Maracaibo, L. Venezuela **76 M2** 10.00N 71.30W
Maracay Venezuela **88 C9** 10.20N 67.28W
Maradi Niger **103 F3** 13.29N 7.10E
Marāgheh Iran **61 G5** 37.25N 46.13E
Marahuaca, Cerro *mtn.* Venezuela **88 C8** 4.20N 65.30W
Marajó I. Brazil **88 E7** 1.00S 49.30W
Maramba Zambia **99 C3** 17.50S 25.53E
Marand Iran **61 G5** 38.25N 45.50E
Marañón *r.* Peru **88 B7** 4.00S 73.30W
Marapi *mtn.* Indonesia **68 C3** 0.20S 100.45E
Marathón Greece **47 K3** 38.10N 23.59E
Marbella Spain **43 C2** 36.31N 4.53W
Marburg W. Germany **48 D5** 50.49N 8.36E
March U.K. **13 H4** 52.36N 0.03E
Marche Belgium **39 D2** 50.13N 5.21E
Marchena Spain **43 C2** 37.20N 5.24W
Marcus I. Pacific Oc. **74 F10** 24.18N 153.58E
Mardān Pakistan **63 D6** 34.14N 72.05E
Mar del Plata Argentina **89 D4** 38.00S 57.32W
Marden U.K. **13 H3** 51.10N 0.29E
Mardin Turkey **60 F5** 37.19N 40.43E

Morcenx France 42 D3 44.02N 0.55W
Morden Canada 81 I2 49.15N 98.10W
Morecambe U.K. 12 E6 54.05N 2.51W
Morecambe B. U.K. 12 E6 54.05N 3.00W
Morelia Mexico 86 D3 19.40N101.11W
Morella Spain 43 E4 40.37N 0.06W
Morelos *d.* Mexico 86 E3 18.40N 99.00W
Morena, Sierra *mts.* Spain 43 C3 38.10N 5.00W
Morez France 42 H4 46.31N 6.02E
Morgan City U.S.A. 83 H2 29.41N 91.13W
Morioka Japan 70 E6 39.43N141.10E
Moriston *r.* U.K. 8 D5 57.12N 4.38W
Morlaix France 42 C5 48.35N 3.50W
Morocco Africa 100 B5 31.00N 5.00W
Moro G. Phil. 69 G5 6.30N123.20E
Morogoro Tanzania 99 D4 6.49S 37.40E
Morón Cuba 87 I4 22.08N 78.39W
Mörön Mongolia 66 F6 49.36N100.08E
Morotai *i.* Indonesia 69 H4 2.10N128.30E
Morpeth U.K. 12 F7 55.09N 1.40W
Mors *i.* Denmark 38 B4 56.50N 8.45E
Morsbach W. Germany 39 F2 50.52N 7.44E
Mortagne France 42 E5 48.32N 0.33E
Morvern *f.* U.K. 14 C3 56.37N 5.45W
Morwell Australia 71 D2 38.14S146.25E
Moscow U.S.S.R. 52 D3 55.45N 37.42E
Mosel *r.* W. Germany 39 F2 50.23N 7.37E
Moselle *r.* see Mosel *r.* France / Lux. 39
Moshi Tanzania 99 D4 3.20S 37.21E
Mosjöen Norway 50 C4 65.50N 13.10E
Moskog Norway 50 A3 61.30N 5.59E
Moskva *r.* U.S.S.R. 33 M6 55.08N 38.50E
Mosquitia Plain Honduras 87 H3 15.00N 84.00W
Mosquito Coast *f.* Nicaragua 87 H2 13.00N 84.00W
Mosquitos, G. of Panama 87 H1 9.00N 81.00W
Moss Norway 50 B2 59.26N 10.41E
Mosso *l.* Denmark 38 C4 56.02N 9.47E
Mossoró Brazil 88 F7 5.10S 37.20W
Most Czech. 48 F5 50.31N 13.39E
Mostar Yugo. 47 H5 43.20N 17.50E
Mosul Iraq 60 F4 36.21N 43.08E
Motagua *r.* Guatemala 87 G3 15.56N 87.45W
Motala Sweden 50 C2 58.34N 15.05E
Motherwell U.K. 14 E2 55.48N 4.00W
Moulins France 42 F4 46.34N 3.20E
Moulmein Burma 68 B7 16.30N 97.40E
Mountain Ash *town* U.K. 13 D3 51.42N 3.21W
Mount Bellew *town* Rep. of Ire. 15 C3 53.29N 8.30W
Mount Gambier *town* Australia 71 D2 37.51S140.50E
Mount Hagen *town* P.N.G. 69 K2 5.54S144.13E
Mount Isa *town* Australia 71 C3 20.50S139.29E
Mount Magnet *town* Australia 71 A3 28.06S117.50E
Mountmellick Rep. of Ire. 15 D3 53.08N 7.21W
Mount Newman *town* Australia 71 A3 23.20S119.39E
Mount's Bay U.K. 13 B2 50.02N 5.25W
Mourne *r.* U.K. 8 C4 54.50N 7.28W
Mourne Mts. U.K. 15 E4 54.10N 6.10W
Moussoro Chad 103 H3 13.41N 16.31E
Moy *r.* Rep. of Ire. 15 B4 54.10N 9.09W
Mozambique Africa 99 D3 18.00S 35.00E
Mozambique Channel Indian Oc. 99 D3 16.00S 42.30E
Mozyr U.S.S.R. 49 N6 52.02N 29.10E
Mtwara Tanzania 99 E3 10.17S 40.11E
Muang Chiang Rai Thailand 68 B7 19.56N 99.51E
Muang Khon Kaen Thailand 68 C7 16.25N102.50E
Muang Lampang Thailand 68 B7 18.16N 99.30E
Muang Nakhon Phanom Thailand 68 C7 17.22N104.45E
Muang Nakhon Sawan Thailand 68 C7 15.35N100.10E
Muang Nan Thailand 68 C7 18.52N100.42E
Muang Phitsanulok Thailand 68 C7 16.50N100.15E
Muang Phrae Thailand 68 C7 18.07N100.09E
Muar Malaysia 68 C4 2.01N102.35E
Muara Brunei 68 F5 5.01N115.01E
Muara Indonesia 68 C3 0.32S101.20E
Mubi Nigeria 103 G3 10.16N 13.17E
Muchinga Mts. Zambia 94 F3 12.00S 31.00E
Muck *i.* U.K. 14 B3 56.50N 6.14W
Mudanjiang China 67 K6 44.36N129.42E
Mudhnib Saudi Arabia 61 G2 25.52N 44.15E
Mugía Spain 43 A5 43.06N 9.14W
Muğla Turkey 47 N2 37.12N 28.22E
Muharraq Bahrain 61 H2 26.16N 50.38E
Mühlhausen E. Germany 48 E5 51.12N 10.27E
Muine Bheag Rep. of Ire. 15 E2 52.41N 6.59W
Mukachevo U.S.S.R. 49 K4 48.26N 22.45E
Mukah Malaysia 68 E4 2.56N112.02E
Mukalla S. Yemen 101 G3 14.34N 49.09E
Mukawa *r.* Japan 70 E8 42.30N142.20E
Mulgrave I. Australia 69 K1 10.05S142.00E
Mulhacén *mtn.* Spain 43 D2 37.04N 3.22W
Mülheim N.-Westfalen W. Germany 39 E3 51.25N 6.50E
Mülheim N.-Westfalen W. Germany 39 F2 50.58N 7.00E
Mulhouse France 42 H4 47.45N 7.21E
Mull *i.* U.K. 14 C3 56.28N 5.56W
Mull, Sd. of U.K. 14 C3 56.32N 5.55W
Mullaghanattin Rep. of Ire. 15 B1 51.55N 9.52W
Mullaghareirk Mts. Rep. of Ire. 15 B2 52.20N 9.10W
Mullaghmore *mtn.* U.K. 15 E4 54.51N 6.51W
Mullet Pen. Rep. of Ire. 15 A4 54.10N 10.05W
Mullingar Rep. of Ire. 15 D3 53.31N 7.21W
Mull of Galloway *c.* U.K. 14 D1 54.39N 4.52W
Mull of Kintyre *c.* U.K. 14 C2 55.17N 5.45W
Multān Pakistan 63 C5 30.10N 71.36E
Multyfarnham Rep. of Ire. 15 D3 53.38N 7.24W
Muna *i.* Indonesia 69 G2 5.00S122.30E
Mundo *r.* Spain 43 E3 38.20N 1.50W
Munich W. Germany 48 E4 48.08N 11.35E
Münster W. Germany 39 F3 51.58N 7.37E
Muntok Indonesia 68 D3 2.04S105.12E
Muonio Finland 50 E4 67.52N 23.45E
Muonio *r.* Sweden / Finland 50 E4 67.13N 23.30E
Murallón *mtn.* Argentina / Chile 89 B3 49.48S 73.26W
Murat *r.* Turkey 33 M2 38.40N 39.30E
Murchison *r.* Australia 71 A3 27.30S114.10E
Murcia Spain 43 E2 37.59N 1.08W
Murcia *d.* Spain 43 E3 39.00N 2.00W
Mureş *r.* Romania 49 J3 46.16N 20.10E
Muret France 42 E2 43.28N 1.19E
Murghab *r.* Afghan. 62 B6 36.50N 63.00E
Muria *mtn.* Indonesia 68 E2 6.30S110.55E
Müritz, L. E. Germany 48 F6 53.25N 12.45E
Murmansk U.S.S.R. 50 H5 68.59N 33.08E
Murom U.S.S.R. 52 D3 55.04N 42.04E
Muroran Japan 70 D8 42.21N140.59E
Murray *r.* Australia 71 C2 35.23S139.20E
Murrumbidgee *r.* Australia 71 D2 34.38S143.10E
Murud *mtn.* Malaysia 68 F4 3.45N115.30E
Murwāra India 63 E4 23.49N 80.28E
Murzuq Libya 100 D4 25.56N 13.57E
Muş Turkey 60 F5 38.45N 41.30E
Musala *mtn.* Bulgaria 47 K5 42.11N 23.35E
Muscat Oman 61 J1 23.36N 58.37E
Musgrave Ranges *mts.* Australia 71 C3 26.30S131.10E
Musi *r.* Indonesia 68 C3 2.20S104.57E
Muskegon U.S.A. 83 I5 43.13N 86.10W
Muskogee U.S.A. 83 G4 35.45N 95.21W
Musselburgh U.K. 14 E2 55.57N 3.04W
Mustang Nepal 63 E5 29.10N 83.55E
Mustjala U.S.S.R. 50 E2 58.30N 22.10E
Mut Turkey 60 D5 36.38N 33.27E
Mutare Zimbabwe 99 D3 18.58S 32.38E
Mutsu wan *b.* Japan 70 E7 41.10N141.05E
Muwai Hakran Saudi Arabia 60 F1 22.41N 41.37E
Muzaffarnagar India 63 D5 29.28N 77.42E
Muzaffarpur India 63 F5 26.07N 85.23E
Mwanza Tanzania 99 D4 2.30S 32.54E
Mwene Ditu Zaïre 99 C4 7.01S 23.27E
Mweru, L. Zambia / Zaïre 99 C4 9.00S 28.40E
Myanaung Burma 63 G3 18.25N 95.10E
Myingyan Burma 63 G4 21.25N 95.20E
Myitkyinā Burma 63 H4 25.24N 97.25E
Mymensingh Bangla. 63 G4 24.45N 90.23E
Myrdal Norway 50 A3 60.44N 7.08E
Mysore India 63 D2 12.18N 76.37E
My Tho Vietnam 68 D6 10.21N106.21E

N

Naas Rep. of Ire. 15 E3 53.13N 6.41W
Nacala Mozambique 99 E3 14.30S 40.37E
Nadiād India 63 D4 22.42N 72.55E
Naestved Denmark 38 E3 55.14N 11.47E
Naft Safid Iran 61 H3 31.38N 49.20E
Naga Phil. 69 G6 13.36N123.12E
Nāgāland *d.* India 63 G5 26.10N 94.30E
Nagano Japan 70 D5 36.39N138.10E
Nagaoka Japan 70 D5 37.30N138.50E
Nāgappattinam India 63 E2 10.45N 79.50E
Nagasaki Japan 70 A3 32.45N129.52E
Nāgercoil India 63 D2 8.11N 77.30E
Nag' Hammadi Egypt 60 D2 26.04N 32.13E
Nagles Mts. Rep. of Ire. 15 C2 52.05N 8.31W
Nagoya Japan 70 C4 35.08N136.53E
Nāgpur India 63 E4 21.10N 79.12E
Nagykanizsa Hungary 49 H3 46.27N 17.01E
Naha Japan 67 K3 26.10N127.40E
Nahāvand Iran 61 H4 34.13N 48.23E
Nahe *r.* W. Germany 39 F1 49.58N 7.54E
Nain Canada 81 L3 56.30N 61.45W
Nairn U.K. 14 E4 57.35N 3.52W
Nairobi Kenya 99 D4 1.17S 36.50E
Nakaminato Japan 70 D5 36.21N140.36E
Nakano shima *i.* Japan 70 A1 29.55N129.55E
Nakatsu Japan 70 A3 33.37N131.11E
Nakhichevan U.S.S.R. 61 G5 39.12N 45.24E
Nakhodka U.S.S.R. 67 L5 42.53N132.54E
Nakhon Pathom Thailand 68 B6 13.50N100.01E
Nakhon Ratchasima Thailand 68 C7 14.59N102.12E
Nakhon Si Thammarat Thailand 68 C5 8.29N100.00E
Naknek U.S.A. 80 C3 58.45N157.00W
Nakskov Denmark 38 E2 54.50N 11.10E
Nakuru Kenya 99 D4 0.16S 36.04E
Nalón *r.* Spain 43 B5 43.35N 6.06W
Nālūt Libya 100 D5 31.53N 10.59E
Namangan U.S.S.R. 66 A5 40.59N 71.41E
Nam Co *l.* China 66 E3 30.40N 90.30E
Nam Dinh Vietnam 68 D8 20.25N106.12E
Namib Desert Namibia 99 B2 22.50S 14.40E
Namibe Angola 99 B3 15.10S 12.10E
Namibia Africa 99 B2 22.00S 17.00E
Namlea Indonesia 69 H3 3.15S127.07E
Namonuito *i.* Pacific Oc. 74 F8 8.46N150.02E
Nampo N. Korea 67 J5 38.40N125.30E
Nampula Mozambique 99 D3 15.09S 39.14E
Namsos Norway 50 B4 64.28N 11.30E
Namuchabawashan *mtn.* China 63 G5 29.30N 95.10E
Namur Belgium 39 C2 50.28N 4.52E
Namur *d.* Belgium 39 C2 50.20N 4.45E
Nanaimo Canada 80 F2 49.08N123.58W
Nanao Japan 70 C5 37.03N136.58E
Nanchang China 67 I3 28.38N115.56E
Nanchong China 66 G3 30.54N106.06E
Nancy France 42 H5 48.42N 6.12E
Nanda Devi *mtn.* India 63 E5 30.21N 79.50E
Nander India 63 D3 19.11N 77.21E
Nānga Parbat *mtn.* Jammu & Kashmir 63 D6 35.10N 74.35E
Nanjing China 67 I4 32.00N118.40E
Nan Ling *mts.* China 67 H2 25.20N110.30E
Nanning China 67 H2 22.50N108.19E
Nanping China 67 I3 26.40N118.07E
Nanshan Is. S. China Sea 68 F6 10.30N116.00E
Nantaise *r.* France 42 D4 47.12N 1.35W
Nantes France 42 D4 47.14N 1.35W
Nantong China 67 J4 32.05N120.59E
Nantucket I. U.S.A. 83 M5 41.16N 70.00W
Nantwich U.K. 12 E5 53.03N 2.29W
Nanumea *i.* Tuvalu 74 H7 5.40S176.10E
Nanyang China 67 H4 33.06N112.31E
Napier New Zealand 71 G2 39.30S176.54E
Naples Italy 46 G4 40.50N 14.14E
Naples, G. of Med. Sea 46 G4 40.42N 14.15E
Nara Mali 102 C4 15.13N 7.20W
Nārāyanganj Bangla. 63 G4 23.36N 90.28E
Narbada *r.* see Narmada *r.* India 63
Narbonne France 42 F2 43.11N 3.00E
Nares Str. Canada 81 K5 78.30N 75.00W
Narmada *r.* India 63 D4 21.40N 73.00E
Narodnaya *mtn.* U.S.S.R. 52 F4 65.00N 61.00E
Narsimhapur India 63 E4 22.58N 79.15E
Narva U.S.S.R. 50 G2 59.22N 28.17E
Narva *r.* U.S.S.R. 50 F2 59.30N 28.00E
Narvik Norway 50 D5 68.26N 17.25E
Naryan Mar U.S.S.R. 52 E4 67.37N 53.02E
Nasarawa Nigeria 103 F2 8.35N 7.44E
Nashville U.S.A. 83 I4 36.10N 86.50W
Näsijärvi *l.* Finland 50 E3 61.30N 23.50E
Nāsik India 63 D4 20.00N 73.52E
Nasratabad Iran 61 J3 29.54N 59.58E
Nassau Bahamas 87 I5 25.03N 77.20W
Nassau I. Cook Is. 74 J6 11.33S165.25W
Nasser, L. Egypt 60 D1 22.40N 32.00E
Nässjö Sweden 50 C2 57.39N 14.40E
Natal Brazil 88 F7 5.46S 35.15W
Natal Indonesia 68 B4 0.35N 99.07E
Natchez U.S.A. 83 H3 31.22N 91.24W
Natitingou Benin 103 E3 10.17N 1.19E
Natron, L. Tanzania 99 D4 2.18S 36.05E
Naumburg E. Germany 48 E5 51.09N 11.48E
Nauru Pacific Oc. 74 G7 0.32S166.55E
Navalmoral de la Mata Spain 43 C3 39.54N 5.33W
Navan Rep. of Ire. 15 E3 53.39N 6.42W
Naver *r.* U.K. 14 D5 58.29N 4.12W
Navojoa Mexico 86 C5 27.06N109.26W
Návpaktos Greece 47 J3 38.24N 21.49E
Návplion Greece 47 K2 37.33N 22.47E
Navrongo Ghana 103 D3 10.51N 1.03W
Nawābshāh Pakistan 62 C5 26.15N 68.26E
Náxos *i.* Greece 47 L2 37.03N 25.30E
Nayarit *d.* Mexico 86 C4 21.30N104.00W
Nazareth Israel 60 D4 32.41N 35.16E
Nazas *r.* Mexico 86 D5 25.34N103.25W
Nazilli Turkey 60 C5 37.55N 28.20E
N'Djamena Chad 103 H3 12.10N 14.59E
Ndola Zambia 99 C3 13.00S 28.39E
Neagh, Lough U.K. 15 E4 54.36N 6.25W
Neath U.K. 13 D3 51.39N 3.48W
Nebraska *d.* U.S.A. 82 F5 41.30N100.00W
Nebrodi Mts. Italy 46 G2 37.53N 14.32E
Neches *r.* U.S.A. 83 H2 29.55N 93.50W
Neckar *r.* W. Germany 48 D4 49.32N 8.26E
Needles U.S.A. 82 D3 34.51N114.36W
Neerpelt Belgium 39 D3 51.13N 5.28E
Nefyn U.K. 12 C4 52.58N 4.28W
Negev *des.* Israel 60 D3 30.42N 34.55E
Negoiu *mtn.* Romania 49 L2 45.36N 24.32E
Negotin Yugo. 47 K6 44.14N 22.33E
Negra, C. Peru 88 A7 6.06S 81.09W
Negrais, C. Burma 63 G3 16.00N 94.30E
Negro *r.* Argentina 89 C3 41.00S 62.48W
Negro *r.* Brazil 88 C7 3.30S 60.00W
Negros *i.* Phil. 69 G6 10.00N123.00E
Neijiang China 66 G3 29.32N105.03E
Nei Monggol *d.* see Inner Mongolia *d.* China 67
Neisse *r.* Poland / E. Germany 48 G6 52.05N 14.42E
Neiva Colombia 88 B8 2.58N 75.15W
Nejd *d.* Saudi Arabia 60 F2 25.00N 42.00E
Nekső Denmark 50 C1 55.04N 15.09E
Nellore India 63 E3 14.29N 80.00E
Nelson Canada 80 G2 49.29N117.17W
Nelson *r.* Canada 81 I3 57.00N 93.20W
Nelson New Zealand 71 G1 41.16S173.15E
Nelson U.K. 12 E5 53.51N 2.11W
Nelson U.S.A. 82 D4 35.30N113.16W
Neman *r.* U.S.S.R. 50 E1 55.23N 21.15E
Nemours France 42 F5 48.16N 2.41E
Nemuro Japan 70 F8 43.22N145.36E
Nemuro kaikyō *str.* Japan 70 F8 44.00N145.50E
Nenagh Rep. of Ire. 15 C2 52.52N 8.13W
Nenana U.S.A. 80 D4 64.35N149.20W
Nene *r.* U.K. 12 H4 52.49N 0.12E
Nenjiang China 67 J6 49.10N125.15E
Nepal Asia 63 E5 28.00N 84.30E
Nephin Beg *mtn.* Rep. of Ire. 15 B4 54.02N 9.38W
Nephin Beg Range *mts.* Rep. of Ire. 15 B4 54.00N 9.40W
Nera *r.* Italy 46 F5 42.33N 12.43E
Neretva *r.* Yugo. 47 H5 43.02N 17.28E
Nes Neth. 39 D5 53.27N 5.46E
Ness, Loch U.K. 14 D4 57.16N 4.30W
Nesterov U.S.S.R. 49 L5 50.04N 24.00E
Netherlands Europe 39 D4 52.00N 5.30E
Netherlands Antilles S. America 87 K2 12.30N 69.00W
Neto *r.* Italy 47 H3 39.12N 17.08E
Neubrandenburg E. Germany 48 F6 53.33N 13.16E
Neuchâtel Switz. 48 C3 47.00N 6.56E
Neuchâtel, Lac de *l.* Switz. 48 C3 46.55N 6.55E
Neuenhaus W. Germany 39 E4 52.30N 6.58E
Neufchâteau Belgium 39 D1 49.51N 5.26E
Neufchâtel France 42 E5 49.44N 1.26E
Neukalen E. Germany 38 F1 53.50N 12.47E
Neumünster W. Germany 48 D7 54.06N 9.59E
Neuquén Argentina 89 C4 38.55S 68.55W
Neuse *r.* U.S.A. 83 K4 35.04N 77.04W
Neusiedler, L. Austria 48 H3 47.52N 16.45E
Neuss W. Germany 39 E3 51.12N 6.42E
Neustadt W. Germany 38 D2 54.07N 10.49E
Neustrelitz E. Germany 48 F6 53.22N 13.05E
Neuwied W. Germany 39 F2 50.26N 7.28E
Nevada *d.* U.S.A. 82 C4 39.00N117.00W
Nevada, Sierra *mts.* Spain 43 D2 37.04N 3.20W
Nevada, Sierra *mts.* U.S.A. 82 C4 37.30N119.00W
Nevers France 42 F4 47.00N 3.09E
Nevşehir Turkey 60 D5 38.38N 34.43E
New Amsterdam Guyana 88 D8 6.18N 57.00W
Newark U.S.A. 83 L5 40.44N 74.11W
Newark-on-Trent U.K. 12 G5 53.05N 0.47W
New Bedford U.S.A. 83 L5 41.38N 70.55W
New Bern U.S.A. 83 K4 35.05N 77.04W
Newbiggin-by-the-Sea U.K. 12 F7 55.10N 1.30W
New Britain *i.* P.N.G. 71 D5 6.00S150.00E
New Brunswick *d.* Canada 81 L2 47.00N 66.00W
Newbury U.K. 13 F3 51.23N 1.20W
New Caledonia *i.* Pacific Oc. 71 F3 22.00S165.00E
Newcastle Australia 71 E2 32.55S151.46E
Newcastle U.K. 15 F4 54.12N 5.54W
Newcastle U.S.A. 82 F5 43.52N104.14W
Newcastle Emlyn U.K. 13 C4 52.02N 4.27W
Newcastle-under-Lyme U.K. 12 E5 53.01N 2.18W
Newcastle upon Tyne U.K. 12 F6 54.58N 1.36W
Newcastle West Rep. of Ire. 15 B2 52.27N 9.04W
New Delhi India 63 D5 28.37N 77.13E
Newent U.K. 13 E3 51.56N 2.25W
New Forest *f.* U.K. 13 F2 50.52N 1.35W
Newfoundland *d.* Canada 81 L3 55.00N 60.00W
Newfoundland *i.* Canada 81 M2 48.30N 56.00W
New Galloway U.K. 14 D2 55.04N 4.08W
New Guinea *i.* Austa. 69 J2 5.00S140.00E
New Hampshire *d.* U.S.A. 83 L5 44.00N 71.30W
Newhaven U.K. 13 H2 50.48N 0.03E
New Haven U.S.A. 83 L5 41.14N 72.50W
New Ireland *i.* P.N.G. 71 E5 2.30S151.30E
New Jersey *d.* U.S.A. 83 L5 40.00N 74.30W
Newmarket Rep. of Ire. 15 B2 52.13N 9.01W
Newmarket U.K. 13 H4 52.17N 0.26E
Newmarket on Fergus Rep. of Ire. 15 C2 52.46N 8.55W
New Mexico *d.* U.S.A 82 E3 34.00N106.00W
New Orleans U.S.A. 83 H3 30.00N 90.03W
New Plymouth New Zealand 71 G2 39.04S174.04E
Newport Tipperary Rep. of Ire. 15 C2 52.42N 8.26W
Newport Mayo Rep. of Ire. 15 B3 53.53N 9.35W
Newport Dyfed U.K. 13 C4 52.01N 4.49W
Newport Essex U.K. 13 H3 51.58N 0.15E
Newport Gwent U.K. 13 E3 51.34N 2.59W
Newport Hants. U.K. 13 F2 50.43N 1.18W
Newport News U.S.A. 83 K4 36.59N 76.26W
New Providence *i.* Bahamas 87 I5 25.03N 77.25W
Newquay U.K. 13 B2 50.24N 5.06W
New Quay U.K. 13 C4 52.13N 4.21W
New Radnor U.K. 13 D4 52.13N 3.09W
New Romney U.K. 13 H2 50.59N 0.58E
New Ross Rep. of Ire. 15 E2 52.23N 6.59W
Newry U.K. 15 E4 54.11N 6.21W
New Scone U.K. 14 E3 56.26N 3.22W
New Siberian Is. U.S.S.R. 53 L4 76.00N144.00E
New South Wales *d.* Australia 71 D2 33.45S147.00E
Newton Abbot U.K. 13 D2 50.33N 3.35W
Newton Aycliffe U.K. 12 F6 54.36N 1.34W
Newtonmore U.K. 14 D4 57.03N 4.10W
Newton Stewart U.K. 14 D1 54.57N 4.29W
Newtown U.K. 13 D4 52.31N 3.19W
Newtownabbey U.K. 15 F4 54.39N 5.57W
Newtownards U.K. 15 F4 54.35N 5.41W
Newtown Butler U.K. 15 D4 54.11N 7.23W
Newtown St. Boswells U.K. 14 F2 55.35N 2.40W
Newtownstewart U.K. 15 D4 54.43N 7.26W
New York U.S.A. 83 L5 40.40N 73.50W
New York *d.* U.S.A. 83 K5 43.00N 75.00W
New Zealand Austa. 71 G1 41.00S175.00E
Nezhin U.S.S.R. 49 O5 51.03N 31.54E
Ngaoundéré Cameroon 103 G2 7.20N 13.35E
Nguigmi Niger 103 G3 14.00N 13.11E
Nguru Nigeria 103 G3 12.53N 10.30E
Nha Trang Vietnam 68 D6 12.15N109.10E
Niagara Falls *town* U.S.A. 83 K5 43.06N 79.04W
Niamey Niger 103 E3 13.32N 2.05E
Niangara Zaïre 99 C5 3.45N 27.54E
Niapa, Gunung *mtn.* Indonesia 68 F4 1.45N117.30E
Nias *i.* Indonesia 68 B4 1.05N 97.30E
Nibe Denmark 38 C4 56.59N 9.39E
Nicaragua C. America 87 G2 13.00N 85.00W
Nicaragua, L. Nicaragua 87 G2 11.30N 85.30W
Nicastro Italy 46 H3 38.58N 16.16E
Nice France 42 H2 43.42N 7.16E
Nicobar Is. India 63 G2 8.00N 94.00E
Nicosia Cyprus 60 D4 35.11N 33.23E
Nicoya, G. of Costa Rica 87 H1 9.30N 85.00W
Nicoya Pen. Costa Rica 87 G2 10.30N 85.30W
Nid *r.* Norway 50 B2 58.26N 8.44E
Nidzica Poland 49 J6 53.22N 20.26E
Niebüll W. Germany 38 B2 54.47N 8.51E
Niers *r.* Neth. 39 D3 51.43N 5.56E
Nieuwpoort Belgium 39 A3 51.08N 2.45E
Nigde Turkey 60 D5 37.58N 34.42E
Niger Africa 100 C3 17.00N 9.30E
Niger *d.* Nigeria 103 F3 9.50N 6.00E
Niger *r.* Nigeria 103 F1 4.15N 6.05E
Niger Delta Nigeria 103 F1 4.00N 6.10E
Nigeria Africa 103 F2 9.00N 9.00E
Nihoa *i.* Hawaiian Is. 74 J10 23.03N161.55W
Niigata Japan 70 D5 37.58N139.02E
Niihama Japan 70 B3 33.57N133.15E

Ringwood U.K. **13 F2** 50.50N 1.49W
Riobamba Ecuador **88 B7** 1.44S 78.40W
Rio Branco Brazil **88 C7** 10.00S 67.49W
Rio de Janeiro Brazil **89 E5** 22.50S 43.17W
Río Gallegos Argentina **89 C2** 51.35S 69.15W
Rio Grande *town* Brazil **89 D4** 32.03S 52.18W
Rio Grande *r.* N. America **76 K4** 25.55N 97.08W
Río Grande *r.* Nicaragua **87 H2** 12.48N 83.30W
Ripon U.K. **12 F6** 54.08N 1.30W
Risha, Wadi *r.* Saudi Arabia **61 F2** 25.40N 44.08E
Rishiri jima *i.* Japan **70 E9** 45.11N141.15E
Risör Norway **50 B2** 58.44N 9.15E
Ristikent U.S.S.R. **50 G5** 68.40N 31.47E
Rivas Nicaragua **87 G2** 11.26N 85.50W
Rivers *d.* Nigeria **103 F1** 4.45N 6.35E
Riyadh Saudi Arabia **61 G2** 24.39N 46.44E
Rize Turkey **60 F6** 41.03N 40.31E
Rizzuto, C. Italy **47 H3** 38.53N 17.06E
Rjukan Norway **50 B2** 59.54N 8.33E
Roag, L. U.K. **14 B5** 58.17N 6.52W
Roanne France **42 G4** 46.02N 4.05E
Roanoke *r.* U.S.A. **83 K4** 36.00N 76.35W
Roberval Canada **81 K2** 48.31N 72.16W
Robin Hood's Bay *town* U.K. **12 G6** 54.27N 0.31W
Robson, Mt. Canada **80 G3** 53.00N119.09W
Roca, Cabo de Portugal **43 A3** 38.40N 9.31W
Roccella Italy **47 H3** 38.19N 16.24E
Rocha Uruguay **89 D4** 34.30S 54.22W
Rochdale U.K. **12 E5** 53.36N 2.10W
Rochechouart France **42 E3** 45.49N 0.50E
Rochefort Belgium **39 D2** 50.10N 5.13E
Rochefort France **42 D3** 45.57N 0.58W
Rochester U.K. **13 H3** 51.22N 0.30E
Rochester U.S.A. **83 K5** 43.12N 77.37W
Rochfort Bridge Rep. of Ire. **15 D3** 53.25N 7.20W
Rockford U.S.A. **83 I5** 42.16N 89.06W
Rockhampton Australia **71 E3** 23.22S150.32E
Rock Springs U.S.A. **82 E5** 41.35N109.13W
Rocky Mts. N. America **76 H7** 42.00N110.00W
Rocroi France **39 C1** 49.56N 4.31E
Rödby Denmark **38 E2** 54.42N 11.24E
Rodel U.K. **14 B4** 57.47N 6.58W
Rodez France **42 F3** 44.21N 2.34E
Rodonit, C. Albania **47 I4** 41.34N 19.25E
Rödvig Denmark **38 F3** 55.13N 12.20E
Roermond Neth. **39 D3** 51.12N 6.00E
Rohtak India **63 D5** 28.54N 76.35E
Rokan *r.* Indonesia **68 C4** 2.00N101.00E
Rokel *r.* Sierra Leone **102 B2** 8.36N 12.55W
Rolla U.S.A. **83 H4** 37.56N 91.55W
Roma *i.* Indonesia **69 H2** 7.45S127.20E
Romain, C. U.S.A. **83 K3** 33.01N 79.23W
Romaine *r.* Canada **81 L3** 50.20N 63.45W
Romania Europe **49 K3** 46.30N 24.00E
Romano, C. U.S.A. **83 J2** 25.50N 81.42W
Romans France **42 G3** 45.03N 5.03E
Rome Italy **46 F4** 41.54N 12.29E
Romilly France **42 F5** 48.31N 3.44E
Romney Marsh *f.* U.K. **13 H3** 51.05N 0.55E
Römö *i.* Denmark **38 B3** 55.10N 8.30E
Romorantin France **42 E4** 47.22N 1.44E
Rona *i.* U.K. **14 C4** 57.33N 5.59W
Ronda Spain **43 C2** 36.45N 5.10W
Rönde Denmark **38 D4** 56.18N 10.30E
Rönne Denmark **50 C1** 55.07N 14.43E
Roof Butte *mtn.* U.S.A. **82 E4** 36.29N109.05W
Roosendaal Neth. **39 C3** 51.32N 4.28E
Roosevelt *r.* Brazil **88 C7** 5.00S 60.30W
Roraima, Mt. Guyana **88 C8** 5.45N 61.00W
Röros Norway **50 B3** 62.35N 11.23E
Rosa, Mt. Italy / Switz. **48 C2** 45.56N 7.51E
Rosario Argentina **89 C4** 33.00S 60.40W
Roscommon Rep. of Ire. **15 C3** 53.38N 8.13W
Roscommon *d.* Rep. of Ire. **15 C3** 53.38N 8.11W
Roscrea Rep. of Ire. **15 D2** 52.57N 7.49W
Roseau Dominica **87 L3** 15.18N 61.23W
Roseburg U.S.A. **82 B5** 43.13N123.21W
Rosenheim W. Germany **48 F3** 47.51N 12.09E
Rosetown Canada **80 H3** 51.34N107.59W
Roshage *c.* Denmark **38 B5** 57.10N 8.30E
Rosières France **39 A1** 49.49N 2.43E
Roskilde Denmark **38 F3** 55.39N 12.07E
Roskilde *d.* Denmark **38 F3** 55.30N 12.05E
Roslags-Näsby Sweden **50 D2** 59.26N 18.02E
Rosslare Rep. of Ire. **15 E2** 52.17N 6.23W
Ross-on-Wye U.K. **13 E3** 51.55N 2.35W
Ross Sea Antarctica **107 R1** 73.00S179.00E
Rössvatnet *l.* Norway **50 C4** 65.50N 14.00E
Rostock E. Germany **48 F7** 54.06N 12.09E
Rostov U.S.S.R. **52 D2** 47.10N 39.45E
Rothbury U.K. **12 F7** 55.20N 1.54W
Rother *r.* U.K. **8 G2** 50.54N 0.48E
Rotherham U.K. **12 F5** 53.26N 1.21W
Rothes U.K. **14 E4** 57.31N 3.14W
Rothesay U.K. **14 C2** 55.50N 5.03W
Roti *i.* Indonesia **69 G1** 10.30S123.10E
Rotterdam Neth. **39 C3** 51.55N 4.29E
Roubaix France **39 B2** 50.42N 3.10E
Rouen France **42 E5** 49.26N 1.05E
Roulers Belgium **39 B2** 50.57N 3.06E
Roundup U.S.A. **82 E6** 46.27N108.34W
Rourkela India **63 F4** 22.16N 85.01E
Rousay *i.* U.K. **14 E6** 59.10N 3.02W
Rouyn Canada **81 K2** 48.15N 79.00W
Rovaniemi Finland **50 F4** 66.29N 25.40E
Rovinj Yugo. **46 F6** 45.06N 13.39E
Rovno U.S.S.R. **49 M5** 50.39N 26.10E
Royale, I. U.S.A. **83 I6** 48.00N 88.45W
Royal Leamington Spa U.K. **13 F4** 52.15N 1.32W
Royal Tunbridge Wells U.K. **13 H3** 51.07N 0.16E
Roye France **39 A1** 49.42N 2.48E
Royston U.K. **13 G4** 52.03N 0.01W
Rub al Khali *des.* Saudi Arabia **101 G3** 20.20N 52.30E
Rubtsovsk U.S.S.R. **52 G2** 51.29N 81.10E
Rūdān *r.* Iran **61 J2** 27.02N 56.53E
Rud-i-Pusht *r.* Iran **61 J3** 29.09N 58.09E
Rudolstadt E. Germany **48 E5** 50.44N 11.20E
Ruffec France **42 E4** 46.02N 0.12E
Rufiji *r.* Tanzania **99 D4** 8.02S 39.17E
Rufisque Senegal **102 A3** 14.43N 17.16W
Rugao China **67 J4** 32.27N120.35E
Rugby U.K. **13 F4** 52.23N 1.16W
Rugby U.S.A. **82 G6** 48.24N 99.59W
Rügen *i.* E. Germany **48 F7** 54.30N 13.30E
Ruhr *f.* W. Germany **39 F3** 51.22N 7.26E
Ruhr *r.* W. Germany **39 E3** 51.27N 6.41E
Rukwa, L. Tanzania **99 D4** 8.00S 32.20E
Ruma Yugo. **47 I6** 44.59N 19.51E
Rum Cay *i.* Bahamas **87 J4** 23.41N 74.53W
Rumoi Japan **70 E8** 43.56N141.39E
Runcorn U.K. **12 E5** 53.20N 2.42W
Ruoqiang China **66 D5** 39.00N 88.00E
Ruo Shui *r.* China **66 F5** 42.15N101.03E
Rur *r.* Neth. **39 D3** 51.12N 5.58E
Rurutu *i.* Pacific Oc. **75 K5** 22.25S151.20W
Ruse Bulgaria **47 L5** 43.50N 25.59E
Rushden U.K. **13 G4** 52.16N 0.33W
Russian S.F.S.R. *d.* U.S.S.R. **52 E3** 62.00N 80.00E
Rustavi U.S.S.R. **52 D2** 41.34N 45.03E
Rütenbrock W. Germany **39 F4** 52.51N 7.06E
Ruteng Indonesia **69 G2** 8.35S120.28E
Ruthin U.K. **12 D5** 53.07N 3.18W
Rutog China **66 C4** 33.30N 79.40E
Ruvuma *r.* Mozambique / Tanzania **99 E3** 10.30S 40.30E
Ruwandiz Iraq **61 G5** 36.38N 44.32E
Ruwenzori Range *mts.* Uganda / Zaïre **99 C5** 0.30N 30.00E
Rwanda Africa **99 C4** 2.00S 30.00E
Ryan, L. U.K. **14 C2** 55.00N 5.05W
Ryazan U.S.S.R. **52 D3** 54.37N 39.43E
Rybachi Pen. U.S.S.R. **50 H5** 69.45N 32.30E
Rybinsk Resr. U.S.S.R. **52 D3** 58.30N 38.25E
Rybnik Poland **49 I5** 50.06N 18.32E
Rybnitsa U.S.S.R. **49 N3** 47.42N 29.00E
Rye U.K. **13 H2** 50.57N 0.44E
Rye *r.* U.K. **12 G6** 54.09N 0.45W
Ryki Poland **49 J5** 51.39N 21.56E
Ryukyu Is. Japan **67 J2** 26.30N125.00E
Ryukyu Is. Trench Pacific Oc. **74 C10** 25.00N129.00E
Rzeszów Poland **49 J5** 50.04N 22.00E

S

Saale *r.* E. Germany **48 E5** 51.58N 11.53E
Saar *r.* W. Germany **39 E1** 49.43N 6.34E
Saarbrücken W. Germany **48 C4** 49.15N 6.58E
Saarburg W. Germany **39 E1** 49.36N 6.33E
Saaremaa *i.* U.S.S.R. **50 E2** 58.30N 22.30E
Saarijärvi Finland **50 F3** 62.44N 25.15E
Saba *i.* Leeward Is. **87 L3** 17.42N 63.26W
Šabac Yugo. **47 I6** 44.45N 19.41E
Sabadell Spain **43 G4** 41.33N 2.07E
Sabana, Archipiélago de Cuba **87 H4** 23.30N 80.00W
Sabinas Mexico **86 D5** 27.51N101.10W
Sabinas Hidalgo Mexico **86 D5** 26.33N100.10W
Sabine *r.* U.S.A. **83 H2** 29.40N 93.50W
Sable, C. Canada **81 L2** 43.30N 65.50W
Sable, C. U.S.A. **76 L4** 25.00N 91.20W
Sable I. Canada **81 M2** 44.00N 60.00W
Sacedón Spain **43 D4** 40.29N 2.44W
Sacramento U.S.A. **82 B4** 38.32N121.30W
Sacramento *r.* U.S.A. **82 B4** 38.05N122.00W
Sacramento Mts. U.S.A. **82 E3** 33.10N105.50W
Sádaba Spain **43 E5** 42.19N 1.10W
Sadiya India **63 G5** 27.49N 95.38E
Sado *i.* Japan **70 D6** 38.00N138.20E
Saeby Denmark **38 D5** 57.20N 10.30E
Safaha *des.* Saudi Arabia **60 E2** 26.30N 39.30E
Safaniya Saudi Arabia **61 H3** 28.00N 48.48E
Säffle Sweden **50 C2** 59.08N 12.55E
Saffron Walden U.K. **13 H4** 52.02N 0.19E
Safi Morocco **100 B5** 32.20N 9.17W
Saga Japan **70 A3** 33.08N130.30E
Sagaing Burma **63 G4** 22.00N 96.00E
Sagamihara Japan **70 D4** 35.35N139.30E
Sāgar India **63 E4** 23.50N 78.44E
Saglouc Canada **81 K4** 62.10N 75.40W
Sagua la Grande Cuba **87 H4** 22.55N 80.05W
Sagunto Spain **43 E3** 39.40N 0.17W
Sahagún Spain **43 C5** 42.23N 5.02W
Sahara *des.* Africa **100 B3** 18.00N 12.00E
Saharan Atlas *mts.* Algeria **100 C5** 34.20N 2.00E
Sahāranpur India **63 D5** 29.58N 77.33E
Sahba, Wadi *r.* Saudi Arabia **61 H1** 23.48N 49.50E
Sāhīwāl Pakistan **63 D5** 30.40N 73.06E
Saïda Lebanon **60 D4** 33.32N 35.22E
Sa'īdābād Iran **61 I3** 29.28N 55.43E
Saidpur Bangla. **63 F4** 25.48N 89.00E
Saimaa *l.* Finland **50 F3** 61.20N 28.00E
Saimbeyli Turkey **60 E5** 38.07N 36.08E
St. Abb's Head U.K. **14 F2** 55.54N 2.07W
St. Albans U.K. **13 G3** 51.47N 0.20W
St. Amand France **39 B2** 50.27N 3.26E
St. Amand-Mont-Rond *town* France **42 F4** 46.43N 2.29E
St. Andrews U.K. **14 F3** 56.20N 2.48W
St. Ann's Bay *town* Jamaica **87 I3** 18.26N 77.12W
St. Anthony Canada **81 M3** 51.24N 55.37W
St. Augustine U.S.A. **83 J2** 29.54N 81.19W
St. Austell U.K. **13 C2** 50.20N 4.48W
St. Barthélemy *i.* Leeward Is. **87 L3** 17.55N 62.50W
St. Bees Hd. U.K. **12 D6** 54.30N 3.40W
St. Boniface Canada **81 I2** 49.54N 97.07W
St. Brides Bay U.K. **13 B3** 51.50N 5.15W
St. Brieuc France **42 C5** 48.31N 2.45W
St. Catharines Canada **81 K2** 43.10N 79.15W
St. Catherine's Pt. U.K. **13 F2** 50.34N 1.20W
St. Céré France **42 E3** 44.52N 1.53E
St. Cloud U.S.A. **83 H6** 45.34N 94.10W
St. Croix *i.* U.S.V.Is. **87 L3** 17.45N 64.35W
St. David's U.K. **13 B3** 51.53N 5.16W
St. David's Head U.K. **13 B3** 51.55N 5.19W
St. Denis France **42 F5** 48.56N 2.21E
St. Dié France **42 H5** 48.17N 6.57E
St. Dizier France **42 G5** 48.38N 4.58E
St. Elias, Mt. U.S.A. **80 D4** 60.20N140.55W
Sainte Marie, Cap *c.* Madagascar **99 G6** 25.34S 45.10E
Saintes France **42 D3** 45.44N 0.38W
St. Étienne France **42 G3** 45.26N 4.26E
St. Feliu de Gixols Spain **43 G4** 41.47N 3.02E
Saintfield U.K. **15 F4** 54.29N 5.50W
St. Flour France **42 F3** 45.02N 3.05E
St. Gallen Switz. **48 D3** 47.25N 9.23E
St. Gaudens France **42 E2** 43.07N 0.44E
St. George's Grenada **87 L2** 12.04N 61.44W
St. George's Channel Rep. of Ire. / U.K. **15 E1** 51.30N 6.20W
St. Germain France **42 F5** 48.53N 2.04E
St. Gheorghe's Mouth *est.* Romania **47 N6** 44.51N 29.37E
St. Gilles-sur-Vie France **42 D4** 46.42N 1.56W
St. Girons France **42 E2** 42.59N 1.08E
St. Gotthard Pass Switz. **48 D3** 46.30N 8.55E
St. Govan's Head U.K. **13 C3** 51.36N 4.56W
St. Helena *i.* Atlantic Oc. **108 I4** 16.00S 6.00W
St. Helena B. R.S.A. **99 B1** 32.35S 18.00E
St. Helens U.K. **12 E5** 53.28N 2.43W
St. Helier U.K. **13 E1** 49.12N 2.07W
St. Hubert Belgium **39 D2** 50.02N 5.22E
St. Hyacinthe Canada **81 K2** 45.38N 72.57W
St. Ives U.K. **13 B2** 50.12N 5.30W
St. Jean Pied-de-Port France **42 D2** 43.10N 1.14W
St. John Canada **81 L2** 45.16N 66.03W
St. John *r.* Canada **81 L2** 45.30N 66.05W
St. John's Antigua **87 L3** 17.07N 61.51W
St. John's Canada **81 M2** 47.34N 52.41W
St. John's Pt. U.K. **15 F4** 54.13N 5.39W
St. Joseph U.S.A. **83 H4** 39.45N 94.51W
St. Kilda *i.* U.K. **8 B5** 57.55N 8.20W
St. Kitts-Nevis Leeward Is. **87 L3** 17.20N 62.45W
St. Lawrence *r.* Canada / U.S.A. **81 L2** 48.45N 68.30W
St. Lawrence, G. of Canada **81 L2** 48.00N 62.00W
St. Lawrence I. U.S.A. **80 A4** 63.00N170.00W
St. Lô France **42 D5** 49.07N 1.05W
St. Louis Senegal **102 A4** 16.01N 16.30W
St. Louis U.S.A. **83 H4** 38.40N 90.15W
St. Lucia Windward Is. **87 L2** 14.05N 61.00W
St. Maixent France **42 D4** 46.25N 0.12W
St. Malo France **42 C5** 48.39N 2.00W
St. Malo, Golfe de *g.* France **42 C5** 49.20N 2.00W
St.-Marc Haiti **87 J3** 19.08N 72.41W
St. Margaret's Hope U.K. **14 F5** 58.50N 2.57W
St. Martin *i.* Leeward Is. **87 L3** 18.05N 63.05W
St. Martin U.K. **13 E1** 49.26N 2.34W
St. Martin's *i.* U.K. **13 A1** 49.58N 6.17W
St. Mary U.K. **13 E1** 49.15N 2.09W
St. Mary's *i.* U.K. **13 A1** 49.55N 6.16W
St. Maurice *r.* Canada **81 K2** 46.20N 72.30W
St. Moritz Switz. **48 D3** 46.30N 9.51E
St. Nazaire France **42 C4** 47.17N 2.12W
St. Neots U.K. **13 G4** 52.13N 0.18W
St. Nicolas Belgium **39 C3** 51.10N 4.09E
St. Omer France **42 F6** 50.45N 2.15E
St. Paul France **42 F2** 42.49N 2.29E
St. Paul U.S.A. **83 H6** 45.00N 93.10W
St. Peter Port U.K. **13 E1** 49.27N 2.32W
St. Petersburg U.S.A. **83 J2** 27.45N 82.40W
St. Pierre and Miquelon *is.* N. America **81 M2** 47.00N 56.15W
St. Pölten Austria **48 G4** 48.13N 15.37E
St. Quentin France **39 B1** 49.51N 3.17E
St. Thomas *i.* U.S.V.Is. **87 L3** 18.22N 64.57W
St. Trond Belgium **39 D2** 50.49N 5.11E
St. Tropez France **42 H2** 43.16N 6.39E
St. Vallier France **42 G3** 45.11N 4.49E
St. Vincent, C. Portugal **43 A2** 37.01N 8.59W
St. Vincent and the Grenadines Windward Is. **87 L2** 13.00N 61.15W
St. Vith Belgium **39 E2** 50.15N 6.08E
St. Wendel W. Germany **39 F1** 49.27N 7.10E
St. Yrieix France **42 E3** 45.31N 1.12E
Sakai Japan **70 C4** 34.37N135.28E
Sakaka Saudi Arabia **60 F3** 29.59N 40.12E
Sakarya *r.* Turkey **60 C6** 41.08N 30.36E
Sakata Japan **70 D6** 38.55N139.51E
Sakété Benin **103 E2** 6.45N 2.45E
Sakhalin *i.* U.S.S.R. **53 L2** 50.00N143.00E
Sakskōbing Denmark **38 E2** 54.48N 11.42E
Sala Sweden **50 D2** 59.55N 16.38E
Salado *r.* La Pampa Argentina **89 C4** 36.15S 66.45W
Salado *r.* Santa Fé Argentina **89 C4** 32.40S 60.41W
Salado *r.* Mexico **86 E5** 26.46N 98.55W
Salala Oman **101 H3** 17.00N 54.04E
Salamanca Spain **43 C4** 40.58N 5.40W
Salar de Uyuni *l.* Bolivia **89 C5** 20.30S 67.45W
Salatiga Indonesia **68 E2** 7.15S110.34E
Salavat U.S.S.R. **52 E3** 53.22N 55.50E
Sala y Gomez *i.* Pacific Oc. **75 P5** 26.28S105.28W
Salbris France **42 F4** 47.26N 2.03E
Salcombe U.K. **13 D2** 50.13N 3.46W
Salekhard U.S.S.R. **52 F4** 66.33N 66.35E
Salem India **63 E2** 11.38N 78.08E
Salerno Italy **46 G4** 40.41N 14.45E
Salerno, G. of Med. Sea **46 G4** 40.30N 14.45E
Salford U.K. **12 E5** 53.30N 2.17W
Salgótarján Hungary **49 I4** 48.07N 19.48E
Salima Malaŵi **99 D3** 13.46S 34.26E
Salina Cruz Mexico **86 E3** 16.11N 95.12W
Salins France **42 G4** 46.56N 5.53E
Salisbury U.K. **13 F3** 51.04N 1.48W
Salisbury U.S.A. **83 K4** 38.22N 75.37W
Salisbury Plain *f.* U.K. **13 F3** 51.13N 1.55W
Salmās Iran **61 G5** 38.13N 44.50E
Salmon *r.* U.S.A. **82 C6** 45.50N116.50W
Salmon River Mts. U.S.A. **82 C5** 44.30N114.30W
Salo Finland **50 E3** 60.23N 23.10E
Salobreña Spain **43 D2** 36.45N 3.35W
Salon France **42 G2** 43.38N 5.06E
Salso *r.* Italy **46 F2** 37.07N 13.57E
Salt Jordan **60 D4** 32.03N 35.44E
Salta Argentina **89 C5** 24.46S 65.28W
Saltee Is. Rep. of Ire. **15 E2** 52.08N 6.36W
Saltfleet U.K. **12 H5** 53.24N 0.12E
Saltillo Mexico **86 D5** 25.30N101.00W
Salt Lake City U.S.A. **82 D5** 40.45N111.55W
Salton Sea *l.* U.S.A. **82 C3** 33.25N115.45W
Salûm Egypt **60 B3** 31.31N 25.09E
Salvador Brazil **88 F6** 12.58S 38.20W
Salwa Qatar **61 H2** 24.44N 50.50E
Salween *r.* Burma **66 F1** 16.30N 97.33E
Salyany U.S.S.R. **61 H5** 39.36N 48.59E
Salzach *r.* Austria **48 F4** 48.35N 13.30E
Salzburg Austria **48 F3** 47.54N 13.03E
Salzgitter W. Germany **48 E6** 52.02N 10.22E
Samaná Dom. Rep. **87 K3** 19.14N 69.20W
Samana Cay *i.* Bahamas **87 J4** 23.05N 73.45W
Samar *i.* Phil. **69 H6** 11.45N125.15E
Samarinda Indonesia **68 F3** 0.30S117.09E
Samarkand U.S.S.R. **52 F1** 39.40N 66.57E
Sāmarrā Iraq **61 F4** 34.13N 43.52E
Samawa Iraq **61 G3** 31.18N 45.18E
Sambalpur India **63 F4** 21.28N 84.04E
Sambor U.S.S.R. **49 K4** 49.31N 23.10E
Sambre *r.* Belgium **39 C2** 50.29N 4.52E
Sam Neua Laos **68 C8** 20.25N104.04E
Sámos *i.* Greece **47 M2** 37.44N 26.45E
Samothráki *i.* Greece **47 L4** 40.26N 25.35E
Sampit Indonesia **68 E3** 2.34S112.59E
Samrong Cambodia **68 C6** 14.12N103.31E
Samsö *i.* Denmark **38 D3** 55.50N 10.35E
Samsö Baelt *str.* Denmark **38 D3** 55.50N 10.50E
Samsun Turkey **60 E6** 41.17N 36.22E
Samui, Ko *i.* Thailand **68 C5** 9.30N100.00E
San Mali **102 D3** 13.21N 4.57W
Şan'ā' Yemen **101 G3** 15.23N 44.14E
Sana *r.* Yugo. **47 H6** 45.03N 16.23E
Sanaga *r.* Cameroon **103 F1** 3.35N 9.40E
San Ambrosio *i.* Chile **89 B5** 26.28S 79.53W
Sanandaj Iran **61 G4** 35.18N 47.01E
San Antonio U.S.A. **82 G2** 29.25N 98.30W
San Antonio, C. Cuba **87 H4** 21.50N 84.57W
San Antonio, Punta *c.* Mexico **86 A5** 29.45N115.41W
San Antonio Oeste Argentina **89 C3** 40.45S 64.58W
San Bernardino U.S.A. **82 C3** 34.07N117.18W
San Blas, C. U.S.A. **83 I2** 29.40N 85.25W
San Carlos Phil. **69 G7** 15.59N120.22E
San Carlos de Bariloche Argentina **89 B3** 41.11S 71.23W
San Cristóbal Dom. Rep. **87 J3** 18.27N 70.07W
San Cristóbal Venezuela **88 B8** 7.46N 72.15W
Sancti Spíritus Cuba **87 I4** 21.55N 79.28W
Sanda *i.* U.K. **14 C2** 55.17N 5.34W
Sandakan Malaysia **68 F5** 5.52N118.04E
Sanday *i.* U.K. **14 F6** 59.15N 2.33W
Sandbach U.K. **12 E5** 53.08N 2.20W
Sande W. Germany **38 B2** 54.44N 8.58E
San Diego U.S.A. **82 C3** 32.45N117.10W
Sandnes Norway **50 A2** 58.51N 5.45E
Sandness U.K. **14 G7** 60.19N 1.40W
Sandö *i.* Faroe Is. **50 M8** 61.50N 6.45W
Sandoway Burma **63 G3** 18.28N 94.20E
Sandown U.K. **13 F2** 50.40N 1.10W
Sandpoint *town* U.S.A. **82 C6** 48.17N116.34W
Sandringham U.K. **12 H4** 52.50N 0.30E
Sandviken Sweden **50 D3** 60.38N 16.50E
San Felipe Mexico **86 B6** 31.03N114.52W
San Félix *i.* Chile **89 A5** 26.23S 80.05W
San Fernando Phil. **69 G7** 16.39N120.19E
San Fernando Spain **43 B2** 36.28N 6.12W
San Fernando Trinidad **87 L2** 10.16N 61.28W
San Fernando de Apure Venezuela **88 C8** 7.53N 67.17W
San Francisco U.S.A. **82 B4** 37.45N122.27W
San Francisco, C. Ecuador **88 A8** 0.38N 80.08W
San Francisco de Macorís Dom. Rep. **87 J3** 19.19N 70.15W
Sanggan He *r.* China **67 I5** 40.23N115.18E
Sangha *r.* Congo **99 B4** 1.10S 16.47E
Sangi *i.* Indonesia **69 H4** 3.30N125.30E
Sangihe Is. Indonesia **69 H4** 2.45N125.20E
Sāngli India **63 D3** 16.55N 74.37E
Sangonera *r.* Spain **43 E2** 37.58N 1.04W
Sangre de Cristo Mts. U.S.A. **82 E4** 37.30N106.00W
Sanjo Japan **70 D5** 37.37N138.57E
San Jordi, G. of Spain **43 F4** 40.50N 1.10E
San Jorge, G. of Argentina **89 C3** 46.00S 66.00W
San José Costa Rica **87 H1** 9.59N 84.04W
San José Guatemala **86 F2** 13.58N 90.50W
San Jose U.S.A. **82 B4** 37.20N121.55W
San Juan Argentina **89 C4** 31.33S 68.31W
San Juan *r.* Costa Rica **87 H2** 10.50N 83.40W
San Juan Puerto Rico **87 K3** 18.29N 66.08W
San Juan *r.* U.S.A. **82 D4** 37.20N110.05W
San Juan del Norte Nicaragua **87 H2** 10.58N 83.40W
San Juan Mts. U.S.A. **82 E4** 37.30N107.00W
Sankt Peter W. Germany **38 B2** 54.19N 8.38E
San Lázaro, C. Mexico **86 B4** 24.50N112.18W
San Leonardo Spain **43 D4** 41.49N 3.04W

Sisak Yugo. **46 H6** 45.30N 16.21E
Sishen R.S.A. **99 C2** 27.48S 22.59E
Sisophon Cambodia **68 C6** 13.37N102.58E
Sisteron France **42 G3** 44.16N 5.56E
Sitka U.S.A. **80 E3** 57.05N135.20W
Sittang *r.* Burma **63 H3** 17.30N 96.53E
Sittard Neth. **39 D3** 51.00N 5.52E
Sivas Turkey **60 E5** 39.44N 37.01E
Sivrihisar Turkey **60 C5** 39.29N 31.32E
Siwa Egypt **60 B3** 29.11N 25.31E
Siwa Oasis Egypt **60 B3** 29.10N 25.45E
Sixmilecross U.K. **15 D4** 54.33N 7.09W
Sjöbo Sweden **38 G3** 55.39N 13.44E
Skaelskör Denmark **38 E3** 55.15N 11.18E
Skaerbaek Denmark **38 B3** 55.09N 8.47E
Skagen Denmark **38 D5** 57.44N 10.37E
Skagerrak *str.* Denmark / Norway **50 B2** 57.45N 8.55E
Skagway U.S.A. **80 E3** 59.23N135.20W
Skaill U.K. **14 F5** 58.57N 2.43W
Skälderviken *b.* Sweden **38 F4** 56.20N 12.40E
Skalintyy *mtn.* U.S.S.R. **53 K3** 56.00N130.40E
Skals Denmark **38 C4** 56.33N 9.23E
Skanderborg Denmark **38 C4** 56.01N 9.53E
Skanör Sweden **38 F3** 55.25N 12.50E
Skara Sweden **50 C2** 58.23N 13.25E
Skarżysko-Kamienna Poland **49 J5** 51.08N 20.53E
Skeena *r.* Canada **80 F3** 54.10N129.08W
Skegness U.K. **12 H5** 53.09N 0.20E
Skellefte *r.* Sweden **50 E4** 64.44N 21.07E
Skellefteå Sweden **50 E4** 64.45N 21.00E
Skelmersdale U.K. **12 E5** 53.34N 2.49W
Skene Sweden **50 C2** 57.30N 12.35E
Skerries Rep. of Ire. **15 E3** 53.34N 6.08W
Skhíza *i.* Greece **47 J2** 36.42N 21.45E
Ski Norway **50 B2** 59.43N 10.52E
Skiddaw *mtn.* U.K. **12 D6** 54.40N 3.09W
Skien Norway **50 B2** 59.14N 9.37E
Skikda Algeria **100 C5** 36.50N 6.58E
Skipness U.K. **14 C2** 55.46N 5.22W
Skipton U.K. **12 E5** 53.58N 2.03W
Skíros *i.* Greece **47 L3** 38.50N 24.33E
Skive Denmark **38 C4** 56.34N 9.03E
Skjálfanda Fljót *r.* Iceland **50 J7** 65.55N 17.30W
Skjern Denmark **38 B3** 55.57N 8.30E
Skjern *r.* Denmark **38 B3** 55.55N 8.22E
Skopje Yugo. **47 J4** 41.58N 21.27E
Skövde Sweden **50 C2** 58.24N 13.52E
Skovorodino U.S.S.R. **53 K3** 54.00N123.53E
Skreia Norway **50 B3** 60.38N 10.57E
Skull Rep. of Ire. **15 B1** 51.31N 9.33W
Skurup Sweden **38 G3** 55.30N 13.31E
Skye *i.* U.K. **14 B4** 57.20N 6.15W
Slagelse Denmark **38 E3** 55.24N 11.23E
Slalowa Wola Poland **49 K5** 50.40N 22.05E
Slamet *mtn.* Indonesia **68 D2** 7.10S109.10E
Slaney *r.* Rep. of Ire. **15 E2** 52.21N 6.30W
Slantsy U.S.S.R. **50 G2** 59.09N 28.09E
Slatina Romania **47 L6** 44.26N 24.23E
Slave *r.* Canada **80 G4** 61.10N113.30W
Slavgorod W.R.S.S.R. U.S.S.R. **49 O6** 53.25N 31.00E
Slavgorod R.S.F.S.R. U.S.S.R. **52 G3** 53.01N 78.37E
Sleaford U.K. **12 G5** 53.01N 0.25W
Sleat, Sound of U.K. **14 C4** 57.07N 5.45W
Sledmere U.K. **12 G6** 54.03N 0.32W
Sleetmute U.S.A. **80 C4** 61.40N157.11W
Sliedrecht Neth. **39 C3** 51.48N 4.46E
Slieve Aughty Mts. Rep. of Ire. **15 C3** 53.05N 8.35W
Slieve Bloom Mts. Rep. of Ire. **15 D3** 53.05N 7.40W
Slieve Callan *mtn.* Rep. of Ire. **15 B2** 52.50N 9.20W
Slieve Donard *mtn.* U.K. **15 F4** 54.11N 5.56W
Slieve Gamph *mts.* Rep. of Ire. **15 C4** 54.08N 8.50W
Slievekimalta *mtn.* Rep. of Ire. **15 C2** 52.45N 8.19W
Slieve Mish *mts.* Rep. of Ire. **15 B2** 52.12N 9.50W
Slieve Miskish *mts.* Rep. of Ire. **15 B1** 51.40N 9.55W
Slievenamon Rep. of Ire. **15 D2** 52.26N 7.37W
Slieve Snaght *mtn.* Rep. of Ire. **15 D5** 55.12N 7.20W
Sligo Rep. of Ire. **15 C4** 54.17N 8.28W
Sligo *d.* Rep. of Ire. **15 C4** 54.10N 8.35W
Sligo B. Rep. of Ire. **15 C4** 54.18N 8.40W
Sliven Bulgaria **47 M5** 42.41N 26.19E
Slonim U.S.S.R. **49 L6** 53.05N 25.21E
Slough U.K. **13 G3** 51.30N 0.35W
Slovechna *r.* U.S.S.R. **49 N5** 51.41N 29.41E
Sluch *r.* U.S.S.R. **49 M6** 52.08N 27.31E
Sluis Neth. **39 B3** 51.18N 3.23E
Słupsk Poland **49 H7** 54.28N 17.01E
Slutsk U.S.S.R. **49 M6** 53.02N 27.31E
Slyne Head Rep. of Ire. **15 A3** 53.25N 10.12W
Slyudyanka U.S.S.R. **66 G7** 51.40N103.40E
Smålandsfarvandet *str.* Denmark **38 E3** 55.05N 11.25E
Smöla *i.* Norway **50 A3** 63.20N 8.00E
Smolensk U.S.S.R. **52 C3** 54.49N 32.04E
Smólikas *mtn.* Greece **47 J4** 40.06N 20.55E
Smolyan Bulgaria **47 L4** 41.34N 24.45E
Smorgon U.S.S.R. **49 M7** 54.28N 26.20E
Snaefell *mtn.* Iceland **32 B7** 64.48N 15.34W
Snaefell *mtn.* U.K. **12 C6** 54.17N 4.29W
Snake *r.* U.S.A. **82 C6** 46.15N119.00W
Snåsa Norway **50 C4** 64.15N 12.23E
Snåsavatn *l.* Norway **50 B4** 64.10N 12.00E
Sneek Neth. **39 D5** 53.03N 5.40E
Sneem Rep. of Ire. **15 B1** 51.49N 9.55W
Snizort, L. U.K. **14 B4** 57.35N 6.30W
Snöhetta *mtn.* Norway **50 B3** 62.15N 9.05E
Snov *r.* U.S.S.R. **49 O5** 51.45N 31.45E
Snowdon *mtn.* U.K. **12 C5** 53.05N 4.05W
Soasiu Indonesia **69 H4** 0.40N127.25E
Sobat *r.* Sudan / Ethiopia **101 F2** 9.30N 31.30E
Sobernheim W. Germany **39 F1** 49.47N 7.40E
Sobral Brazil **88 E7** 3.45S 40.20W
Sochi U.S.S.R. **52 D2** 43.35N 39.46E
Society Is. Pacific Oc. **75 K6** 17.00S150.00W
Socorro I. Mexico **86 B3** 18.45N110.58W
Socotra *i.* S. Yemen **101 H3** 12.30N 54.00E
Sodankylä Finland **50 F2** 67.21N 26.31E
Söderhamn Sweden **50 D3** 61.19N 17.10E
Södertälje Sweden **50 D2** 59.11N 17.39E
Soest W. Germany **39 G3** 51.34N 8.06E
Sofia Bulgaria **47 K5** 42.41N 23.19E
Sognefjorden *est.* Norway **50 A3** 61.10N 5.50E
Sögüt Turkey **60 C5** 40.02N 30.10E
Sohag Egypt **60 C2** 26.33N 31.42E
Sohar Oman **61 J2** 24.23N 56.43E
Soignies Belgium **39 C2** 50.35N 4.04E
Soissons France **42 F5** 49.23N 3.20E
Söke Turkey **47 M2** 37.46N 27.26E
Sokodé Togo **103 E2** 8.59N 1.11E
Sokółka Poland **49 K6** 53.25N 23.31E
Sokolo Mali **102 C3** 14.53N 6.11W
Sokoto Nigeria **103 F3** 13.02N 5.15E
Sokoto *d.* Nigeria **103 F3** 11.50N 5.05E
Sokoto *r.* Nigeria **103 E3** 11.23N 4.05E
Solikamsk U.S.S.R. **52 E3** 59.40N 56.45E
Solingen W. Germany **39 F3** 51.10N 7.05E
Sollefteå Sweden **50 D3** 63.09N 17.15E
Sóller Spain **43 G3** 39.47N 2.41E
Solomon Is. Pacific Oc. **71 E5** 8.00S160.00E
Šolta *i.* Yugo. **46 H5** 43.23N 16.17E
Solway Firth *est.* U.K. **12 D6** 54.50N 3.30W
Soma Turkey **47 M3** 39.11N 27.36E
Somali Republic Africa **101 G2** 5.30N 47.00E
Sombor Yugo. **47 I6** 45.48N 19.08E
Somerset *d.* U.K. **13 D3** 51.09N 3.00W
Somerset I. Canada **81 I5** 73.00N 93.30W
Somes *r.* Hungary **49 K4** 48.04N 22.30E
Somme *r.* France **42 E6** 50.01N 1.40E
Son *r.* India **63 F4** 25.55N 84.55E
Sönderborg Denmark **38 C2** 54.55N 9.48E
Sonderjyllands *d.* Denmark **38 C3** 55.10N 9.10E
Songhua Jiang *r.* China **67 L6** 47.46N132.30E
Songkhla Thailand **68 C5** 7.13N100.37E
Son La Vietnam **68 C8** 21.20N103.55E
Sonneberg E. Germany **48 E5** 50.22N 11.10E
Sonora *d.* Mexico **86 B5** 29.20N110.40W
Sonora *r.* Mexico **86 B5** 28.45N111.55W
Sonsorol *i.* Caroline Is. **69 I5** 5.20N132.13E
Son Tay Vietnam **68 D8** 21.06N105.32E
Sopron Hungary **48 H3** 47.41N 16.36E
Soria Spain **43 D4** 41.46N 2.28W
Sor Kvalöy *i.* Norway **50 D5** 69.45N 18.20E
Sorocaba Brazil **89 E5** 23.30S 47.32W
Soroki U.S.S.R. **49 N4** 48.08N 28.12E
Sorol *i.* Caroline Is. **69 K5** 8.09N140.25E
Sorong Indonesia **69 I3** 0.50S131.17E
Soroti Uganda **99 D5** 1.42N 33.37E
Söröya *i.* Norway **50 E5** 70.30N 22.30E
Sorraia *r.* Portugal **43 A3** 39.00N 8.51W
Sorsele Sweden **50 D4** 65.32N 17.34E
Sortavala U.S.S.R. **50 G3** 61.40N 30.40E
Sosnowiec Poland **49 I5** 50.18N 19.08E
Sotra *i.* Norway **50 A3** 60.20N 5.00E
Soure Portugal **43 A4** 40.04N 8.38W
Souris *r.* Canada **82 G6** 49.38N 99.35W
Sous le Vent, Îles *is.* Society Is. **75 K6** 16.30S151.30W
Sousse Tunisia **100 D5** 35.48N 10.38E
Soustons France **42 D2** 43.45N 1.19W
South America 88
Southampton U.K. **13 F2** 50.54N 1.23W
Southampton I. Canada **81 J4** 64.30N 84.00W
South Atlantic Ocean 89
South Australia *d.* Australia **71 C3** 29.00S135.00E
South Beveland *f.* Neth. **39 B3** 51.30N 3.50E
South Carolina *d.* U.S.A. **83 J3** 34.00N 81.00W
South Cerney U.K. **13 F3** 51.41N 1.54W
South China Sea Asia **68 E7** 12.30N115.00E
South Dakota *d.* U.S.A. **82 F5** 44.30N100.00W
South Dorset Downs *hills* U.K. **13 E2** 50.40N 2.20W
South Downs *hills* U.K. **13 G2** 50.54N 0.34W
South Eastern Atlantic Basin Atlantic Oc. **106 I3** 20.00S 0.00
Southend-on-Sea U.K. **13 H3** 51.32N 0.43E
Southern Alps *mts.* New Zealand **71 G1** 43.20S170.45E
Southern Uplands *hills* U.K. **14 E2** 55.30N 3.30W
Southern Yemen Asia **101 G3** 16.00N 49.30E
South Esk *r.* U.K. **14 F3** 56.43N 2.32W
South Fiji Basin Pacific Oc. **107 R3** 27.00S176.00E
South Flevoland *f.* Neth. **39 D4** 52.22N 5.22E
South Georgia *i.* Atlantic Oc. **89 F2** 54.00S 37.00W
South Glamorgan *d.* U.K. **13 D3** 51.27N 3.22W
South-haa U.K. **14 G7** 60.37N 1.19W
South Holland *d.* Neth. **39 C4** 52.00N 4.30E
South Honshu Ridge Pacific Oc. **74 E9** 22.00N141.00E
South I. New Zealand **71 G1** 43.00S171.00E
South Korea Asia **67 K4** 36.00N128.00E
South Molton U.K. **13 D3** 51.01N 3.50W
South Nahanni *r.* Canada **80 F4** 61.00N123.20W
South Orkney Is. Atlantic Oc. **89 E1** 60.50S 45.00W
Southport U.K. **12 D5** 53.38N 3.01W
South Ronaldsay *i.* U.K. **14 F5** 58.47N 2.56W
South Sandwich Is. Atlantic Oc. **89 G2** 58.00S 27.00W
South Sandwich Trench *f.* Atlantic Oc. **89 G2** 57.00S 25.00W
South Shetland Is. Antarctica **106 F1** 62.00S 60.00W
South Shields U.K. **12 F6** 54.59N 1.22W
South Tyne *r.* U.K. **12 E6** 54.59N 2.08W
South Uist *i.* U.K. **14 A4** 57.15N 7.20W
South Western Pacific Basin Pacific Oc. **106 A3** 39.00S148.00W
South West Peru Ridge Pacific Oc. **75 R5** 20.00S 82.00W
Southwold U.K. **13 I4** 52.19N 1.39E
South Yorkshire *d.* U.K. **12 F5** 53.28N 1.25W
Sovetsk U.S.S.R. **50 E1** 55.02N 21.50E
Sovetskaya Gavan U.S.S.R. **53 L2** 48.57N140.16E
Sozh *r.* U.S.S.R. **49 O5** 51.57N 30.48E
Spa Belgium **39 D2** 50.29N 5.52E
Spain Europe **43 B4** 40.00N 4.00W
Spalding U.K. **12 G4** 52.48N 0.10W
Spandau W. Germany **48 F6** 52.32N 13.13E
Spárti Greece **47 K2** 37.04N 22.28E
Spartivento, C. Calabria Italy **46 H2** 37.55N 16.04E
Spartivento, C. Sardinia Italy **46 D3** 38.53N 8.51E
Spátha, C. Greece **47 K1** 35.42N 23.43E
Spence Bay *town* Canada **81 I4** 69.30N 93.20W
Spencer G. Australia **71 C2** 34.30S136.10E
Sperrin Mts. U.K. **15 D4** 54.49N 7.06W
Spey *r.* U.K. **14 E4** 57.40N 3.06W
Spiekeroog *i.* W. Germany **39 F5** 53.48N 7.45E
Spilsby U.K. **12 H5** 53.11N 0.07E
Spithead *str.* U.K. **13 F2** 50.45N 1.05W
Spitsbergen *is.* Arctic Oc. **54 D10** 78.00N 19.00E
Spittal an der Drau Austria **48 F3** 46.48N 13.30E
Split Yugo. **47 H5** 43.32N 16.27E
Spodsbjerg Denmark **38 D2** 54.57N 10.50E
Spokane U.S.A. **82 C6** 47.40N117.25W
Spratly I. S. China Sea **68 E5** 8.45N111.54E
Spree *r.* E. Germany **48 F6** 52.32N 13.15E
Sprenge W. Germany **38 D2** 54.15N 10.04E
Springfield Ill. U.S.A. **83 I4** 39.49N 89.39W
Springfield Miss. U.S.A. **83 H4** 37.11N 93.19W
Springs *town* R.S.A. **99 C2** 26.15S 28.26E
Spurn Head U.K. **12 H5** 53.35N 0.08E
Sredne Kolymskaya U.S.S.R. **53 M4** 67.27N153.35E
Sri Lanka Asia **63 E1** 7.30N 80.50E
Srīnagar Jammu & Kashmir **63 D6** 34.08N 74.50E
Stadskanaal Neth. **39 E5** 53.02N 6.55E
Stadtkyll W. Germany **39 E2** 50.21N 6.32E
Staffa *i.* U.K. **14 B3** 56.26N 6.21W
Stafford U.K. **12 E4** 52.49N 2.09W
Staffordshire *d.* U.K. **12 E4** 52.40N 1.57W
Staines U.K. **13 G3** 51.26N 0.31W
Stainforth U.K. **12 F5** 53.37N 1.01W
Stamford U.K. **13 G4** 52.40N 0.28W
Stanley Falkland Is. **89 D2** 51.45S 57.56W
Stanley U.K. **12 F6** 54.53N 1.43W
Stanley, Mt. Uganda / Zaïre **94 E5** 0.20N 30.50E
Stanovoy Range *mts.* U.S.S.R. **53 K3** 56.00N125.40E
Stara Zagora Bulgaria **47 L5** 42.26N 25.37E
Starbuck I. Kiribati **75 K7** 5.37S155.55W
Stargard Poland **48 G6** 53.21N 15.01E
Starogard Gdański Poland **49 I6** 53.59N 18.33E
Starokonstantinov U.S.S.R. **49 M4** 49.48N 27.10E
Start Pt. U.K. **13 D2** 50.13N 3.38W
Staryy Oskol U.S.S.R. **52 D2** 51.20N 37.50E
Stavanger Norway **50 A2** 58.58N 5.45E
Stavelot Belgium **39 D2** 50.23N 5.54E
Staveren Neth. **39 D4** 52.53N 5.21E
Stavropol' U.S.S.R. **52 D2** 45.03N 41.59E
Steenbergen Neth. **39 C3** 51.36N 4.19E
Steenvorde France **39 A2** 50.49N 2.35E
Steenwijk Neth. **39 E4** 52.47N 6.07E
Steinkjer Norway **50 B3** 64.00N 11.30E
Stenay France **39 D1** 49.29N 5.12E
Stendal E. Germany **48 E6** 52.36N 11.52E
Stepanakert U.S.S.R. **61 G5** 39.48N 46.45E
Sterling U.S.A. **82 F5** 40.37N103.13W
Sterlitamak U.S.S.R. **52 E3** 53.40N 55.59E
Stevenage U.K. **13 G3** 51.54N 0.11W
Stevenston U.K. **14 D2** 55.39N 4.43W
Stewart Canada **80 F3** 55.56N129.59W
Stewart I. New Zealand **71 F1** 47.02S167.51E
Steyr Austria **48 G4** 48.04N 14.25E
Stikine *r.* Canada **80 E3** 56.45N132.30W
Stikine Mts. Canada **80 E4** 59.00N129.00W
Stilton U.K. **13 G4** 52.31N 0.18W
Stinchar *r.* U.K. **14 C2** 55.06N 5.01W
Stirling U.K. **14 E3** 56.07N 3.57W
Stjördalshalsen Norway **50 B3** 63.30N 10.59E
Stockbridge U.K. **13 F3** 51.07N 1.29W
Stockholm Sweden **50 D2** 59.20N 18.05E
Stockport U.K. **12 E5** 53.25N 2.11W
Stocksbridge U.K. **12 F5** 53.29N 1.35W
Stockton U.S.A. **82 B4** 37.59N121.20W
Stockton-on-Tees U.K. **12 F6** 54.33N 1.20W
Stoke-on-Trent U.K. **12 E5** 53.01N 2.11W
Stolin U.S.S.R. **49 M5** 51.52N 26.51E
Stone U.K. **12 E4** 52.55N 2.10W
Stonehaven U.K. **14 F3** 56.58N 2.13W
Stony Tunguska *r.* U.S.S.R. **53 H3** 61.40N 90.00E
Storå *r.* Denmark **38 B4** 56.20N 8.19E
Stora Lulevatten *l.* Sweden **50 D4** 67.00N 19.30E
Storavan *l.* Sweden **50 D4** 65.45N 18.10E
Storby Finland **50 D3** 60.14N 19.36E
Stord *i.* Norway **50 A2** 59.50N 5.25E
Store Baelt *str.* Denmark **38 D3** 55.30N 11.00E
Stören Norway **50 B3** 63.03N 10.16E
Stornoway U.K. **14 B5** 58.12N 6.23W
Storsjön *l.* Sweden **50 C3** 63.10N 14.20E
Storstroms *d.* Denmark **38 E2** 55.00N 11.30E
Storuman Sweden **50 D4** 65.05N 17.10E
Storuman *l.* Sweden **50 D4** 65.14N 16.50E
Stour *r.* Dorset U.K. **13 F2** 50.43N 1.47W
Stour *r.* Kent U.K. **13 I3** 51.19N 1.25E
Stour *r.* Suffolk U.K. **13 I3** 51.56N 1.03E
Stourport-on-Severn U.K. **13 E4** 52.20N 2.18W
Stövring Denmark **38 C4** 56.53N 9.53E
Stow in the Wold U.K. **13 F3** 51.56N 1.41W
Stowmarket U.K. **13 H4** 52.11N 0.59E
Strabane U.K. **15 D4** 54.50N 7.30W
Stradbally Rep. of Ire. **15 D3** 53.01N 7.11W
Stralsund E. Germany **48 F7** 54.18N 13.06E
Strangford Lough U.K. **15 F4** 54.28N 5.35W
Stranraer U.K. **14 C1** 54.54N 5.02W
Strasbourg France **42 H5** 48.35N 7.45E
Stratford-upon-Avon U.K. **13 F4** 52.12N 1.42W
Strathclyde *d.* U.K. **14 D2** 55.45N 4.45W
Strathmore *f.* U.K. **14 E3** 56.44N 3.15W
Strathspey *f.* U.K. **14 E4** 57.25N 3.25W
Straubing W. Germany **48 F4** 48.53N 12.35E
Straumnes *c.* Iceland **50 I7** 66.30N 23.05W
Street U.K. **13 E3** 51.07N 2.45W
Stromboli *i.* Italy **46 G3** 38.48N 15.14E
Stromeferry U.K. **14 C4** 57.20N 5.34W
Stromness U.K. **14 E5** 58.58N 3.19W
Strömö *i.* Faroe Is. **50 L9** 62.08N 7.00W
Strömstad Sweden **50 B2** 58.56N 11.11E
Ströms Vattudal *l.* Sweden **50 C3** 63.55N 15.30E
Stronsay *i.* U.K. **14 F6** 59.07N 2.36W
Stroud U.K. **13 E3** 51.44N 2.13W
Struer Denmark **38 B4** 56.30N 8.37E
Struma *r.* Greece **47 K4** 40.45N 23.51E
Strumica Yugo. **47 K4** 41.26N 22.39E
Stryn Norway **50 A3** 61.55N 6.47E
Stryy U.S.S.R. **49 K4** 49.16N 23.51E
Stubbeköbing Denmark **38 F2** 54.53N 12.04E
Sturminster Newton U.K. **13 E2** 50.57N 2.28W
Stuttgart W. Germany **48 D4** 48.47N 9.12E
Styr *r.* U.S.S.R. **49 M6** 52.07N 26.35E
Suakin Sudan **101 F3** 19.04N 37.22E
Subotica Yugo. **47 I7** 46.04N 19.41E
Suceava Romania **49 M3** 47.39N 26.19E
Suck *r.* Rep. of Ire. **15 C3** 53.16N 8.03W
Sucre Bolivia **89 C6** 19.05S 65.15W
Sudan Africa **101 E3** 14.00N 30.00E
Sudbury Canada **81 J2** 46.30N 81.01W
Sudbury U.K. **13 H4** 52.03N 0.43E
Sudd *f.* Sudan **101 E2** 7.50N 30.00E
Sudeten Mountains Czech. / Poland **48 H5** 50.30N 16.30E
Sudirman Mts. Indonesia **69 J3** 3.50S136.30E
Suez Egypt **60 D3** 29.59N 32.33E
Suez, G. of Egypt **60 D3** 28.48N 33.00E
Suez Canal Egypt **60 D3** 30.40N 32.20E
Suffolk *d.* U.K. **13 H4** 52.16N 1.00E
Suhl E. Germany **48 E5** 50.37N 10.43E
Suir *r.* Rep. of Ire. **15 D2** 52.17N 7.00W
Sukabumi Indonesia **68 D2** 6.55S106.50E
Sukadana Indonesia **68 E3** 1.15S110.00E
Sukaraja Indonesia **68 E3** 2.23S110.35E
Sukhona *r.* U.S.S.R. **52 D3** 61.30N 46.28E
Sukhumi U.S.S.R. **52 D2** 43.01N 41.01E
Sukkertoppen Greenland **81 M4** 65.40N 53.00W
Sukkur Pakistan **62 C5** 27.42N 68.54E
Sulaimaniya Iraq **61 G4** 35.32N 45.27E
Sulaimān Range *mts.* Pakistan **63 C5** 30.50N 70.20E
Sulaimiya Saudi Arabia **61 G2** 24.10N 47.20E
Sula Is. Indonesia **69 H3** 1.50S125.10E
Sulawesi *d.* Indonesia **69 G3** 2.00S120.30E
Sulina Romania **47 N6** 45.08N 29.40E
Sullana Peru **88 A7** 4.52S 80.39W
Sulmona Italy **46 F5** 42.04N 13.57E
Sulu Archipelago Phil. **69 G5** 5.30N121.00E
Sulu Sea Pacific Oc. **69 G5** 8.00N120.00E
Sumatra *i.* Indonesia **68 B4** 2.00S102.00E
Sumba *i.* Indonesia **68 F2** 9.30S119.55E
Sumbawa *i.* Indonesia **68 F2** 8.45S117.50E
Sumburgh Head U.K. **14 G6** 59.51N 1.16W
Sumgait U.S.S.R. **61 H6** 40.35N 49.38E
Summan *f.* Saudi Arabia **61 G2** 27.00N 47.00E
Sumy U.S.S.R. **52 C2** 50.55N 34.49E
Sunagawa Japan **70 E8** 43.30N141.55E
Sunart, L. U.K. **14 C3** 56.42N 5.45W
Sundarbans *f.* India / Bangla. **63 F4** 22.00N 89.00E
Sunda Str. Indonesia **68 D2** 6.00S105.50E
Sunderland U.K. **12 F6** 54.55N 1.22W
Sundsvall Sweden **50 D3** 62.22N 17.20E
Sungaipenuh Indonesia **68 C6** 2.00S101.28E
Sungguminasa Indonesia **68 F2** 5.14S119.27E
Sungurlu Turkey **60 D6** 40.10N 34.23E
Sunwu China **67 K6** 49.40N127.10E
Sunyani Ghana **102 D2** 7.22N 2.18W
Suomussalmi Finland **50 G4** 64.52N 29.10E
Suō nada *str.* Japan **70 A3** 33.45N131.30E
Suonenjoki Finland **50 F3** 62.40N 27.06E
Superior U.S.A. **83 H6** 46.42N 92.05W
Superior, L. N. America **83 I6** 48.00N 88.00W
Süphan Daglari *mtn.* Turkey **60 F5** 38.55N 42.55E
Şur Oman **61 J1** 22.23N 59.32E
Sura *r.* U.S.S.R. **33 O6** 56.10N 46.00E
Surabaya Indonesia **68 E2** 7.14S112.45E
Surakarta Indonesia **68 E2** 7.32S110.50E
Surat India **63 D4** 21.10N 72.54E
Sûre *r.* Lux. **39 E1** 49.43N 6.31E
Surgut U.S.S.R. **52 G3** 61.13N 73.20E
Surigao Phil. **69 H5** 9.47N125.29E
Surin Thailand **68 C6** 14.50N103.34E
Surinam S. America **88 D8** 4.30N 56.00W
Surrey *d.* U.K. **13 G3** 51.16N 0.30W
Surtsey *i.* Iceland **50 I6** 63.18N 20.37W
Sutlej *r.* Pakistan **63 C5** 29.26N 71.09E
Sutton U.K. **13 G3** 51.21N 0.10W
Sutton in Ashfield U.K. **12 F5** 53.08N 1.16W
Suva Fiji **74 H6** 18.08S178.25E
Suwałki Poland **49 K7** 54.07N 22.56E
Suwon S. Korea **67 K4** 37.16N126.59E
Suzhou China **67 J3** 31.21N120.40E
Suzu misaki *c.* Japan **70 C5** 37.30N137.21E
Svartisen *mtn.* Norway **50 C4** 66.30N 14.00E
Svedala Sweden **38 G3** 55.30N 13.11E
Sveg Sweden **50 C3** 62.02N 14.20E
Svendborg Denmark **38 D3** 55.04N 10.38E
Svenstrup Denmark **38 C4** 56.58N 9.52E
Sverdlovsk U.S.S.R. **52 F3** 56.52N 60.35E
Svetogorsk U.S.S.R. **50 G3** 61.07N 28.50E
Svishtov Bulgaria **47 L5** 43.36N 25.23E

Tomsk U.S.S.R. **52 H3** 56.30N 85.05E
Tona, G. of U.S.S.R. **53 L4** 72.00N136.10E
Tonalá Mexico **86 F3** 16.08N 93.41W
Tonbridge U.K. **13 H3** 51.11N 0.16E
Tondano Indonesia **69 G4** 1.19N124.56E
Tönder Denmark **38 B2** 54.57N 8.53E
Tonekābon Iran **61 H5** 36.49N 50.54E
Tonga Pacific Oc. **74 I6** 20.00S175.00W
Tongatapu Group *is.* Tonga **74 I6** 21.10S175.10W
Tonga Trench *f.* Pacific Oc. **74 I5** 20.00S173.00W
Tongguan China **67 H4** 34.36N110.21E
Tonghua China **67 K5** 41.40N126.52E
Tongking, G. of Asia **68 D8** 20.00N107.50E
Tongling China **67 I3** 30.57N117.40E
Tongres Belgium **39 D2** 50.47N 5.28E
Tongue U.K. **14 D5** 58.28N 4.26W
Tonk India **63 D5** 26.10N 75.50E
Tônlé Sap *l.* Cambodia **68 C6** 12.50N104.00E
Tonnerre France **42 F4** 47.51N 3.59E
Tönning W. Germany **38 B2** 54.20N 8.58E
Tönsberg Norway **50 B2** 59.16N 10.25E
Toowoomba Australia **71 E3** 27.35S151.54E
Top, L. U.S.S.R. **50 H4** 65.45N 32.00E
Topeka U.S.A. **83 G4** 39.03N 95.41W
Topko, Mt. U.S.S.R. **53 L3** 57.20N138.10E
Torbay *town* U.K. **13 D2** 50.27N 3.31W
Tordesillas Spain **43 C4** 41.30N 5.00W
Töre Sweden **50 E4** 65.55N 22.40E
Torhout Belgium **39 B3** 51.04N 3.06E
Tormes *r.* Spain **43 B4** 41.18N 6.29W
Torne *r.* Sweden **50 E4** 67.13N 23.30E
Torneträsk *l.* Sweden **50 D5** 68.15N 19.20E
Tornio Finland **50 F4** 65.52N 24.10E
Tornio *r.* Finland **50 F4** 65.53N 24.07E
Toro Spain **43 C4** 41.31N 5.24W
Toronaíos, G. of Med. Sea **47 K4** 40.05N 23.38E
Toronto Canada **81 K2** 43.42N 79.25W
Torre de Moncorvo Portugal **43 B4** 41.10N 7.03W
Torrelavega Spain **43 D5** 43.21N 4.00W
Torreón Mexico **86 D5** 25.34N103.25W
Torres Str. Pacific Oc. **69 K1** 10.30S142.20E
Torres Vedras Portugal **43 A3** 39.05N 9.15W
Torrevieja Spain **43 E2** 37.59N 0.40W
Torridge *r.* U.K. **13 C3** 51.01N 4.12W
Torridon U.K. **14 C4** 57.32N 5.30W
Torridon, L. U.K. **14 C4** 57.35N 5.50W
Törring Denmark **38 C3** 55.50N 9.30E
Torsminde Denmark **38 B4** 56.22N 8.09E
Tortola *i.* B.V.Is. **87 L3** 18.28N 64.40W
Tortosa Spain **43 F4** 40.49N 0.31E
Tortue *i.* Haiti **87 J4** 20.05N 72.57W
Toruń Poland **49 I6** 53.01N 18.35E
Tory I. Rep. of Ire. **15 C5** 55.15N 8.15W
Tory Sound Rep. of Ire. **15 C5** 55.12N 8.10W
Tosan *d.* Japan **70 C5** 36.00N138.00E
Tosa wan *b.* Japan **70 B3** 33.10N133.40E
Totana Spain **43 E2** 37.46N 1.30W
Tottori Japan **70 B4** 35.32N134.12E
Touba Ivory Coast **102 C2** 8.22N 7.42W
Toubkal *mtn.* Morocco **100 B5** 31.03N 7.57W
Touggourt Algeria **100 C5** 33.08N 6.04E
Toul France **42 G5** 48.41N 5.54E
Toulon France **42 G2** 43.07N 5.53E
Toulouse France **42 E2** 43.33N 1.24E
Toungoo Burma **63 H3** 19.00N 96.30E
Tourcoing France **39 B2** 50.44N 3.09E
Tournai Belgium **39 B2** 50.36N 3.23E
Tournus France **42 G4** 46.33N 4.55E
Tours France **42 E4** 47.23N 0.42E
Tovada *r.* U.S.S.R. **52 F3** 57.40N 67.00E
Towcester U.K. **13 G4** 52.09N 0.59W
Townsville Australia **71 D4** 19.13S146.48E
Towyn U.K. **13 C4** 52.36N 4.05W
Toyama Japan **70 C5** 36.42N137.14E
Toyohashi Japan **70 C4** 34.46N137.22E
Trabzon Turkey **60 E6** 41.00N 39.43E
Trafalgar, C. Spain **43 B2** 36.10N 6.02W
Trail Canada **80 G2** 49.04N117.39W
Trajan's Gate *f.* Bulgaria **47 K5** 42.13N 23.58E
Tralee Rep. of Ire. **15 B2** 52.16N 9.42W
Tralee B. Rep. of Ire. **15 B2** 52.18N 9.55W
Tranås Sweden **50 C2** 58.03N 15.00E
Trang Thailand **68 B5** 7.35N 99.35E
Trangan *i.* Indonesia **69 I2** 6.30S134.15E
Transylvanian Alps *mts.* Romania **49 K2** 45.35N 24.40E
Trapani Italy **46 F3** 38.02N 12.30E
Trasimeno, Lago *l.* Italy **46 F5** 43.09N 12.07E
Traverse City U.S.A. **83 I5** 44.46N 85.38W
Travnik Yugo. **47 H6** 44.14N 17.40E
Třebíč Czech. **48 G4** 49.13N 15.55E
Trebišov Czech. **49 J4** 48.40N 21.47E
Třeboň Czech. **48 G4** 49.01N 14.50E
Tredegar U.K. **13 D3** 51.47N 3.17W
Treene *r.* W. Germany **38 C2** 54.22N 9.07E
Tregaron U.K. **13 D4** 52.14N 3.56W
Trelew Argentina **89 C3** 43.13S 65.15W
Trelleborg Sweden **50 C1** 55.22N 13.10E
Tremadog B. U.K. **12 C4** 52.52N 4.14W
Trenque Lauquen Argentina **89 C4** 35.56S 62.43W
Trent *r.* U.K. **12 G5** 53.41N 0.41W
Trento Italy **46 E7** 46.04N 11.08E
Trenton U.S.A. **83 L5** 40.15N 74.43W
Três Marias Dam Brazil **89 E6** 18.15S 45.15W
Treuchtlingen W. Germany **48 E4** 48.57N 10.55E
Treviso Italy **46 F6** 45.40N 12.14E
Trier W. Germany **39 E1** 49.45N 6.39E
Trieste Italy **46 F6** 45.40N 13.47E
Triglav *mtn.* Yugo. **46 F7** 46.21N 13.50E
Tríkkala Greece **47 J3** 39.34N 21.46E
Trincomalee Sri Lanka **63 E2** 8.34N 81.13E
Trinidad Bolivia **88 C6** 15.00S 64.50W
Trinidad Cuba **87 H4** 21.48N 80.00W
Trinidad U.S.A. **82 F4** 37.11N104.31W
Trinidad & Tobago S. America **87 L2** 10.30N 61.20W
Trinity *r.* U.S.A. **83 H2** 29.55N 94.45W
Tripoli Lebanon **60 D4** 34.27N 35.50E
Tripoli Libya **100 D5** 32.58N 13.12E
Tripolitania *f.* Libya **100 D4** 29.45N 14.30E
Tripura *d.* India **63 G4** 23.45N 91.45E
Tristan da Cunha *i.* Atlantic Oc. **108 I3** 38.00S 12.00W
Trivandrum India **63 D2** 8.41N 76.57E
Trnava Czech. **49 H4** 48.23N 17.35E
Troisdorf W. Germany **39 F2** 50.50N 7.07E
Trois-Rivières *town* Canada **81 K2** 46.21N 72.34W
Troitsko-Pechorsk U.S.S.R. **52 E3** 62.40N 56.08E
Troitskoye U.S.S.R. **49 O3** 47.38N 30.19E
Trollhättan Sweden **50 C2** 58.17N 12.20E
Tromsö Norway **50 D5** 69.42N 19.00E
Trondheim Norway **50 B3** 63.36N 10.23E
Trondheimsfjorden *est.* Norway **50 B3** 63.40N 10.30E
Troon U.K. **14 D2** 55.33N 4.40W
Trostan *mtn.* N. Ireland **15 E5** 55.03N 6.10W
Trowbridge U.K. **13 E3** 51.18N 2.12W
Troyes France **42 G5** 48.18N 4.05E
Trujillo Peru **88 B7** 8.06S 79.00W
Trujillo Spain **43 C3** 39.28N 5.53W
Truk Is. Pacific Oc. **74 F8** 7.23N151.46E
Truro Canada **81 L2** 45.24N 63.18W
Truro U.K. **13 B2** 50.17N 5.02W
Trust Territory of the Pacific Is. Pacific Oc. **74 E8** 10.00N155.00E
Trysil *r.* Norway **50 C3** 61.03N 12.30E
Trzemeszno Poland **49 H6** 52.35N 17.50E
Tsaratanana, Massif de *mts.* Madagascar **99 G9** 14.00S 49.00E
Tselinograd U.S.S.R. **52 F2** 51.10N 71.28E
Tsimlyansk Resr. U.S.S.R. **33 N4** 48.00N 43.00E
Tsna *r.* W.R.S.S.R. U.S.S.R. **49 M6** 52.10N 27.03E
Tsna *r.* R.S.F.S.R. U.S.S.R. **33 N5** 54.45N 41.54E
Tsu Japan **70 C4** 34.43N136.35E
Tsuchiura Japan **70 D5** 36.05N140.12E
Tsugaru kaikyō *str.* Japan **70 D7** 41.30N140.50E
Tsumeb Namibia **99 B3** 19.13S 17.42E
Tsuruga Japan **70 C4** 35.40N136.05E
Tsuruoka Japan **70 D6** 38.44N139.50E
Tsushima *i.* Japan **70 A4** 34.30N129.20E
Tsuyama Japan **70 B4** 35.04N134.01E
Tuam Rep. of Ire. **15 C3** 53.32N 8.52W
Tuamotu Archipelago *is.* Pacific Oc. **75 L6** 16.00S145.00W
Tuapse U.S.S.R. **52 D2** 44.06N 39.05E
Tubbercurry Rep. of Ire. **15 C4** 54.03N 8.47W
Tubja, Wadi *r.* Saudi Arabia **60 E2** 25.35N 38.22E
Tubuai *i.* Pacific Oc. **75 L5** 23.23S149.27W
Tubuai Is. Pacific Oc. **75 K5** 23.00S150.00W
Tucson U.S.A. **82 D3** 32.15N110.57W
Tucumcari U.S.A. **82 F4** 35.11N103.44W
Tudela Spain **43 E5** 42.04N 1.37W
Tuguegarao Phil. **69 G7** 17.36N121.44E
Tukangbesi Is. Indonesia **69 G2** 5.30S124.00E
Tukums U.S.S.R. **50 E2** 56.58N 23.10E
Tula *r.* Mongolia **66 G6** 48.53N104.35E
Tula U.S.S.R. **52 D3** 54.11N 37.38E
Tulcea Romania **47 N6** 45.10N 28.50E
Tulchin U.S.S.R. **49 N4** 48.40N 28.49E
Tuli Indonesia **69 G3** 1.25S122.23E
Ţulkarm Jordan **60 D4** 32.19N 35.02E
Tullamore Rep. of Ire. **15 D3** 53.17N 7.31W
Tulle France **42 E3** 45.16N 1.46E
Tullins France **42 G3** 45.18N 5.29E
Tullow Rep. of Ire. **15 E2** 52.48N 6.43W
Tuloma *r.* U.S.S.R. **50 H5** 68.56N 33.00E
Tulsa U.S.A. **83 G4** 36.07N 95.58W
Tulun U.S.S.R. **53 I3** 54.32N100.35E
Tulungagung Indonesia **68 E2** 8.03S111.54E
Tumaco Colombia **88 B8** 1.51N 78.46W
Tummel, Loch U.K. **14 E3** 56.43N 3.55W
Tummo Niger **100 D4** 22.45N 14.08E
Tump Pakistan **62 B5** 26.06N 62.24E
Tunceli Turkey **60 E5** 39.07N 39.34E
Tundzha *r.* Bulgaria **47 M4** 41.40N 26.34E
Tungabhadra *r.* India **63 E3** 16.00N 78.15E
Tunis Tunisia **100 D5** 36.47N 10.10E
Tunisia Africa **100 C5** 34.00N 9.00E
Tunja Colombia **88 B8** 5.33N 73.23W
Tupelo U.S.A. **83 I3** 34.15N 88.43W
Tura U.S.S.R. **53 I4** 64.05N100.00E
Turgutlu Turkey **47 M3** 38.30N 27.43E
Türi U.S.S.R. **50 F2** 58.48N 25.28E
Turia *r.* Spain **43 E3** 39.27N 0.19W
Turin Italy **46 C6** 45.04N 7.40E
Turkana, L. Kenya **99 D5** 4.00N 36.00E
Turkestan *f.* Asia **101 H5** 40.00N 56.00E
Turkestan U.S.S.R. **52 F2** 43.17N 68.16E
Turkey Asia **60 C5** 39.00N 35.00E
Turkmenistan S.S.R. *d.* U.S.S.R. **52 E2** 40.00N 60.00E
Turks Is. Turks & Caicos Is. **87 J4** 21.30N 71.10W
Turku Finland **50 E3** 60.27N 22.15E
Turneffe Is. Belize **87 G3** 17.30N 87.45W
Turnhout Belgium **39 C3** 51.19N 4.57E
Tŭrnovo Bulgaria **47 L5** 43.04N 25.39E
Turnu Măgurele Romania **47 L5** 43.43N 24.53E
Turnu-Severin Romania **47 K6** 44.37N 22.39E
Turov U.S.S.R. **49 M6** 52.04N 27.40E
Turpan China **66 D5** 42.55N 89.06E
Turpan Pendi *f.* China **66 D5** 42.40N 89.00E
Turquino *mtn.* Cuba **87 I4** 20.05N 76.50W
Turriff U.K. **14 F4** 57.32N 2.29W
Tuscaloosa U.S.A. **83 I3** 33.12N 87.33W
Tuticorin India **63 E2** 8.48N 78.10E
Tuttlingen W. Germany **48 D3** 47.59N 8.49E
Tutuila *i.* Samoa **74 I6** 14.18S170.42W
Tuvalu Pacific Oc. **74 H7** 8.00S178.00E
Tuxpan Mexico **86 E4** 21.00N 97.23W
Tuxtla Gutiérrez Mexico **86 F3** 16.45N 93.09W
Tuz, L. Turkey **60 D5** 38.45N 33.24E
Tuzla Yugo. **47 I6** 44.33N 18.41E
Tweed *r.* U.K. **14 F2** 55.46N 2.00W
Twin Falls *town* U.S.A. **82 D5** 42.34N114.30W
Twyford U.K. **13 F3** 51.02N 1.20W
Tyler U.S.A. **83 G3** 32.22N 95.18W
Tyne *r.* U.K. **12 F7** 55.00N 1.25W
Tyne and Wear *d.* U.K. **12 F6** 54.57N 1.35W
Tynemouth U.K. **12 F7** 55.01N 1.24W
Tyr Lebanon **60 D4** 33.16N 35.12E
Tyrone *d.* U.K. **15 D4** 54.35N 7.15W
Tyrrhenian Sea Med. Sea **46 E4** 40.00N 12.00E
Tyumen U.S.S.R. **52 F3** 57.11N 65.29E
Tywi *r.* U.K. **13 C2** 51.46N 4.22W

U

Ubaiyidh, Wadi *r.* Iraq **60 F4** 32.04N 42.17E
Ubangi *r.* Congo / Zaïre **99 B4** 0.25S 17.50E
Ube Japan **70 A4** 34.00N131.16E
Ubeda Spain **43 D3** 38.01N 3.22W
Uberaba Brazil **89 E6** 19.47S 47.57W
Uberlândia Brazil **89 E6** 18.57S 48.17W
Ubon Ratchathani Thailand **68 C7** 15.15N104.50E
Ubsa Nur *l.* Mongolia **66 E7** 50.30N 92.30E
Ucayali *r.* Peru **88 B7** 4.00S 73.30W
Uchiura wan *b.* Japan **70 D8** 42.20N140.40E
Udaipur India **63 D4** 24.36N 73.47E
Udbyhöj Denmark **38 D4** 56.37N 10.17E
Uddevalla Sweden **50 B2** 58.20N 11.56E
Uddjaur *l.* Sweden **50 D4** 65.55N 17.50E
Udine Italy **46 F7** 46.03N 13.15E
Udon Thani Thailand **68 C7** 17.29N102.46E
Uele *r.* Zaïre **99 C5** 4.08N 22.25E
Uelzen W. Germany **48 E6** 52.58N 10.34E
Ufa U.S.S.R. **52 E3** 54.45N 55.58E
Uffculme U.K. **13 D2** 50.55N 3.20W
Uganda Africa **99 D5** 1.00N 33.00E
Ughelli Nigeria **103 F2** 5.33N 6.00E
Uglegorsk U.S.S.R. **53 L2** 49.01N142.04E
Uig U.K. **14 B4** 57.35N 6.22W
Uinta Mts. U.S.A. **82 D5** 40.45N110.30W
Uithuizen Neth. **39 E5** 53.24N 6.41E
Ujjain India **63 D4** 23.11N 75.50E
Ujpest Hungary **49 I3** 47.33N 19.05E
Ujung Pandang Indonesia **68 F2** 5.09S119.28E
Uka U.S.S.R. **53 N3** 57.50N162.02E
Ukiah U.S.A. **82 B4** 39.09N123.12W
Ukraine *f.* U.S.S.R. **33 L4** 48.50N 33.00E
Ukraine S.S.R. *d.* U.S.S.R. **52 C2** 49.00N 30.00E
Ulan Bator Mongolia **66 G6** 47.54N106.52E
Ulan Göm Mongolia **66 E6** 49.59N 92.00E
Ulan-Ude U.S.S.R. **66 G7** 51.55N107.40E
Ulfborg Denmark **38 B4** 56.16N 8.20E
Uliastaj Mongolia **66 F6** 47.42N 96.52E
Ulla *r.* Spain **43 A5** 42.38N 8.45W
Ullapool U.K. **14 C4** 57.54N 5.10W
Ullswater *l.* U.K. **12 E6** 54.31N 2.50W
Ulm W. Germany **48 D4** 48.24N 10.00E
Ulsan S. Korea **67 K4** 35.32N129.21E
Ulsberg Norway **50 B3** 62.45N 10.00E
Ulstrup Denmark **38 D3** 55.44N 10.55E
Ulúa *r.* Honduras **87 G3** 15.50N 87.38W
Ulverston U.K. **12 D6** 54.11N 3.05W
Ul'yanovsk U.S.S.R. **52 E3** 54.19N 48.22E
Uman U.S.S.R. **49 O4** 48.45N 30.10E
Ume *r.* Sweden **50 E3** 63.43N 20.20E
Umeå Sweden **50 E3** 63.50N 20.15E
Umiat U.S.A. **80 C4** 69.25N152.20W
Umm-al-Gawein U.A.E. **61 I2** 25.32N 55.34E
Umm Lajj Saudi Arabia **60 E2** 25.03N 37.17E
Umm Sa'id Qatar **61 H2** 24.47N 51.36E
Umtata R.S.A. **99 C1** 31.35S 28.47E
Umuahia Nigeria **103 F2** 5.31N 7.26E
Una *r.* Yugo. **47 H6** 45.16N 16.55E
Uncompahgre Peak U.S.A. **82 E4** 38.04N107.28W
Ungava B. Canada **81 L3** 59.00N 67.30W
Union of Soviet Socialist Republics Europe / Asia **52 E4** 64.00N 84.00E
United Arab Emirates Asia **61 I1** 24.00N 54.00E
United Kingdom Europe **18** 54.00N 3.00W
United States of America N. America **82 C4** 39.00N100.00W
Unna W. Germany **39 F3** 51.32N 7.41E
Unst *i.* U.K. **14 H7** 60.45N 0.55W
Ünye Turkey **60 E6** 41.09N 37.15E
Unza *r.* U.S.S.R. **33 N6** 57.40N 43.30E
Upernavik Greenland **81 M5** 72.50N 56.00W
Upolu *i.* W. Samoa **74 I6** 13.55S171.45W
Upper Egypt *f.* Egypt **60 D2** 26.00N 32.00E
Upper Lough Erne N. Ireland **15 D4** 54.13N 7.32W
Upper Taymyr *r.* U.S.S.R. **53 I4** 74.10N 99.50E
Upper Tean U.K. **12 F4** 52.58N 1.58W
Uppsala Sweden **50 D2** 59.55N 17.38E
Ur *ruins* Iraq **61 G3** 30.55N 46.07E
Ural *r.* U.S.S.R. **52 E2** 47.00N 52.00E
Ural Mts. U.S.S.R. **52 E3** 55.00N 59.00E
Ural'sk U.S.S.R. **52 E2** 51.19N 51.20E
Uranium City Canada **80 H3** 59.32N108.43W
Urbino Italy **46 F5** 43.43N 12.38E
Ure *r.* U.K. **12 F6** 54.05N 1.20W
Urfa Turkey **60 E5** 37.08N 38.45E
Urgench U.S.S.R. **52 E2** 41.35N 59.58E
Ürgüp Turkey **60 D5** 38.39N 34.55E
Urlingford Rep. of Ire. **15 D2** 52.43N 7.35W
Urmia, L. Iran **61 G5** 37.40N 45.28E
Uruapan Mexico **86 D3** 19.26N102.04W
Uruguaiana Brazil **89 D5** 29.45S 57.05W
Uruguay S. America **89 D4** 33.00S 55.00W
Uruguay *r.* Uruguay **89 D4** 34.00S 58.30W
Ürümqi China **66 D5** 43.43N 87.38E
Uryu ko *l.* Japan **70 E9** 44.22N142.15E
Uşak Turkey **60 C5** 38.42N 29.25E
Ushant *i. see* Ouessant, Île d' *i.* France **42**
Ushnuiyeh Iran **61 G5** 37.03N 45.05E
Usk *r.* U.K. **13 E3** 51.34N 2.59W
Üsküdar Turkey **47 N4** 41.00N 29.03E
Ussuriysk U.S.S.R. **67 K5** 43.48N131.59E
Ustica *i.* Italy **46 F3** 38.42N 13.11E
Ústí nad Labem Czech. **48 G5** 50.41N 14.00E
Ustinov U.S.S.R. **52 E3** 56.49N 53.11E
Ust'kamchatsk U.S.S.R. **53 N3** 56.14N162.28E
Ust-Kamenogorsk U.S.S.R. **52 G2** 50.00N 82.40E
Ust Kut U.S.S.R. **53 I3** 56.40N105.50E
Ust'Maya U.S.S.R. **53 L3** 60.25N134.28E
Ust Olenëk U.S.S.R. **53 J4** 72.59N120.00E
Ust'Tsilma U.S.S.R. **52 E4** 65.28N 53.09E
Ust Urt Plateau *f.* U.S.S.R. **52 E2** 43.30N 55.20E
U.S. Virgin Is. C. America **87 L3** 18.30N 65.00W
Utah *d.* U.S.A. **82 D4** 39.00N112.00W
Utica U.S.A. **83 K5** 43.06N 75.05W
Utiel Spain **43 E3** 39.33N 1.13W
Utrecht Neth. **39 D4** 52.04N 5.07E
Utrecht *d.* Neth. **39 D4** 52.04N 5.10E
Utrera Spain **43 C2** 37.10N 5.47W
Utsunomiya Japan **70 D5** 36.40N139.52E
Uttaradit Thailand **68 C7** 17.38N100.05E
Uttar Pradesh *d.* India **63 E5** 27.40N 80.00E
Uttoxeter U.K. **12 F4** 52.55N 1.49W
Uusikaupunki Finland **50 E3** 60.48N 21.30E
'Uwaina Saudi Arabia **61 H2** 26.46N 48.13E
Uwajima Japan **70 B3** 33.13N132.32E
Uyo Nigeria **103 F2** 5.01N 7.56E
'Uyun Saudi Arabia **61 F2** 26.32N 43.41E
Uyuni Bolivia **89 C5** 20.28S 66.47W
Uzbekistan S.S.R. *d.* U.S.S.R. **52 E2** 42.00N 63.00E
Uzda U.S.S.R. **49 M6** 53.28N 27.11E
Uzhgorod U.S.S.R. **49 K4** 48.38N 22.15E

V

Vaagö *i.* Faroe Is. **50 L9** 62.03N 7.14W
Vaasa Finland **50 E3** 63.06N 21.36E
Vác Hungary **49 I3** 47.49N 19.10E
Vadodara India **63 D4** 22.19N 73.14E
Vaduz Liech. **48 D3** 47.08N 9.32E
Vaggeryd Sweden **50 C2** 57.30N 14.10E
Váh *r.* Czech. **49 I3** 47.40N 18.09E
Vaitupu *i.* Tuvalu **74 H7** 7.28S178.41E
Valdai Hills U.S.S.R. **33 L6** 57.00N 33.00E
Valdemarsvik Sweden **50 D2** 58.13N 16.35E
Valdepeñas Spain **43 D3** 38.46N 3.24W
Valdez U.S.A. **80 D4** 61.07N146.17W
Valdivia Chile **89 B4** 39.46S 73.15W
Valença Portugal **43 A5** 42.02N 8.38W
Valence France **42 G3** 44.56N 4.54E
Valencia Spain **43 E3** 39.29N 0.24W
Valencia *d.* Spain **43 E3** 40.00N 0.40W
Valencia Venezuela **88 C9** 10.14N 67.59W
Valencia, G. of Spain **43 F3** 39.38N 0.20W
Valencia de Alcántara Spain **43 B3** 39.25N 7.14W
Valenciennes France **39 B2** 50.22N 3.32E
Vale of Evesham U.K. **13 F4** 52.05N 1.55W
Vale of Pewsey *f.* U.K. **13 F3** 51.20N 1.45W
Vale of York *f.* U.K. **12 F6** 54.15N 1.22W
Valga U.S.S.R. **50 F2** 57.44N 26.00E
Valinco, G. of Med. Sea **42 I1** 41.40N 8.50E
Valjevo Yugo. **47 I6** 44.16N 19.56E
Valkeakoski Finland **50 F3** 61.17N 24.05E
Valkenswaard Neth. **39 D3** 51.21N 5.27E
Valladolid Spain **43 C4** 41.39N 4.45W
Valledupar Colombia **88 B9** 10.10N 73.16W
Valletta Malta **46 G1** 35.53N 14.31E
Valley City U.S.A. **82 G6** 46.57N 97.58W
Valmiera U.S.S.R. **50 F2** 57.32N 25.29E
Valnera *mtn.* Spain **43 D5** 43.10N 3.40W
Valognes France **42 D5** 49.31N 1.28W
Valparaíso Chile **89 B4** 33.05S 71.40W
Vals, C. Indonesia **69 J2** 8.30S137.30E
Valverde Dom. Rep. **87 J3** 19.37N 71.04W
Valverde del Camino Spain **43 B2** 37.35N 6.45W
Van Turkey **60 F5** 38.28N 43.20E
Van, L. Turkey **60 F5** 38.35N 42.52E
Vancouver Canada **80 F2** 49.13N123.06W
Vancouver I. Canada **80 F2** 50.00N126.00W
Vänern *l.* Sweden **50 C2** 59.00N 13.15E
Vänersborg Sweden **50 C2** 58.23N 12.19E
Vanimo P.N.G. **69 K3** 2.40S141.17E
Vännäs Sweden **50 D3** 63.56N 19.50E
Vannes France **42 C4** 47.40N 2.44W
Vanua Levu *i.* Fiji **74 H6** 16.33S179.15E
Vanuatu Pacific Oc. **74 G6** 16.00S167.00E
Var *r.* France **42 H2** 43.39N 7.11E
Vārānasi India **63 E4** 25.20N 83.00E
Varangerfjorden *est.* Norway **50 G5** 70.00N 29.30E
Varaždin Yugo. **46 H7** 46.18N 16.20E
Varberg Sweden **50 C2** 57.06N 12.15E
Vardar *r.* Greece **47 K4** 40.31N 22.43E
Varde Denmark **38 B3** 55.37N 8.29E
Varel W. Germany **39 G5** 53.24N 8.08E
Varennes France **42 F4** 46.19N 3.24E
Varkaus Finland **50 F3** 62.15N 27.45E
Varna Bulgaria **47 M5** 43.13N 27.57E
Varnaes Denmark **38 C3** 55.01N 9.34E
Värnamo Sweden **50 C2** 57.11N 14.03E
Várpalota Hungary **49 I3** 47.12N 18.09E
Vascongadas *d.* Spain **43 D5** 43.00N 2.00W
Vasilkov U.S.S.R. **49 O5** 50.12N 30.15E
Vaslui Romania **49 M3** 46.38N 27.44E
Västerås Sweden **50 D2** 59.36N 16.32E
Västerdal *r.* Sweden **50 C3** 60.32N 15.02E
Västervik Sweden **50 D2** 57.45N 16.40E
Vatnajökull *mts.* Iceland **50 J7** 64.20N 17.00W
Vättern *l.* Sweden **50 C2** 58.30N 14.30E
Vaughn U.S.A. **82 E3** 34.35N105.14W
Vavuniya Sri Lanka **63 E2** 8.45N 80.30E
Växjö Sweden **50 C2** 56.52N 14.50E

Wolverhampton U.K. **13 E4** 52.35N 2.06W
Wonsan N. Korea **67 K5** 39.07N127.26E
Woodbridge U.K. **13 I4** 52.06N 1.21E
Woodstock U.K. **13 F3** 51.50N 1.20W
Wooler U.K. **12 E7** 55.32N 2.01W
Worcester R.S.A. **99 B1** 33.39S 19.26E
Worcester U.K. **13 E4** 52.12N 2.12W
Worcester U.S.A. **83 L5** 42.14N 71.48W
Workington U.K. **12 D6** 54.39N 3.34W
Worksop U.K. **12 F5** 53.19N 1.09W
Worland U.S.A. **82 E5** 44.01N107.58W
Worms W. Germany **48 D4** 49.38N 8.23E
Worthing U.K. **13 G2** 50.49N 0.21W
Worthington U.S.A. **83 G5** 43.37N 95.36W
Wowoni i. Indonesia **69 G3** 4.10S123.10E
Wragby U.K. **12 G5** 53.18N 0.17W
Wrangel I. U.S.S.R. **53 O4** 71.00N180.00
Wrangell U.S.A. **80 E3** 56.28N132.23W
Wrangle U.K. **12 H5** 53.03N 0.10E
Wrath, C. U.K. **14 C5** 58.37N 5.01W
Wrexham U.K. **12 D5** 53.05N 3.00W
Wrigley Canada **80 F4** 63.16N123.39W
Wrocław Poland **49 H5** 51.05N 17.00E
Wuhan China **67 I3** 30.35N114.19E
Wuhu China **67 I3** 31.23N118.25E
Wu Jiang r. China **66 G3** 30.10N107.26E
Wuliang Shan mts. China **66 F2** 24.27N100.43E
Wuppertal W. Germany **39 F3** 51.15N 7.10E
Würzburg W. Germany **48 D4** 49.48N 9.57E
Wutongqiao China **66 G3** 29.21N103.48E
Wuwei China **66 G5** 38.00N102.54E
Wuxi China **67 J3** 31.35N120.19E
Wuzhou China **67 H2** 23.30N111.21E
Wye U.K. **13 H3** 51.12N 0.57E
Wye r. U.K. **13 E3** 51.37N 2.40W
Wyk W. Germany **38** 54.42N 8.32E
Wymondham U.K. **13 I4** 52.36N 1.09E
Wyndham Australia **71 B4** 15.29S128.05E
Wyoming d. U.S.A. **82 E5** 43.00N108.00W

X

Xánthi Greece **47 L4** 41.07N 24.55E
Xiaguan China **66 F2** 25.33N100.09E
Xiamen China **67 I2** 24.26N118.07E
Xi'an China **67 H4** 34.16N108.54E
Xiangfan China **67 H4** 32.20N112.05E
Xiangtan China **67 H3** 27.55N112.47E
Xiangyang China **67 H4** 32.00N112.00E
Xianyang China **67 H4** 34.23N108.40E
Xiao Hinggan Ling mts. China **67 K6**
 48.40N128.30E
Xieng Khouang Laos **68 C7** 19.11N103.23E
Xigazê China **66 D3** 29.18N 88.50E
Xi Jiang r. China **67 H2** 22.23N113.20E
Xingtai China **67 H4** 37.08N114.29E
Xingu r. Brazil **88 D7** 2.00S 52.30W
Xining China **66 G4** 36.35N101.55E
Xinjiang-Uygur d. China **66 C5** 41.15N 87.00E
Xinjin China **67 J5** 39.25N121.58E
Xinxiang China **67 H4** 35.16N113.51E
Xinzhou Taiwan **67 J2** 24.48N120.59E
Xizang d. see Tibet d. China **66**
Xuanhua China **67 I5** 40.36N115.01E
Xuchang China **67 H4** 34.03N113.48E
Xueshuiwen China **67 K6** 49.15N129.39E
Xugou China **67 I4** 34.42N119.28E
Xuzhou China **67 I4** 34.17N117.18E

Y

Yablonovy Range mts. U.S.S.R. **53 J3**
 53.20N115.00E
Yacheng China **67 H1** 18.30N109.12E
Yakima U.S.A. **82 B6** 46.37N120.30W

Yaku jima i. Japan **70 A2** 30.20N130.40E
Yakujima kaikyo str. Japan **70 A2** 30.10N130.10E
Yakutsk U.S.S.R. **53 K3** 62.10N129.20E
Yalong Jiang r. China **66 F3** 26.35N101.44E
Yamagata Japan **70 D6** 38.16N140.19E
Yamaguchi Japan **70 A4** 34.10N131.28E
Yamal Pen. U.S.S.R. **52 F4** 70.20N 70.00E
Yaman Tau mtn. U.S.S.R. **52 E3** 54.20N 58.10E
Yambéring Guinea **102 B3** 11.49N 12.18W
Yambol Bulgaria **47 M5** 42.28N 26.30E
Yamethin Burma **63 H4** 20.24N 96.08E
Yamoussoukro Ivory Coast **102 C2** 6.49N 5.17W
Yamuna r. India **63 E4** 25.20N 81.49E
Yana r. U.S.S.R. **53 L4** 71.30N135.00E
Yanbu Saudi Arabia **60 E2** 24.07N 38.04E
Yancheng China **67 J4** 33.23N120.10E
Yanchuan China **67 H4** 36.55N110.04E
Yangquan China **67 H4** 37.52N113.29E
Yangtze r. see Chang Jiang r. China **67**
Yanji China **67 K5** 42.45N129.25E
Yanqi China **66 D5** 42.00N 86.30E
Yantai China **67 J4** 37.30N121.22E
Yao Chad **100 D3** 12.52N 17.34E
Yaoundé Cameroon **103 G1** 3.51N 11.31E
Yap i. Caroline Is. **74 D8** 9.30N138.09E
Yaqui r. Mexico **86 B5** 27.40N110.30W
Yare r. U.K. **13 I4** 52.34N 1.45E
Yariga daki mtn. Japan **70 C5** 36.21N137.39E
Yarkant He r. China **66 C5** 40.30N 80.55E
Yarlung Zangbo Jiang r. see Brahmaputra r. China **63**
Yarmouth Canada **81 L2** 43.50N 66.08W
Yaroslavl U.S.S.R. **52 D3** 57.34N 39.52E
Yarrow r. U.K. **14 F2** 55.36N 2.48W
Yartsevo U.S.S.R. **53 H3** 60.17N 90.02E
Yaselda r. U.S.S.R. **49 M6** 52.07N 26.28E
Yatakala Niger **103 E3** 14.52N 0.22E
Yatsuo Japan **70 C5** 36.35N137.10E
Yatsushiro Japan **70 A3** 32.32N130.35E
Ya Xian China **67 H1** 18.20N109.31E
Yazd Iran **101 H5** 31.54N 54.22E
Ydby Denmark **38 B4** 56.42N 8.25E
Ye Burma **68 B7** 15.15N 97.50E
Yegorlyk r. U.S.S.R. **53 N4** 47.10N 40.20E
Yell i. U.K. **14 G7** 60.35N 1.05W
Yellowknife Canada **80 G4** 62.30N114.29W
Yellow Sea Asia **67 J4** 35.00N123.00E
Yellowstone r. U.S.A. **82 F6** 47.55N103.45W
Yellowstone L. U.S.A. **82 D5** 44.30N110.20W
Yellowstone Nat. Park U.S.A. **82 D5**
 44.35N110.30W
Yell Sound U.K. **14 G7** 60.35N 1.15W
Yelsk U.S.S.R. **49 N5** 51.50N 29.10E
Yelwa Nigeria **103 E3** 10.48N 4.42E
Yemen Asia **101 G3** 15.15N 44.30E
Yenagoa Nigeria **103 F1** 4.59N 6.15E
Yenisei r. U.S.S.R. **53 H4** 69.00N 86.00E
Yenisei G. U.S.S.R. **52 G4** 73.00N 79.00E
Yeniseysk U.S.S.R. **53 H3** 58.27N 92.13E
Yeovil U.K. **13 E2** 50.56N 2.39W
Yerevan U.S.S.R. **61 G6** 40.10N 44.31E
Yeu Burma **63 G4** 22.49N 95.26E
Yeu, Île d' i. France **42 C4** 46.43N 2.20W
Yibin China **66 G3** 28.50N104.35E
Yichang China **67 H3** 30.43N111.22E
Yilan China **67 K6** 46.22N129.31E
Yinchuan China **66 G5** 38.30N106.19E
Yingde China **67 H2** 24.20N113.20E
Yingkou China **67 J5** 40.40N122.17E
Yining China **66 C5** 43.57N 81.23E
Ylikitka l. Finland **50 G4** 66.10N 28.30E
Yogyakarta Indonesia **68 E2** 7.48S110.24E
Yokadouma Cameroon **103 H1** 3.26N 15.06E
Yokkaichi Japan **70 C4** 34.58N136.38E
Yoko Cameroon **103 G2** 5.29N 12.19E
Yokohama Japan **70 D4** 35.28N139.28E

Yokosuka Japan **70 D4** 35.20N139.32E
Yola Nigeria **103 G2** 9.14N 12.32E
Yonago Japan **70 B4** 35.27N133.20E
Yonne r. France **42 F5** 48.22N 2.57E
York U.K. **12 F5** 53.58N 1.07W
York, C. Australia **71 D4** 10.58S142.40E
York Factory town Canada **81 I3** 57.08N 92.25W
Yorkshire Wolds hills U.K. **12 G6** 54.00N 0.39W
Yorkton Canada **80 H3** 51.12N102.29W
Yoshino r. Japan **70 B4** 34.03N134.34E
Yoshkar Ola U.S.S.R. **52 D3** 56.38N 47.52E
Yosu S. Korea **67 K4** 34.46N127.45E
Youghal Rep. of Ire. **15 D1** 51.58N 7.51W
You Jiang r. China **67 H2** 23.25N110.00E
Youngstown U.S.A. **83 J5** 41.05N 80.40W
Yoxford U.K. **13 I4** 52.15N 1.29E
Yozgat Turkey **60 D5** 39.50N 34.48E
Ypres Belgium **39 A2** 50.51N 2.53E
Ystad Sweden **50 C1** 55.25N 13.50E
Ythan r. U.K. **14 F4** 57.20N 2.01W
Yuan Jiang r. see Red r. China **66**
Yuan Jiang r. China **67 H3** 29.20N112.12E
Yubari Japan **70 E8** 43.04N141.59E
Yucatán d. Mexico **87 G4** 20.30N 89.00W
Yucatan Channel Carib. Sea **87 G4** 21.30N 86.00W
Yucatan Pen. Mexico **86 F3** 19.00N 90.00W
Yuci China **67 H4** 37.40N112.44E
Yugoslavia Europe **47 H6** 44.00N 20.00E
Yukon r. U.S.A. **80 B4** 62.35N164.20W
Yukon Territory d. Canada **80 E4** 65.00N135.00W
Yuma U.S.A. **82 D3** 32.40N114.39W
Yumen China **66 F5** 40.19N 97.12E
Yunnan d. China **66 F2** 24.30N101.30E
Yunnan Plateau mts. Asia **54 M5** 24.00N107.00E
Yushu China **66 F4** 33.06N 96.48E
Yuzhno Sakhalinsk U.S.S.R. **67 M6** 46.58N142.45E
Yvetot France **42 E5** 49.37N 0.45E

Z

Zaandam Neth. **39 C4** 52.27N 4.49E
Zabrze Poland **49 I5** 50.18N 18.47E
Zacapa Guatemala **87 G2** 15.00N 89.30W
Zacatecas Mexico **86 D4** 22.48N102.33W
Zacatecas d. Mexico **86 D4** 24.00N103.00W
Zadar Yugo. **46 G6** 44.08N 15.14E
Zafra Spain **43 B3** 38.25N 6.25W
Zagazig Egypt **60 C3** 30.36N 31.30E
Zagorsk U.S.S.R. **52 D3** 56.20N 38.10E
Zagreb Yugo. **46 G6** 45.49N 15.58E
Zagros Mts. Iran **101 G4** 32.00N 51.00E
Zähedän Iran **61 K3** 29.32N 60.54E
Zahle Lebanon **60 E4** 33.50N 35.55E
Zaïre Africa **99 C4** 2.00S 22.00E
Zaïre r. Zaïre **99 B4** 6.00S 12.30E
Zaïre Basin f. Africa **99 C4** 0.30N 22.00E
Zaječar Yugo. **47 K5** 43.55N 22.15E
Zakataly U.S.S.R. **61 G6** 41.39N 46.40E
Zákinthos i. Greece **47 J2** 37.46N 20.46E
Zakopane Poland **49 I4** 49.19N 19.57E
Zalaegerszeg Hungary **48 H3** 46.51N 16.51E
Zambezi r. Mozambique / Zambia **99 D3** 18.15S
 35.55E
Zambia Africa **99 C3** 14.00S 28.00E
Zamboanga Phil. **69 G5** 6.55N122.05E
Zamfara r. Nigeria **103 E3** 12.04N 4.00E
Zamora Mexico **86 D4** 20.00N102.18W
Zamora Spain **43 C4** 41.30N 5.45W
Zamość Poland **49 K5** 50.43N 23.15E
Záncara r. Spain **43 C3** 38.55N 4.07W
Zanjän Iran **61 H5** 36.40N 48.30E
Zanzibar Tanzania **99 D4** 6.10S 39.12E
Zanzibar I. Tanzania **99 D4** 6.10S 39.12E
Zaozhuang China **67 H4** 34.40N117.30E
Zapala Argentina **89 B4** 38.55S 70.10W
Zaporozhye U.S.S.R. **52 C2** 47.50N 35.10E

Zara Turkey **60 E5** 39.55N 37.44E
Zaragoza Spain **43 E4** 41.39N 0.54W
Zardeh Kuh mtn. Iran **61 H4** 32.21N 50.04E
Zaria Nigeria **103 F3** 11.01N 7.44E
Zarqa Jordan **60 E4** 32.04N 36.05E
Zary Poland **48 G5** 51.40N 15.10E
Zatishye U.S.S.R. **49 N3** 47.20N 29.58E
Zaysan U.S.S.R. **66 D6** 47.30N 84.57E
Zaysan, L. U.S.S.R. **66 C6** 48.00N 83.30E
Zduńska Wola Poland **49 I5** 51.36N 18.57E
Zealand i. Denmark **38 E3** 55.30N 12.00E
Zealands Odde pen. Denmark **38 E4** 56.00N 11.18E
Zeebrugge Belgium **39 B3** 51.20N 3.13E
Zeeland d. Neth. **39 B3** 51.30N 3.45E
Zeila Somali Rep. **101 G3** 11.21N 43.30E
Zeist Neth. **39 D4** 52.03N 5.16E
Zeitz E. Germany **48 F5** 51.03N 12.08E
Zelenogorsk U.S.S.R. **50 G3** 60.15N 29.31E
Zelenogradsk U.S.S.R. **52 B3** 54.57N 20.28E
Zemio C.A.R. **101 E2** 5.00N 25.09E
Zenne r. Belgium **39 C3** 51.04N 4.25E
Zevenbergen Neth. **39 C3** 51.41N 4.42E
Zeya r. U.S.S.R. **53 K2** 50.20N127.30E
Zêzere r. Portugal **43 A3** 39.28N 8.20W
Zhanghua Taiwan **67 J2** 24.06N120.31E
Zhangjiakou China **67 I5** 41.00N114.50E
Zhangzhou China **67 I2** 24.57N118.36E
Zhanjiang China **67 H2** 21.05N110.12E
Zhdanov U.S.S.R. **52 D2** 47.05N 37.34E
Zhejiang d. China **67 I3** 29.15N120.00E
Zhengzhou China **67 H4** 34.35N113.38E
Zhenjiang China **67 I4** 32.05N119.30E
Zhitkovichi U.S.S.R. **49 M6** 52.12N 27.49E
Zhitomir U.S.S.R. **49 N5** 50.18N 28.40E
Zhlobin U.S.S.R. **49 O6** 52.50N 30.00E
Zhmerinka U.S.S.R. **49 N4** 49.00N 28.02E
Zhob r. Pakistan **63 C5** 31.40N 70.54E
Zhuzhou China **67 H3** 27.53N113.07E
Zibo China **67 I4** 36.50N118.00E
Zielona Góra Poland **48 G5** 51.57N 15.30E
Zigong China **66 G3** 29.20N104.42E
Ziguinchor Senegal **102 A3** 12.35N 16.20W
Zile Turkey **60 D6** 40.18N 35.52E
Zilfi Saudi Arabia **61 G2** 26.15N 44.50E
Žilina Czech. **49 I4** 49.14N 18.46E
Zimatlán Mexico **86 E3** 16.52N 96.45W
Zimbabwe Africa **99 C3** 18.00S 30.00E
Zimbor Romania **49 K3** 47.00N 23.16E
Zimnicea Romania **49 L1** 43.38N 25.22E
Zinder Niger **103 F3** 13.46N 8.58E
Zingst E. Germany **38 F2** 54.27N 12.41E
Zlatoust U.S.S.R. **52 F3** 55.10N 59.38E
Złotów Poland **49 H6** 53.22N 17.02E
Znojmo Czech. **48 H4** 48.52N 16.05E
Zomba Malawi **99 D3** 15.22S 35.22E
Zonguldak Turkey **60 C6** 41.26N 31.47E
Zoutkamp Neth. **39 E5** 53.21N 6.18E
Zrenjanin Yugo. **47 J6** 45.22N 20.23E
Zug Switz. **48 D3** 47.10N 8.31E
Zuhreh r. Iran **61 H3** 30.04N 49.32E
Zújar r. Spain **43 C3** 38.58N 5.40W
Zújar Dam Spain **43 C3** 38.57N 5.30W
Zungeru Nigeria **103 F2** 9.48N 6.03E
Zunyi China **66 G3** 27.41N106.50E
Zürich Switz. **48 D3** 47.23N 8.33E
Zutphen Neth. **39 E4** 52.08N 6.12E
Zvenigorodka U.S.S.R. **49 O4** 49.05N 30.58E
Zvolen Czech. **49 I4** 48.35N 19.08E
Zwickau E. Germany **48 F5** 50.43N 12.30E
Zwolle Neth. **39 E4** 52.31N 6.06E
Zyryanovsk U.S.S.R. **52 H2** 49.45N 84.16E